# Practical
# Criminal
# Investigation

**Fifth Edition**

# Manuel S. Peña

DELMAR
CENGAGE Learning™

Australia • Brazil • Japan • Korea • Mexico • Singapore • Spain • United Kingdom • United States

**DELMAR**
CENGAGE Learning·

**Practical Criminal Investigation, Fifth Edition**
Manuel S. Pena

For product information and technology assistance, contact us at **Cengage Learning Customer & Sales Support, 1-800-354-9706**

For permission to use material from this text or product, submit all requests online at **www.cengage.com/permissions**
Further permissions questions can be emailed to **permissionrequest@cengage.com**

Library of Congress Control Number: 82-70470

ISBN-13: 978-1-928916-11-6

ISBN-10: 1-928916-11-2

**Delmar**
Executive Woods
5 Maxwell Drive
Clifton Park, NY 12065
USA

Cengage Learning is a leading provider of customized learning solutions with office locations around the globe, including Singapore, the United Kingdom, Australia, Mexico, Brazil, and Japan. Locate your local office at **international.cengage.com/region**

Cengage Learning products are represented in Canada by Nelson Education, Ltd.

For your lifelong learning solutions, visit **delmar.cengage.com**

Visit our corporate website at **www.cengage.com**

Printed in the United States of America
10 11 12 13 14 15 11 10 09 08

To my wife, Olga

# TABLE OF CONTENTS

*Chapter 6*
# THE CRIMINALISTICS LABORATORY ................... 111

## *Chapter 9*
## SURVEILLANCE AND
## UNDERCOVER INVESTIGATION ......................... 177

## *Chapter 10*
## INTERROGATION PRINCIPLES ............................... 199

*Chapter 11*
## WRITTEN STATEMENTSand CONFESSIONS ........ 223

*Chapter 12*
## INVESTIGATIVE GUIDELINES FOR
##    SELECTED CRIMES AND SCENES ........................ 229

*Chapter 14*
## TERRORISM, BOMBINGS, AND HOSTAGE INCIDENTS

## Chapter 17
## INNOVATIONS IN INVESTIGATIVE
##     TECHNOLOGY ........................................................ 387

# PREFACE

The arrangement of material in this unique and comprehensive text leads the student from the beginning stages of basic criminal investigation through the more advanced techniques for handling cases involving all major crimes. Preparing cases for presentation to the prosecutor, a grand jury, or a court of law is also fully covered. In addition to basic fundamentals, this book features material on the latest laboratory services, sources of investigative information, and scientific techniques available to assist the investigator.

Because *Practical Criminal Investigation* presents a profusion of time-tested investigative procedures for a wide variety of crimes, along with specific techniques and new innovations in criminal investigation, it is also an excellent reference resource.

The author, Manuel S. Peña, has an extensive background of thirty years experience in municipal and military criminal investigation. He has worked as a chief agent in the Criminal Investigation Detachment of the U.S. Army and as a divisional detective commander of the Los Angeles Police Department. He was a supervising investigator of the assassination of Senator Robert F. Kennedy.

Professor Pena has taught criminal investigation for over two decades and for fifteen years served as professor and chairman of the Administration of Justice Department, East Los Angeles College.

*Derald D. Hunt*
Developmental Editor

# ACKNOWLEDGMENTS

During the past 40 years, I have been privileged to have been associated with scores of skilled professionals in the criminal investigation and criminal justice education fields. My investigative assignments, over a period of 30 years, have included the Los Angeles Police Department; the United States Army, Criminal Investigation Division (CID); and the Office of Public Safety, U.S. State Department.

This diverse experience has afforded me a unique opportunity to learn and practice criminal investigation techniques in this and several foreign countries. I gratefully acknowledge all the above for providing me with the knowledge-base for this text.

I also wish to express my gratitude to the following law enforcement agencies, industries and colleges whose cooperation, instructional materials and suggestions contributed greatly to the breadth and scope of this text:

- California State Department of Justice
- East Los Angeles Community College
- Federal Bureau of Investigation
- Hughes Aircraft Company
- Los Angeles Police Department
- The Rand Corporation
- Rockwell International
- Santa Barbara County, California, District Attorney's Office
- Sony Corporation of America
- United States Drug-Enforcement Administration (DEA)
- Sirchie Fingerprint Laboratories Inc.
- United States Department of State

*Manuel S. Peña*

# FUNDAMENTALS
# OF INVESTIGATION

## KEY TERMS AND CONCEPTS

Investigation (definition of)
Criminal investigation (objectives of)
Overview of methods
*Corpus delicti*
*Modus operandi*
Complaint evaluation
Suspect identification
Collection/preservation/handling of evidence
Recovery of property
Records availability
Arrest of suspect
Spontaneous remarks
Interrogation of suspect
Presentation of case to prosecutor/court/grand jury

An investigation is a systematic, methodical, and detailed inquiry and examination of all components, circumstances, and relationships pertaining to an incident. The objective of a criminal investigation is to establish the truth or falsity of a complaint, basing conclusions on facts derived through a complete and impartial investigation. If a crime has been committed, it is essential to establish the *corpus delicti* or elements of the crime in a court of law and to prove beyond a reasonable doubt that the accused committed the crime.

# OVERVIEW OF METHODS

An investigation can be successful only if it is conducted in a sequential and thorough manner. Knowledge of the basic criminal laws, investigative principles, case preparation methods, and the procedures of the criminal justice system is most essential to investigators. In order to facilitate the in-depth study of the materials contained in succeeding chapters, this overview of methods is offered.

## Crime Elements (*Corpus Delicti*)

### Corpus Delicti

In order that investigators understand what is necessary to successfully prove a case in court, they must first know the *corpus delicti* (elements) of the many crimes contained in various municipal, county, state and federal codes.

Every crime consists of a combination of elements, all of which must be present for a particular crime to be proven. That combination of elements is known as the *corpus delicti* of a crime. Examples of some crimes that are a common occurrence throughout the world are listed below. The statutory modifications as to exceptions, degrees or lesser or included offenses within each crime, may vary with each country or state.

- **Burglary:** *(Breaking and entering in some states)* The elements of the crime of burglary generally consist of: (1) the entering, (2) of a dwelling or other building, (3) with the intent to commit grand or petty theft, or (4) any felony therein. In common law one additional element is required to complete the crime of burglary. The offense must be committed in the nighttime. The criminal codes of some states still require this additional element to constitute the crime of burglary. Forced entry is not an element of burglary in most states, but may be an element of breaking and entering.

- **Robbery:** The elements of the crime of robbery generally consist of: (1) the felonious taking, (2) of personal property, (3) in the possession of another, (4) from his person or immediate presence, (5) by means of force or fear.

- **Murder:** The elements of the crime of murder generally consist of: (1) the unlawful killing, (2) of a human being, (3) by another, (4) with malice aforethought or premeditated design.

*Evaluation*

An *evaluation* is the act of carefully studying an object, situation or set of circumstances, for the purpose of determining its value, worth or credibility.

Initially all complaints must be evaluated with great care. The first information received from an alleged victim or witness may be erroneous, colored or too brief. The complainant or witness may be influenced by emotions such as fear or anger, or by a financial interest in the subject matter of the complaint or may be very confused and unfamiliar with police procedures and terminology. On occasion it may well be that the individual giving information to the investigator is dishonest. Any one of the above influences can, if not carefully considered, mislead an investigation and cost a considerable loss of time.

If no crime has been committed, the incident may well be a civil matter; such as a business dispute between partners over the sale of property that is jointly owned. In this event the complainant should be referred to an attorney for advice.

In the case where a specific crime has been committed and the suspect is known or identifiable and probable cause for an arrest exists, an apprehension on occasion is made at the scene of the crime or as a result of an immediate pursuit. Unfortunately, in many cases involving both felony and misdemeanor crimes, the immediate identification and arrest potential of the suspect does not exist. The unknown or unidentified suspect has fled the scene with or without the victim's property. An identification thus becomes more difficult, but not impossible, because the investigation of the crime scene will generally yield leads as to the identification of the suspect.

## Crime Scene and Identification of Suspect

All major crime scenes require a preliminary and a follow-up investigation. The investigation techniques utilized may be similar whether the case involves an arrest of the suspect at the scene or results from an immediate pursuit or even if the suspect is unknown or has fled the scene. They will vary primarily in the order and depth to which they are applied, in keeping with the circumstances of the particular case. The identification of the suspect is a prime objective in all cases. Police efforts to effect an identification may vary from minimal to extensive. To illustrate this point, the following hypothesis is offered.

A suspect wearing a mask and gloves and armed with a shotgun, enters a bank and holds up a teller. While the robbery is in progress a second teller manages to press the silent alarm, alerting the police. Before the suspect finishes emptying the one teller's cage of all the money, the blaring sirens of police cars are heard as they approach the bank. The suspect panics, shoots and kills the teller and runs toward the front door of the bank, with the shotgun in one hand and the bank bag with money in the other. As the suspect exits the door, he confronts the police and is captured. This is a major crime scene which will be handled as a homicide and robbery.

The identification of the suspect and the arrest and recovery of the money is no great problem. If the suspect had escaped arrest by making a getaway, the investigative techniques used by the police would vary, in that much more in-depth follow-up investigation would be required to effect an identification of the suspect, than where the suspect was captured at the scene. The preliminary investigation of a major crime scene is as follows: The crime scene must be isolated by the first officers on the scene. This means that order must be restored as quickly as possible. Victims and witnesses must be separated for independent interviews. Nothing is touched or moved so that the value of physical evidence, such as latent prints, footprints or glass fractures, is not negated. If the first officers on the scene are to handle the investigation they will proceed immediately. In cases where other investigators will assume investigative responsibility, the first officers to arrive will protect the scene. Protection and isolation of a crime scene means that no one except those allowed by the investigators will enter or disturb a crime scene in any way. The only valid reason for disturbing a scene is to render aid to the injured or in an attempt to save a human life.

A systematic evaluation of the crime scene will be conducted by the officers or investigators responsible. The usual first step is a careful walk-through by one or two persons, one of whom may be the criminologist or an evidence technician. Chronological notes are taken of the observations in general. Necessary photos, latent print potentials, and other laboratory and coroner services are needed in homicides.

If enough investigators are available, the independent and in-depth interview of all victims and witnesses can proceed while the crime scene search is in progress. Individual witnesses' perceptions, with word and picture descriptions, must be obtained from those interviewed. All details derived must then be collectively dovetailed into a composite of the occurrence. The interviews are included in the file of notes taken during the crime search.

The search of the crime scene and the collection, handling and preservation of evidence is conducted utilizing standard search methods and full use of all needed laboratory services (See Chapters 5 and 6).

Some police departments require the patrol officer or field investigator to conduct all preliminary investigations including all crime scene functions. Some departments employ evidence technicians or criminalists for this duty, and these specialists work with the investigators. Also involved in the identification of suspects will be the use by investigators of municipal, county, state and federal law enforcement records system. These record systems include extensive *modus operandi* files. The term *modus operandi* means method of operation. The development of police "MO" files is based on the theory that a criminal, like other human beings, develops habits. The criminal who is successful with a particular method in committing a crime will likely continue to use the method in committing future crimes. As a result of the success factor, the particular method can become a lasting part of the offender's criminal behavior. It is through these MO files that the crime patterns of an individual suspect or a group of suspects can be evaluated and followed or at times predicted as to a forthcoming occurrence. A brief example of some of the information contained in these files is as follows: (1) the name, address, and phone number, (2) race, sex and age, (3) occupation of the person attacked, (4) the property attacked by type of premises, (5) method of attack, (6) means of attack, (7) object of attack or property taken, (8) trademarks of the suspect (anything unique), (9) words spoken by the suspect, and (10) transportation used, if any. This phenomena, *modus operandi*, is only briefly mentioned in this overview of methods of investigation. Full coverage is offered in Chapter 3.

There are numerous other private and non-police recorded sources of information. Several examples are credit bureaus, department store credit records, bank records, and public records, such as schools, license and regulatory agencies. A simple common investigative factor applies to these records. They generally contain much more valid information as to names, current and former addresses of family, relatives, references, schools, births and marriages, than do many police records. The prime reason for this is that if persons want loans from banks or credit from department stores or need licenses, they aren't likely to file applications loaded with false information, such as vacant lots for addresses or nonexistent references. A suspect under arrest and being questioned by an officer is very apt to give much misleading information that will become an integral part of police files. Personal informants are also a good source of information and, at times, may be the only source by which a suspect may be identified. The collaboration and aid from other law enforcement agencies, including, on occasion, out of state and foreign countries, is required. This assistance is usually obtained via radio, teletypes, computers, bulletins, telephone, correspondence and personal visits by investigators.

Detailed coverage of the use of police records and other sources of information is contained in following chapters. When the suspect has been identified and there is sufficient cause, the investigator will proceed with the arrest.

## Arrest of Suspect

The suspect may be arrested at the scene, as mentioned in the prior bank robbery homicide example. The arrest may occur as a result of an immediate pursuit from or near the scene of the crime or the arrest may be preceded by a follow-up investigation, as in the example where the suspect fled from the bank before the police arrived.

In any case, the arrest procedure is very important to the final disposition of the case. The suspect and location of the arrest, as well as the vehicle and residence involved (including the route of escape in immediate pursuit cases) must be searched for weapons and evidence in the case. A search might produce the bank bag and money as in the robbery that has been given as an example.

All arrests of suspects as well as searches and seizures of evidence must be in keeping with current laws and court decisions. Many county and state prosecutors provide police agencies and college criminal justice programs with monthly digests of the latest appellate and Supreme Court decisions (case law), changes, or sustaining laws in pertinent criminal codes. Included in the digests will be the prosecutor's interpretation of each court decision and often a recommended procedure for police to follow in enforcing the particular law. In as much as criminal codes are generally published on a yearly basis, these digests have proven very valuable in keeping police current, particularly in the area of arrest, search and seizure.

### *Spontaneous Remarks*

The arresting officers must be alert for spontaneous remarks or admissions by suspects, which may be admissible as evidence in court. They must note the actions and evaluate the emotional and physical condition of the arrestees, as these factors may have a bearing on future defenses of "diminished capacity." For example, the late Senator Robert F. Kennedy's assassin, Sirhan Sirhan, was noted to be very alert, calculating, and even, at times, cunning in his conduct, following his removal from the crime scene and while being booked and interviewed at the station. Officers' testimony to this effect proved valuable during the subsequent trial in rebutting his defense, that he lacked the mental capacity to premeditate murder.

Advising arrestees of their constitutional rights under the Fifth Amendment is required, if they are to be questioned regarding an offense. In 1966 the United States Supreme Court concluded in *Miranda v. Arizona*, 384 U.S.436, that if officers intended to question suspects who are in custody or who have been significantly deprived of their freedom of action, they must advise the suspects of: (1) their right to counsel before any questions are asked (2) their right to remain silent at all times (3) the fact that if they gave up the right to remain silent, any statements they make may be used as evidence against them in court and (4) their right to have counsel present during questioning by officers and that if they cannot afford counsel, one will be appointed to represent them free of charge. Some states require that juveniles must be advised of their rights under the Fifth Amendment upon arrest, whether they are to be questioned or not. Provided the circumstances of the case warrant, and the arrestee, after being advised, waives all rights under the Fifth Amendment, an interrogation by the officers may proceed.

### Interrogation of the Suspect

The interrogation of suspects may occur wherever and whenever the time and location offers the greatest potential of deriving admissions or confessions from them. If the crime has just occurred and the suspect is arrested shortly thereafter, the circumstances may indicate that then is the time to interrogate. The location of the interrogation may be on the scene, or nearby, or in a police car en route to the police station. Many cases go to trial with no more statements from the accused than those obtained by the arresting officers. This may well be the *only* time a suspect will talk. Many times following incarceration the suspect has time to react, talk to other prisoners or a lawyer, and thereafter remain silent or at least become a poor interrogation subject.

If a period of time has passed and a follow-up investigation has occurred between the crime and the arrest, it may harm the investigation for any person, other than the investigator directly working the case, to interrogate the subject. The circumstances of the case may be that only the investigator will have intimate knowledge of all known details of the crime, the *modus operandi* and other confidential facts. It is possible that only the investigator knows what specific questions to ask the suspect or can recognize what information elicited or volunteered during questioning is relevant, material or otherwise important to the investigation. For example, a suspect in a murder may have violated the body of the victim in a depraved manner—a fact known only to the suspect, the key investigator, the case supervisor and the coroner. Someone questioning a suspect, who was not familiar with such intimate details, could overlook a very meaningful slip or even an intentional comment by the suspect. A detailed treatment of the techniques of interrogation is contained in Chapter 10.

### Recovery of Property

Property recovered in an investigation is not limited to that stolen from victims, but may well include weapons, tools, vehicles and numerous other items used in the commission of crimes.

The important fact to be established, if possible, is to connect the recovered property to the suspect and the crime. Suspects may retain jewelry, heirlooms, rare coins or other identifiable property of their victims. It is not uncommon for the police to recover victims' vehicles, weapons, and credit cards in the possession of suspects. Recovery may occur at the scene of an arrest or result from the interrogation of the suspect or the questioning of relatives or associates.

A search of a suspect's residence, vehicle or other location not accomplished at the time of the arrest, may require a search warrant and result in additional recovery of property. Stolen property is often located in pawnshops by use of computerized records maintained by law enforcement agencies. Secondhand stores, junkyards and receivers of stolen property (fences) often prove productive in this effort as well. The use of the many sources of recorded information, of which property files are but one, will be discussed in Chapters 7 and 8.

### Personal Identification of the Suspect

Personal identification of the suspect by the victim and witnesses is not always possible nor required to substantiate a case against the offender in some crimes. For example, in a murder where the victim is alone in an isolated area when he or she is killed by the suspect, there are no witnesses to make a personal identification of the suspect. Yet a case may be substantiated against the offender, through latent prints, footprints, foot imprints, a weapon, or items of clothing left by the suspect at the scene.

Often items of evidence that will establish a case for the prosecution may be obtained during the follow-up investigation and the arrest, including the admission of statements of suspects. Much the same as in murders, the investigation of many burglaries and thefts requires the police to develop cases primarily based on physical evidence.

In the crimes of robbery, assault, and rape, personal identification of the suspects by victims and witnesses is generally essential to the prosecution of the case. If the arrest of the suspect occurs on the scene or nearby shortly after the occurrence, it may be acceptable to allow the victim or witness to view the suspect for identification purposes. This obviously is not in keeping with the formal representative lineup procedure. In a formal lineup, the suspect is viewed, by the victim and witnesses in a line accompanied by at least eight or ten other persons of the same sex, race, and age group and approximate height, weight, build, and clothing etc., as that of the subject. Many lineup rooms or stages are a part of the jail facilities of the police station. The room or stage may be equipped with a large two-way mirror or screen that shields the viewers from view by those in the lineup.

The lighting conditions under which the suspect was seen can be simulated by the use of stage lights of various combinations. It may be desirable to photograph or shoot a color and sound videotape or film of the lineup in select cases. Defense attorneys are normally notified in advance that their client will appear in a formal lineup.

Attorneys have a right to attend lineups to protect their clients against improperly conducted lineups. However, an attorney may decline to be present. The final test of whether this identification procedure was properly conducted is a question of fact to be decided by the court.

## Presentation of the Case to the Prosecutor

Upon completion of the follow-up phase of the investigation, the investigator will usually submit the case file complete with all pertinent reports to either the city, county, state or federal prosecutor depending on the specific crime and jurisdiction involved. The file should contain, in addition to the reports, a list of all victims, witnesses, exhibits, and a summary of facts and witnesses' statements.

If the facts substantiate the offense, the prosecutor will then file a complaint charging the suspect with a specific offense. The prosecutor may deny the complaint for causes of insufficient evidence to prosecute and convict, or may request that further information be developed by additional investigation.

It is not uncommon for felony cases to be referred by the district attorney to the city attorney for reduction to misdemeanors. In highly sensitive and other selected felony cases, prosecutors may proceed via the grand jury indictment procedure in lieu of the complaint. This procedure is discussed in the following section.

## Presentation of the Case to a Grand Jury or Court

The prosecutor may elect to present a felony case, complete with all data, to a grand jury for consideration of an indictment. Examples of circumstances that may justify this approach in many jurisdictions are as follows:

- The statute of limitations is running out on the case and the suspect is not in custody. Laws in most states require that a criminal action be commenced against an accused within a given number of years after the commission of the crime. The statute of limitations for the typical felony is three years in most jurisdictions. If a jurisdiction fails to initiate a criminal action against an accused within the three years (may be more in some crimes), the accused could be free from prosecution.

- Some cases involving reluctant victims or witnesses in a rape or homicide, wherein threats of death or violence have been made against them, may be taken to the grand jury.

- The case may be highly sensitive, as in a political scandal or a major narcotics smuggling ring, wherein it is desired to eliminate exposure of witnesses to harassment and cross-examination by the defense. This factor is assured in the grand jury procedure because neither the accused nor his attorney has the right to be present at the hearing.

It is important to point out that a grand jury hearing is not a legal criminal trial, although all testimony is under oath and rules of evidence are followed. The grand jury hearing serves much the same purpose as the preliminary hearing, more commonly used in felony cases. Jurors can ask questions of the witnesses and often do. As a body, they can request the accused to testify; however, he or she can refuse to do so. Otherwise the presentation of testimony and evidence by the prosecutor follows the same procedure as in a court hearing or trial.

If the grand jury indicts the accused, the judge of the superior court will issue a bench warrant charging the specific offenses and setting bail. This indictment has the same force and effect as a preliminary hearing wherein the defendant is held to answer and an *information* is filed in superior court. Like the grand jury hearing, the preliminary hearing is not a criminal trial, but is rather for the purpose of determining if a crime was in fact committed and if there is reasonable cause to believe that the accused committed the crime. Once an indictment has been rendered and the warrant issued or the accused has been held to answer and the information is filed in superior court, the running of the statute of limitations is stopped.

The advantages of the grand jury process to the prosecution are obvious, yet the powers of the prosecutor are more limited compared to the complaint procedure. For example, in the grand jury method the prosecutor cannot directly "charge" the accused with any specific crime, even if the evidence substantiates it. The prosecutor can only *request* an indictment. It is the exclusive province of the grand jury to render the indictment it finds applicable.

If the prosecutor files a felony complaint against an accused, he or she is then arrested and arraigned on the charges. The case will be processed through the preliminary hearing and the superior court, or other court as appropriate. As in the grand jury process, the investigators, other law enforcement personnel involved in the case, the victim, and the witnesses will be called to testify; the rules of evidence are followed. However, the accused in this case is present with defense counsel and may cross-examine all witnesses and present a defense.

## Specialized Assignments—General Assignments

It would be difficult for one investigator to attain a great degree of expertise in the investigation of all types of crimes such as homicide, robbery, burglary, auto theft, narcotics, larceny and confidence games, during an average period of service with a law enforcement agency. This is because each of these categories of investigation includes a variety of specific offenses. In addition, the types of offenders, *modus operandi*, rates of occurrence, loss of property and degrees of public toleration are all variable. Each individual law enforcement agency typically evaluates the overall crime rate it is responsible for investigating. Due consideration is given to the variables in the light of the level of law enforcement demanded by the community. A determination is then made as to how much investigative time will be dedicated to each activity.

For example, some police departments devote very little investigative time to minor larcenies, particularly where the stolen property cannot be identified by serial numbers or other effective means. It is not uncommon for some agencies to receive reports of larcenies from victims via the telephone without a personal contact with the victim. The logic of this practice is obvious since very few departments have sufficient personnel to render full scale investigative services to all crimes committed in their jurisdiction. Available personnel is concentrated in the areas of greatest demand. Too often, in minor larcenies, the chances of arresting the right suspect, recovering identifiable property and returning it to the victims are very slim. Police auctions that periodically sell hundreds of thousands of dollars in unidentified stolen and lost property that has been recovered are evidence of this factor.

So it is that many investigators in large departments will spend a majority of their careers specializing in one or two areas of investigation, such as homicide, robbery, burglary, larcenies or confidence games. Investigators in smaller departments may work a broader field of assignments in keeping with the volume of cases in the various categories of crimes. Investigative expertise can be attained on either a large department or a smaller one depending on the time and effort expended. Many smaller departments train investigators to function proficiently as evidence technicians at crime scenes, unlike investigators with many larger departments, that have criminalists and other laboratory personnel at their disposal for the majority of the crime scene work. In either case, whether an investigator works specialized assignments or a general assignment, both endeavors can be very challenging and interesting. Chapters which follow will explore, in detail, qualifications and fundamental investigation techniques only touched on in this chapter. Every effort has been made to include the latest technological and scientific development in each technique discussed.

With respect to the area of crime scene investigation, this text's emphasis is on homicide which lends itself to better demonstrating a broad utilization of criminalistic functions. These same laboratory services are often used in whole or in part in the processing of crime scenes in the majority of all other crimes. As to the remaining techniques involved in the complete follow-up investigation and preparation of a case for trial, many investigations will involve similar functions. It is fully appreciated that the immensely broad field of criminal investigation will continue to improve and that material offered here is not beyond addition.

## SUMMARY

A successful criminal investigation can best be achieved if it is conducted in a sequential and thorough manner, beginning with the preliminary stage at the crime scene and continuing through the complete follow-up phases. It is essential that investigators have knowledge of the various combinations of elements that constitute the basic criminal laws. In addition, investigators should develop proficiency in evaluating complaints received from the public before taking appropriate action. If the complaint involves a civil matter, referral to an attorney would be in order. However if a crime has been committed, a preliminary investigation should be initiated. To insure the maximum probability of obtaining all evidence and identifying the suspect, the preliminary investigation of a crime scene should be systematic and in proper sequence.

The first officers arriving should isolate the scene, bearing in mind that the only valid reason for disturbing a crime scene is to render aid to the injured or to save a human life. Victims and witnesses must be separated for independent interviews. The scene should be evaluated as to the need for laboratory or other specialists and for selection of a standard search method to be used. Proceeding beyond the crime scene, the identification of the suspect may require collaboration from other agencies via teletypes and broadcasts and the use of various law enforcement records systems, including *modus operandi* files. Numerous other private and non-police recorded sources of information may also be used in the identification of the suspect.

When the suspect is identified, an arrest and a further search for evidence may follow, all performed in keeping with current laws. Investigators should be alert for spontaneous pre-interrogation statements made by suspects, which may be admissible as evidence in court. If arrestees are to be questioned regarding an offense, they must be advised of their constitutional rights under the Fifth Amendment.

The interrogation of suspects may occur wherever and whenever the time and location offers the greatest potential for deriving admissions or confessions from them. In complicated cases there may be some key information as to *modus operandi* that only the right suspect, the investigators, the victim, and perhaps a few other law enforcement personnel know. If this is the case, it may be advisable that only the investigators conduct the interrogation. They may be the best equipped to ask specific questions and evaluate information received.

The recovery of property may occur at various locations and may require a search warrant. The preparation of the case for presentation to a prosecutor may include physical evidence recovered at the crime scene and other locations. Statements and personal identification of the suspect by the victim and/or witnesses and any admission or confession made by the suspect, are also part of case preparation.

A prosecutor may proceed with a criminal action against a suspect by filing a complaint which will be followed by an arraignment of the suspect (if in custody), followed by a preliminary hearing. If the suspect who is now a defendant is "held to answer," the case would then move into the superior court for trial. In sensitive cases, the prosecutor may select to proceed via a grand jury indictment. The fundamentals and methods of investigation discussed are applicable whether investigators are working specialized assignments in larger departments or general assignments in smaller departments.

## DISCUSSION QUESTIONS

1. Define *investigation* in your own words.
2. What is the primary objective of a criminal investigation?
3. What is the *corpus delicti* of a crime? Give an example.
4. Why must an investigator evaluate a complaint from an alleged victim prior to initiating action?
5. How is a composite perception of an occurrence obtained from victims and witnesses?
6. How is the crime scene coverage important to the identification of the suspect?
7. How do investigators obtain information from recorded sources?
8. Explain the importance of the overall circumstances of the arrest of the suspect relative to the outcome of a criminal case in court.
9. Where should the interrogation of a suspect take place? Why?
10. Do arresting officers ever obtain incriminating statements from suspects? Why?

11. When may it be advisable for only the investigators directly working the case to interrogate a suspect?

12. What is the most important fact to be established regarding recovered property?

13. Identify several locations where property may likely be recovered.

14. Is personal identification of a suspect by the victim or witness always required to make a case on a suspect? Explain and give an example.

15. Describe a formal lineup and several types of crimes the suspect could be involved in.

16. What is the main advantage to the prosecution of filing a felony case via the prosecutor, as opposed to presenting the case to a grand jury for indictment?

17. What are several of the advantages to the prosecution in presenting a case to a grand jury for indictment?

18. Is a grand jury hearing a criminal trial? Why? Why not?

19. What is a specialized investigative assignment?

20. What is a general investigative assignment?

# CHARACTERISTICS OF INVESTIGATORS  2

## KEY TERMS AND CONCEPTS

Development of characteristics
"Search for truth"
Bump of suspicion
Unfounded complaint syndrome
Rapid decision vs. hasty conclusion
Factors of observation
Rapport
Bias and prejudice
Patience and courtesy
Exhibitionism
Ethics
Remaining qualified

Knowledge of the basic fundamentals, methods, and techniques of investigation is obviously essential for anyone who is preparing for this field. In addition, there are a number of characteristics that investigators must develop in order to perform their duties properly.

## THE DEVELOPMENT OF CHARACTERISTICS

The search for facts in cases is often confused, if not stifled, by a lack of objectivity on the part of investigators. They may be well versed in the law and investigative techniques, yet may overdevelop one characteristic to the detriment of others, thus limiting their effectiveness.

Investigators, therefore, should strive to be objective, keeping in mind that a criminal investigation can affect the lives of all those involved, both guilty and innocent. Being objective includes maintaining a reasonable balance between each of the following essential characteristics.

## Suspicion

To investigators, *suspicion* means taking nothing for granted, yet not making it overly obvious to those they contact. Investigators may find that victims and witnesses, as well as suspects, may be motivated by various physiological, psychological and sociological needs that "color" the information they give. In developing ways of satisfying the basic need for food, sex, love, security, economic and social status, some people, unfortunately, identify with values that encourage deceit. "Higher animals,especially man, acquire the need for many conditions not originally related to survival (i.e., approval by others, status symbols, etc.) and his internal equilibrium is upset in the absence of these conditions." Therefore, investigators should, when possible, develop proof of all that is alleged to them and be constantly wary of things that appear too obvious.

The following actual case illustrates the need to be suspicious of that which is too obvious:

> The bullet-riddled body of a male victim was found in some brush. The bereaved wife of the victim was showing investigators around the family business, which was a paint store. The investigators noticed that while the exterior and interior of the building were in dire need of a new paint job, the floor of the interior was freshly painted in red. Further investigation by criminalists, at the request of the investigators, revealed blood stains of the victim's type on the floor underneath the fresh paint. A follow-up of this lead revealed that the victim was slain in the store by the wife's lover.

## Curiosity

Another characteristic that is closely related to suspicion is curiosity. Curiosity means a desire to investigate and learn the facts or truth about people, places or objects. To investigators this means being habitually curious of such things as spontaneous statements made by suspects, an unusual amount of money in the possession of a person of moderate means, or the presence of a highly expensive business machine in an otherwise modest business office. For example, investigation may reveal that a spontaneous statement made by a suspect is admissible as evidence in court. An unusual amount of money in the possession of a person of otherwise moderate means, may be completely legal. It could also be stolen. Investigation may reveal that the modest business mentioned has purchased an expensive business machine for a fraction of its true value from a burglar.

## Observation

Still another characteristic that should be developed along with curiosity is observation. Investigators should be trained observers. They should develop the ability to take accurate notice of, keep in view and give attention to, that which is present to their five senses. This is a prime and important function of investigation. The physical factors of the senses involved in observation are sight, hearing, smell, touch and taste.

### *Sight*

It is widely accepted that the most important and accurate aspect of observation is sight, and yet, what we perceive via our senses can be erroneous. Research in physiology and psychology reveals that: "Sensations do not impinge on a totally naive nervous system. Sensations, therefore, interact with the memory traces of past-experience to form perceptions." This principle in psychology is often expressed in law enforcement circles as our eyes often see only what they look for and look for what is already in our minds.

It is possible to train our powers of observation by making a concerted effort to see and recall more of what we look at. Thus, the average person may look at something but does not really see it and cannot describe in any detail what he or she has just looked at. On the other hand, a trained observer will make an effort not to miss anything, especially if it is the least bit suspicious, unusual or out of place. An officer on patrol should develop the habit of glancing down every alley and side street he or she passes. One should also make a mental note of the people, vehicles, etc., as he or she goes by. Most of us see but do not observe (i.e., we do not let enough of what we see consciously register on our minds).

There are a variety of factors that also affect proper vision. The distance and light conditions involved in the perception, as well as the size of the object observed, are important factors. It is generally accepted that dimly lighted objects are indistinct, that a person already in a dark hallway can see better than one who has just entered the hallway, and that objects directly in front of one's view are the clearest.

With continued practical application, the investigator can develop this side vision to a level of proficiency that will enable him or her to observe movements in stores and parking lots as he or she drives by in a vehicle. In searching crime scenes, following the systematic procedure, discussed in later chapters, can train the eye to observe detail.

### Hearing

Another important aspect of observation is hearing. Too often, the observation of sound is unclear and subjective. It is difficult to estimate the distance, place and direction of sound. We generally relate a sound to a series of sounds previously heard. The same principle of sensations and perceptions referred to in the discussion of the sight aspect of observation would apply here. An investigator should make an effort to remember the source of sounds (e.g., breaking glass, automotive engines, motorcycles, running footsteps, etc.) which he or she hears.

Voice clarification can often present problems. It may be somewhat difficult for a witness to identify the voice of a person positively, unless that person is known to the witness. Now and then a crime will occur wherein the suspect's voice is unusual (such as shrill or cackling), particularly when the suspect is under tension during the commission of the crime. Yet the chance that the witness will again hear the suspect's voice under tension is remote, even when the suspect is apprehended, placed in a lineup, and asked to answer routine, irrelevant questions.

Scientific studies on recognizing voices, have tested how likely it is that a listener's judgment might be in error. One such study by McGhee, reported in his article, "The Reliability of the Identification of the Human Voice, *General Psychology*, vol. 17, pages 249-251, reported on groups of listeners who participated in two experimental sessions that were separated in time from one day to several months. During the first session, participants heard an unfamiliar speaker read a paragraph of text. During the second session, they heard the same paragraph read by five speakers, including the speaker from the first session. The ability of the listeners to recognize the speaker whom they heard in the first session was investigated as a function of the time interval between the two sessions. The investigation revealed that the reliability of recognition decreases rapidly as the time interval between sessions is extended beyond two weeks. For example, the decrease ranged from 83 percent recognition on the first day to 81 percent recognition at the end of the first week. Thereafter, recognition dropped rapidly from 69 percent at the end of the second week to 51 percent recognition at the end of the third week. By the end of the second month, recognition dropped to 35 percent, and by the end of the third month, it was down to only 13 percent.

It was also discovered that increasing the number of speakers heard during the sessions and using vocal disguise, effectively lowered recognition scores. A police lineup may contain as many as 12 or more suspects. If a witness were to hear each suspect speak in turn and one or more disguised voice, a positive recognition may be difficult unless, as previously stated, the suspect was apprehended shortly after the crime.

### Smell

Investigators should also utilize their sense of smell which is very useful in identifying such things as gases, inflammables, poisons and other substances involved in arson and suicide investigations. The following suicide case illustrates the importance of recognizing odors.

A truck driver employed by an electroplating company had access to cyanide from their plating section. He was undergoing marital problems and decided the only way out was suicide. He took some cyanide home, dissolved it in a pan of water in his garage, closed the doors and inhaled the fumes. He probably collapsed immediately and died within minutes. When the investigators arrived at the scene, responding to a call, the garage door was open. As they stepped into the garage they smelled a bitter-almond odor. Recalling prior training on poisons, they immediately smelled the deceased's mouth which reeked of the bitter-almond odor. This, of course, meant a strong possibility of cyanide poisoning. They immediately left the garage, locked the door and called the fire department that aired the garage thoroughly. Investigators carefully removed the pan with the cyanide prior to a search of the scene. Is this too much concern over a little gas in a garage with an open door? The investigators obviously did not think so. Cyanide, a compound (as potassium cyanide) of cyanogen and used in electroplating processes, is deadly poisonous. It is rapidly absorbed by the skin and most dangerous when inhaled. A .2 to .3 mg. per liter concentration is immediately fatal. Collapse is usually instantaneous, and a .13 mg. per liter concentration would be fatal in an hour.

### Touch

The sense of touch has several applications in the field of investigation. A fast heartbeat, pulse or breathing rate can indicate whether a person has very recently experienced exertion (e.g., running or altercation). Whether the tires, engine or radiator of a vehicle are hot or cold will indicate if it has recently been in motion. Various types of cloth have a distinctive feel to the touch (e.g., silk is very smooth, soft and flexible when twisted; wool on the average is soft and fibrous with body, and its fibers will crisp and curl when touched by flame). The sense of touch, however, can be deceptive unless controlled by eyesight.

### Taste

The sense of taste must be used with discretion, as is the case with the sense of smell, for obvious safety reasons. Taste is quite subjective and more often individual than not.

### Summary

To insure maximum effectiveness as an observer, investigators must memorize and associate observations, and evaluate them in terms of violations of the law or as indicators of investigative needs. They must remain cognizant of all suspicious persons, vehicles, lights, movements and actions.

## Bias And Prejudice

An unbiased and unprejudiced mind is very difficult to develop, yet it is essential to investigators if they are to establish the truth or facts in a case. A discussion of bias and prejudice will, it is hoped, offer some assistance in this effort.

Definitions for bias and prejudice are varied, according to the context with which the terms are associated. In criminal investigation, *bias* means a highly personal and unreasoned distortion of judgment. *Prejudice* means an opinion or leaning adverse to anything without just grounds or before sufficient knowledge.

Neither bias nor prejudice has any place in an investigation. To allow either attitude to be involved in a case will result in a sloppy investigation, incorrect conclusions and unfairness to victims and suspects.

It is imperative that the investigator maintain an open mind, regardless of the circumstances. At times, conditions may require the denial of an assignment or the removal of an investigator from a case for reasons of emotional or other interests that do not serve the cause of justice. Through training and experience one can overcome predisposed attitudes towards certain types of situations, people, places and objects that otherwise can be misleading.

One must remember that even a "chronic complainant" can make a legitimate complaint. A prostitute can be the victim of a rape, and a drunk can be robbed like any sober person. The search for facts can be greatly facilitated if investigators develop rapport with those they contact, particularly victims and witnesses. *Rapport* means a feeling of ease and harmony in a contact or relationship between people. This can be accomplished through the use of patience, courtesy, sympathy and empathy.

## Patience, Courtesy, Sympathy and Empathy

Establishment of rapport with victims and witnesses is one of the prime facilitators of an investigation. With few exceptions, this can be accomplished by being patient, courteous and sympathetic with persons contacted during an investigation. This does not mean that investigators are to be beguiled or mislead. They are seeking rapport not conversation. It is important to remember that all persons have their own reality, which is a product of their life experiences.

Values differ; what is important to an investigator is not necessarily important to a victim. It is often necessary to empathize with the victim or witness which means to put yourself in their place. Remember, an investigation may be routine to the police, but utter bewilderment and confusion to others. Investigators can make a more positive impression with the public they serve by producing results, rather than by being exhibitionists or show-offs. A few comments that may assist investigators in developing credibility and avoiding exhibitionism are offered below.

## Credibility vs. Exhibitionism

Investigators should beware not to attempt to exhibit expertise in all fields of law enforcement. It is entirely possible that the person they talk to may actually be an expert in the area being discussed. One should not tell a victim that certain evidential factors are present at the crime scene, such as latent prints, unless they have developed, photographed and lifted the prints or were present when it was done. Otherwise, when an evidence technician or criminalist arrives at the scene and can't find prints to develop, the police will lose face regardless of whom the victim believes. In addition, investigators should not discuss case details with anyone outside of police or other authorized circles. This practice can be prejudicial and compromising to both the prosecution and the defense. The sensitivity of this issue is manifested daily by allegations of pretrial publicity of defendants by the media and courts ordering "gags" in cases. Investigators should also develop the use of reason in making decisions or conclusions, and thus facilitate logical deductions. The following comparison between a rapid decision and a hasty conclusion illustrates this point.

## A Rapid Decision vs. A Hasty Conclusion

A rapid decision by a seasoned investigator can be based on experience and training, while a hasty conclusion is often based on a superficial investigation or a preconceived idea. For example, an investigator is conducting a preliminary walk-through of a murder scene in a high crime frequency rooming house. The victim is lying nude on the floor face down. There is evidence of post-mortem lividity on the victim's back, yet the discoverer of the scene has stated that nothing has been moved. The investigator knows from experience and training that the lividity visible on the body appeared some time after death. The blood drained down by force of gravity to those parts of the body nearest the floor and remained. A rapid decision to immediately pursue this issue may well be in order. It is obvious that the deceased laid face up for several hours after death, yet now lies face down. However, a conclusion at this point that the discoverer of the scene has lied to the investigator or is involved in the death would be hasty. It would not be a logical deduction. Some one else could have turned the body over hours after death or the deceased could have been brought there from another location, several hours after the murder.

The remaining characteristics of investigators are also applicable to most professions. They must be dedicated, industrious, innovative and persevering, thus assuring complete investigations. They must also be loyal to the ethics of law enforcement and constantly strive to maintain the highest professional standards. A coverage in this area would be incomplete without mentioning *intuition*—the innate or instinctive knowledge often referred to as a "gut feeling." Intuition can be a valuable tool to investigators, however it must be accompanied by reasoning and objectivity.

## SUMMARY

Knowledge of the fundamentals and methods of investigation is essential for persons who are preparing for assignments in investigation. In addition, investigators must develop a number of professional characteristics in order to perform their duties effectively. They must strive for objectivity and avoid the overdevelopment of any one characteristic discussed in this chapter. They must be suspicious of that which is too obvious and take nothing for granted. In addition, investigators should be curious of and investigate such things as spontaneous statements by suspects or the sudden wealth of a person of usually modest means. They must develop and make full use of the five senses—sight, hearing, smell, touch, and taste—and become trained observers.

Also essential to investigators is an unbiased and unprejudiced mind. The use of patience, courtesy, sympathy and empathy when dealing with victims and witnesses will help establish rapport. The development of credibility can be enhanced by avoiding exhibitionism. The use of reason in making decisions and conclusions is also an essential characteristic, as is dedication, industriousness, innovativeness, perseverance and the use of intuition. In conclusion, investigators must be loyal to the ethics of law enforcement and constantly strive to maintain the highest professional standards.

## DISCUSSION QUESTIONS

1.  Why is it imperative that an investigator not take anything for granted when dealing with victims, witnesses and suspects?
2.  What is the prime disadvantage to an investigation caused by an investigator having an "unfounded complaint" syndrome?
3.  What is the difference between a rapid desision and a hasty conclusion? Review a case in example from the text or other sources.

4.  In connection with the five senses, what ability must the investigator develop?

5.  Give some examples of physical conditions that may exist in situations that affect proper vision.

6.  Why would one subjectively relate a sound heard? Give some examples.

7.  With regard to sounds, what must the investigator exercise care in remembering? Give examples.

8.  How is the sense of smell useful in investigations? Give an example.

9.  How is the sense of touch useful in investigations? Give an example.

10. How can an investigator insure maximum effectiveness as an observer?

11. Define *bias* in its relationship to a criminal investigation.

12. Define what *prejudice* means in a criminal investigation.

13. What affect will the involvement of bias or prejudice likely have on an investigation?

14. How can an investigator overcome predisposed detrimental attitudes about situations, people, places, and objects? Give examples.

15. How can an investigator help to establish rapport with victims and witnesses?

16. Give some examples of exhibitionism that are to be avoided by the investigator while on a case.

17. Give examples of other ideal characteristics and attitudes for investigators that are applicable and important to most professions.

# NOTES AND REPORTS

**3**

---

## KEY TERMS AND CONCEPTS

Chronological notes
Principles of reporting
*Modus operandi*
Description of property
Brevity
Aid to Law Enforcement

It is generally accepted that most persons would find it difficult, if not impossible, to commit to memory all investigative details that are necessary for a complete report. Therefore, upon first notification or receipt of a complaint of an alleged offense, investigators must begin taking written chronological (in order of occurrence) notes of all information received, actions taken, and observations made. It is imperative to maintain this written record of all phases of an investigation, including the preliminary and follow-up procedures. These notes will be the basis for all narrative reports. Notes are used in connection with the investigator's future testimony in court and may be entered as evidence.

## NOTES

Written chronological notes establish a permanent record of all official notifications received and made by investigators. In addition, the following preparatory, preliminary and follow-up investigation activities are also recorded:

- Ambulance or other medical aid at the scene
- Laboratory services at the scene
- Assistance from other investigators, officers or persons at the scene
- Assistance from other public agencies, such as the fire department
- Coroner or medical examiner services
- News media (photos and press releases)
- Complete crime scene search and neighborhood canvass
- Statements from victims and witnesses
- Identification, apprehension and interrogation of suspects
- Recovery of evidence or other property
- Preparation of the case for the prosecutor

The materials needed for notetaking are very basic. A lined paper tablet, a ball-point pen and a plastic scaled rule are ideal for notes and rough sketches. A clipboard with a battery powered light or the tablet clipboard will also prove advantageous. Taking notes in a structured chronological order, covering all activities from the first notification received to the conclusion of the case, has been proven to be very desirable. Each entry should be prefaced by an identification of the subject matter, the date, time, location and persons present or involved. Whether the notes are totally narrative or in part in outline form will depend on the subject matter.

Brevity in notes is desirable, but not at the sacrifice of pertinent and relevant material. The recording of spontaneous declarations, admissions and confessions by suspects (in lieu of formal statements) should be as verbatim as possible. Chronological coverage will facilitate dictating the narrative report by merely embellishing on the notes obtained. On occasion it may be advantageous to use a stenographer or an electronic device, either overt or covert, for recording an interview or an interrogation. All investigators' and stenographers' notes and recordings of interviews, admissions or confessions, which are highly sensitive or have special value as evidence, should be maintained in a secure place. It may be difficult for investigators not to avoid overlooking an important step or item in the course of an investigation. This is particularly true in the first minutes of a highly sensitive or otherwise tension producing case. Some investigators prepare formats (prepared notes with blank spaces) and notification or check sheets for the crime scene and immediate follow-up investigation of several specific crimes. Examples of these guidelines are offered in Chapter 12.

## INVESTIGATIVE CHECKLIST FOR KIDNAP— HOSTAGE CASES

The following investigative checklist was developed to serve as a reminder to investigators involved in major kidnap-hostage crimes. The list is the product of years of experience and represents the input of scores of specialized investigators. Much like a commercial airline pilot, it is difficult for an investigator to remember to do everything necessary in a lengthy or complicated procedure without a checklist.

For the reader's benefit, acronyms used in this checklist are in alphabetical order and have the following meaning: BAD - Burglary/Auto theft Division; CNT—Crisis Negotiation Team; CRASH—Gang Detail; DHD/CO—Detective Headquarters, Commanding Officer; RHD—Robbery-Homicide Division; SID—Scientific Investigation Division; SIS—Special Investigation Section; SWAT—Special Weapons and Tactics Team.

1.  The Victim(s)

    *   Obtain complete identity and description (oddities such as scars, birthmarks, jewelry, clothing last worn) of victim.

    *   Obtain victim's vehicle description if applicable.

    *   Obtain most recent photograph of victim.

    *   Obtain copies via photo lab.

    *   Obtain medical information on victim (i.e., present physical condition, health and if presently taking medication).

    *   Run victim for warrants and criminal history.

    *   Obtain copy of prints.

    *   Crime victim check.

- Determine victim's normal daily routine and backtrack to locate where victim was kidnapped (if known). If kidnap site is located, canvas area for evidence and witnesses to be interviewed.

- Obtain as much information on victim as possible (i.e., specific information only the victim would know or be able to acknowledge). This requires suspect to take some type of action in most cases.

- Require proof victim is still alive. This proof should be absolute and on an ongoing basis.

- Anticipate what you will do if emergencies arise, such as death threats, sudden changes, arrest of only one suspect and victim still outstanding, etc.

- Ascertain if victim has had any disagreements lately. If businessman or executive, is there a partner dispute or disgruntled past or present employees.

- Check victim's residence and consider a stakeout.

- If contact for ransom not made, anticipate and be at victim's residence.

- Attempt to locate all vehicles that victim uses or are registered to him. If any are missing, send teletype.

- Record, on paper, exact statements of all participants. If exact verbiage is unknown, so indicate.

- If victim and suspects are located, remember SWAT is at your disposal.

2. Suspects

- Check any known locations where victim was taken for any evidence to identify suspect(s).

- Setup surveillance of suspect (if known) or person who will make money drop.

- Have any item that suspect and/or victim may have touched printed.

- When suspect(s) are arrested, isolate them. Have SID, Crime Lab, process their clothing and person for evidence that may connect them **with** the victim or locations where victim was held or injured.

- Search and photograph any locations used by suspect(s), i.e., residence, work, hangouts, etc.
- Contact duty district attorney for warrants if time permits. Locate judge to sign warrants.
- Consider voice print corroboration.
- Utilize a profile assessment when time and data permit.
- Assess any threat, will it be carried out, is suspect knowledgeable about how to carry the threat out.
- Anticipate suspect utilizing someone not involved in crime to make money pick up.

3. Notifications

- Staff personnel (DHD C/O)
- RHD Rape Section and Child Abuse if victim is a child
- SIS (seek input for any surveillance)
- SID
  1. Electronics (tape equipment)
  2. Explosives (exploding package or if there is a bomb involved)
- DHD (Has list of officers who speak other languages)
- Metro
  1. SWAT
  2. CNT officer
  3. Dog
- Air Support
- FBI (If interstate transport or escape probable)
- Other local law enforcement agencies.

4. Investigative

- Phone tap where suspect(s) will call.

- Tape record all conversations to that phone.

- Maintain constant contact and control of person to receive calls from suspect(s).

- Reduce police visibility (vehicles and personnel).

- Anticipate need for rental equipment (vehicles, trucks, uniforms, etc.)

- Spanish speaking detective if needed.

- Obtain funds if needed from DHD.

- Obtain exploding package if needed from SID, Explosives Unit.

- Make facsimile package if needed.

- Anticipate long term investigation and make up detective relief roster (overlap watches). Give complete briefing.

- Build in flexibility to your plans. At the mercy Of suspect(s) and everything is subject to     immediate change.

- Deployment should provide reserve capability 24-hours a day. Utilize all specialized details (NARC, BAD,

- Vice Units, Gangs, CRASH, etc. Select someone to deal with suspect(s) on phone or meet in person. Someone who is up on current street jargon. Consider "CNT" officer input and SIS input.

- Anticipate need for SWAT, bomb squad, dogs, and air support to counter terrorist types.

- Nuclear or chemical threat requires special handling; consider military, etc.

- Plan ahead. Control the exchange or money drop if possible. This requires tune and coordination. Utilize SIS input.

- Centralize control of all information gathered. This allows all personnel to get information immediately.

- Utilize all department resources and experts in their field. DO NOT hesitate to call them.

- PRIMARY OBJECTIVE IS ALWAYS THE SAFE RETURN OF THE VICTIM.

# REPORTS

Information obtained by investigators is of little use unless it is properly communicated to appropriate persons. The identification, apprehension, and successful prosecution of criminals and the recovery of stolen property depends on a carefully planned strategy. The investigators' reports, as well as all other law enforcement reports, constitute the core of the record systems that is an integral part of this planned strategy. The many complete and productive police record bureaus in various jurisdictions in the United States and foreign countries represent several hundred years of collective investigative and technical staff experience. The prevailing objective in developing these massive reservoirs of information is the efficient and effective identification, apprehension and prosecution of criminals and the recovery of stolen property. Record systems have improved dramatically from their modest inception to today's computerized mode. The stature investigators achieve in agencies will be greatly influenced by the caliber of the reports they write. The original reporting officers' thoroughness and ability are indicated by their reports. If the original report is incomplete, reporting officers must be contacted by the investigators, witnesses must be re-interviewed and supplementary efforts made. This is a wasteful expenditure of personnel and resources which can be avoided.

Original reporting officers have the best opportunity to obtain all the facts at the crime scene immediately following the occurrence, while the incident is fresh in the minds of the victims and witnesses. It is generally an accepted practice that in serious or complicated cases, where investigators assigned to the case are not the original reporting officers, the investigators will re-interview victims and witnesses. This may be done even when the original report appears complete. It is frequently imperative that the investigators who are directly working the case, evaluate the quality of all persons making accusations or offering other evidence. On occasion the stories of these persons may change after they have had time to "think things over." Re-interviews may also reveal something that was overlooked by the original reporting officers.

## Principles of Reporting

The most important principle in reporting is accuracy. It is therefore imperative that investigators do not confuse hearsay with facts.

Basically, *hearsay* is a statement or a story given by a person who did not witness or experience the occurrence. The person giving the statement or story is merely repeating what he or she was told about the occurrence by someone else. This kind of a statement is not admissible as evidence because it is not based on something that was personally witnessed or experienced by the declarant.

This is not a full treatment of the *hearsay rule* and does not identify the several exceptions to the rule. However this information suffices for the purpose of this chapter. A thorough investigator will use hearsay information received as a lead to the person that can relate facts. As the investigation progresses, hearsay, facts, opinions and conclusions will be related by many of those interviewed. Hearsay and facts have been briefly defined, now let's consider opinions and conclusions. An opinion is a general conclusion made by a person about another person, place or object, however lacking certainty. Opinions may be arrived at as the result of either subjective or objective evaluation of information or experience. In brief, *subjective* relates to something within the mind, while *objective* relates to something outside of the mind. What this means to investigators is that if they allow their own emotions, bias or prejudice to enter into an opinion, then that opinion is clearly subjective, and has no place in an investigative report.

Investigators may form an objective opinion of a person, place, situation, or object, providing they consider facts only. Their experience may have established certain facts that may also properly be a part of that opinion. Objective opinions can be included in reports, but must be clearly identified as such. To investigators, a conclusion is a practical determination or a final decision and can be based only on objective facts.

Completeness in an investigational report is a "must." Partial facts tell only a part of the story and may well create a false picture in the mind of the reviewer. If essential information is missing in the report, the investigator must explain why it was not obtained. An incomplete report may be avoided if the who, what, where, when, why and how of a case is established and no verbal explanation by the investigator is required.

Investigators should strive for brevity in writing their reports, but not at the sacrifice of any pertinent and relevant material. They should eliminate all unnecessary material, thus condensing the narrative and facilitating an objective evaluation of the investigation.

### *Reports Aid Direction of Law Enforcement*

Identification, statistics, *modus operandi*, crime summary, engineering, and other investigational information from reports is part of the data used by chiefs of police and sheriffs in the overall administration of their departments. To achieve the most effective use of all available resources, such as personnel and equipment, in the battle against crime, these administrators are constantly involved in short, medium and long range planning. This planning can be most meaningful if administrators have current, precise and complete data readily available to them. These requisites are basic to administration and mentioned here primarily for the purpose of prefacing a description of the pioneering efforts of many police agencies in designing report forms, from which this needed data can be retrieved.

For many years data from police reports was converted to code numbers and symbols for IBM and other punch card input and retrieval. Identification, statistical, property, crime and other modus operandi information retrievals from these systems had proven very useful. However, data was not fully correlated or always current. Population growths in many cities and a disproportionate increase in crime emphasized the need for more effective systems of input and retrieval. Many systems have since been developed throughout the United States to meet the need for greater correlation and currency of data.

For example, the Los Angeles Police Department has developed a computerized information processing system that provides current crime pattern recognition by correlating information on crimes, property and suspects. The daily input into this processing system is comprised of information from crime reports, property reports, pawnshop reports, investigators' final reports and automated field interview cards. The retrieval of this correlated information is very simple. An investigator can ask the computer questions. The computer can supply a crime pattern in a matter of minutes. The correlating capability of the system reveals possible tie-ins between each suspect, each element of his modus operandi in various crimes, separate items of property taken in different crimes, pawnshop records, and suspect and vehicle information from field interview cards on a day-to-day basis.

Since much of the *modus operandi* information which investigators work with is derived from police reports, it is logical to treat modus operandi at this point.

### Modus Operandi

*Modus operandi* is the method of operation used by a criminal in committing a crime. The theory of *modus operandi* is based on the premise that we all acquire habits, traits or mannerisms, thus establishing a behavior pattern which is individual. Many investigators have encountered any number of situations which validate this theory. All cases necessitate an evaluation as to which elements of the overall modus operandi are characteristic, accidental or individual. In the commission of a certain crime or series of similar crimes by a single suspect or group of suspects, the same modus operandi elements may be individual in one case and accidental in the other.

The socioeconomic background of the suspect or the victim may be a factor in the evaluation also, particularly in tying in a series of crimes to one suspect or a group of suspects. Behavioral scientists state that our traits, habits and mannerisms stem from the fact that we all develop our own ways of satisfying our basic physiological, psychological and sociological needs. Further, the overall environment from birth throughout life greatly influences individual development and change. To illustrate why *modus operandi* elements require an evaluation to determine which are characteristic, accidental, or individual, the following cases are offered.

This first case illustrates that in spite of the suspect's high intelligence, a prior prison term served for the same crime, and a cunning flexibility in general *modus operandi*, he could not overcome the desire to obtain even an inexpensive item for nothing. The suspect was on parole from the state prison and decided to commit a series of armed robberies of markets. His intelligence and experience directed him to supermarkets, since the prison term for armed robbery does not differentiate as to the amount of money or other property taken. He was clever in switching personal disguises, weapons, briefcases and vehicles. He widely dispersed his pattern of attack and did not leave latent prints, notes or other physical evidence at the crime scenes. However, he had long before developed a taste for a particular brand of scotch whiskey and took a bottle from the liquor section of each market he robbed. The bottles contained serial numbers on the tax seals that could be traced to the individual markets. A statewide broadcast included information relative to his taking the scotch whiskey on each robbery, brought about his arrest. Following a traffic accident, a partially consumed bottle of scotch was found in his car. Another bottle and some holdup paraphernalia was found in his apartment. This suspect was trapped by a bottle of whiskey he could have easily purchased with loot from any of the prior robberies. The *modus operandi* elements were characteristic as to the weapons, disguises, and other paraphernalia, yet individual as to the taking of the whiskey. The element of accident was not present in the commission of these crimes.

In another case, investigators were required to use flexibility in interpreting the *modus operandi* factors. The suspects all came from a ghetto area, where a divergence of values and a devil-may-care attitude was prevalent. This case involved a holdup gang that committed a series of robberies of armored trucks, a variety of major business houses, hot dog stands, taxi cabs, busses and pedestrians. The ethnic backgrounds of the victims were as varied as the types of businesses attacked. The gang frequently switched members, cars and weapons. Investigators first assumed that they were dealing with a number of different gangs. However, as the investigation progressed, it was clear that individual participating gang members used the same spoken phrases, threats, and brutality, regardless of the combination of suspects, weapons or cars used on particular individual robberies. The final identification and roundup of the suspects revealed family relationships, regular crime partners, or just strays, who happened to be in the local pool hall when the group decided to commit a particular robbery. The *modus operandi* elements were characteristic as to weapons and cars used, as well as to the money taken. The elements were individual as to the spoken phrases, threats and brutality used, yet a combination of characteristic and accidental depending on what group of suspects comprised the gang on any one of the particular robberies. The only constant factor in the case was the ethnic background of the suspects, which was attributable to the area they all lived in.

The *modus operandi* examples given relate to only one class of crime. In the overall field of criminal investigation there are as many interesting or bizarre examples as there are types of crimes and suspects. Because of this phenomenon, many police agencies have for many years utilized the experience of investigators to aid staff units in developing and periodically revising crime reporting forms and procedures to improve the collection of *modus operandi* information.

Although this reporting system includes forms for all arrests and investigative activities, only the robbery report is offered as an illustration under Figure 3-1. Other forms are illustrated in Chapter 7.

### *Description of Property*

When reporting the theft or loss of property, the investigator should, if possible, indicate the current market value of the property;

Page 1 of _____    03.01 0 (6-75)    LOS ANGELES POLICE DEPARTMENT
**PRELIMINARY INVESTIGATION of**
**ROBBERY**    DR    TEAM OF OCCUR

| PREMISES | CRIME OCCURRED IN/ON (St, Bar, Bank, Veh, Resid, Vac Lot) | | | | | | |
|---|---|---|---|---|---|---|---|
| | IF RESIDENCE GIVE TYPE (Apt., Single Family, Hotel) | | | | LAST NAME, FIRST, MIDDLE (Firm Name if Business) | SEX | DESCENT | AGE | DOB |

VICTIM

R/B-RESIDENCE/BUSINESS ADDRESS    PHONE    X

| VEHICLE | ☐ Susp's ☐ Vict's | YEAR | MAKE | MODEL | TYPE |
|---|---|---|---|---|---|
| | COLOR | VEH LIC NO | | | STATE |

R-
B-

LOCATION OF OCCURRENCE    RD    VICT'S OCCUPATION

| Interior | Exterior | Body | Windows |
|---|---|---|---|
| INSIDE COLOR | 1 CUSTOM WHLS | 1 DAMAGE | 1 DAMAGE |
| 1 BUCKET SEATS | 2 PAINTED INSCR | 2 MODIFIED | 2 CUST. TINT |
| | 3 LEVEL ALTERED | 3 STICKER | 3 CURTAINS |
| 2 DAMAGED INSIDE | 4 RUST/PRIMER | 4 LEFT | 4 LEFT |
| | 5 CUSTOM PAINT | 5 RIGHT | 5 RIGHT |
| | 6 VINYL TOP | 6 FRONT | 6 FRONT |
| | | 7 REAR | 7 REAR |

DATE & TIME OF OCCURRENCE    DATE & TIME REPORTED TO PD

TYPE OF PROPERTY TAKEN    STOLEN $    RECOVERED $

NOTIFICATIONS - Persons & Division    CONNECTED REPORTS - Type & Dr No.

| ENTRY | Point of entry (FRONT DOOR, SIDE WINDOW, SKYLIGHT, ETC) | Method of entry (PRIED LOCK, CUT SCREEN, SMASHED WINDOW, ETC) | Instrument/tool used (SCREWDRIVER, BODILY FORCE, KEY, ETC) | Type window or door (WOOD PANEL, SLIDING GLASS, WOOD SASH, ETC) |
|---|---|---|---|---|

M. O.    UNIQUE OR UNUSUAL ACTIONS THAT MAY TEND TO IDENTIFY THIS SUSPECT'S M O

SUSPECTS

| | SEX | DESC | HAIR | EYES | HEIGHT | WEIGHT | AGE | CLOTHING | NAME & ADDRESS IF KNOWN; NAME, BKG NO & CHARGE IF ARRESTED |
|---|---|---|---|---|---|---|---|---|---|
| 1 | | | | | | | | | |

Personal oddities (Unusual Features, Scars, Tattoos, etc)    Weapon (IF GUN, DESCRIBE FULLY)

| | SEX | DESC | HAIR | EYES | HEIGHT | WEIGHT | AGE | CLOTHING | NAME & ADDRESS IF KNOWN; NAME, BKG NO & CHARGE IF ARRESTED |
|---|---|---|---|---|---|---|---|---|---|
| 2 | | | | | | | | | |

Personal oddities (Unusual Features, Scars, Tattoos, etc)    Weapon (IF GUN, DESCRIBE FULLY)

INVOLVED PERS.

Codes:    W - WITNESS    R - PERSON REPORTING    S - PERSON SECURING    D - PERSON DISCOVERING    P - PARENT

NAME    R/B-RESIDENCE/BUSINESS ADDRESS & PHONE    X

R –
B –
R –
B –

(1) LIST ADDIT'L SUSP'S, VICT'S, INVOLVED PERSONS  (2) RECONSTRUCT THE CRIME, INCL ALL ELEMENTS OF CORPUS DELECTI,  (3) DESCRIBE ANY EVIDENCE, STATE LOCATION FOUND & BY WHOM, GIVE DISPOSITION  (4) SUMMARIZE OTHER DETAILS, INCL WHEN AND WHERE PERSONS WITH NO PHONE CAN BE LOCATED  (5) LIST STOLEN ITEMS

| ITEM NO | QUAN | ARTICLE | SERIAL NO. | BRAND | MODEL NO. | MISC. DESCRIPTION (COLOR, SIZE, INSCRIPTIONS, CALIBER, ETC) | DOLLAR VALUE |
|---|---|---|---|---|---|---|---|

VICTIM INDEMNIFICATION INFORMATION (IF APPLICABLE):

| SUPERVISOR APPROVING | SERIAL NO. | INVESTIGATING OFFICERS | SERIAL NO. | AREA/TEAM OR DIV./DETAIL | PERSON REPORTING (SIGNATURE) |
|---|---|---|---|---|---|
| | | | | | X |
| DATE & TIME REPRODUCED | DIV. | CLERK | | | CLEARED BY ARREST ☐ Yes ☐ No |

*Left margin:* Altercation ☐   Shots Fired (5/3.20) ☐   Extra Copies ↑

*Figure 3-1 Sample M.O. (Robbery) Form Report*

otherwise inaccurate property loss statistics will result. For example, a victim may suffer the loss of an artifact, family heirloom or other keepsake, which he feels is priceless. Sentimental value does not justify inflated figures on a report. However, historical value is another question. It may be necessary to consult an expert to establish an appropriate market value of certain unusual or unique items.

1. Minimum description on report should include:
    a.  Quantity of items
    b.  Kind of items
    c.  Style, shape, size, model
    d.  Material; gold, silver, wool, silk, etc.
    e.  Color
    f.  Condition (age if the information is available)
    g.  Value (current market)
    h.  Serial numbers, initials, marks or trade name

2. Firearms:
    a.  Manufacturer's name and code mark
    b.  Type (e.g., revolver, automatic, rifle, etc.)
    c.  Caliber, gauge, barrel length
    d.  Serial number and/or frame number
    e.  Finish (e.g., blue steel, nickel plated)
    f.  Stock or grips (e.g., metal, wood, plastic, bone or ivory)
    g.  Initials or engraving *Note:* Very important, because duplication of identifying numbers has occurred within same manufacturer's name; some foreign-made guns have no numbers
    h.  Value and condition

3. Rings:
    a.  Man's, woman's or child's
    b.  Kind of metal or material, modern or antique mounting and type of setting, plain or engraved
    c.  Manufacturer's code marks, initials or inscriptions
    d.  Kind, number cut, size and weight of stones
    e.  Value and condition

4. Watches:
    a.  Manufacturer's name, material, size, color and shape
    b.  Type; wrist, pocket, lapel, man's or woman's
    c.  Kind of metal or material

    d.  Number of jewels, size, cut, number and weight of stones

    e.  Value and condition

5.  Miscellaneous jewelry:

    a.  Name of item

    b.  Manufacturer's name, material, size color and shape

    c.  Stones, kind, number, size, cut, color and weight

    d.  Setting, design, initials, engravings, marks and scratches

    e.  Value and condition

6.  Silverware:

    a.  Name and number of items, manufacturer's trade name

    b.  Solid or plated

    c.  Monograms, engravings or initials. *Note:* check manufacturers' catalogues for photos and details

    d.  Value and condition

7.  Clothing:

    a.  Kind; suit, dress, hat, etc., man's, woman's or child's

    b.  Manufacturer's trade name; size, style, color and material

    c.  Laundry or cleaners marks, (contact shop), initials or monograms sewn into clothing

    d.  Value and condition

8.  Miscellaneous:

    a.  Manufacturer's name, model, serial numbers or other identifying characteristics (e.g., cracks, cigarette burns, torn areas, missing parts), repairs on: cameras, TV's typewriters, adding machines, radios, power tools, bicycles, washers, dryers, etc.

# SUMMARY

Most persons would find it difficult, if not impossible, to commit to memory all investigative details required for a complete report. Investigators must, therefore, from the first notification or receipt of a complaint, take written chronological notes of all information received, actions taken and observations made. This notetaking must be continued through the preliminary and follow-up investigation process. Notes are the basis for all reports; they are used in connection with the investigator's future testimony in court and may be used as evidence. All entries should be prefaced by an identification of the subject matter, the date, time, location and persons present or involved. Notes may be totally narrative or in part in outline form. Brevity is desirable but not at the sacrifice of pertinent material.

Statements by suspects should be recorded as verbatim as possible. Information in written reports is of little use unless it is properly communicated to appropriate interested persons. Investigators' reports are the core of police record systems; serving a major role in the identification, apprehension and successful prosecution of criminals and the recovery of stolen property. The principles of good report writing are accuracy, completeness and brevity. A report that requires a verbal explanation is an incomplete report. Reports aid in directing law enforcement by providing identification, statistical *modus operandi*, crime summary, engineering and other investigational information. To effect proper planning and continue meaningful daily efforts in the battle against crime, police agencies need current, precise, complete and fully correlated crime information from their reports. Many agencies have developed computerized police information processing systems that meet this need. By requiring specific report writing forms, this system makes all the needed data available and, in addition, provides excellent *modus operandi* information to investigators.

# DISCUSSION QUESTIONS

1. What are notes the basis for and how may they be used in court?
2. What do notes establish a permanent record of?
3. Describe the proper method of taking notes.
4. What security measures should be exercised with notes on sensitive cases?

5.  What characteristics of an officer or an investigator can be measured by the reports they write?

6.  When is the first opportunity for the officer or investigator to obtain all the facts in the case? Explain why.

7.  Why is it imperative that the caliber of the victim or witness be evaluated? Give an example.

8.  Differentiate between hearsay vs. fact.

9.  Discuss opinion vs. conclusion.

10. Discuss subjective vs. objective.

11. Discuss the importance of completeness and brevity in reports.

12. Define *modus operandi*? Review case examples in text.

13. Discuss the strategy of the structure of the sample report form in Figure 3-1.

14. What minimum descriptions should reports include regarding property?

# INTERVIEWING

4

## KEY TERMS AND CONCEPTS

Interviewing (definition of)
Age and sex factors
Motivating factors
Untrained observer factor
Intelligence and stability factors
Interviewing techniques
Personal evaluation of interviewee
The "kinesics" technique

*Interviewing* is the questioning of persons who may possess direct informational evidence through personal perceptions or who may contribute leads and other valuable assistance in a criminal investigation. Much like other sensitive interfacing experiences, interviewing requires the use of sound human relations principles and continued practical application of techniques. Interviewing can be developed to a fine art. An interview is unlike an interrogation. However, the investigator must recognize and remain aware that the receptiveness and reliability of subjects being interviewed may be affected by a variety of factors.

### Age and Sex Factors

Young children of both sexes are imaginative and susceptible to suggestion, particularly from parents whom they tend to emulate. A child will generally identify with values he/she has been taught or has assimilated through environmental exposure. Great care must be exercised in interviewing and evaluating information supplied by children, particularly if the child is also the victim in the case. Objectivity often escapes the emotional, concerned and protective parent. If a parent and child have discussed the information prior to the interview, the investigator may eventually learn that the child's story was subconsciously influenced by the parent.

The aforementioned potentials are not interview "rules of thumb" to be applied to children arbitrarily, but rather precautions of which the experienced investigator must remain aware. Children often are very aware of their observations and experiences and can relate them accurately. Physical demonstration or reproduction of the objects, persons and circumstances that were perceived or otherwise experienced by the child during an occurrence can result in meaningful recall. The following case is offered as an example: This case involved a male parolee from an out-of-state prison who served a term for robbery; however, he had no prior record for sex crimes. He was married, employed and ostensibly rehabilitating himself. However, he began exposing himself to young females. Before long he "graduated" to kidnapping, robbing, and beating and sexually attacked 15 females between the ages of 12 and 73 over a seven month period. His last victim, a five-year-old child, was brutally beaten and sexually assaulted. She was left for dead in a canyon but later found there alive by investigators. The younger victims in this series of crimes experienced great emotional tension at having male investigators present while being interviewed by a female investigator. With the help from a female physician and female psychiatrist, investigators received good cooperation from the parents.

The male investigators, whose very presence in the hospital room terrified this five-year-old victim, very wisely allowed their female partner and the psychiatrist to work alone with the victim during a very productive interview. The victim viewed comparative identification manuals of male suspects, automobiles and colors. A good description of the suspect and his car was obtained. An artist was able to draw a composite picture of the suspect which, coupled with other information, resulted in the arrest of the suspect. An example of an identification aid that is very useful in interviewing is offered in Figure 4-1.

Teenagers of both sexes are generally aware of their daily surroundings and can readily separate imagination from reality. Although their values are greatly influenced by the home, as well as peers, they can independentcly evaluate and reliably relate what they perceive. Male teenagers are particularly effective in recalling perceptions involving mechanical objects, autos, motorcycles, boats, aircraft, sports, etc. Female teenagers are particularly effective in noting and describing persons voices, clothing, jewelry, etc. and are generally current on neighborhood events and gossip.

Many sensitive investigations, including felonious assaults and killings resulting from youth gang activity in various jurisdictions have been materially aided by teenage witnesses. Young adults of both sexes, whether married or single, are generally involved in their own objectives and unlike the teenagers, do not maintain a broad scope of interest in their surroundings. However, if personally involved in an incident they can accurately perceive and relate accordingly.

Mature adults of both sexes, whether married or single, have generally made the necessary adjustments to their surroundings, and have broadened their perspectives. Many are at the peak of intellectual and emotional maturity, thus this group represents the greatest potential

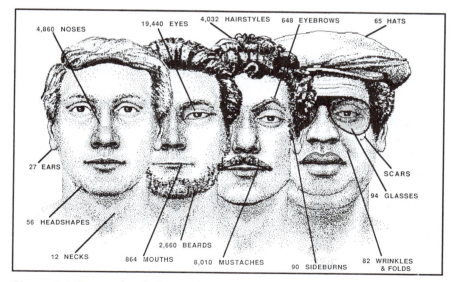

*Figure 4-1 Compusketch feature library for computer generated composite sketches (Courtesy of VISATEX Corporation)*

for reliable witnesses. Elderly people of both sexes, whether married or single, may regress to childlike behavior. However, the investigator must bear in mind that many of this group are in good health and maintain an active interest in their surroundings and can render reliable information.

## Motivating Factors

The vulnerability of a victim or witness to these common pressures, particularly in sensitive cases, must be recognized. The subject of the intended interview may seek to protect himself or another person, hurt another person, confuse or negate the investigation. The investigator must carefully evaluate each situation individually with empathy, and proceed with caution, if he or she is to achieve the objective of the interview. The following motivators often affect human behavior in our everyday life.

Fear, love and hate can motivate a victim or witness to go into hiding, remain silent, relate only partial information, alter information given, or tell an outright lie, depending on the circumstances. Revenge and jealousy are other common motivators that can affect the reliability of the subject in an interview.

The foregoing are not all the possible emotional motivators, but rather those most commonly encountered. For example, in juvenile gang cuttings, shootings and murders, too often the motives are jealousy and revenge which rotate from one gang to the other. Fear for their lives, love for those on their side of the fence, and hate for the sake of hate are also descriptive of the state of mind of most victims and witnesses in this kind of an investigation. Yet much success has been realized by skilled investigators in cases of this type, partially by the use of sound interviewing techniques.

Financial interests of a victim or witness in a case may motivate an attempt to defraud a partner, an insurance company, or the government. Doubtless the series of examples could go on and on, yet for purposes of this section, it suffices to quote one of Webster's New Collegiate Dictionary's definitions of *motive* as, "a need or desire that causes a person to act."

## The Untrained Observer Factors

Most victims and witnesses are not trained observers. Many will experience difficulty in effectively describing or identifying suspects of certain ethnic groups. On many occasions, suspects with dark hair, olive skin and dark eyes are described as Latins, yet they actually are Armenian, Syrian, Italian, Hawaiian, African-American, Gypsy or Anglo. A fair-complexioned Mexican with light hair and eyes can be, and has been, mistaken for an Anglo. An original description calling for an African-American may often result in a Puerto Rican suspect.

Many interviewees can not identify the various speech accents peculiar to the Anglo from certain areas of the United States and foreign countries. The Spanish that is spoken by a Mexican National, a Central or South American, a Cuban, a Puerto Rican, or a Spaniard will differ. Those that come to live in the United States for a long period of time, tend to assimilate and use the colloquial Spanish phrases peculiar to the area where they live. They, like other ethnic groups, also tend to develop the accent with which English is spoken in their respective areas.

No doubt the aforementioned physical description, weapon and language characteristics can, with appropriate variations, apply to investigative problems throughout the world. Being able to determine the subject's ethnic group and get a physical description of the suspect, the weapon, and a reasonable idea as to the country or area the suspect is from, has resulted in many successful investigations. This is primarily due to the fact that most police records and other sources of information on an international basis are filed and cross-indexed by ethnic group and other factors and also contain valuable information on weapons. Centralized repositories of records at state or even federal levels do not always contain information on suspects from other states and countries. It is, therefore, often imperative to know where the suspect is from.

### Examples

This case involved a long series of armed robberies of plush supper clubs in Las Vegas, Nevada, by a two-person team wearing paper sacks with peepholes over their heads. They were consistently described as Latins because of the brown skin revealed by their short sleeve shirts and their English, spoken with an accent. They fared well until they held a Mexican-American woman hostage in an office. They spoke to her, yet upon leaving, one suspect said to his partner, "Come on brudda." In relating her observations, this witness doubted the Latin heritage of the suspect because she did not recall ever hearing any Mexican speak in English in that manner. The word "brudda" was the key, as this is colloquial for brother in the Hawaiian Islands. Fortunately, latent prints were left by the bandits in several of the robberies and within days they were identified as parolees from Oahu Prison in Hawaii. When arrested in Las Vegas, the weapons and sufficient physical evidence were recovered to assure their conviction.

Another case involved a long series of armed robberies of finance companies and loan offices in Southern California. The lone suspect was consistently described as a male Anglo. His *modus operandi* was characteristic, with the exception that he was always charming if not flirtatious with the female victims and witnesses. He generally took a hostage with him, whom he released a block or so away from the scene. He also did well until he flirted in Spanish with a Mexican-American female victim in San Diego. She not only recognized that he spoke English with an accent similar to that used in Texas, but also felt he was a Latin in spite of his fair coloring. Another witness noticed a slight bow in his left leg. A good composite description of the bandit, and his M.O. was wired to the Arizona, New Mexico, Texas and Colorado authorities requesting information and a check of all parolees from state prisons; including those with Latin surnames. Shortly thereafter detectives from Denver, Colorado forwarded photos, prints and information on a very Anglo-appearing parole violator named Gonzalez. He was identified and captured in San Diego, based on the information from Denver, Colorado.

Investigators should, if at all possible, go through a physical reconstruction of the perceptions of victims and key witnesses. This should be done at the actual crime scene or under physical, climatic, lighting and other conditions as closely like those factors existing at the time the crime was committed, as possible. It is imperative to determine if it was physically possible for the interviewee to have perceived what he or she is relating. Many well-meaning witnesses have sincerely believed they have seen or heard a variety of often very important details relative to the suspect(s) and the crime that proved to be physical impossibilities. Some instances have involved eyesight, particularly when the interviewee was not wearing his or her glasses at the time the perception was made. A polite observation or question during the interview can determine this factor. Other instances have involved the distance at which the perception was made, the lighting or the emotional stability of the interviewee.

An interesting example of a mistaken hearing perception in a New York City case involved a lone male deaf-mute suspect in the mugging and beating of an elderly lady on a dark street. When originally interviewed after the occurrence, she stated that when the suspect grabbed her around the neck from behind, he stated, "Give me your purse." When she resisted, he beat her and took the purse. She could not identify the suspect other than to give an impression as to his ethnic origin. The location of occurrence, the other *modus operandi* factors and limited description fit a lone deaf-mute and the area he operated in. He was on parole for the same offense and although suspected in other similar cases, the victims could never identify him. Fortunately, in this case, he pawned the victim's lapel watch that was in the purse and used his own name and address. A subsequent search of his room at the time of his arrest revealed several old coins that were also the property of the victim. The suspect admitted the offense when interrogated via sign language.

Notwithstanding a delicate re-interview of the elderly victim, wherein it was explained that the suspect was raised in the area and had never been known to speak in or out of prison, she still believed, in spite of her poor hearing, that he said, "give me your purse." What she probably heard was a very effective growl the suspect was capable of uttering. Fortunately, the victim's testimony was not tested in court. The suspect's parole was violated, based on the evidence, and he was returned to prison.

It is interesting to note that this case exemplifies the importance of evaluating hearing, age, physical stability and fear as affecting perceptions. It also serves to remind us of the phenomenon of modus operandi. Here we have an ex-offender going back to prison for an offense identical to the first conviction, in practically the same area of occurrence and the same type and age of victim. Also, he signed his own name and address on the pawn ticket. It almost seems as if he wanted to be caught.

Additional specific case examples regarding the importance of a physical reconstruction of perceptions of victims and witnesses would be redundant. However, it is important to cite some general areas of concern with the distances at which perceptions are made, the lighting conditions, visual problems and unfamiliarity with guns and other weapons. Many investigators have found that short victims and witnesses, particularly when under the stress of fear, are prone to exaggerate the height and sometimes the weight of suspects. Under the stress of fear, victims may also exaggerate the size and possible caliber of handguns, shotguns or rifles, or the length of a knife or blade. In the area of weapons, the problem may be due to an unfamiliarity factor. Some persons have never been tested for color blindness. Yet it is believed that approximately 3 percent of our population suffers this disadvantage. With respect to lighting conditions and distance, it is important that the lighting and distance be duplicated if at all possible, when evaluating the perception of the interviewee. This is imperative in an identification of a suspect situation. No doubt many experienced investigators can cite a case of mistaken identity.

A recent case in Inglewood, California, involved the robbery of a dimly-lit cocktail lounge. The bartender was shot to death in the presence of 11 witnesses. Some months after the occurrence, a suspect was arrested following a series of bar robberies. He fit the general description of the robbery-murder suspect and was positively identified by the 11 witnesses in the robbery-murder. Although the witnesses were seated at various locations at the bar and the lighting varied, they all steadfastly insisted this was the man. At the time of his arrest, he had a different caliber gun than that used in the murder, and there was no physical evidence to connect him with the murder. He was charged and convicted. As one might suspect, he denied the murder, and it was reasonably presumed that he got rid of the murder weapon. He was sentenced to life imprisonment. Several years later a bar-bandit was captured in San Francisco. Among the crimes he confessed to was the aforementioned robbery-murder. As it turned out, he closely resembled the other bandit erroneously convicted of his murder. With action initiated by the prosecutors and the police agencies involved, the wrong man was cleared of the murder and the right one was charged. Cases like this have happened. It is difficult to rebut the cumulative weight of a series of witnesses all positive of their identification. Yet witnesses can be mistaken!

The investigator must show extra concern in regard to interviewees with marked emotional instability or mental deficiencies. These areas are naturally very delicate and require professional evaluation by a psychologist or psychiatrist for other than a common sense approach by the investigator. Generally, a calm, constrained interview with an avoidance of "high tension" questions is best with subjects that exhibit marked emotional instability.

In the case of the obviously mentally deficient, it is important to remember that, like children, they can provide valuable information if handled intelligently. Simple tests in perception can be given as to these witnesses' ability to make distinctions as to size, color, weight, height, etc. Dependent on the determination, the investigator may delicately proceed with an interview.

Experienced investigators have found that the one most important factor in establishing rapport with any person is to recognize that
every other person has his or her own "reality." Two brothers or sis-
ters, raised in the same family, will have different realities. If meaningful rapport is to be established, one must recognize the other's reality and try, by means of empathy, sympathy and objectivity, to find a
happy medium where they can relate.

## THE INTERVIEW

Victims of crimes and witnesses to actions, statements or other
evidential matters occurring before, during or after the act can be found
on, near or some distance from the scene. The following combination
outline and narrative is offered as a guide to conducting an interview;
with appropriate notes.

1. Introduce yourself by full name and title, explain your role and
   purpose.

2. If applicable, acknowledge the ordeal the victim or witness has
   been through and reassure their immediate safety i.e., an armed
   robbery and shooting in a bank or supermarket, etc.

3. Determine whether the victim or witness has any physical injuries, if so arrange for appropriate aid.

4. Explain the reasons for questions that are asked i.e., sexual assault victims often feel humiliated, powerless and out of control.

5. Do not cut off the expression of feelings by victims and/or witnesses. Validate them if possible (i.e., anger and blame towards
   others).

6. Indicate the date, time, location and subject matter, as first entry
   on notes.

7. Obtain complete identification i.e., name, address, telephone number etc. of the person interviewed. A special precaution should
   be taken, particularly at crime scenes. Verify the identification,
   if possible, via operator's license, etc. The witness may later come
   to be a suspect and the investigator may have a false name and
   address given at the time of interview.

8. Victims and witnesses at a crime scene should be separated and removed from the scene as soon as possible. They should be kept separated and interviewed individually, out of hearing of each other. This is important in order to prevent one interviewee influencing the other.

9. Obtain an independent account from each person interviewed as to their perceptions, using singular questions that do not result in a yes or no answer unless this is required. Allow witnesses to tell their own story.

10. Determine if witnesses are related or in any way connected or acquainted with the victim or suspect.

11. Note where the victim or witnesses were located during the commission of the crime, if applicable.

12. Check perceptions as to eyesight, hearing, distance, etc. Be alert for unguarded statements (e.g., "I knew this was going to happen").

13. Determine who left the crime scene and why, if applicable.

14. Be certain that the interviewee knows whom he or she is talking about, when referring to another person.

15. If an accusatory statement is made, attempt to record it as verbatim as possible.

16. If the interviewee is one who left the crime scene, determine why he or she left and treat the witness the same as the others who were at the scene.

17. Leave the interviewee with the impression that a subsequent interview may be required.

## Kinesics

*Kinesics* ("body language") is a systematic study of the relationship between non-linguistic body motions and communication. This writer would be remiss if mention were not made of an excellent work titled *The Kinesic Interview Technique* by Frederick C. Link and D. Glen Foster, published by Frederick Link and Associates Inc.

These authors are highly experienced practitioners and teachers of the technique in connection with interviews and interrogations. They describe their technique as based on the concept of stress that an interviewee or the subject of an interrogation experiences, as a result of words or actions of the interviewer/interrogator or by the inner feelings of the interviewee/subject toward the situation. The verbal or non-verbal behavior caused by the stress is diagnosed, with the objective of making an analysis as to whether or not the interviewee or subject is being deceptive. If the analysis indicates deception, then that factor can be used by the interviewer/interrogator to facilitate obtaining the information desired. For a comprehensive treatment on this technique, Link and Foster's work is highly recommended.

## Cognitive Interview

The cognitive interview is very different than what you would typically expect to see in the movies. It involves the use of a secluded and quiet place that is free from distractions. The interview is calm, and the subject is urged to speak slowly and recall the event by "focused retrieval" which helps take the interviewee mentally back to the scene.

It is suggested that a skilled interviewer who conducts this type of interview can elicit up to 50 percent more information using this technique. The technique allows the interviewee to do most of the talking asking mostly open-ended questions, allowing more time to answer each question and encouraging more details in answers, and avoiding interruptions in order to perpetuate the flow of details.

The drawbacks of this type of interview are in the amount of time it takes to conduct the interview and the higher level of skill that is required of the interviewer (it is not an interrogation). Coupled with this is the fact that sometimes the environment that is required for this type of interview is simply not available or impractical to provide.

## The Neighborhood Canvass for Witnesses

Begin with residences, buildings, businesses, apartments, etc. that are in view of the crime scene or in the area. Persons who were at home, or in their business, on a coffee break, or sitting on a fire escape, or in a parking lot, for example, may be able to render a description of the suspect. They may have seen the suspect enter or leave the scene of the crime. Persons convalescing from an illness or who are shut-in for other reasons, often sit at windows and look out. You may find that almost every residential block or apartment house canvassed has at least one resident who is very interested in knowing what is going on.

Some spend more time minding other people's affairs than they do their own, up to and including leaving drapes or window shades adjusted to facilitate observation of the outside. These persons are often valuable sources of good information and, on occasion, of good identification.

The value of a thorough neighborhood canvass cannot be over emphasized. For example, it is a common practice following a bank robbery (manpower permitting) to saturate the area with investigators in a neighborhood canvass. Many times this technique has paid off. In one case the suspect held up a bank, left the scene and ran through an alley where he discarded an army fatigue jacket and cap in a trash can. He then got into a car that was parked there and drove off. A factory worker who was on a break, sitting on a fire escape in the alley, observed the unusual conduct of the suspect. When interviewed, this witness indicated that he became suspicious (i.e., who would throw away a good jacket and cap?). This prompted him to take a good look, which resulted in his being able to describe the suspect, car and the emblem of a local car company on the back of the suspect's shirt. A check of the car company resulted in the suspect's arrest, recovery of the stolen money and the gun used in the robbery. The car turned out to be a "loaner" borrowed by the suspect without his employer's permission.

A bizarre example of the importance of a neighborhood canvass was encountered in Washington, D.C., the case involved the strangulation and rape of an elderly woman with a telephone cord. A neighborhood canvass revealed a resident who spent much time observing the neighborhood through her front window. On the day of the occurrence she noted a solicitor ask three different females who were working in their yards for a glass of water. She reasoned logically that the solicitor was either very thirsty or was up to something. She actually saw him enter and leave the home of the victim around the estimated time the death occurred. The rest was simple. Other interviews of neighbors revealed an excellent description of the suspect and the company he solicited for. He was subsequently arrested. Physical evidence developed at the scene linked him with the murder and he confessed. His confession revealed that the reason he asked several women for a glass of water prior to the murder was that he became sexually aroused by sipping water from a glass while looking at a woman. By the time he reached the victim's house he was aroused and she, like an innocent good samaritan, invited him in for a glass of water.

Other checks to be made during a canvass are for persons who live or work in a building with the victim. Particular attention is to be given to intimate relationships between the victim and others. Sudden departures from employment or the place of residence may tie into the case. Remember the emotional motivators: hate, fear, anger and jealousy. For example, a check of all persons who live or work in a building, including the taverns or bowling alleys where people go to relax and often make acquaintances, have revealed relationships between victims and others that were a complete surprise to the families of victims. The relationships may be sexual, criminal, etc. Such relationships have often furnished precisely the leads that were needed to solve the case.

Other important sources to check for possible witnesses are all the persons regularly in the crime scene area (e.g., milkmen, newspaper carriers, garbage collectors, neighborhood children, people on their way to work, loiterers, etc.). The time and manpower to be used on a neighborhood canvass will be determined by the overall situation. Care must be exercised not to delay action, otherwise it might come too late to be of real value. One last precaution. The investigator who is taking the case to court should personally have evaluated each victim and witness who is going to testify via interview or re-interview. It is not a good practice to accept someone else's evaluation of victims or witnesses. Additional techniques to be employed, regarding witnesses and their testimony are covered in Chapter 15 under Case Preparation.

## SUMMARY

Interviewing is a sensitive interfacing experience that can be developed to an art with continued practical application of sound human relations principles and interviewing techniques. The investigator must remain aware that the receptiveness and reliability of subjects of interviews may be affected by a variety of factors. Young children of both sexes, although imaginative and susceptible to suggestion, are often very cognizant of their perceptions and can relate them accurately. Teenagers of both sexes can also reliably relate what they perceive, particularly in the areas of most interest to them. Young adults can make reliable witnesses if personally involved in the incident. Because of a more complete adjustment to their surroundings and their intellectual and emotional maturity, the more mature adults represent the greatest potential for reliable witnesses. Elderly people may sometimes regress to childlike behavior. However, many are in good health and are active and can render reliable information.

Fear, love, hate, revenge and jealousy can motivate a witness or interviewee to give unreliable information. An interviewee who is an untrained observer may encounter difficulty in effectively describing or identifying suspects of certain ethnic groups, weapons used or language spoken by the suspects. Other interviewees may be handicapped by poor hearing, sight, emotional instability or mental deficiency. To appropriately evaluate the reliability of the information received from an interviewee, an investigator should, whenever possible, physically reconstruct the attendant surroundings of the scene where the perception was made. This helps to determine if it was physically possible for the witness to have perceived what is being related. This reconstruction, coupled with a consideration of the characteristic and motivating factors which can affect an interviewee, can lead to a complete interview and a valid evaluation of the information received using the outline guide offered in this chapter.

# DISCUSSION QUESTIONS

1. How can an investigator become a proficient interviewer?
2. How does an interview basically differ from an interrogation?
3. Discuss the various age and sex factors of subjects of interviews.
4. Explain how fear, love and hate affect the subject of an interview?
5. How can revenge and jealousy affect the subject of an interview?
6. Discuss the various problems that are likely to be encountered by the untrained observer.
7. Why should the investigator evaluate the physical, intelligence and stability factors in witnesses?
8. Why is it important that the investigator obtain a full identification of the subject of an interview?
9. Discuss the recommended guide to conducting an interview.
10. Discuss the importance of the neighborhood canvass for witnesses.

# THE CRIME SCENE

5

## KEY TERMS AND CONCEPTS

Crime scene (definition of)
First officer at scene (duties of)
Isolation and protection of crime scene
Walk-through
Crime scene search
Chain of custody

## PROCESSING THE CRIME SCENE—GUIDELINES

The *crime scene* is the locale within the immediate vicinity of the occurrence wherein evidence may be found. It may contain much of the evidence and information that is essential to a successful investigation. A methodical and detailed evaluation, examination and search of the crime scene may establish the *corpus delicti* of the crime, the modus operandi used and evidence that connects the suspect or suspects to the crime. The investigative principles and techniques applied will not materially differ with the type and size of the scene, whether it is in an indoor or outdoor locale. These factors will only affect the required number of personnel (technical or otherwise) and the time required to process the scene. All investigative activities regarding the crime scene must be carefully recorded and documented.

### First Officer or Investigator at the Scene

The initial thoughts and efforts of the first officer or investigator at the crime scene must be directed to the welfare of the victim. All activities from his or her first notification of the crime, date and time of arrival and location of the scene, condition of the weather, condition and type of lighting, position of the sun or moon, direction of the wind, and visibility must be recorded in his or her notes. The full identification of the person discovering or reporting the scene, as well as the person(s) who meet the officer-investigator at the scene, should also be recorded as soon as possible.

Dependent on the type of crime scene involved and when applicable, the investigator must determine if the victim is alive or injured. If the victim is dead the body is not generally moved except by a coroner or medical examiner who will be called to the scene at a later time. If the victim is injured, the investigator or officer must immediately call for an ambulance or paramedic unit and render all first aid that is possible. Isolation and protection of the scene is a desirable must, yet the preservation of human life is most important. A determination must be made if a crime has been committed and the appropriate notifications made to the supervisor at the station. The officer or investigator must then proceed to isolate and protect the immediate scene. This will involve clearing the immediate scene of witnesses and unauthorized personnel, except those injured. In the case of death, only unusual circumstances will justify moving a dead body without the coroner. If a body is in the middle of a heavily traveled street, and traffic is backed up, moving the body may be required in the interest of public welfare.

Although the above rules are standard, experience indicates it is not always possible to expediently clear and protect crime scenes. For example, assassinations and other major crimes committed in public places, in the presence of or within the hearing of hundreds of people, are most difficult to clear. A classic illustration of this problem occurred in the assassination of Senator Robert F. Kennedy. The shooting took place in a hotel pantry in the immediate presence of a number of people. The bedlam that immediately followed, with people from the adjoining packed ballroom screaming and running in and out of the already crowded pantry, presented a most difficult crime scene for anyone to isolate and protect. In situations like this, common sense must rule, as it did in the Kennedy case. The officers isolated and protected the scene as expeditiously as the circumstances allowed.

The techniques and conditions discussed thus far apply to most crimes, as will the following material. Special guidelines for use in several selected crimes (i.e., homicide, robbery, burglary, rape, auto theft, and the battered child will be covered in Chapter 12).

Before proceeding with a crime scene the officer or investigator must remember that the rules of evidence require a crime scene be "reproduced" in court as it existed when discovered. As collectors of fact, police are charged with the responsibility of meeting the above requirement. For this reason the crime scene must be protected until all possible evidence, testimony, photos, prints and sketches are collected or accomplished. Some major cases may require a follow-up by a surveyor and a professional drawing or an engineer's mock-up of the scene to augment the reproduction in court.

The officer or investigator must also be aware of unintentional and intentional acts of nature that disturb crime scenes. Curious well-meaning citizens, members of the news media and fellow officers or supervisors, if not controlled by set outer perimeters, may wander around and unintentionally damage or destroy evidence such as footprints, fingerprints, etc. They may also leave debris, cigarette butts or prints on the scene that will cause confusion and loss of investigative time. This problem was illustrated in a case wherein a bartender was shot and killed by a bandit in a plush, well upholstered cocktail lounge. At the time of the shooting, according to witnesses, he stood directly in front of a certain stool at the bar. Unfortunately, there were unauthorized persons on the scene while it was being searched (i.e., two police onlookers, one member of the press and a politician). The print man found a complete handprint on the seat of the certain stool. There was some temporary enthusiasm enjoyed by the investigators until elimination prints were taken of all people known to be at the bar on the evening of the killing. The handprint turned out to belong to one of the above mentioned unauthorized persons.

In another case, a well-meaning neighbor of a murder victim came on the scene and happened to spot the murder weapon in the backyard grass before the police did. He picked it up and put it in his pocket and continued the search until he was noticed and politely removed. Before leaving, he handed the weapon to the officer indicating that he was just trying to help.

Intentional disturbances to crime scenes may occur in a variety of ways and for various reasons. A suspect may alter the scene or attempt to destroy it by fire or explosion to conceal a crime (e.g., a major burglary or a murder). It may be that the alteration of evidence is for the purpose of making a murder look like suicide. Now and then a concerned family member may alter a suicide scene in an attempt to make it took like an accident, or even a murder, for insurance purposes or other reasons.

Alteration and damages to crime scenes and evidence are  also caused by nature. Weather conditions and natural elements, such as air, water and fire can and have seriously disturbed crime scenes. Wild animals have moved or partially destroyed bodies of murder victims who were either killed or dumped in isolated areas. The following are examples of both intentional acts by people and acts of nature that caused disturbances to crime scenes.

A father and son, who lived together, had been fighting and bickering for days. This fact was attested to by neighbors as was the fact that this condition depressed the father very much. On the evening of the killing, neighbors heard a shot fired and called the police. When the police arrived they found the father sitting on the couch dead with a bullet wound in his chest and a handgun lying just under the front edge of the couch on the floor between his feet. The son was sobbing and relating that his father had been depressed lately because they had been fighting a lot. The son also stated that he was in the kitchen making a sandwich when he suddenly heard a shot ring out. He ran into the living room and saw his father sitting obviously dead on the couch. He further volunteered that the gun was his and that he kept it in his dresser drawer.

While evaluating the scene, one of the officers kneeled at the end of the couch and took a close look at how far back under the edge of the front of the couch the handgun was lying. It was obviously too far under to assume it slid out of the hand of the dead man, who was sitting on the couch. It was also unrealistic to assume that the victim shot himself through the heart and then carefully leaned over, tucked the gun under the front edge of the couch between his feet and then sat back and died. A look at the entry hole in the victim's shirt did not give the appearance of a contact wound, typical in suicides. It was also unrealistic to assume the father shot himself with the gun in his hand with his arm in an outstretched position. If so, the gun would have probably fallen to the floor out in front of his feet.

Needless to say, the officers acted promptly and had a confession from the son before the coroner arrived. The son admitted he shot his father from a distance of five feet while the father dozed on the couch in a sitting position. He then placed the weapon where it was found. He figured he could explain his prints on his gun if they were found by police. This suspect had not planned an explanation for the absence of his father's prints on the gun nor did he know of laboratory tests for nitrates on gun hands or nitrates around bullet holes. Tests for nitrates will be discussed in the succeeding chapters.

A suicide is a tragic experience for any family and with just a little empathy, an investigator can understand, but not condone, an attempt by a family member to alter a suicide scene. For example, the emotional or other pressures that a suicide victim had been under prior to the death, have, in many cases, been concealed or denied by families. On occasion a suicide note will be concealed or a story fabricated to the effect that the victim frequently cleaned his gun or rifle. It is very important to remember that the investigator has a responsibility to learn the truth whether or not it serves the emotional or other needs of a family, an insurance company or a religious faith. For this reason, it is recommended that when at all possible, apparent suicide scenes should be handled with the same degree of attention given a homicide.

An example of how the forces of nature can disturb a crime scene is illustrated by the following example. In this case two young males kidnapped a university coed, took her to a lonely canyon and murdered her by smashing her head with a large rock. They left the clothed body, the rock and the victim's purse at the scene. Some 18 months later an informant accompanied one of the suspects and several investigators to the scene to recover the remains of the victim and any evidence possible. The body was totally mummified and the head and feet and had been chewed off by wild animals. Pieces of bones and hair were dragged and scattered for a mile up the canyon. Only tiny shreds of clothing and the victim's purse were left. Mummification of the body was caused by the hot and dry weather in the canyon.

# METHODS, PERSONNEL AND EQUIPMENT FOR ISOLATING AND PROTECTING A CRIME SCENE

Evaluation of the crime scene and perimeters is required. The first officer or investigator at the crime scene must quickly evaluate the scene as to the crime that has been committed, whether the location is indoors, outdoors or a combination of both. The type of residence or building, open yard or street, field or canyon and possible routes of entry and escape used by the suspect(s) must be also considered in terms of establishing the perimeter of the scene to be protected.

## Methods and Personnel

It is obvious that an outdoor scene, involving a field or a canyon may represent a greater problem in terms of manpower and equipment needs, as opposed to a scene in an average residence. Once the perimeter of the scene is established, the immediate scene and area must be cleared. All persons present or in progress of leaving the scene or area at the time of arrival of the first officer or investigator must be detained for questioning. As previously indicated, all victim(s) and witnesses must be separated and kept so, for independent interviews. Again a reminder—the only valid reason for disturbing a crime scene are efforts to render aid to the injured or circumstances where public safety and welfare are involved.

## Isolation and Protection

Continued isolation and protection of the scene may require obtaining additional personnel for guarding doors, gates, entryways and selected positions in the perimeter. For outdoor scenes, portable transceivers (walkie-talkies) are desirable for communication between investigators and guard posts. The situation may also require obtaining portable barricades, ropes, tarps or boxes to block off roads, streets, open areas and protect evidence such as, footprints, tire tracks, weapons, etc. The scene may require a portable generator for lights in the event of darkness, scuba divers to recover a body or evidence from water, or the aid of a fire department or rescue unit to scale difficult heights or drain a body of water.

# SELECTION OF SEARCH METHODS

The search of a crime scene must be done methodically and thoroughly. For this reason it is necessary to select and use a search method or combination of methods, whichever is the most practical and potentially productive to the situation. The investigator must visualize the scene as it was before the crime occurred and try to visualize what has taken place.

### The Grid Search Method: (Figure 5-1)
This technique is an augmentation of the Strip Method and provides a double coverage of the area; thus possibly increasing the potential of finding evidence.

### The Zone Search Method: (Figure 5-2)
The Zone Method is generally used when a large area is involved in the search and several investigators are participating. In this method

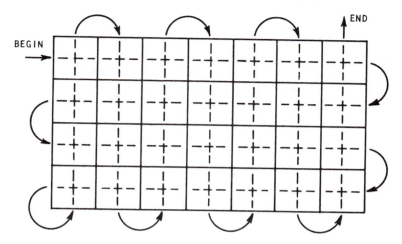

*Figure 5-1 Grid Search Method*

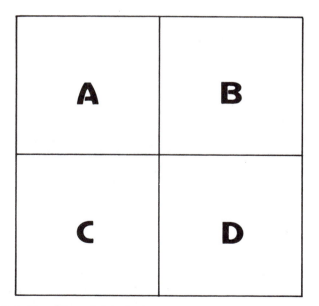

*Figure 5-2  Zone Search Method*

the crime scene is divided into zones, and each investigator is assigned a zone, which will be searched via the method most practical.

### The Spiral Search Method: (Figure 5-3)

This method provides an effective method for a crime scene that is to be searched by one investigator. Following the spiral from the outermost edge to the center provides a minute search and low risk of damaging or destroying evidence. A reversal of this pattern (i.e., working from the center out) is not recommended. The risk of damaging or destroying evidence in walking from the center is too high. The spiral search method is used in both indoor and outdoor scenes, depending on the locale and circumstances.

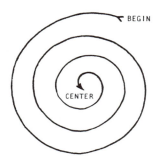

Figure 5-3 Spiral Search Method

### The Strip Search Method: (Figure 5-4)

This procedure involves dividing the crime scene by visualization into strips. One or more investigators participate by proceeding through an assigned strip, then reversing direction and continuing in sequence until the search is complete. The strip search method is more commonly used on outdoor scenes.

### The Wheel Search Method: (Figure 5-5)

This is a variation of the zone search method, however it is not generally used because of the basic disadvantages involved. An investigator starting from the outside and working towards the center encounters a gradually narrowing area, which would normally be searched via the strip method. If the investigator were to start from the center in the wheel search method he or she should encounter the same disadvantage in a reverse spiral method (i.e., damaging evidence by walking into the center). If the crime scene is circular, it is still more practical to use the spiral search method (Figure 5-3).

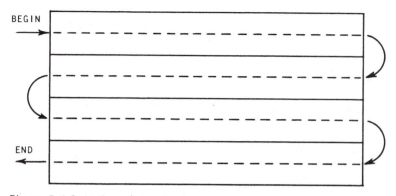

*Figure 5-4 Strip Search Method*

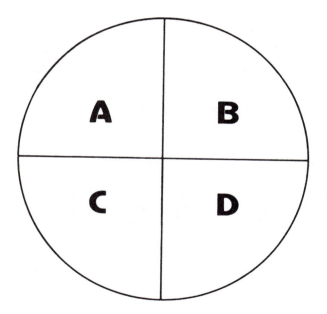

*Figure 5-5 Wheel Search Method*

# CRIME SCENE WALK-THROUGH

The walk-through is a very desirable procedure that is a preliminary to the actual full-scale search of the crime scene. It should be conducted by the coordinating investigator or officer. If applicable he or she should be accompanied by an evidence technician or criminalist.

## Purpose of Walk-through

1. Visualization of what the scene looked like before the crime occurred

2. Visualization of what took place during the crime

3. Identifying all evidence potentials, prints, weapons, etc. and possible perishable evidence

4. Identifying laboratory service and other equipment needs— barricades, lights, etc.

5. Identifying manpower needs

6. Establishing a practical path through the scene, that affords the lowest risk factor in terms of damaging or destroying evidence

*Note:* The investigator or officer conducting the walk-through must record all these activities in his or her chronological notes. He or she must identify the locations of potential evidence at the scene by placing a card or sign or evidence envelope alongside the item or print potential, whichever is the case. Empty cardboard boxes, barricades or even tarps in the case of inclement weather conditions, are used to protect footprints, imprints, tire tracks, etc., outside.

When the walk-through is completed, the investigator-officer should know what the personnel, laboratory and other equipment needs are. As coordinator of the search, he or she is responsible for obtaining the services and equipment needed. This person should assign and coordinate any others participating in the scene as guards, searchers and those providing laboratory or other services, and should correlate all notes taken into one comprehensive, thoroughly written report.

# PRE-SEARCH PHOTOGRAPHY OF CRIME SCENE

Prior to beginning the search, the entire scene must be photographed, (in color if possible) as it was found. This will include general identification shots of residences, buildings, vehicles, street signs, persons loitering around or interested citizens. If possible the photos should include addresses, license numbers and street names. In one case reviewed in research, a teenage murder suspect returned to the scene and was photographed in front of a house. These identification photos are in keeping with a standard principle in crime scene searches that nothing should be touched or moved until it has been identified, measured, printed and photographed. The walk-through will provide the identification of potential evidence. The processing of the scene by the investigator, evidence technician and/or criminalist will accomplish the measurements, prints and close-up identification photos of evidence.

The immediate scene should be photographed from the perimeters inward in overlapping shots in sequence, along the path set by the walk-through. Location shots should be taken of all evidence identified such as a body, weapons and all potential evidence located via the walk-through. Aerial photographs may also be desirable for overall detail of the outdoor scene and the surrounding area.

## THE CRIME SCENE SEARCH

The coordinating investigator-officer, who is responsible for the overall scene, must make the assignments of other investigators, technicians, or criminalists, etc. who will participate in processing and guarding the scene. He or she will divide the scene in specified areas, if the size, circumstances and choice of search methods, so indicate, He or she must maintain an accurate record of all assignments, the detail of what is accomplished by each of those assigned and a record of all persons who have been on the scene officially or otherwise. This latter point is of utmost importance in terms of the eventual elimination of prints, footprints, tire tracks, debris, etc.

In the past much time has been wasted in trying to identify the source of the above mentioned items of evidence found on crime scenes. For example, a Manhattan cocktail glass, with excellent latent prints on it, and a cigarette butt in an ash tray were found on a table in a home where a housewife was raped and strangled. These items disclaimed by the victim's husband, gave the impression that the victim may have had a welcome visitor, prior to being murdered. Eventual elimination of the prints on the glass proved that an ambulance driver who was on the scene had helped himself to a drink and a cigarette.

## Methodical Steps of Searching

1.  Each participant must insure that debris is not tracked into an indoor scene by his or her shoes. (Paper slippers may be used in homicides). Record all activities in the notes.

2.  Conduct inch-by-inch search for all clues and evidence with first attention to floor, or ground of the crime scene.

3.  Be alert for possible alterations to the crime scene, such as a nude body lying on its stomach, with post mortem lividity apparent on its back. After death, blood will drain in a body by force of gravity to those portions of the body closest to the floor or ground the body is lying on. Within approximately two to four hours a reddish-purple discoloration of the flesh will appear, usually bordering the portions of the body closest to the floor or ground. This blood coagulates and, once set, will not drain in the opposite direction. It is obvious that the body in this example was turned over after lividity set in. Another example may be a case where the exterior temperature is 70°, interior temperature is 95° and a dead body is present. Check the thermostat (if applicable). It may have been turned up in the belief that heat slows down rigor mortis by keeping a body warmer, thus altering an estimated time of death. Heat actually speeds up rigor mortis.

4.  Examine all floors or base, doors, windows, walls, mail boxes, trash cans, entry and exit ways, furniture etc. and record all findings.

5.  Do not confine the search to too small an area. The area surrounding the scene (neighborhood canvass) may reveal discarded evidence or evidence moved by the wind.

6.  Obtain the license numbers and descriptions of all vehicles parked at the scene within a reasonable distance surrounding the scene. This practice has yielded the suspect in many cases. For example, running a police record and other checks on the registered owners of vehicles in the vicinity may reveal a suspect who has a criminal background with the same M.O. as used in the case being investigated.

7.  When evidence is located, it must not be touched or moved until it has been identified, measured, recorded and photographed.

8. All perishable evidence such as blood, etc., must be given prompt attention.

# CRIME SCENE PHOTOGRAPHY

Crime scene photographs are admissible as evidence in court, if testimony can be offered by the investigator or technician to the effect that they accurately depict the scene or item as it was observed, i.e., objects, distances, scale, and perspective. Although a camera may record all that is in focus, it may not correctly depict distances between objects. It is critical that photographs provide a proper perspective. O'Hara states, the incorrect selection of photographic angle (formed by the camera axis and the horizontal) often results in a distorted and false impression of the scene. (See Figure 5-6).

The crime scene sketch and the investigator's notes augment the photographs and provide the required accuracy in depicting distances between objects, scale and the overall proper perspective.

## Guidelines for Photographing Crime Scenes

In addition to the pre-search photography information offered previously, the following guidelines are recommended:

1. When in doubt, take a picture. It is better to expend some film than to pass up evidence which may be otherwise lost forever.

2. Record all camera locations and photographs in the investigator's notes and, if practical, in the sketch. This will insure proper identification.

3. Include a ruler in the photograph when it is desired to depict scale or distance.

4. Color photos are desirable to depict blood or wounds, etc., but not required. Black and white photos are standard.

5. Take area or general scene photographs in overlapping sequence.

6. Take the necessary number of close-up shots of entrances and exits to the scene, bodies, wounds, weapon, fingerprints, footprints, tire tracks, tool marks, points of impact, skid marks, glass fractures, debris and damages to safes, etc.

7.  Use aerial photography for overall detail of outdoor scenes and surrounding area of an indoor scene, if applicable and available.

8.  Use video camera to record a scene if applicable and available.

9.  Maintain proper custody of prints and negatives; book as evidence if possible.

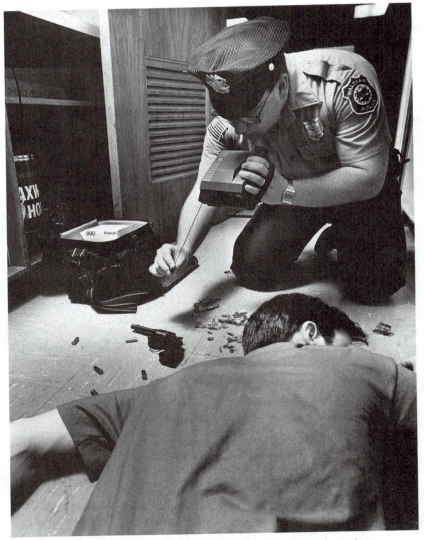

Figure 5-6 *Photographing crime scene with close-up Polaroid Spectra System (Courtesy of the Polaroid Corporation)*

# CRIME SCENE SKETCHING

The crime scene sketch augments the investigator's notes and photographs by providing an accurate record of the distances and relationships between the essential evidential components. It can be used in the follow-up investigation to orient witnesses as to their perceptions on the crime scene and, most importantly, in the preparation and presentation of the case in court. An adequate sketch will include the following:

1.  Name, rank and agency of the investigator

2.  Date, time, case number and type of crime

3.  Location of crime (e.g., address, etc.)

4.  Compass direction

5.  Accurate distances and relationships between the essential evidential components

6.  The entrances and exits to the scene

7.  Name, rank and agency of person(s) participating in the measurements and/or preparation of the sketch

8.  A legend for identifying each piece of evidence and camera positions

9.  The scale used, if applicable

## Methods of Sketching

There are several methods of sketching that can be used depending on the particular case.

### *Rectangular Coordinates (Figure 5-7)*

This method uses two walls in a room as fixed points, from which distances are measured at right angles.

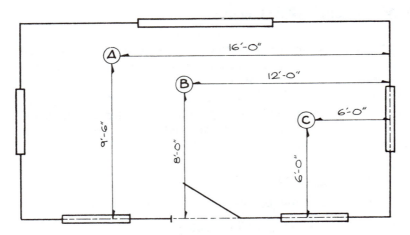

Figure 5-7 Rectangular Coordinate Method

### Triangulation Method (Figure 5-8)

In this method an object is located by drawing two straight lines from two fixed points creating a triangle; the object is in the angle formed by the lines.

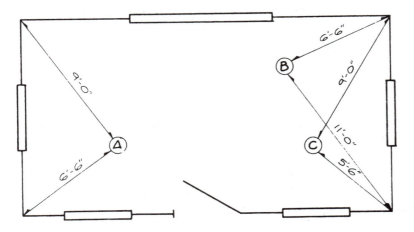
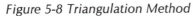

Figure 5-8 Triangulation Method

### Baseline Method: (Figure 5-9)

In this method a straight line is established from one fixed point to another fixed point. Using one end of the line as a starting point, an object can be located by measuring along either side of the baseline to the point at a right angle to the object.

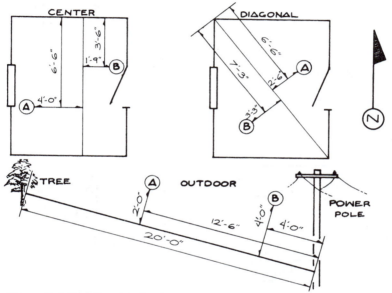

Figure 5-9 Baseline Method

### Compass Point Method: (Figure 5-10)

In this method a protractor is used to measure the angle between two lines. One point along a wall is selected as the origin. An axis line drawn from the origin is the line from which the angle is measured.

### Cross Projection Method (Figure 5-11)

In this method, the sketch is drawn so that the ceiling, floor and walls are on one surface, as if one took a box, lifted the top, cut the four corners and flattened it all out.

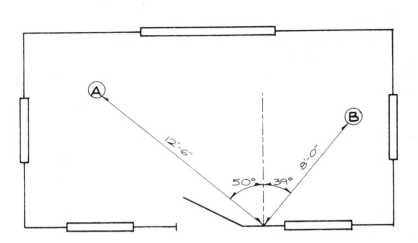

Figure 5-10 Compass Point Method

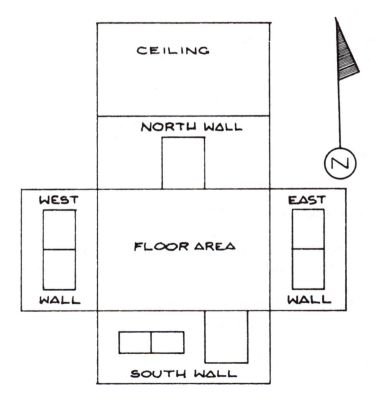

Figure 5-11 Cross Projection Method

### *Rough Sketch and Scale Drawing: (Figures 5-12 and 5-13)*

A rough sketch is drawn by the investigator or evidence technician at the scene (not to scale). A scale drawing is usually accomplished by a draftsman or technician at a police facility.

### *Materials Needed:*

A sketch kit is ideal but not required for a rough sketch. At minimum, the investigator or technician should have the following: 1) plain or graph paper, 2) soft lead pencil & eraser, 3) ruler, 4) clipboard, 5) compass, and 6) 100 ft. steel tape. The scale drawing will require the sketch kit or like drafting materials.

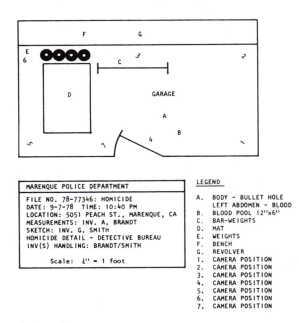

*Figure 5-12 Rough sketch*

# COLLECTION, RECORDING, PRESERVATION AND DISPOSITION OF PHYSICAL EVIDENCE

The term, *physical evidence*, includes any physical thing that may be found at the crime scene or found at another location, yet having a direct connection or relationship with the scene, the suspect or the vic-

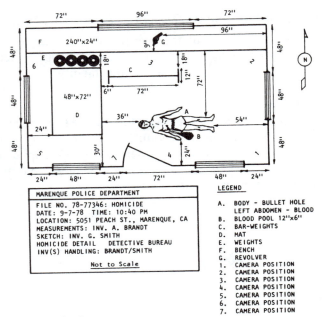

Figure 5-13 Scale drawing

MARENQUE POLICE DEPARTMENT

FILE NO. 78-77346: HOMICIDE
DATE: 9-7-78  TIME: 10:40 PM
LOCATION: 5051 PEACH ST., MARENQUE, CA
MEASUREMENTS: INV. A. BRANDT
SKETCH: INV. G. SMITH
HOMICIDE DETAIL   DETECTIVE BUREAU
INV(S) HANDLING: BRANDT/SMITH

Not to Scale

LEGEND

A.  BODY - BULLET HOLE
    LEFT ABDOMEN - BLOOD
B.  BLOOD POOL 12"x6"
C.  BAR-WEIGHTS
D.  MAT
E.  WEIGHTS
F.  BENCH
G.  REVOLVER
1.  CAMERA POSITION
2.  CAMERA POSITION
3.  CAMERA POSITION
4.  CAMERA POSITION
5.  CAMERA POSITION
6.  CAMERA POSITION
7.  CAMERA POSITION

tim. The proper locating, collecting, handling and preservation of evidence will many times be the determining factor in establishing guilt or innocence of an accused.

## Chain of Custody

The chain of custody must be maintained unbroken from the time of the collection of the evidence until it is presented in court. This chain (custodians) must be kept to a minimum, ideally one person. However, this is not normally practical in large crime scenes. One must remember a chain is only as strong as its weakest link. If one person involved in the custodial chain allows the evidence to become contaminated, altered, misplaced or lost for any period of time, the evidence, once this factor is known, will probably not be admitted in court.

Anything which might lead to the identification of the suspect to clarify how the crime was committed is important as evidence. It is not the purpose of this section to attempt a full treatment of the vast field of physical evidence. Such would deeply involve criminalistics and its many areas of scientific application. It is more appropriate here to offer some basic examples of physical evidence, its collection, recording, preservation and disposition. The sources of the information and illustrations will be identified.

## Fingerprints—Basic Techniques for Discovering and Preserving

Fingerprints are one of the most common types of physical evidence found at crime scenes and often prove to be the most valuable in terms of identifying the suspect and placing him or her on the scene, at the time of the crime. The term, *fingerprint*, normally includes palm prints and prints of the feet. Fingerprints are generally left on objects that have been handled. They may be visible or invisible. Perspiration from the human body is principally water and a minute percentage of salt, urea, oils and acids. The friction ridges on the inside of the fingers, palms and on the soles of the feet contain sweat pores that excrete a small quantity of perspiration. This perspiration is transferred to an object in the form of a fingerprint when the object is touched. These "latent" impressions are normally invisible or, at best, partially visible. They are discovered by the use of an oblique (angled) light shined on the surface involved and are recorded in the notes and the sketch.

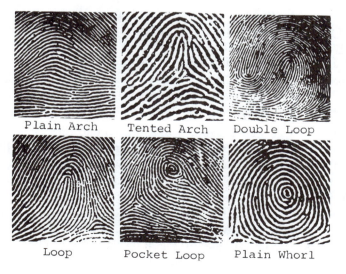

| Plain Arch | Tented Arch | Double Loop |
|---|---|---|
| Loop | Pocket Loop | Plain Whorl |

*Figure 5-14 Common fingerprint patterns*

More visible prints are generally left by fingers, palms or feet that have been impregnated with grease, dirt, blood, etc., or when the ridge structures have come into contact with soft putty, soap, paint or wax. These impressions are normally photographed for preservation and recorded in the notes and sketch since no powder or chemical development is necessary.

### Brush and Powder Techniques

Fingerprint powder is brushed lightly, evenly and smoothly with the tip of the brush over the potential print, in short quick strokes. When the print becomes clearly visible (caused by powder adhering to the print), any further brushing to improve the development must be with the flow of the ridge pattern. Excess powder that adheres between the ridges should be gently brushed away.

Normally black powder is used on light objects and silver powder on dark objects. When dealing with multicolored objects, fluorescent powder and ultraviolet light is used to make the print visible for photographing. Another powder technique involves the use of a magnet (Magna-Brush). This magnet lifts the powder allowing only powder to come in contact with the print. This eliminates the contact of the bristles with the print, which is present in the conventional brush technique. Once the latent print is developed, it should be photographed immediately then recorded in the notes and on the sketch.

An additional method of preserving and collecting latent prints, developed with powder is the lifting process. This lifting process will not destroy the print or damage the surface it is on. If this danger exists, the entire object containing the print is collected (if possible) for examination.

### Latent Print Lifting

This is a relatively simple matter of using a broad adhesive plastic tape similar to Scotch Brand tape, touching one end of it to the surface not covered by the dusted print, and lowering the tape from this anchorage so that it covers the print smoothly. The tape is then stroked down uniformly on the dusted print, after which it is carefully pulled loose from one end. The dust will be retained on the sticky surface of the tape without distortion or damage. The tape can then be placed on a paper or glass surface, so that it is available for photography or direct examination. Rubber lifting tapes similar to a tire patch are also available for this purpose. In either case, the paper, card, or glass that the lifted print is mounted on should be properly marked with the date, time, location the print was lifted from, the case number and identification of the print technician.

*Inked Fingerprint*                     *Latent Fingerprint*

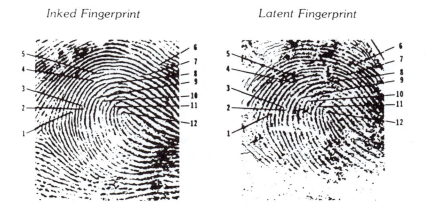

*Figure 5-15 Some common points of comparison between a fingerprint lifted from a crime scene (latent) and a test print from a suspect.*

### Elimination Prints

The fingerprints of all persons who are known to have had access to the scene must be taken for comparison against all latent prints developed. In this way, prints left at the scene by the persons other than the suspect are eliminated.

## Chemical Techniques

Chemical techniques are normally used to develop latent prints on paper, cardboard, unpainted wood and other absorbent surfaces. Some of the common chemical techniques are described below.

### Iodine Fuming

This technique employs the use of an iodine gun which is standard in most crime scene kits or an iodine pumping cabinet made of glass, usually found in any laboratory. Normally, specimens subjected to this technique are handled with tweezers or gloves, avoiding touching more than the edges of the object. Iodine crystals are placed in the fuming gun or the cabinet and subjected to mild heat. The heat causes the crystals to vaporize and produce violet fumes, which are absorbed by the fats or oils (if present) in the latent print. If the fats or oils are there, the ridges will appear in a yellow/brown color against the respective background. These prints, once developed, must be photographed immediately because they fade once the process is discontinued. The item containing these prints must also be properly marked for identification as indicated, for the print lifts.

### Ninhydrin Method

This method of developing latent prints is dependent upon traces of amino acids in human perspiration. Ninhydrin solution is available from fingerprint laboratories and is applied by spraying, dipping or brushing. Spraying appears to be the most effective method of application. After treatment, latent prints may begin to appear at room temperature in two hours. Normally, most will develop within 24 hours. However, exceptions have been noted where a much longer period of time was required for such prints to develop. Ninhydrin development is often used on old prints and can be expedited by application of heat by the use of an electric steam iron or the blowing of hot air on the object. Care must be taken with the use of heat, otherwise the sample is scorched or is ignited by the richly flammable solvents used in the solution. These prints, once developed, must be photographed and the item containing them properly marked for identification.

### Silver Nitrate Method

This method of developing latent prints is dependent on the sodium chloride (salt) content in human perspiration. The silver nitrate solution transforms the sodium chloride present in the print to silver chloride. The sheet of paper etc., can be dipped into the solution (3%) or the solution may be sprayed on with a fuming gun, and hung to dry in a dark room. Once dry, it is exposed to bright light and the latent print appears in a reddish-brown color. The prints must be photographed and the item containing them properly marked for identification. A precaution regarding the three chemical methods discussed—if an item is to be processed via all three methods, the processing must be in the following order: 1) Iodine Fuming, 2) Ninhydrin, 3) Silver Nitrate. This is required because silver nitrate destroys the fats, oils and amino acids on which the first two methods are dependent.

## Cases Involving Fingerprint Evidence

There is no doubt that law enforcement agencies throughout the world can cite case examples of outstanding accomplishments by their latent print technicians. For illustration purposes, three cases involving a police department's Latent Print Section are cited below. The first was a series of burglary-murders, wherein the suspect was finally placed on a burglary-murder scene by a partial palm print developed on the inside wooden wall of a milk delivery door. The opening was seemingly too small for a child to get through, let alone a six foot, 200 pound burglar. The suspect wore leather gloves, laid on his back and pushed himself backwards through the chute to enter the apartment. As he did so, his right-hand glove became unbuttoned allowing his palm to touch the wooden surface and leave a print. He was convicted and executed for murder. The second example involved a series of bar robberies and a murder wherein one of the suspects made a series of purchases with a Sears Roebuck credit card stolen from one of the victims. When the sales slips were obtained from Sears, it was determined that 38 persons had handled the slips during the credit processing. Notwithstanding this discouraging factor, the print technician tenaciously processed the slips via chemical methods and developed seven latent prints left by the suspect when he handled and signed the slips. He was convicted of murder and robbery. The third case was a sexual assault and strangulation murder of a housewife by a TV serviceman. His partial palm print, developed on the lower portion of a wall in a hallway next to where the victim was found, broke his story that he was never in that part of the house. This evidence was a major factor in his trial, and he was convicted of murder.

## Automated Fingerprint Identification System (AFIS)

Automated Fingerprint Identification System (AFIS) has emerged as the latest in innovative technology to access fingerprints from a network database. Fingerprints no longer need to be manually matched to files. Time is often the critical factor in determining the success of a criminal investigation. The use of this computerized technology not only saves time but significantly increases the old accuracy match rate of 1.5 percent. Using AFIS, the positive IDs compared to the number of latent prints submitted is 20-25 percent. Because of this, AFIS is rapidly being implemented throughout law enforcement agencies.

The AFIS process involves using a latent fingerprint image from a crime scene which is then enlarged and traced by hand to highlight the minutiae/relation data which serve as reference points for the system to identify when matching prints. The image is then reduced to the original size and scanned into the computer. This print is then compared to several hundred thousand prints contained in a database of fingerprints of known offenders. This process usually takes from five to ten minutes to match a print from the file. The computer assigns a percentage of probability on the matches generated. If a print registers an 85 percent probability or greater, you are almost assured this is the perpetrator. The system is also able to match imperfect latent prints found at the crime scene in a slightly longer amount of time (20 minutes). This compares to manual searches which could takes days to months. It should be noted, however, that final determination is always left up to a professional print examiner and not only the computer.

An example of how this technology was currently put to use was dramatically portrayed when California used the NEC ID system to match latent prints found on an automobile against a database of 380,000 known offenders. In just three minutes, the system produced a list of possibles. In only two days, the primary suspect was in custody. Ultimately charged with having committed 15 murders during a seven-month terror spree, the infamous Night Stalker was apprehended.

It is anticipated that soon this technology will be increasingly fine-tuned and networks from various agencies will be linked so that a fingerprint will be compared to one large database connected to local, state and FBI systems.

## Foot and Tire Prints and Imprints

Footprints and tire prints are produced when material that is adhering to the sole and heel of the shoe or the tread of the tire is deposited on a hard base or surface. For example, dust, paint, blood, etc., adhering to a shoe or tire may leave a print on paper or a polished wooden base. Great care should be taken to protect these prints, as in the case of latent fingerprints. A cardboard box may be used as an interim cover. Such prints should be photographed with an oblique (angled) light, with a scale in the picture, then measured and recorded in the notes. If practical, these prints should be included in the sketch.

If the item containing the prints can be removed in total, it should be appropriately marked for identification and transported to the laboratory. Shoe and tire prints can occasionally be lifted by use of finger-print lifting tape or rubber lifting pads if the material the print is composed of is sturdy enough (e.g., paint); otherwise these photos will be used for comparison with photos of prints made in the laboratory with a shoe or tire suspected of having been at the crime scene.

### Imprints

Foot and tire imprints are produced when the sole and heel of a shoe or the tread of a tire is pressed into a moldable substance, such as soil, sand, snow, mud, etc. Again, it is imperative to protect imprints from alteration or destruction. Cardboard boxes may be used as an interim protective cover. The imprints should be measured and photographed with a scale in the photo and their locations recorded in the notes. If practical, imprints should be included in the sketch. In outdoor locations it may be necessary to use barriers to keep pedestrian and vehicular traffic away.

## Casting Imprints

It is not the purpose of this section to treat the entire area of casting imprints or tool marks, but rather to discuss a few examples of imprints found on crime scenes (e.g., shoe imprints in dry soil). As in any technique, there are certain basic materials which one should have assembled prior to making an imprint cast. These are listed below.

### Basic Casting Materials:

- Plaster of Paris (free from lumps or sifted if possible)
- Rubber mixing bowl
- Water
- Metal casting frame
- Wire mesh strips for reinforcement
- Soft brush (baby bottle brush)

*Note:* The casting of tool marks and other microscopically detailed imprints require the use of silicone rubber rather than plaster. Commercial preparations are available for this process. Tool marks must be photographed, measured and included in the notes and sketch. If possible, the item containing the tool mark should be taken to the laboratory for preservation, examination and casting. In the event the item cannot be removed, the casting should be done by a criminalist or an evidence technician who will be familiar with the special materials and techniques required. In this way, the preservation of the tool mark for presentation in court can be assured.

1. Preparing a Shoe Imprint: The imprint must be cleaned of all debris, leaves and other foreign material.

2. Photographing a Shoe Imprint: The imprint is measured and photographed with a scale included in the photo and the location and measurements recorded in the notes and sketch.

3. Casting Frame and Silicone Spray: A metal casting frame is placed around the imprint. If the impression is in loose or sandy soil it should be sprayed with a silicone preparation to reinforce the details and allow 15 to 20 minutes for the silicone to dry.

4. Preparing the Plaster for Casting: Calculate how much water it will take to fill the impression up to the borders of the frame. Pour that much water into the mixing bowl and add plaster until the majority of the water is absorbed and then mix by hand.

5. Pouring the Plaster: The plaster is poured from one end of the imprint to the other using one hand as a baffle to lighten the fall of the plaster. When the plaster reaches a thickness of approximately 1/2 inch, wire mesh may be laid on the plaster for reinforcement. The remainder of the plaster mixture is then added until the plaster fills the casting frame.

6. Marking the Cast for Identification: The cast must be marked for identification before it hardens. The date, case number and the name of the person casting the imprint is appropriate.

7. Retrieving the Hardened Cast: When the cast has dried for at least one hour, it can be turned over and the casting frame carefully removed. Some of the soil adhering to the bottom of the cast can be removed with a soft brush and preserved for future laboratory comparison with soil taken from the suspect's shoes, clothing, etc.

8. Cleaning the Cast: The cast should be allowed to thoroughly dry at room temperature for 24 hours. It can then be cleaned by stroking it gently with a soft brush under a trickle of water.

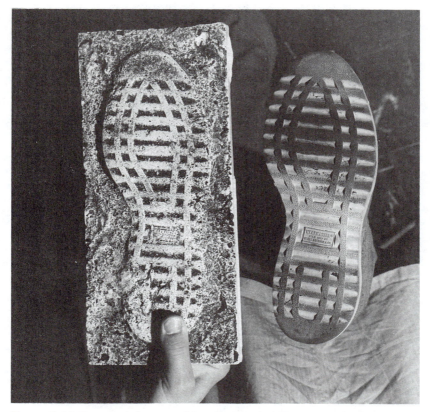

*Figure 5-16 Cast and shoe used for the imprint (Courtesy of East Los Angeles College)*

### *Special Situations*

Although the casting of imprints is normally done with plaster of Paris, special situations may arise where the imprints are in snow, dust, ash, are water-filled or in mud or sludge. In these cases special techniques and other materials are required. For an in-depth treatment of casting foot imprints with paraffin wax, sulfur, silicone rubber, as well as the techniques of comparing foot imprints; the student is referred to Arne Swenson and Otto Wendell's text *Techniques of Crime Scene Investigation*, 2nd edition, American Elsevier Publishing Co. Inc., New York, pp. 75-90.

## Blood Stains

Studies of blood stains are frequently of importance in a wide variety of criminal investigations. In some cases, particularly homicide, crime scene examinations by a criminalist may be required to establish direction of origin of blood spatters, show movements of individuals, establish sequence of deposit of stains and to develop other necessary information. The more common type of blood studies are laboratory operations involving analysis of recovered stains.

The following guidelines and illustrations are from the State of California, Department of Justice, Division of Law Enforcement, Investigative Services Branch.

### *Fresh Moist Stains:*

1. Do not heat stained material or place it in bright sunlight to dry. Hang clothing and similar articles in a room where there is a rapid air movement, such as in front of a fan. Caution: a fan should not be used if foreign material has potential significance.

2. If items containing fresh moist stains are not completely dried before packaging, decomposition will occur which will prevent complete testing.

3. When the stain is dry, label the item and roll it in paper or place it in a paper bag or box; seal and label the container. Do not put stained objects into plastic bags.

### *Dried Stains:*

1. On cloth: label the article, roll in paper or place it in a bag or box, seal and label the container. Do not attempt to remove the stain from the cloth.

2. On small solid objects: send entire object to the laboratory, after labeling and packaging it.

3. On large solid objects: if it is practical, the whole object should be delivered to the laboratory, with areas containing dry stains covered with paper, with the edges sealed with tape to prevent loss or contamination. If it is impractical to deliver the whole object to the laboratory, the stain should be scraped onto a clean piece of paper, which can be folded into a bundle and placed in

an envelope. A freshly washed and dried knife or similar instrument can be used to scrape blood from an object. The instrument must be washed and dried before each stain is scraped off so as not to cross-contaminate the contaminate samples with traces of blood on the instrument used. Seal and mark the container for identification; enter in notes. Do not mix separate dried stains. Place each stain in a separate container.

4.  If the stain cannot be removed in any other manner, use a piece of gauze dampened with distilled water to absorb the stain. Make a similar swab of an unstained area. Dry the gauze pads, place them in separate envelopes, mark for identification and seal.

### *Comparison Specimens:*

1.  If grouping of stains is desired, always obtain fresh known samples of all subjects involved. Grouping of dried stains seldom has any significance unless the blood groups of the subjects involved in the case are known. Information concerning the blood groups of subjects involved in all investigation may also assist the laboratory in selecting the more suitable test method or methods.

2.  It is usually possible to obtain known blood specimens from defendants if requested soon after the arrest. Often the subject will consent to the withdrawal of a specimen if he is advised that the results may prove that the stains in question are not his blood type and that in any event it is not possible to prove that such stains are his blood.

3.  Submit fresh blood samples from subject in two separate vials. One sample must be in a sterile vial containing a preservative and an anticoagulant. The other sample must be in a sterile vial without added preservatives. Label each vial with the name of the subject, date, name of person withdrawing specimen and officer's name or initials. Submit such specimens to the laboratory as soon as possible.

### *Types of Tests Conducted:*

1.  Proof of presence of human blood

2.  Detection of human origin of blood

3.  Detection of some types of animal bloods

4.  Determination of basic ABO blood groups

5.  It is not possible to prove that a blood stain came from a specific individual. It may be possible however, to demonstrate that all blood groups presented in the stain and in the blood of a subject are alike. When this is the case it must be realized that many other persons will also have blood of the same groups. In other cases, it may be possible to demonstrate that the stain could not have come from a specific person.

6.  Recent developments in genetic typing of bloodstains have succeeded in breaking blood down into many more components than previously identified. These refinements make it possible to pinpoint certain key characteristics of an individual. Now, for example, serologists can identify not only the blood type, but the race and sex of the person it came from and even the drug habits, if any, of the individual in question.

The laboratory should be informed of the race of all individuals known to be involved in crimes when blood stain evidence is present. Transfusions of persons seriously injured will alter their blood chemistry and obscure their true blood groups. In these cases it is necessary to wait at least 60 days after the transfusion to obtain a valid blood sample.

## Blood Spatter Analysis

The field of blood spatter analysis is perhaps one of the most misunderstood and neglected forms of forensic physical evidence presently available to investigators of violent crime. Often called a "new science," blood spatter analysis existed and was recognized as essential knowledge a millennia ago for prehistoric hunters in their tracking of wounded animals. The type and amount of blood relate a great deal of information as to the location of the wound and what the victim was doing at the time of the incident.

By analyzing blood spatter marks left at a crime scene a trained investigator can objectively reconstruct the crime scenario and offer supporting data to other forms of evidence found at the scene. Through use of computer aided graphics programs or the string approach (see Figure 5-17) an investigator can, in many cases, determine:

1. Point of origin of the wound(s)

2. Type of object used to produce the wound(s)

3. Relative position of victim and assailant

4. The degree of the assault

These determinations can be made by the trained investigator because blood is predictable. Blood from vessels and veins have different characteristics which will result in appearance and droplet array peculiarity. Classified as rain, gush, spurt, initial breech, rate of bleed, cast off and spurt, impact and spurt, etc., blood spatter analysis can offer enormous evidence potential.

Blood also acts as a transferring agent. Examples of this are: swipes, wipes, smudges, direct transfer (foot, hand and fingerprints), victim's blood on the assailant's clothes, weapon and other personal or traceable objects, etc. The lack of blood on a suspect's person or items may also constitute irrefutable evidence as to a suspect's innocence as with the classic case of Lizzy Borden who was acquitted of the vicious assault on her parents on the basis of not having blood on her dress.

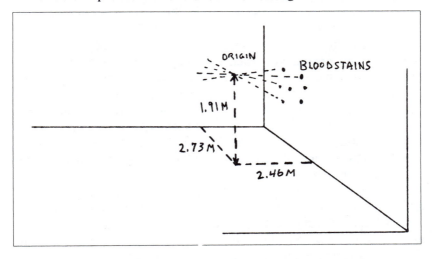

*Figure 5-17 Example of blood spatter analysis to determine point of blood origin (wound)*

Blood stain analysis is still a developing technology. After thousands of years of history, 400 years of application to investigation, and 30 years of investigator training, we are now arriving at a new beginning for this type of evidence. With the current demonstrated abilities to produce objective evidence from blood spatter analysis and the rapidly accelerating technological advances in this area, investigators are now being trained to take advantage of this commonly available evidence.

## Seminal Stains

*Semen* is the male reproductive fluid. It normally contains spermatozoa, which are reproductive cells, as well as other substances. An ultraviolet lamp may be useful in the preliminary search for an indication of semen, because of the bluish-white fluorescence of semen stains. It should be noted that materials which have been laundered will often carry highly fluorescent brighteners derived from detergents and even a fluorescence of the right color is not proof, but only an indication, of the presence of semen.

However, it is possible to identify dried semen by either chemical test or the microscopic identification of characteristically shaped spermatozoa. Seminal stains are often, but not always, found on clothing, blankets, sheets or other materials in rape and other sex offenses. When dry they may have a stiff, starchy feel and can often be located by the sense of touch.

In sex offense cases the victim should always be examined by a physician and a vaginal or rectal specimen taken. The laboratory can examine such specimens for sperm cells. Vaginal specimens can be submitted either as smears, swabs or aspirates, although the collection of a vaginal aspirate in a clean glass vial is the preferred method. Time is of the essence in obtaining vaginal specimens as bacterial action rapidly destroys the sperm cells. The victim should be examined as soon as possible after the incident and the vaginal specimen kept refrigerated until delivery to the laboratory.

Submit all suspected stained materials to the laboratory. If possible, always include the underwear and other clothing from the victim. All garments should be placed in separate packages. The packages containing the victim's clothing should be kept separate from those containing the suspect's clothing. Label all garments or other exhibits.

If damp, always allow fabric to dry completely before packaging to prevent decomposition. When the stain is dry, roll the garments gently in paper, place in paper bags and then seal and label the container. Do not put such stained objects into plastic bags. Handle fabrics as little as possible. Under special circumstances, seminal stains may be analyzed for the blood group factors: A, B, AB or O. If this type of testing is requested, contact the laboratory by telephone prior to shipping exhibits. This is essential since other biological samples are required.

## Fibers and Threads

Clothing, rugs, blankets, curtains and other fabrics are common articles, yet contain a variety of animal, vegetable and synthetic fibers of numerous colors; thus threads and individual fibers frequently are useful evidence in criminal cases. Fibers and threads are often found in fabric abrasions, torn metal or in other areas on hit and run vehicles. In burglary cases, such evidence may be located on torn screens, broken glass, or metal or safes, or other locations. Fibers may be important in homicides, rapes and other assaults.

Examinations of fibers or threads usually establish their type and color or may indicate the type of garments or fabric from which the fibers or threads originated. Also, fibers and threads can be compared with the fibers or clothing of suspects to determine if they originated from such garments. In many cases, threads or long fibers can be picked up with fingers or tweezers and placed in plastic envelopes or glass or plastic vials. Never place loose fibers in mailing envelopes or other paper containers; they are difficult to locate and remove and the paper itself may contain fibers, thus contaminating the evidence.

If the fibers are short, few in number or firmly adhering to an exhibit, try to remove the complete object containing the fibers, place it in a plastic envelope and send it to the laboratory. Never attempt to remove the fibers with gummed tape; it is almost impossible to remove fibers from the tape later for effective study. Always submit all clothing of persons the fibers might have originated from. Each garment should be packaged in a separate bag or wrapped in large, clean sheets of paper. Each package should be properly marked for identification.

The following Houston, Texas, case dramatically illustrates the importance of fiber evidence. The crime involved a robbery and strangulation murder of a hotel manager. The suspect tore a strip of fabric from a tablecloth from the crime scene and used it to strangle the victim. He then used the remaining portion of the tablecloth to bundle up the loot—money, a coin collection and some silver. Fortunately, the suspect left a few latent prints behind, and when he was located, he was still in possession of the stolen property. He was tried and convicted for murder. The conviction was based primarily on the testimony of the criminalist who matched a strip of torn fabric recovered from the victim's neck to the remaining portion of the tablecloth (bundle) recovered at the time of the suspect's arrest.

## Hair Strands

Although hair is a frequently encountered type of evidence, it has real evidentiary value in only a limited number of cases, usually for determinations as to possible source. Yet such studies require fairly large samples if the laboratory results are to be of real significance.

### Human Hair

Hair samples can be identified as human and some indication of the part of the body from which they originated can frequently be established. Hair color can be determined and some information developed concerning bleaching, dyeing or related treatment. In many instance, the race of the individual from whom head hairs originated can be determined. Study of hairs can frequently establish whether or not they fell out naturally, were pulled out or if they have been cut or crushed.

At present it is not possible to conclusively prove that two specimens of hair came from the same individual. In the case of head hair, however, the laboratory may be able to indicate a possible common origin. The evidentiary value of laboratory tests on hair will vary greatly depending upon the quantity of hair recovered as well as the uniqueness of the characteristics found during the examination.

### Animal Hair

Animal hair samples can sometimes be identified as to the genus or species of animal from which they originated. While animal hair can be compared with specimens from specific animals, this type of examination will only serve to establish similarities in structure and animal type. It is never possible to prove that recovered animal hairs came from a specific animal.

### Recovery of Hair Evidence

If hair is firmly attached, such as in dry blood or caught in metal or a crack in glass, do not attempt to remove it, but rather leave the hair intact on the object. If the object is small, mark and seal it in an envelope. If the object is large, wrap the area containing the hair in cellophane to prevent loss of the hairs during shipment. Recover all hairs present. If possible, use the fingers to pick up the hair and place in a vial or plastic envelope. Do not mix samples recovered at different locations. Label and seal the container. Never use gummed tape to pick up hairs or fibers.

### Standards for Comparison

If injuries to a victim are at a point where hair exists, secure hair specimens from as near this location as possible. When the point of injury is unknown, secure samples from various locations, and keep the samples separate. In the case of human head hair, it is important to obtain samples from different areas on the head since variations in structure or color of head hair frequently occur on the same individual. Likewise, there is a major difference in human head, pubic, arm, beard and other hair from different parts of the body.

Animal hair secured from different areas on the animal body will also vary greatly in structure. Whenever possible obtain large samples from each area. It is desirable that each of these contain at least several dozen hairs. Attempt to pull out standard samples which will be used for comparison purposes. If this is not possible, cut the hair as close to the skin as possible.

Always obtain samples from all individuals involved. In many investigations the laboratory is requested to determine if a sample in question originated from a specific individual when there are only a limited number of persons from whom the hair could have come. In the case of hair samples from vehicles in accidents, beds in sex offense cases and similar investigations, it is important to have standard samples from all possible occupants and not just from the individual from whom the hairs are believed to have originated.

### Blood Group From Hair

In certain instances it is possible to determine ABO blood type from human hair as an additional means of individualization. Submit samples of blood from the individuals involved to assist the laboratory in making this analysis. Contact the laboratory by telephone for special instructions prior to submitting hair specimens if blood group determinations are desired.

## Tool Marks

Tool marks are encountered most frequently in burglary cases but may also be found in many other types of crimes. The evidence consists of abrasions or impressions left by tools on objects at the crime scene and various types of tools found in the possession of suspects. In many cases, it is possible to identify the specific tool which made the questioned marks by means of laboratory comparison of tools and marked objects. In some instances, it is also possible to prove that marks on tools were produced by objects which they contacted at crime scenes. In other cases it is possible to prove, by means of physical or other comparisons, that parts of tools left at crime scenes were broken from damaged tools found in the possession of suspects.

### *Preservations and Packaging of Tools*

All areas on recovered tools which contain transferred paint, building materials or other contamination should be wrapped in plastic so that such substances will not be lost. After marking, tools should be wrapped or packaged to prevent the prying blades or edges from contacting any other surface or object. Care should be taken that no tape is placed on the mark or questioned area of the tool when packaging.

### *Make No Tests With Tools*

Attempts should never be made to fit tools into questioned marks or to make test marks prior to laboratory examination. If done, the questioned mark or the tool may be altered and this may make any laboratory examination valueless. In addition, traces of transferred paint or other substances on the tool may be lost or additional material may be transferred to the tool.

### *Preservation of Tool Marks*

Whenever possible send the whole object containing tool marks to the laboratory instead of just removing the area containing the mark. This is important since to make satisfactory test marks with the tool, it is necessary to determine the direction of motion and the vertical and horizontal angle at which the questioned mark was made. A study of all impressions and abrasions present on an object, such as a door jamb or safe, will often indicate the method in which the tool was used much better than an examination of just a small section removed from the safe or other object.

If it is impossible to submit the whole object to the laboratory, remove the tool mark itself. In such cases, care should be taken to prevent any damage or alteration of the questioned mark. Always remove sufficient surrounding material and the tool mark so that no damage will occur. A photograph showing the original location of the mark and its relation to its environment should accompany any removed marks.

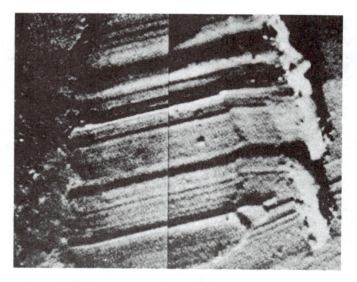

*Figure 5-18 Comparison of a tool abrasion mark on a door lock (left) and a test mark made on lead with suspect's wrench (right)*

While photographs of tool marks at crime scenes may have value in some investigations, they rarely have any value in identifying the particular tool used. The laboratory cannot accurately compare suspected tools with photographs of tool marks, even when the exact magnification of the photographs is known. Photographs which show the whole object as well as the tool mark, however, may be of value to indicate methods by which the marks were produced by the tool. This information may assist in producing satisfactory test marks in the laboratory; therefore, such photographs should be included.

Mark the object containing tool marks in some area where the questioned impression or abrasion will not be damaged. Pack the object containing tool marks so that no alteration or damage will occur during shipment. Small objects may be placed in envelopes or boxes while important areas on larger objects can be protected with plastic, paper or cardboard. Large objects may be packed in cartons or crates if not delivered in person.

### Examples of Tools as Evidence

While all applications of tool mark evidence cannot be covered here, a few illustrations may indicate its value as evidence.

1.  Hammers may often be identified as being the specific tools which made impressions on safes and other objects.

2.  Screwdriver scrape marks on lock boxes and other objects are often identifiable as having been made by tools found in the possession of suspects. It has also been possible to identify the tool used to remove metal screws at the crime scene.

3.  Pry bars and other similar tools can frequently be identified as having been used to produce marks on doors, window frames, safes and other objects.

4.  Knives have been identified as having made cuts on wood.

5.  Bolt cutters, pliers, tin snips and similar tools can often be identified as being the specific tools used to cut wires, lock hasps, metal bars, sheet metal, etc.

6.  Pipe wrenches can sometimes be identified as having been used to disconnect pipes or twist off other objects such as door knobs.

7.  Axes and hatchets can be compared with cut marks on wood. In several cases, tools have been identified as lethal weapons by comparison with marks on the skulls of victims.

## Firearm Evidence

Firearms are involved in an appreciable percentage of both major and minor crimes. The evidence in such cases is frequently very broad and investigations of the weapons themselves, as well as the events which occurred, may be quite varied. The laboratory is able to assist in many phases of such investigations.

### Ballistics

The word ballistics is frequently used incorrectly when reference is made to studies of weapons and cases involving firearms. *Ballistics* is the science that deals with the motion and flight of projectiles. Such studies are of importance in only a limited number of criminal investigations. The laboratory is capable of furnishing scientific aid in connection with some problems related to ballistics. Examples are the establishment of the range, trajectory or penetration power of fired bullets, ricochet pattern studies and the like

### Crime Scenes

When a firearm is recovered at a crime scene, the investigator must note the position of the hammer (down, halfcocked or cocked) if the weapon has one, before picking it up. Care must be taken to preserve prints when picking up weapons. Rough surfaces that usually do not retain prints are safest for touching. When unloading a revolver it must be noted whether or not the cartridge under the firing pin has been fired or not. The investigator must also note the position of other fired or unfired cartridges in the cylinder. In the case of automatics, notes must be made of the rounds left in the magazine and the chamber.

The findings that may result from a laboratory examination of firearms evidence is treated in the succeeding chapter. The following information is limited to the handling of firearms at crime scenes.

### Firearms Precautions Check List

1. Never submit a loaded gun to the laboratory unless it is delivered in person. Unfired cartridges may be left in the magazine provided the magazine is removed from the gun. A firearm with a cartridge in the chamber should never be shipped by any method, even if the weapon is not cocked or is on safety.

2. Never clean the bore, chamber or cylinder before submitting a firearm and never attempt to fire the gun before it is examined in the laboratory.

3. Never pick up a weapon by placing a pencil or other object in the end of the barrel.

4. Record serial number, make and model of the weapon and mark it in some inconspicuous manner before sending it to the laboratory. The marking of many firearms is important since duplicate serial numbers are sometimes found on different guns of the same make and general type.

5. Place the weapon in a strong cardboard or wooden box well-packed to prevent shifting of the gun in transit.

6.  Rifles or shotguns may be taken apart to make it easier to package and ship, but do not disassemble more than necessary.

7.  If blood or other material of interest is present on the muzzle of the gun, place a small paper bag around the muzzle and seal it to the barrel with plastic tape to prevent loss of the sample during shipment.

### Bullets as Evidence

1.  Never mark a bullet on or near the rifling markings on the bullet side, even if they are not clearly defined. Certain examinations may not be possible if the base or nose is marked even though these are the preferred marking locations. If there is any question don't mark the bullet but seal it in a marked container.

2.  Wrap recovered bullets individually in tissue paper and seal in separate pill boxes or envelopes.

3.  Submit all evidence bullets recovered to the laboratory. A conclusive identification may be possible on only one of several bullets recovered even when they all appear to be in good condition.

4.  Do not attempt to clean recovered bullets before sending them to the laboratory except in the case of bullets removed from a body. The latter may be washed off immediately in running water and dried by blotting on a soft dry towel in those cases where the study of fiber and other evidence adhering to the bullet nose is not important.

5.  Handle fired evidence bullets as little as possible to prevent damage to the identification characteristics in the rifling markings or loss of material adhering to the bullets. Never use forceps or other tools to handle bullets.

### Cartridge Cases as Evidence:

1.  Mark cartridge cases on the inside of the open end, if possible. Use initials or other characteristic marks which are kept as small as possible. Cases may be marked on the outside near the open end, but care must be taken not to damage clip or other markings which may be present. Never mark on or near the primer end of the case. Again, if there is any question, seal the cartridge in a marked container.

2.   Fired shotgun shells may be marked either on the inside or the outside of the paper or plastic portion of the shell.

3.   Submit all evidence cartridge cases or shotgun shells recovered to the laboratory. Frequently some cases contain more identifying detail than do others.

4.   Do not attempt to clean recovered cartridge cases before submitting them to the laboratory.

5.   Wrap each cartridge case separately in tissue paper to prevent damage to breech block, firing pin or other markings by contact with other cartridge cases.

6.   Place wrapped cartridge case in envelopes or pill boxes, label and seal the container.

### Ammunition as Evidence

1.   Always attempt to recover unused ammunition for comparison purposes when firearms are obtained as evidence. If not in the weapon itself, suspects often have additional ammunition in their car, clothing, house or at other locations. While the laboratory maintains an adequate supply of cartridges of all types for test purposes, some types are not always available. In addition, it may be important for test purposes to duplicate exactly the make, type and age of the ammunition used in the crime. Other ammunition in the possession of the suspect frequently is identical to that fired at the time of the crime.

2.   Unfired ammunition may be marked on the side of the cartridge case, near the bullet end.

3.   Ammunition may be compared to establish similarities in type and manufacturer. It is sometimes possible to show that a particular bullet or cartridge came from cartridges manufactured within a specific time period.

4.   In some instances it is possible to prove that hand loaded bullets had a common source or that the cartridges were reloaded with the same tools.

# MARKING EVIDENCE—GENERAL COMMENTS

Evidence must be marked to assure that its identity can be legally established in court. When evidence is produced in court, it is imperative to prove it is the same as that found at the scene. Normal descriptions of items are not sufficient; distinctive symbols or initials should be used. These marks can be written, scratched or carved; however, they should be as small as possible and in manner and location so as not to damage the item or alter its evidential value. For example, a watch can be marked on the inside of the back of the case or jewelry can be sketched or photographed and packaged rather than risk damage by marking.

A piece(s) of broken glass may be traced on a piece of paper and the paper properly marked for identification and packaged. All persons who came into possession of the evidence for storage or examination, etc., should mark the articles or containers for identification and to verify the unbroken chain of custody. The container of evidence must be marked for identification even if the item inside is marked. When tags are used on large objects, the tag must be securely attached and marked as well as the item of evidence. All items of evidence, their serial numbers and distinctive characteristics, identification markings by investigators, etc. must be recorded in the investigator's notes.

# PRESERVING EVIDENCE-GENERAL COMMENTS

Physical evidence may be most effectively presented in court if it has been properly handled and preserved. An analysis of evidence by the laboratory may be impossible, if the evidence has been altered or contaminated. Conclusions drawn from such evidence may be erroneous or invalid. Evidence must be preserved in its natural state. Each item must be preserved as a separate sample. There can be no mixing of the unknown and the known. For example, a knife which is to be examined for traces of copper screen wire must not be placed in the same container with samples of the copper screen wire.

## Containers

Various types of containers can be used for items of physical evidence. Several different packaging methods are listed here. The investigator should try to suit his containers to the sample. Due to bacte-

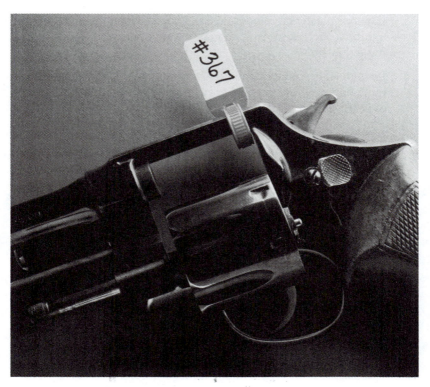

*Figure 5-19  ID tag correctly placed on a gun used for evidence*

rial or fungal actions it is imperative that one does not put damp or biological evidence in plastic bags. The following is suggested:

1.  Plastic or cellophane envelopes are suitable for small dry objects.

2.  Paper envelopes are suitable for folded paper bundles containing very small or powdery material if all corners are sealed. Do not use paper envelopes for fiber evidence, a vial or pill box is preferred.

3.  Vials, pill boxes, capsules and like containers are frequently suitable, depending upon the exhibit and its condition.

4.  Garments and large exhibits can be placed in bags or rolled in paper.

5.  Paper or plastic envelopes can be sealed around the ends of large exhibits, such as tools, with plastic tape to prevent loss of adhering evidence.

6.  Loss of adhering evidence on large exhibits, such as safes, vehicle bumpers, etc., can be prevented by placing plastic or paper over the evidence and sealing it with tape.

7.  Always use clean and new containers to prevent contamination.

## Storing Evidence

Evidence should be stored in a safe, evidence vault, locker or some other location where unauthorized persons do not have access to it. This applies to both temporary and long range storage.

# DELIVERY OF EVIDENCE TO THE LABORATORY FOR EXAMINATION

## Recommended Procedures

1.  **Personal delivery of evidence** is the best method, where the investigation or the evidence involved is complex or the exhibits are large or perishable, or there are many separate items. This personal contact will permit a consultation between the criminalist and the investigator, which may be very beneficial.

2.  **Mail shipments of evidence**. Use registered or certified mail if evidence is of high monetary value or if it is small and of critical value. Otherwise, first or fourth class mail is satisfactory.

3.  **Prevent damage.** Package contents so that breakage or contamination will not occur during shipment.

4.  **Restrictions.** Follow postal regulations. Do not mail explosives and other prohibited items.

5.  **Seal package completely**, even if fourth class mail is employed. Do not just tie with string, but rather employ tape which meets postal service regulations (masking tape is not authorized).

6. **Place the cover letter on the outside of package.**
7. **Express shipments** packaging procedures are the same as for regular mail shipments.

CALIFORNIA DEPARTMENT OF JUSTICE
DIVISION OF LAW ENFORCEMENT
INVESTIGATIVE SERVICES BRANCH

ISB CASE NO. ..................
ISB use only — New ☐ Additional ☐ Resubmittal ☐

**REQUEST FOR PHYSICAL EVIDENCE EXAMINATION**

REQUESTING AGENCY: ........................ (Location) ........ COUNTY OF: ........

OFFENSE: .................. DATE OF OFFENSE: .......... AGENCY NO.: ........

SUSPECT(S): (Include ID No. if any) ..................................

VICTIM(S): ..................

BRIEF SUMMARY OF CIRCUMSTANCES:

EVIDENCE SUBMITTED: (Packages, containers, etc.) ...

PURPOSE OF EXAMINATION: ...

CHAIN OF CUSTODY

| EVIDENCE RECEIVED FROM | EVIDENCE DELIVERED TO | DATE | TIME |
|---|---|---|---|
| | | | |

If further information is needed concerning this case, the following official should be contacted:
.................................... Phone No.: ..................

ISB Report to be sent to the attention of: ..................

Evidence should be returned to the attention of: ..................

Officer investigating this case: ..................

Date results needed by: .......... For (type of court and location) ..........

IS ABOVE LISTED EVIDENCE PROPERLY MARKED AND PACKAGED?
PLACE THIS FORM IN ENVELOPE ON OUTSIDE OF EVIDENCE PACKAGE

*Figure 5-20 Request for Physical Evidence Examination Form*

Evidence Requiring Special Handling:

1. Explosives: Do not deliver or ship explosives to the laboratory without contacting the criminalist by telephone first; he will evaluate the situation and indicate the procedures to be followed.

2. Dangerous Materials: The same telephonic contact must be made prior to delivering loaded weapons, dangerous chemicals, etc.

3. Perishable Materials: Deliver only during working hours. If the items are to be shipped, the laboratory must be contacted first, except in the case of blood related specimens which are sent for alcohol, drug or grouping tests.

### *Disposal of Evidence*

Some evidence is declared contraband or a nuisance by law. As such it may be confiscated by the court and ordered destroyed by a chief of police or sheriff, once its evidentiary need or value is terminated. This applies most frequently to certain guns, knives, drugs, etc. Some evidence must be returned to its owner when it is no longer needed for court trial purposes. In any case, no evidence should be disposed of until the case is finally terminated by the court.

## SUMMARY

The crime scene is the locale within the immediate vicinity of the occurrence wherein evidence may be found. It may contain much of the evidence and information required for a successful investigation; therefore, a methodical and detailed evaluation and search of the scene is imperative. All of the investigator's activities from the first notification of the crime's occurrence, through the entire processing of the scene must be recorded in the investigator's notes. The initial thoughts and efforts of the first officer or investigator at the scene must be directed to the welfare of the victim.

Isolation and protection of the scene is necessary; however, preservation of human life is most important. Rendering first aid or calling for medical assistance may, on occasion, precede the actual isolation and protection of a scene. The rules of evidence require that a crime scene be "reproduced" in court as it existed when discovered. It is therefore necessary to protect the scene until all possible evidence is collected. Investigators must remain aware of the possibility of unintentional and intentional acts by humans and acts of nature that disturb crime scenes.

An evaluation of the crime scene and its perimeters is required, so that the appropriate search method(s), personnel and equipment needs for processing the scene can be determined. Once the evaluation is completed and appropriate decisions are made, the processing of the crime scene should proceed as expeditiously as circumstances allow.

A full scale search of the crime scene may he preceded by a walk-through, preferably by the coordinating investigator (if applicable) accompanied by the evidence technician or criminalist. The walk-through can provide an intimate visualization of the scene before the crime occurred and a feeling for what took place during the crime. Evidence potentials, laboratory equipment and personnel needs can be determined by this procedure. In the process, one can establish a practical path through the scene that affords the lowest risk of damaging or destroying evidence.

Prior to beginning a full scale search, the entire scene must be photographed in color (if possible) as it was found. The methodical full-scale search must be supervised by the coordinating investigator-officer who should make the assignments of any other investigators, technicians, or criminalists participating in the processing of the scene. An accurate record of all persons who have been on the scene officially or otherwise will be invaluable in terms of eliminating latent prints, footprints, tire tracks, debris, etc., found on the scene.

Crime scene photographs are admissible as evidence in court, if testimony can be offered by the investigator or technician to the effect that they accurately depict the scene or item as it was observed. A camera may record all that is in focus, yet it may not correctly depict distances between objects. Therefore, the investigator must depend on the crime scene sketch and notes to provide accuracy as to distances between objects, the scale and overall perspective.

General guidelines for photographing a crime scene indicate that, when in doubt, take photos. It is better to expend some film than to pass up valuable evidence. Also included in these guidelines is a reminder that the investigator must record all camera locations and photos in the notes and if practical, in the sketch. A ruler should be included in a photograph when it is necessary to depict scale or distance. Color photos are desirable but not required to show blood or wounds. Area or scene-as-a-whole photos are taken in overlapping sequence.

Close-up photos should be taken of entrances and exits to crime scenes and of bodies, wounds, weapons and various trace evidence potentials. Aerial photography may be useful for overall detail of outdoor scenes and surrounding area of indoor scenes. A videotape record of the scene may be useful if applicable and available. The investigator must insure proper custody of all photos and negatives and book them as evidence if possible.

A rough sketch is drawn by the investigator or evidence technician at the crime scene but not to scale. The sketch will provide an accurate record of the distances and relationships between the essential evidential components of the crime scene. The scale drawing is usually accomplished by a draftsman or technician utilizing the crime scene and the rough sketch.

The proper locating, collecting, handling and preservation of evidence will many times be the determining factor in establishing the guilt or innocence of the accused. The chain of custody must be maintained unbroken from the time of the collection of the evidence until it is presented in court. The chain of custodians must be kept to a minimum.

Many kinds of evidence can be recovered at crime scenes. Fingerprints are one of the most common types of physical evidence found at crime scenes and may prove of value in identifying the suspect and placing him and her on the crime scene. The term, *fingerprint*, normally includes palm prints and prints of the feet. Fingerprints may be visible, i.e., perspiration accumulated on the friction ridges on the inside of the fingers, palms and soles of the feet is transferred to an object when touched. Prints may also be visible because fingers, palms or feet have been impregnated with grease, dirt or blood or when the ridges are pressed into soft putty, soap or wax. The basic techniques for discovering, developing, recording and preserving prints include oblique lighting, photography, brush and powder developing, and chemical techniques, such as iodine fuming, ninhydrin method and the silver nitrate method.

The relatively new method of comparing fingerprints using state of the art technology is called the Automated Fingerprint Identification System. This new method uses high tech photography and computer programs to match fingerprints found at a crime scene to fingerprints on file with the agency. It is expected that law enforcement agencies will soon be able to network their systems so that all data on file is available to any given law enforcement agency.

Foot and tire prints are produced when material that is adhering to the sole and heel of the shoe or the tread of the tire is deposited on a hard surface or base. Foot and tire imprints are produced when the sole and heel of a shoe or the tread of a tire is pressed into a soft substance, such as soil, sand, snow or mud. These prints and imprints are measured and photographed with a scale in the photo and recorded in the notes. In the case of prints, the photos are taken with an oblique light and imprints are included in the sketch if practical. Shoe and tire prints can occasionally be lifted as fingerprints are, using tape or pads. Imprints are further preserved for laboratory comparison by casting with plaster of Paris, paraffin wax, sulfur and silicone rubber.

Blood stains are frequently of importance in a wide variety of criminal investigations. Blood stains should be allowed to completely dry before items containing the stains are packaged for transporting to a laboratory.

If grouping of stains is desired, fresh known blood samples must be obtained from the subject(s) involved in two sterile vials. One sample must contain a preservative and an anticoagulant and the other must be without the added preservatives. The more common types of tests conducted with blood stains are proof of presence of blood, detection of human or animal origin of the blood, and determination of the basic ABO blood groups. To date, it is impossible to prove that a blood stain came from a specific individual. It may be possible, however, to demonstrate that all blood groups presented in the stain and in the blood of the subject are alike.

It must be realized that many other persons will also have blood of the same groups, yet it may be possible to demonstrate that the stain could not have come from a specific person. Some blood group factors have been found in certain racial groups. For this reason, the laboratory should be informed of the race of all individuals known to be involved in crimes, when blood stain evidence is present. Blood spatter marks left at a crime scene can also aid the trained investigator in determining many factors relating to a crime.

Seminal stains are often, but not always, found on clothing, blankets, sheets or other materials in rape and other sex offenses. If dry, the stains may have a stiff, starchy feel. An ultraviolet lamp may be useful in the preliminary search for an indication of semen because of the bluish-white fluorescence of these stains. In sex offense cases, the victim should always be examined by a physician and a vaginal or rectal smear taken for laboratory examination. It may be possible to obtain blood group factors from semen stains.

Fibers and threads are often found in fabric abrasions, torn metal or in other areas on hit-and-run vehicles or on torn screens, broken glass, or metal or safes in burglary cases. Fibers may also be important evidence in homicides, rapes and other assaults.

Laboratory examination of fibers or threads may establish their type, color and the fabric from which they originated. Laboratory examination of hair can identify hair samples as human, determine their color, provide some indication as to the part of the body from which they originated. Information as to bleaching, dying, racial origin and whether the hair fell out, was pulled out or was cut or crushed may also be determined. At present, it is impossible to conclusively prove that two specimens of hair came from the same individual. ABO blood type may be determined in some cases by testing human hair. In the case of animal hairs, it is sometimes possible to identify the genus or species of the animal from which they originated; however, it is impossible to prove that certain hairs came from a specific animal.

Tool marks (abrasions or impressions) found in burglary cases and other types of crimes can be important evidence. It is possible to identify the specific tool which made the questioned marks or prove that marks on tools were produced by objects they contacted at the crime scene.

Firearms are involved in a large percentage of both major and minor crimes. When firearms evidence is found at crime scenes, the investigator must practice appropriate techniques of collecting, handling and preserving this evidence, thus enhancing the possibilities of connecting a suspect to the evidence through laboratory examination.

Evidence must be marked with distinctive symbols or initials by all persons who come into possession of it in order to verify the unbroken chain of custody and to assure that its identity can be legally established in court. All evidence must be preserved in its natural state, free from alteration or contamination. No evidence should be disposed of until the case is finally terminated by the courts.

## DISCUSSION QUESTIONS

1. Discuss the duties of the first officer at a crime scene.
2. Explain the importance of the isolation and protection of a crime scene.
3. Describe both intentional and unintentional acts nature that may disturb crime scenes.
4. What are the traditional search methods for crime scenes?

5. What is the purpose of the crime scene walk-through?
6. Explain the purpose and importance of the crime scene sketch.
7. Explain the purpose and importance of crime scene photography.
8. Discuss the importance of physical evidence in a case. Give examples.
9. Give examples of physical evidence and explain why some require special attention.

# THE CRIMINALISTICS LABORATORY

**6**

## KEY TERMS AND CONCEPTS

Firearms identification and ballistics
Trace analysis
Scanning electron microscope
Gas chromatograph
Emission spectrometer
Forensic photography
Latent prints
Voice Identification Unit

A criminalistics laboratory utilizes the skills of professional criminalists, technical assistants, questioned document and latent fingerprint examiners, photographers, and polygraph examiners. Criminalists are university graduates holding degrees in criminalistics and related physical sciences. Other staff members may hold various degrees in connection with the duties they perform. All staff members must eventually be qualified to present expert testimony before courts in connection with the services they render. Some laboratories may also include a surveyor and a composite artist as staff members. Many laboratories are organized in sections, each responsible for specific functions. *Note:* A major portion of the information and illustrations in this chapter are from the *Physical Evidence Manual*, State of California, Department of Justice, Division of Law Enforcement, Investigative Services Branch, with permission from that agency.

# THE FIREARMS SECTION

This section conducts firearms identification examinations, comparisons of firearms and bullets, studies to determine trigger pull, operation of safety devices, alteration or modification of weapons or any condition of the weapon that might cause accidental fire or make it unsafe.

## Functions

The Firearms Section is responsible for:

- Test firing of all firearms.

- Comparisons of bullets and cartridge casings to evidence guns.

- Securing all firearms.

- Restoration of serial numbers.

- Clothing analysis for gunshot evidence.

- Analysis of any firearms-related evidence.

## Firearms Identification

Each firearm has an individual set of characteristics which can serve to identify it, even though it is compared with one of the same type, model, caliber and manufacturer. Individual characteristics will be found as follows:

1. Barrels: No two barrels are microscopically identical. Rifling (which consists of a number of spiral grooves) is cut into the surface of the bore to provide the fired projectile with rotation, stability and direction in motion. This rifling is individual with each barrel, and leaves raised portions ("lands") which are actually original surfaces of the bore before the rifling is cut. Both grooves and lands will contain identifiable characteristics due to the individual cutting (boring) process and the character of the steel tubing the barrel was made from. The rifling may have a right-handed or left-handed twist. Either twist may be constant throughout the bore or increase from the breach to the muzzle. The number of grooves may vary from four to six. The grooves and lands of the bore may be of equal width, or broad grooves and narrow lands, depending on the manufacturer. Other characteristics of rifling are the pitch, the measure of the rate at which

the direction of the groove changes; diameter bore, the distance from land to land; and groove diameter, the distance from bottom to bottom of opposite grooves.

2.  Caliber: This is the diameter of the bore measured in hundredths of an inch. Example: A .30 caliber gun is one in which the bore has a diameter of 30 one hundredths of an inch.

3.  Firing Pins: These are individually finished during manufacture and contain file marks and pit marks which will leave an impression on the primer of the bullet when it is fired.

4.  Extractor Marks: These marks are produced when the extractor under spring tension is forced over the rim of the case in loading the cartridge into the chamber. This occurs in the use of automatic, self-loading, bolt, pump and lever action rifle and shotguns and automatic pistols.

5.  Ejector Marks: These are produced on the base of a casting, or the rim or flange, when the fired cartridge is drawn from the chamber by the extractor. They are normally found on cartridges fired from self-loading and automatic weapons.

6.  Breech Face Marks: These are produced on the primer of the cartridge when the gas pressure generated at the time of firing forces the cartridge against the breech face, or in the case of rifles, the bolt head. Again, the principle of individual characteristics applies to extractor and ejector marks, as well as breech face mark. File marks as a result of manufacturing are present, often augmented by marks acquired through the use in firing (see Figure 6-1).

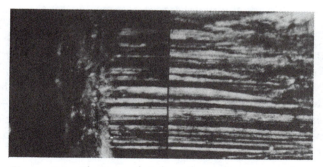

*Figure 6-1 Photograph taken through a comparison microscope showing matching rifling markings on test and questioned .25 Cal. automatic bullet*

7.  Ballistics: All tests concerning ballistics and bullets would also be a function of the Firearms Identification Section of the crime laboratory.

8.  Experts: It is not uncommon to find that the firearms expert is also the explosives expert charged with the highly hazardous duty of handling and disposing of explosives. Some agencies are equipped with an explosives van and specialized equipment for this service.

9.  Trace Metal Detection Technique: It is possible to demonstrate that a person has recently held a gun in his hand. Research has determined that metal objects leave traces on skin and clothing surfaces in characteristic patterns with intensities proportional to the interaction of weight, friction, or duration of contact with metal objects. The trace metal detection technique makes such metal trace patterns visible when skin or clothing is treated with a test solution (hydroxyquinoline) and then is illuminated by ultraviolet light. A spray container is generally the most suitable method of applying the test solution. Test areas are allowed to dry thoroughly prior to examination. The parts of a test area that have been in contact with metal objects give off fluorescent colors that are unique to each metal:

Iron, steel = blackish-purple

Copper, brass = purple

Galvanized iron (tin) = bright yellow

Aluminum = mottled dull yellow

Lead = buff (flesh tone)

The pattern of the metal traces as revealed by the fluorescent colors is traced. Handguns leave distinctive patterns which are specific to types, makes, models and calibers of these weapons. The shape, size and weight of the gun or metal object, the duration of contact and the use of the metal object all combine to produce the location and intensity of metal traces and their patterns on the hands. It has been found that metal trace patterns have developed up to 36 to 48 hours after contact when the suspect has followed a normal routine of daily hand washings. Fluorescence photography reveals the preserved metal tracings.

## Restoration of Obliterated Serial Numbers

It is, on occasion, possible to restore serial numbers that were originally imprinted on metal (i.e., engine blocks, guns, etc). When the number was originally stamped into the metal, the molecules of the immediate area became compressed, "crushed," and otherwise distorted and the metal molecules were thrown out of line to varying degrees. This compression actually leaves a shadow below the original numbers, approximately half the original depth of the pressed number. When the serial number is ground off, this shadow remains below the surface, unnoticed, undisturbed.

### Etching

This method is applied if the serial number has been ground off. The area where the original number was located is cleaned and then highly polished with an abrasive (emery cloth). The area is then surrounded with a mound of putty to contain the etching solution. The solution can be nitric, hydrochloric or sulfuric acid in a reagent, and is applied with a swab. With care and patience the original number may appear if the acid does not eat away the shadow position. It is obvious that the experienced laboratory technician with the knowledge of the various reagents and their affects on various metals is required for this testing. If the number is restored, it must be promptly photographed for recording purposes.

### Magnaflux

This method is also used if the serial number has been ground off, though reports of success with it are not as frequent as with acid etching. In this technique the metal surface is prepared in the same manner as with the acid etching. The metal is then magnetized, wherein the crystalline structure (shadow) below the visible surface draws the iron oxide in the applied flux (solution) and forms the numbers which are then photographed for recording purposes. It is important to note that these methods of restoration are useless if the serial numbers have been ground off too deeply or below the shadow area. On occasion, serial numbers are burned off with a torch or punched out which also makes restoration impossible. Examples of successful restoration are offered (see Figure 6-2).

## Firearms Tests

### Dermal Nitrate Tests

Many research studies have clearly confirmed that the dermal nitrate paraffin cast technique is worthless for determining whether or not an individual has fired a weapon. In this technique the suspect's shooting hand is coated with melted paraffin, and a reagent (dipheny-

Figure 6-2 Restoration of the last four serial numbers which had been filed off on a 30.06 rifle. Restoration was by means of acid etching.

lamine) is dropped on the paraffin mold. The appearance of dark blue specks ostensibly indicates a positive reaction, i.e., presence of nitrates from gunpowder residue on the suspect's hand. The great problem is that bleach, fertilizers, tobacco, urine and other oxidizing compounds will cause the same reaction, thus proving only that an oxidizing substance—not necessarily nitrates—is present on the suspect's hand.

### Powder or Shot Pattern Tests

An approximation as to the distance from which a gun was fired when inflicting a wound can be obtained by powder or shot pattern tests conducted in a laboratory. These tests are based primarily on the spread of gunpowder residues on the skin or clothing of the victim. A contact or near contact wound will often cause a scorching of the flesh or cloth around the entrance, in addition to depositing gunpowder residue. Weapons fired at a distance greater than twenty-four inches will not normally deposit gun powder residue at a point of contact (entrance of bullet). The same weapon and same type of ammunition used in the crime is fired into white artist's sketching paper from various distances until the approximate powder residue and shot pattern desired is achieved (see Figure 6-3).

### Neutron Activation Analysis

Only a few major laboratories are equipped to conduct these studies. Neutron Activation Analysis involves the irradiation of any unknown material with neutrons (nuclear particles). Some of the irradiated atoms in the unknown material become radioactive and disintegrate, giving off gamma rays. The energy of the ray is measured with a Gamma Ray Spectrometer. The energy values are used to identify the element(s) in the original material. Quantitative measurement of the elements present can be made by comparing the radioactivity of the elements in the evidentiary material with the radioactivity of known amounts of these elements. Extensive studies have been conducted of paraffin casts made on hands of individuals who have fired various weapons; however, to date this analysis cannot always establish whether or not an individual has fired a gun.

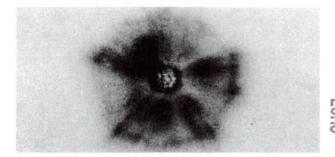

*Figure 6-3 Muzzle discharge residue left on victim's outer garment as a consequence of a close range firearms discharge.*

### Atomic Absorption Method

Atomic Absorption is now replacing neutron activation analysis and the dermal nitrate paraffin test for determining whether or not a subject has recently fired a handgun. Neutron activation analysis is quite expensive, and the paraffin test is not always effective.

Atomic absorption analysis for detecting gunpowder residue on a suspect's hands is relatively inexpensive. It not only detects antimony and barium (as does neutron activation analysis) but also lead. Collection of gunshot residue is accomplished by spraying the hands of the suspected shooter with a five percent solution of nitric acid. The hands are then swabbed with a dry cotton-tipped applicator. Any gunshot residue (particles) that adhere to the swab are then analyzed. The analysis involves burning the test swab and comparing the frequency of the light given off by the sample with a known standard.

# THE TRACE ANALYSIS SECTION

Trace analysis involves the examination, identification and evaluation of numerous types of physical evidence collected in criminal investigations. The studies conducted by this section would include the microscopic examination of slides taken from rape victims during the pelvic examination conducted by a physician. The microscopic examination and comparison of fibers, hair, tool marks, pry marks and wood chips are other examples of the studies conducted in this section. The shoe and tire prints and imprints obtained at crime scenes by investigators or criminalists, as well as soil samples, debris, paint, glass and plastic fragments collected during the investigation are also analyzed and compared by this section (see Figures 6-4 and 6-5).

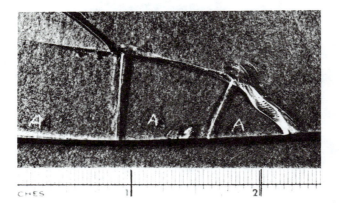

*Figure 6-4 Three pieces of glass found in suspect's vehicle(A) matched with larger pieces from broken window at burglary scene.*

# THE SEROLOGY SECTION

The Serology Section conducts all ABO typing of blood, semen and other body fluids. The following describes several basic tests for these.

*Figure 6-5  Paint from a safe of a burglarized store (left) and chips of paint found in vehicle of suspect (right). Corresponding abrasion markings on the paint show that all came from the same source.*

## Tests for Presence of Blood

- Presumptive Test (Benzidine TMB Reagent): This is a presumptive test: it does not establish the presence of blood. It is used as a screening test to determine if a stain may be blood. If the test is negative, this would eliminate the stain as not being blood.

  Method: Moisten a piece of clean filter paper with distilled water and touch the edge of the stain. Apply a drop of the reagent to the absorbed stain on the filter paper. If a blue coloration appears, this indicates a positive reaction.

- Confirmatory Test (Hemin): This test is used to establish the presence of hemoglobin in a suspected blood stain.

  Method: A small portion of the suspected blood stain is placed on a slide and intermittently treated with drops of saline solution and glacial acetic acid. When dry, the substance is examined under a microscope. If blood is present, brown rhombic hemin chloride crystals have formed.

- Biological Perciptin (Ring Perciptin): This test is used to establish the origin of blood stain as to species, human or animal; and if animal, what kind: dog, cat, hog, chicken, etc.

    Method: This test is conducted in a test tube, and a positive reaction can be observed as a ring of precipitate which transforms at the interface of an extract of the blood stain and the antiserum. Note: To identify a stain as human blood, an antihuman serum is used. This antiserum factor applies to the testing of animal blood as well.

- Blood Grouping: Blood grouping tests will establish which of the four major blood groups a stain belongs in (i.e., O, A, B, or AB). Blood grouping involves the agglutination, or clumping, of erythrocytes (red blood cells). Note: The author will not attempt to treat the methods of analysis involved in blood grouping, as they are beyond the intent of this text.

## Tests for Presence of Semen

- Preliminary Test (Florence): This test is used to determine the presence of choline. Seminal plasma is one of the richest sources of choline. A strong positive reaction indicates the stain may contain semen, though this is not a specific test as a positive reaction may also be produced by tissue extracts. In addition, false negative reactions may be caused by blood in the semen or if the semen is low in choline.

    Method: The test is conducted by adding a drop of Florence Reagent to an extract of a suspected seminal stain. If dark brown choline-periodide crystals form, they can be viewed under a microscope.

- Confirmatory Test (Microscopic Examination): The conclusive identification of a stain as semen depends on the presence of male reproductive cells (spermatozoa) in the stain. This is determined by microscopic examination of the stain.

    Other Body Fluids: Many human beings secrete the blood group substance(s) corresponding to their major blood group in their body fluids (e.g., semen, saliva, vaginal secretions, etc.). These persons are known as "secretors." Those persons whose body fluids do not contain the major blood group substance(s) are called "nonsecretors." It is, therefore, possible to establish the presence of the ABO blood group from stains of semen, saliva, vaginal fluid, etc., derived from secretors. Approximately sixty percent of the population are secretors.

# THE BLOOD ALCOHOL ANALYSIS SECTION

This section conducts quantitative analysis of alcohol levels in blood and urine.

## Gas Chromatography

An accurate and expedient method of analysis, widely used today, is gas chromatography. The gas chromatograph is an instrument that separates complex mixtures of substances into component parts, identifying and quantifying them. The sample to be processed is placed in the injector port where it is vaporized (usually by burning), then swept into a column by a carrier gas. Each sample component emerges separately and is identified according to the time it has taken to traverse the column. The concentration of the component is sensed by a detector, which translates the information via electrical impulses, which are recorded on a graph. The column is operated isothermally or by programmed heat. This instrument is also used to analyze organic substances, such as narcotics, paints, petroleum products, etc.

# THE TOXICOLOGY SECTION

*Toxicology* is the study of poisons and their action on the living organism. It is a very complex science that is divided into two areas: clinical and chemical. *Clinical toxicology* deals primarily with the recognition of poisoning symptoms, remedial treatment, and actions of poison in the body. *Chemical toxicology* focuses mainly on the detection of poison in stomach contents, blood, etc. The two areas of study naturally will overlap in a criminal investigation. A Toxicology Section in a police laboratory can normally conduct the following tests for:

A. Opiate in urine

B. Toluene in a substance

C. Tests for drugs in biological fluids

1. Acid drugs: barbiturates in blood or urine

2. Basic drugs: Methaqualone in blood or urine

3. Codeine or morphine in urine

4. Methadone in urine

5. Phencyclidine (PCP) in urine

6. Ethchlorvynol in blood

## Death Cases—Crime Suspected

Toxicological analysis of human body fluids and organs, including pathological studies of tissue to aid in determining the cause of death, is normally a responsibility of the coroner or medical examiner.

# THE NARCOTICS SECTION

This section conducts qualitative and quantitative analysis of controlled substances. The term, *controlled substances*, for the purpose of this section, refers to prohibited drugs and narcotics.

### *Techniques Used*

Most police laboratories utilize various wet chemical tests involving reagents, and microscopic examination for analysis. Some laboratories also use the gas chromatograph as an adjunct to the above methods, and it is considered very reliable for this purpose.

# OTHER TESTING UNITS

## The Scanning Electron Microscope

This powerful microscope is used to study soils, metals, fibers, tool marks, paint, hair, glass, explosive residue and gunshot residue, where high magnification and detail is required. The illumination source for this microscope is an electron gun. It magnifies the item being examined over 100,000 times, as compared to the light microscope which only magnifies 2,000 times. Additionally, the scanning electron microscope gives a three dimensional impression of the specimen (item), whereas a light microscope gives only a two dimensional impression (see Figure 6-6).

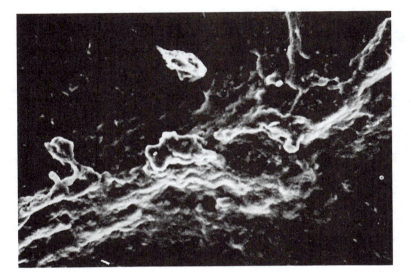

*Figure 6-6 A magnified pore on the ridge of a finger (Courtesy of East Los Angeles College)*

## The Emission Spectrometer

This instrument is used to analyze metals, minerals, paints and some nonmetallic substances. It can be substituted for wet chemistry or used as an adjunct to it. The basic principle underlying the arc-spark emission spectrographic method may be described as follows. A minute part of the sample is vaporized and excited to the point of light emission. This may be done by means of an electric arc (5,000 to 8,000 C) or spark (7,000 to 20,0001 C). Excitation parameters are selected according to the material to be analyzed. The light derived from the vaporized, excited material is dispersed into its component parts in the spectrograph. The medium of diffraction is either a prism or a grating. At the exit aperture this light is either photographed on a plate or film, or recorded by means of photoelectric devices. Since each element produces a spectrum (or rather a series of spectral lines of specific wave lengths), which is characteristic of itself, the identification of an element is possible by studying the lines according to their respective locations. Determination of quantity is made according to the intensity of the lines.

# LATENT PRINT SECTION

The latent print analysts of this section provide the field investigator with the following services:

1. Searches for, develops, photographs, and lifts latent prints at the scene of investigations.
2. Compares suspect's prints with latent prints obtained from crime scenes.
3. Takes plaster casts of footprints, tire tracks, etc.
4. Conducts fingerprint examinations of various items of evidence (e.g., guns and other weapons, papers, glass, metal, etc).
5. A service available to investigators is a computer terminal that records fingerprints electronically, without ink or smudges. The fingerprints are captured by an optical disk, when the finger is pressed on the screen. The prints can be compared in minutes against those in the state and federal files.

# QUESTIONED DOCUMENT SECTION

This section conducts examinations and comparisons of forged and questioned documents (see Figures 6-7 and 6-8.) It also examines and compares handwriting exemplars (samples) made by suspects with handwriting on questioned documents; examines and compares exemplars made on typewriters and check protectors for comparison with questioned documents; and restores or deciphers altered, obliterated or erased writing. The physical matching of cut or torn paper of various types is also conducted by the questioned document examiner.

## Functions

The Questioned Document Section is responsible for examining and comparing forged or quesitoned documents, including:

• Anonymous letters
• Bills of sale

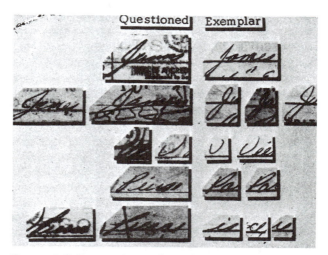

*Figure 6-7 Comparison of signatures on questioned checks and credit card invoices*

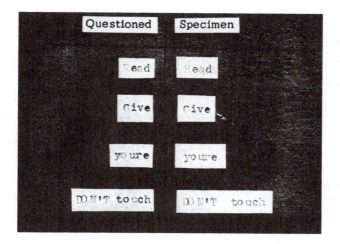

*Figure 6-8 Comparison of typewritten robbery demand note with the typing of a typewriter found in the residence of the suspect. Note: light strike of the letter "R" and "G" and the word "DON'T."*

- Checks
- Holdup notes
- Hotel registers
- Narcotic prescriptions
- Pawnshop tickets
- Receipts
- Traffic citation signatures
- Typewritten documents
- Wills

## FORENSIC PHOTOGRAPHY SECTION

This section performs a very critical service to criminal investigation. Through the use of forensic photography, many items of physical evidence, that are the prime incriminating factors in cases, are graphically depicted in trial courts. (See "Physical Evidence Examples" in Chapter 5 and Figure 6-9).

### *Services Performed:*

- Crime scene documentation and recording
- Physical evidence still photography and videotaping
- Infrared, ultraviolet and infrared-luminescent photographic examination
- Trace evidence photography
- Aerial photography
- Image enhancement techniques
- Specialized identification and surveillance photography
- Crime reconstruction, reenactment, etc., via motion picture or videotape procedures
- A new forensic camera custom built by the Bureau of Organized Crime and Intelligence, California State Attorney General's Office. The camera is contained in a briefcase; one corner contains a lens that captures images and transmits them to a remote television via microwaves

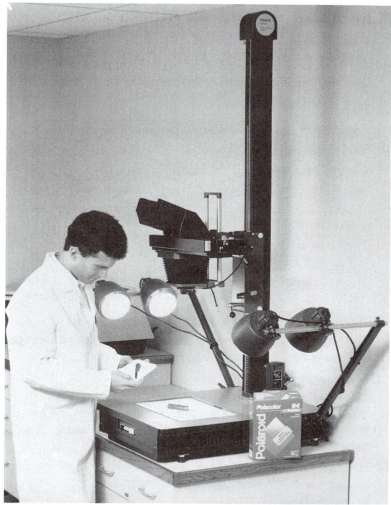

Figure 6-9 A forensic technician photographing evidence

## POLYGRAPH SECTION

This section is responsible for the instrumental detection of deception. Note: There is no instrument that detects lies. The instrument commonly called a *lie detector* is actually a scientific diagnostic instrument (similar to the electrocardiograph) and is referred to in many police circles as the *polygraph*. A competent examiner can diagnose truth or deception.

### Theory of the Examination

- It is based on the emotion of fear.
- Fear of detection by an untruthful subject will cause physiological changes to occur in the subject's body at the point of deception.
- Physiological changes can be diagnosed by a trained, competent examiner.
- The subject must have something to gain or lose by submitting to the examination.

### Components of the Polygraph

- The pneumograph component: records changes in respiration.
- The galvanograph component: records changes in the electrical resistance of the skin.
- The cardiosphygmograph component: records changes in blood pressure and pulse rate.
- The kymograph components: move the chart paper at the timed rate of speed, under the pens of the other three components.

### Basic Uses of the Polygraph

- The polygraph is an excellent aid and a valuable tool if properly utilized during the conducting of an investigation.
- The polygraph, however, will never be able to take the place of good, thorough investigative methods.
- The final results of a polygraph examination will be based, in great measure, upon the thoroughness of the investigation prior to having a subject take the examination.
- In criminal investigation, examinations will be conducted upon suspects, victims, witnesses and informants.

## Stipulated Polygraph Examination

The results of a polygraph examination are admissible evidence in court on stipulation only. A stipulation is a written agreement signed by the district attorney, the defendant and the defense attorney before the defendant submits to a polygraph examination. The stipulation will state that the defendant will submit voluntarily to a polygraph examination, to be administered by a particular polygraph examiner or agency. If the test results are conclusive, the examiner's opinion as to the truth or deception, and the charts, will be admitted as evidence in court. If the results are inconclusive, no testimony by the examiner will be admitted. Even though the examiner is known as an expert in his field, he must still prove his expertise each time he testifies in court.

## Factors That May Prohibit Polygraph Examination

A polygraph examination should not be conducted on any subject who has been physically abused, or on any person that the examiner feels will be an unfit subject, nor on any subject who has been questioned extensively, immediately prior to the time for testing. Only those who voluntarily agree and will sign a statement of consent can be examined. Juvenile subjects under 14 years of age are very difficult subjects to examine due to a lack of maturity, both physical and mental. Many times, conclusive results cannot be obtained by the use of the polygraph because of these factors. Consent forms for juveniles must be signed by either the parent or guardian prior to the examination. The investigator must keep in mind that there are several factors, especially of a physical or psychological nature, that sometimes preclude the use of the polygraph on a subject. Questionable subjects and conditions include:

- Females during menstrual period

- Females who are more than 90 days in pregnancy

- Subjects with amputations that affect the placement of instruments on his or her person

- Subjects with paralysis

- Recent surgery or major injury or illness. The human body usually requires at least six months to recover fully

- Physical disabilities (i.e., skull or spine injuries, high or low blood pressure, and cardiac trouble)

- Certain types of drugs and medication preclude the use of the polygraph

- Emotional instability

- A subject who has not had sufficient nourishment

- Subject suffering from a severe cold or respiratory disorder

- Subjects with low mental ability (i.e., idiots, imbeciles, and morons). However, these should not be confused with persons lacking academic education

- Mental illness—either pathological or psychological

### Investigator's Procedure—Preparing a Subject for Examination

The investigator should keep in mind from the very inception of the investigation that it may be necessary to request the aid of the polygraph; it should not be used only as a last resort. It may also be necessary to withhold key information from the subject and the press. This does not mean that the press should not be informed of the circumstances of a crime; but, rather, that certain "catch phrases" or "peculiar acts," etc., on the part of the suspect could be withheld without materially affecting a press release. Do not ask your subject to agree to a polygraph examination merely as a bluff, then when he or she agrees, forget it. This does not mean the person is innocent at all. Do not ask the subject to submit to a polygraph examination unless you intend to administer it.

The polygraph examiner should be supplied with all the following information and records prior to the administration of the test:

1. Crime reports of suspected offense(s)

2. Investigation reports to date

3. Background information of the suspect to be examined

4. Brief resume of the reason for the examination

5. Brief resume of statements or denials made by the suspect

### Interrogation Prior to Time of Examination

Extensive interrogation of the subject within fours hours prior to the examination should be avoided so that an accurate determination of truthfulness or untruthfulness of the subject can be accomplished. The subject may be questioned briefly prior to examination but only to determine opportunity to commit the crime, motive and desire. This should not be misinterpreted as meaning that the investigator should not interrogate during the investigation, but only applies to that period of time just before the examination. Prolonged interrogation produces an exhausted or antagonistic subject who may then not be a fit subject for the examination.

The chances of a successful conclusion to an investigation are great when the suspect is made available for a polygraph examination before the final stage of the investigation. It is desirable that the subject have a normal amount of food and sleep during the twenty-four hour period preceding the polygraph appointment. A person suffering from the influence of alcohol, sedatives, opiates, physical pain, severe cold or respiratory disorder (as indicated in the preceding section) is not ordinarily considered to be in a fit condition for a polygraph examination.

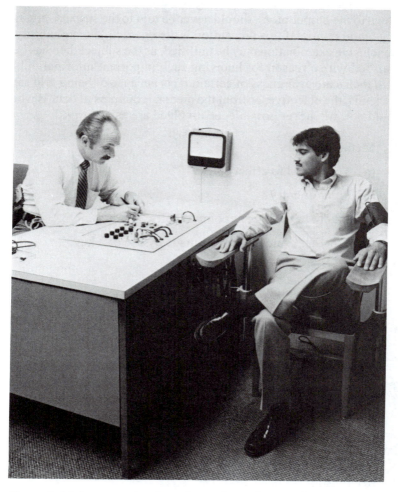

*Figure 6-10 An example of a polygraph test being administered*

### *Suggested Information to be Withheld from Subject*

The subject of a polygraph examination should not be advised of the method in which the examination is to be conducted. The subject should only be told that he or she will suffer no discomfort, will not be subjected to injections of any type, and that the entire process will be explained to him or her by the examiner prior to being examined. The investigating officer, field as well as detective, should avoid disclosure to the subject or suspect of any details of facts established during the investigation. Facts concerning the crime, which could only be known to the perpetrators, should never be told to the suspect, press, or the general public. If this precaution is disregarded, the probability of a conclusive examination may be nullified, as the subject then has been furnished with a reason for knowing such important information. He could then state awareness of certain facts because of being told same by friends, the detective, or from the media. Examples of details which should not, whenever possible, be divulged are as follows:

1. Method of entry
   (a) Tools used to effect entry
   (b) Point of entry
   (c) Extent of damage at point of entry
   (d) Whether or not entry was made by use of a key.

2. Property taken
   (a) Specific amount taken
   (b) Denominations of currency taken
   (c) Unusual articles taken
   (d) Description of articles taken

3. Weapons or force used to commit crime: specific
   (a) Club
   (b) Gun
   (c) Knife
   (d) Poison
   (e) Number and location of wounds and bruises

4. Evidence left at the scene of the crime by suspects (i.e., tools, weapons, articles of clothing, etc).

5. Unusual acts by suspect before, during, or after the commission of the crime.

(a) Conversation or commands

(b) Peculiar habits, actions or characteristics of the suspects

6. Means of exit from the scene

(a) If by vehicle, anything unusual about same, such as dents, missing portions, loud muffler, damage, etc.
(b) If on foot, direction taken from scene, if noted

7. Location from which property was taken.

(a) Where safe or cash box was located in the building

(b) Type of container from which money or articles were taken, such as green metal cash box, cigar box, laundry bag, paper sack, etc.

8. Homicide weapons used

(a) Make and type of gun, such as .38 caliber Smith and Wesson, 4-inch chrome plate with plastic grips, if it is found at crime scene

(b) Weapon believed to have caused death

(c) Detailed description of knives and other weapons

### *Administering the Examination*

The investigator(s) who actually participated in the investigation should be present at the time of the examination to turn the subject over to the examiner, and should remain available to the examiner in order to discuss any pertinent information which may result from the testing sequences. It is necessary for the investigator(s) to be present as they are most familiar with the facts and case information. The polygraph examination is a time-consuming process, and the investigator(s) and subject should expect it to take a minimum of two hours to complete. The examiner, at any stage of the examination, will advise the investigator(s) of the desire of a subject who may wish to make admissions of participation in a crime, and will then turn the subject over to the investigator(s) for further investigation.

## Summary

Polygraph examinations are *not* a substitute for thorough preliminary investigation. They should be regarded only as a supplement to a thorough and complete investigation. Never withhold any pertinent information on either the crime or the subject from the polygraph examiner. The effectiveness of the polygraph examination is dependent upon the investigator(s) and the polygraph examiner working together in cooperation.

## SURVEY AND COMPOSITE ARTIST SECTION

This section provides schematic drawings to scale of areas and crime scenes that are under police investigation. It can also provide maps, graphs, charts, and other drafts that may be needed by investigators. On occasion, a major case may require a mock-up of the crime scene or the surrounding area, in order to facilitate the reconstruction of the occurrence before a court of law. The mock-up augments the testimony of witnesses, photographs, sketches and physical evidence presented, by giving the judge and jury a three dimensional view of the crime scene or area in question. (See Figure 6-11).

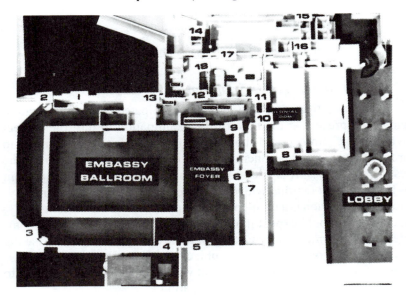

Figure 6-11 Mock-up of crime scene area and lobby floor—The Ambassador Hotel, Los Angeles, CA. Assassination of Senator Robert F. Kennedy (Courtesy Los Angeles Police Dept.)

## Composite Artist

Many police agencies utilize a composite artist to work with victims and witnesses and compose, from their descriptions, excellent likenesses of suspects or missing persons (see Figure 6-12).

*Figure 6-12 Left—The composite drawing of the suspect. Right— Photo of the suspect when arrested. (Courtesy Los Angeles Police Dept.)*

# VOICE IDENTIFICATION SECTION

"I've planted a bomb inside the First National Bank on Main Street. If you don't pay me $100,000 in cash by noon today, I'll set it off." "If you want to see your kid alive again, take the money to Pier 5 and leave it in the abandoned office."

Verbal threats can indicate a very real and dangerous criminal intention. Just like physical evidence found at a crime scene—hair, fibers, blood, etc.—recording of a suspect's voice can become an extremely valuable piece of evidence.

Like fingerprints, which are unique to each person and have various points of identification, the image left by the human voice also has its own identifiable patterns that experts can say, with a high degree of certainty, came from one individual.

To compare a suspect's voice with a recorded criminal's voice, the suspect must repeat the message as it was first recorded. If necessary, investigator's can get a court order which forces the suspect to say the exact words spoken in the original threat or statement. If the suspect refuses to comply, he or she can be held in contempt of court and kept in jail until he or she complies.

Law enforcement can now use a recorded sample of an unknown suspect's voice to locate and identify suspects and use the samples as evidence in court proceedings. The current state of the art for handling voice evidence is *voiceprint analysis*.

Voiceprint analysis uses a sound spectrograph in combination with an expert examiner. Every two and one half seconds, the spectrograph visibly displays on paper a speaker's tonal quality, voice pitch, and pauses between sounds. An examiner then interprets the data from the spectrograph to help pinpoint a suspect (see Figure 6-7).

## Computerized Technology

Rutgers University has developed a new speaker verification and identification system using two patented technologies. The system uses a computer and more effectively discriminates between two similar speakers, such as identical twins.

## FBI Laboratory

The largest voice and sound identification lab in the country is at FBI headquarters in Washington D.C. This national availability has helped solve a number of difficult cases. The most often asked question about voice comparisons concerns mimicry or impersonations. An accomplished impersonator like Rich Little can indeed mimic another person's voice closely enough to fool the human ear. However, even a good impersonator doesn't approach another's voice closely enough to fool current computer technology using Computer Assisted Voice Identification System (CAVIS).

# ELECTRONICS SECTION

## Functions

The Electronics Section is responsible for the following special duties:

- Construction of special equipment—designing constructing, and modifying electronic investigation equipment.

- Special files—maintaining a file of information pertaining to electronic investigation equipment issued or installed by the Electronics Section.

- Special logs—maintaining special logs of

  √ Tape recordings made throughout the department.

  √ Electronic equipment borrowed from the Electronics Section.

  Other functions are as follows:

- Maintaining electronic laboratory equipment used by Scientific Investigation Division.

- Installing and removing electronic investigation equipment.

- Temporary issuance of electronic investigation equipment to other divisions.

- Maintaining inventory records for, and repairing all, department electronic investigation equipment.

- Issuing, restoring and recycling Departmental recording tapes.

- Operating and maintaining the public address system at the Parker Center Auditorium.

- Instruct at department schools on availability and use of electronic investigation equipment.

- Provide electronic countermeasure sweeps (debugging) for department entities and city government.

## SUMMARY

A criminalistics laboratory utilizes the skills of professional criminalists who hold university degrees and other technicians who hold various degrees in connection with the duties they perform. All staff members of a laboratory must be qualified to present expert testimony in court, in connection with the services they render.

Many laboratories are organized into sections which are each responsible for specific functions. A Firearms Section conducts firearms identification examinations, which include comparisons of firearms and bullets, and studies to determine trigger pull, operation of safety devices, alteration or modification of weapons, or any condition of the weapons that might cause accidental fire or make it unsafe. Each firearm has an individual set of characteristics which can serve to identify it, even when it is compared with another of the same type, model, caliber and manufacturer. Of prime importance are barrels, which are microscopically individual. The caliber of the weapon, although not individual, is also important. Other unique characteristics are found in firing pins, extractor marks, and breech face marks. The Firearms Section also conducts studies concerning ballistics (i.e., the study of a projectile in motion).

In many large laboratories, the Firearms Section handles all explosives, as well as conducting powder and shot pattern tests, plus the tests to determine and demonstrate whether a person has held a gun in his or her hand (trace metal detection technique and neutron activation analysis).

Another basic section of a laboratory deals with trace analysis. This analysis involves the examination of various types of physical evidence, such as slides taken from rape victims, fibers, hair, tool marks, shoe and tire imprints, soil, debris, glass and plastics taken from crime scenes. Basic to the laboratory is the Serology Section, which conducts all ABO typing of blood, semen and other body fluids. The Blood-Alcohol Section conducts quantitative analysis of alcohol levels in blood and urine. Then there is the Toxicology Section, which tests for the presence of opiates in urine, toluene in a substance, and acid or basic drugs in blood and urine. This section also tests to determine the presence of codeine, morphine, methadone or phencyclidine (PCP) in urine or ethchlorvynol in blood.

A Narcotics Section is an active component of most police laboratories, utilizing various wet chemical tests involving reagents and microscopic examination for analysis. Some larger laboratories use the gas chromatograph as an adjunct to these methods.

Other testing units are: the scanning electron microscope for studying soils, metals, fibers, tool marks, hair, etc., where high magnification (100,000 times) and a three-dimensional impression is desired; and the emission spectrometer, which is used as a substitute for wet chemistry to analyze metals, minerals, paints and some nonmetallic substances. In this latter process, a sample that is vaporized or excited to a point of light emission produces a spectrum or series of lines of specific wave lengths, which are photographed or recorded, to provide identification of the element and its quantity.

Some laboratories have a Voice Identification Unit which conducts voice comparisons of unknown and known voices by three methods (i.e., recognition by listening, by visual comparisons of spectrograms and speaker, and by machine). All methods are based on the fact that a given word or phrase tends to be uttered differently by different speakers.

The Latent Print Section of a laboratory assists the field investigator by searching for, developing, photographing, and lifting latent prints at crime scenes. This section also prints comparisons, takes plaster casts of footprints and tire tracks, and conducts fingerprint examinations of various types of physical evidence.

There may be a Questioned Document Section which examines forged and questioned documents, compares handwriting, typewriting, printing by check protectors, and restores or deciphers obliterated or erased writing.

A Forensic Photography Section may also be a basic component of a laboratory. This section performs infrared, ultraviolet, and infrared-luminescent photographic examination of evidence; and provides the necessary display photos for court, as well as crime scene documentation and recording in major cases.

The Polygraph Section conducts examinations with instruments to detect deception on the part of suspects and other subjects. A polygraph examination is based on the emotion of fear. Fear of detection by an untruthful subject will cause physiological changes in his or her respiration (breathing), electrical resistance of the skin, and changes in blood pressure and pulse rate. The polygraph is an excellent aid to an investigation, however, only those who sign a statement of consent may be examined; moreover, there are various physical and psychological factors that may preclude these examinations. From the inception of the investigation, the investigator should withhold key information in the case from a possible subject as well as from the press in the event it becomes necessary to request a polygraph examination. The results of an examination are admissible as evidence in court only on stipulation by the district attorney, the defendant and the defense attorney.

The laboratories of many large agencies have a Survey and Composite Artist Section. A surveyor assigned to the section provides schematic drawings to scale of areas or crime scenes, as well as mockups of crime scenes for presentation in court. A composite artist assigned to the section works with victims and witnesses to compose likenesses of suspects and missing persons from descriptions given.

# DISCUSSION QUESTIONS

1.  Describe the typical staff members of a criminalistics laboratory (i.e., classifications and education required).
2.  Discuss firearms identification (i.e., the individual characteristics of a firearm that serves to identify it).
3.  What is the trace metal detection technique? Explain the process.
4.  Describe the molecular disturbance that occurs when a serial number is imprinted on metal.
5   What is acid etching? Explain the process.
6.  Describe the magnaflux technique? Explain the process.
7.  What is the dermal nitrate paraffin test? Explain its limitations.
8.  Explain how powder or shot pattern tests are conducted.
9.  Explain the process of neutron activation analysis.
10. Discuss the various types of physical evidence studied by the trace analysis section.
11. Discuss the blood testing techniques described in this chapter.
12. Discuss the semen tests described in this chapter.
13. What is a "secretor?"
14. Describe how the gas chromatograph functions to analyze a substance. Identify several of its uses in instrumental analysis.
15. Define "toxicology," and identify the tests conducted by the toxicology section.
16. Discuss how controlled substances are analyzed.
17. On what fact is speaker recognition based?
18. Describe the three speaker recognition methods (i.e., by listening, by visual comparisons of spectrograms, by machine).
19. Define the theory of the polygraph examination.
20. What is a "stipulated" polygraph examination?
21. Define the uses of the polygraph.
22. Summarize the services of the survey and composite artist section.

# USE OF
# POLICE RECORDS

7

## KEY TERMS AND CONCEPTS

Police records (purpose of)
Confidentiality
General access policy
Organization of police records
Crime and miscellaneous reports
Criminal records (location of)
Automated Field Interview System
Network Communication System
California Law Enforcement Telecommunications System
Rap sheet
Final report

Police records are often useless unless needed information can be readily located. Records assist police agencies in gathering information on crimes, arrests and complete *modus operandi* data that may serve in the identification and apprehension of wanted suspects. This information, as gathered by the police, is indexed and systematically stored via computers for future retrieval.

Records are also maintained of other police services provided to a community. The above combined information is frequently used in detecting and analyzing police problems such as, crime trends, personnel, and other resource needs and in aiding in their solution. Since police planning relies heavily on statistics and other data provided by its records systems, records must be kept as up-to-date as possible.

Records are the heart of a police department, providing a permanent record of activities.

Information contained in police records is confidential in nature. In some jurisdictions, it is a criminal offense to release information from these records to unauthorized personnel. Through close supervision of concerned personnel, many agencies maintain a tight administrative control over information contained in their files. A number of police agencies have adopted a "general access policy" with regard to releasing information contained in their records systems. If the requester and the situation fit the following criteria, the information may be released: The information requested has a bearing on an investigation in progress, and the requester is an authorized person or agency. The term *authorized agency* may include peace officers and criminal justice agency personnel on a municipal, county, state, federal or international level.

In cases in which vehicles and other personal property are stolen, or which involve traffic accidents, the victims or parties to an accident (or their insurance companies) may be authorized to receive information relevant to their case. The military services, many public service agencies (i.e., police departments, fire departments, schools, and private corporations engaged in governmental contracts involving national security) are authorized by law to require fingerprinting of all applicants as a condition of recruitment or employment. These fingerprints are used in connection with a background investigation conducted of each recruit or applicant by authorized investigators who may have access to police records, in conformance with specific laws.

Most police agencies try to protect the privacy of persons with records of arrest or investigation, as well as the officers and their sources of information. The previously cited examples of the general access policy attest to that fact. However, the advent of centralized, automated reservoirs of criminal information, collected from police agencies on a state and nationwide basis, has presented a potential for problems of control over the information. For example, although most agencies may adhere to an appropriate access policy to prevent abuses in the release of criminal information, all it takes is for one agency in the chain of participants to falter and an abuse occurs. The old adage that a chain is only as strong as its weakest link applies. Computers have proven to be very effective aids to police records systems. Therefore, all participating agencies must collectively insure that the security and confidentiality of the information contained in the system is maintained; otherwise, public demands may seriously diminish this service to criminal investigation.

# ORGANIZATION OF A POLICE RECORDS DIVISION

The key or organizational center of a police records system is the master index card or computer file. This file is normally arranged alphabetically by name, and will include victims, arrestees, wanted persons, missing persons (both adult and juvenile); stolen, lost, impounded and recovered vehicles; as well as persons and locations licensed by the agency. The size of the record division and the volume of its records will generally be in conformance with the size of the agency and the volume of police services provided to the community it serves. It may vary from a few files up to a large computerized system. The practice of cross-indexing name records, location, case numbers, arrestee numbers, license numbers, property, aliases, etc., will vary according to the needs of the particular agency. The organization of a records division will normally be by sections, each charged with specific functions. The listing below is offered as an example.

## Crime and Miscellaneous Reports Section

Maintains the following records:
1. Crime report records and related files—indexed by case number, victim, location of occurrence, property (if taken)
2. Vehicle report records and related files; stolen, lost, recovered, and impounded vehicles—indexed by case number, victim, location of occurrence, license and engine number
3. Stolen, lost and found property files—indexed by case number, item, identifiable serial number, engraving, etc.
4. Gun record files—indexed and cross-indexed, caliber, manufacturer, type, serial number, registered owner, purchaser, person pawning
5. Missing persons file—indexed by case number, victim, location of occurrence
6. Dead body files—indexed by case number, victim, and location of occurrence
7. Stolen and lost license plate files—indexed by case number, victim, license number, and location of occurrence

8. Vice location files—indexed by case number, arrestee and location of occurrence-used for abatement proceedings to close undesirable businesses

9. Traffic accident files—indexed by case number, names of parties involved, location of occurrence and vehicles involved

## Criminal Records Section

Maintains the following records:

1. Criminal records packages on all arrestees—indexed by key name (name first arrested under), agency record number (retains same number regardless of how many times arrested under the same name or alias), charge, and location of arrest. An adequate criminal records package will include (a) copies of all arrest reports, (b) fingerprints, (c) photographs, (d) list of known aliases, monikers and oddities, (e) physical description and date of birth, (f) personal and criminal history including *modus operandi* information.

2. Identification unit files—indexed by fingerprint classification, name(s) and agency number. This unit classifies all fingerprint cards taken on arrestees and searches existing agency files for a prior record.

3. Registration files on sex offenders and other convicted persons, as may be required by law—indexed by agency number, name(s) and crime.

4. Oddity file—indexed first by criminal background, then name(s) and agency number. The effectiveness of an oddity file will depend primarily on how thorough, observant and proficient the arresting, booking and investigating officers are in obtaining the desired (i.e., valid) information on their agency report forms during the booking and investigative interviews of a suspect. The word "valid" is used, because experience indicates that suspects often lie to police.

An oddity file will contain the name(s), complete physical description, criminal background and agency number of any prior arrestee, male/female, who has any of the following characteristics:

a.   Ambidextrous or left-handed

b.   Amputations

c.   Deformities, ("cauliflower" ears, one green and one brown eye, hare lip, etc.)

d.   Impairments (speech impediment, deaf mute, cast eye, etc.)

e.   Marks (birthmarks, pock marks, etc.)

f.   Scars (cuts, burns, narcotic scars, etc.)

g.   Tattoos

h.   Monikers (nicknames, e.g., "Fitz," "Rocky," "Red," "Beto," "Chuy," "Kiki," etc.)

An ideal way to further break down an oddity file is by race, age, height, weight, etc. No doubt any police agency that has maintained an oddity file for a number of years will attest to its effectiveness in identifying suspects through oddities observed by victims and witnesses during the commission of crimes. Many investigators have found that the moniker and tattoo sections of the file have been the most effective with the general run of criminals, since so many of them have nicknames and tattoos. It is not uncommon for these suspects to refer to one another constantly by nickname, even when in disguise, during the commission of the crime. Case examples of identifications could be given for each category of oddities listed, covering all ethnic groups and various types of crimes; however, in the interest of space, it will suffice to state that truth is much stranger than fiction. Literally thousands of suspects with very obvious physical oddities and easy to remember nicknames commit crimes daily, wherein they run the risk of being observed and heard.

## Warrant and Teletype Unit

This unit usually has the responsibility for the receiving, rerouting and transmitting of arrest warrants and want information, teletypes, telegrams, radiograms and correspondence within the agency and to outside agencies. It also mails fingerprint cards of arrestees to the respective state and federal criminal records repositories (if applicable). These repositories (systems) will connect the record of the arrest as reflected on the fingerprint cards forwarded (by a municipal or county agency), with any record in their files. These repositories will then forward all available accumulated arrest and disposition and other information on the arrestee to the contributing agency. This information is usually in chronological order by name, date of occurrence, criminal charge (e.g., burglary) or reason for fingerprinting (e.g., license, employment, etc.), arresting or contributing agency by location, and disposition information if known (e.g., "sentenced to state prison"). This record of criminal or other history of an arrestee is commonly referred to in police circles as a "kickback" or "rap sheet." It is a very valuable tool to criminal investigators as well as to those agencies or employers who are authorized by law to require fingerprinting and background investigations of applicants as a prerequisite of employment.

Prior to the inception of centralized criminal records repositories (keyed by fingerprints) at state and federal levels, it was not uncommon for fugitives, ex-offenders and other persons with criminal records to change their identity and move from area to area, or state to state, and suffer other arrests without being connected to their prior criminal background. During this author's several tours of duty as an agent serving the U.S. Government in foreign countries, I participated in the discovery of several wanted fugitives working in highly sensitive positions. One case, for example, involved a wanted narcotics peddler who was serving as chief of detectives in a municipal police department. I am pleased to note, at this point, that great strides have been made in the collection, centralization and exchange of criminal information on nationwide levels here and abroad. Several examples of the many automated criminal record and information systems in operation in law enforcement are discussed below.

# AUTOMATED CRIMINAL RECORD AND INFORMATION SYSTEMS

This system contains information recorded on field interview cards by police when a contact is made in the field with a person or persons whose conduct or presence in an area or at a location is unlawful, suspicious or unusual (i.e., loitering, prowling, soliciting, hitchhiking, gang-related activity), and who may have a criminal record or is on parole or probation.

## Method

The information from the cards is stored in a computer. FIS (Field Identification System) contains detailed data on persons and vehicles obtained on a city-wide basis. The active file is normally composed of some 300,000 records covering the most recent 18 months of field activity.

FIS has been very effective in providing investigators with leads or identifications of suspects and vehicles. For example, a witness may give only a partial description of two suspects observed leaving the scene of a crime; however, this witness clearly observed the getaway car and can describe the vehicle in fair detail as to year, make, model, type, color, custom paint job, mag-wheels, inscription painted on the body and partial license number. If the vehicle has been the subject of a previous entry to FIS, the above description given by the witness would probably have been sufficient to effect a connect-up. Thus, it is an excellent lead, if not an identification. This hypothetical case reflects actual gang shootings in Los Angeles, wherein vehicles and suspects have been identified through FIS.

FIS can also be effective in furnishing investigative leads in cases where no descriptions of the suspects or vehicles are available. For example, the investigator can request a computer run of all recent interviews conducted at or near the location, prior to the commission of the crime. An individual evaluation of the subjects, their backgrounds and the conditions under which the interviews are conducted will determine if an investigative lead is there. Perhaps one of the subjects has a criminal record with the same M.O. as in the crime that is under investigation, and prints may have been left at the scene that can be compared with those of the subject of the interview. Many residential burglary investigators have had success with such "runs" and, on occasion, have solved burglary-murders.

# COUNTY WARRANT SYSTEM

This system maintains a county-wide centralized records file for Los Angeles County on (1) felony wants for investigation, (2) felony warrants of arrest, (3) misdemeanor warrants of arrest, and (4) traffic warrants of arrest. Some fifty police agencies in Los Angeles County have access to the system via either a Cathode Ray Tube (like a TV set with a typewriter keyboard at the bottom) or by teletype or telephone to a computer terminal. The file contains approximately 1,000,000 records, and the flexibility of the system provides for searching for a record by (1) name and description of subject, (2) system identification number, (3) warrant number, and (4) vehicle license number.

## Method

A radiotelephone operator at a terminal types a subject's name and description or other information being used for the search on a keyboard connected with the computer. In essence, the computer is asked if the subject has an outstanding "want" or warrant file. This operation takes approximately forty seconds. The computer searches the file and responds in approximately eight seconds. If an outstanding warrant is located in the file, the terminal operator can direct the computer to transmit a teletyped warrant booking abstract back to the terminal requesting the search.

## Additional Features

Each terminal on the County Warrant System also has a direct access to the California Highway Patrol's "Auto-Statis System" (a file of stolen, recovered, repossessed and impounded vehicles). Auto-Statis, in turn, interfaces these terminals with the Federal Bureau of Investigation's National Crime Information Center's (NCIC) stolen vehicle file and the California Department of Motor Vehicle's file on vehicle registrations.

*Note:* Prior to the implementation of the County Warrant System, information on wants and warrants was obtained by searching files manually at a considerable cost of personnel hours. Additionally, any number of persons who were either wanted for investigation, or were named on a warrant of arrest by a particular police agency in Los Angeles County, were arrested, even served sentences in other cities in that county, and released by those jurisdictions, without ever knowing of another agencies' want(s).

# (NECS) NETWORK COMMUNICATION SYSTEM

This computerized system allows multiple inquiries to County Warrant System to be interfaced with the California Department of

Justice, California Law Enforcement Telecommunications System (CLETS), and the Federal Bureau of Investigation's National Crime Information Center (NCIC). The CLETS system maintains computerized access to the following information on a statewide basis.

1. Persons wanted for felonies and high-grade misdemeanors

2. Stolen, recovered, pawned and lost firearms with a record of gun dealers' sales, all firearm registrations, including those registered to police officers and departments

3. Stolen, pawned and lost property containing serial numbers or identifiable engravings, etc.

4. Stolen, recovered and lost vehicles

5. Criminal history records, including name, physical description, I.D. number from arresting police agency, fingerprint classification, California Department of Justice I.D. number, and the Federal Bureau of Investigation I.D. number. The record also contains the arrestees associates, occupations, aliases, miscellaneous I.D. numbers, number of arrests, number of convictions, category of offenses, date and the agency involved in the last arrest. Probation and parole data on an arrestee is also included if such information has been forwarded to the system

## Kick-Back or Rap Sheet

The criminal record or other history of an arrestee, previously mentioned in this chapter, can be provided via NECS to a high-speed printer, making it readily available to the investigator. Note: Municipal and county agencies are responsible for updating their entries to this system in order to maintain current records.

The National Crime Information Center (NCIC) of the Federal Bureau of Investigation augments individual municipal and state automated records systems by storing criminal information contributed by police agencies nationwide. Readily accessible data is available on:

1. Wanted persons, if a warrant of arrest is issued and the demanding state will extradite

2. Stolen, lost and recovered firearms

3. Stolen property containing serial numbers or identifiable engravings, etc.

4. Stolen vehicles

5. Criminal history records (kickback, rap sheet)

## Investigator's Final Report
(5.10 Form of the Los Angeles Police Department)

This form is completed by investigating officers on all suspects arrested for felonies or misdemeanors that require follow-up investigation, such as assaults, batteries, etc. It is retained in the criminal record packages mentioned in this chapter. The follow-up investigative value of the form will depend primarily on thorough and astute interviewing techniques practiced by the investigator. The 5.10 Form (and similar forms used by other agencies) has been particularly useful in developing leads with which to locate a suspect at a later date. For example, a suspect may be arrested on a charge and released (e.g., "victim refuses to prosecute"). One year later, this same suspect is wanted on a new and more serious charge. Valid information from the 5.10 Form could prove critical in locating the suspect. Such information might include:

1. Address: may still be current.

2. Vehicle license number: may still be current, and provides access to vehicle registration records, traffic citations or accidents; plus addresses and other pertinent information.

3. Birthplace: may have relatives or friends there who may provide leads, or suspect may return there.

4. Probation Investigative Unit: provides access to those files. Suspect may have given much valid information to enhance probation potential.

5. Bail information: bondsman may be able to provide valuable information.

6. Complaint filed: defense counsel may provide information as to suspect's whereabouts.

7. Occupation: his or her occupation may require a license or membership in a union. The information in those files is available.

8. Employer: employer personnel files contain much personal information. It is likely to be valid, because a person who wants employment does not give false addresses, credit references, character references, etc.

9. Special medical problem: diabetes, hemophilia, etc. Suspect may need continuing medication. Provides leads to pharmacies and/or hospitals.

10. In case of emergency notify: this person may provide lead.

11. Relatives and associates: can provide much information and, on occasion, a relative or associate may turn out to be an accomplice.

12. Additional occupations: same as #7, above.

13. Union and Local No.: Union files contain much information. It is possible to run a nationwide check on a subject.

14. B.P.A. Relief No.: Welfare files contain relevant data.

15. Credit and Bank references: these records are very valuable, persons seeking credit and/or loans do not usually give false information.

16. Unemployment Office: a suspect on the run needs money; he may try to stop to pick up a check.

17. Checks cashed at: may provide information, including time when suspect will arrive.

18. Schools attended: school records contain a great deal of valid data, i.e., addresses, family, teams, fraternities and clubs that provide names of persons to interview for leads.

19. Name and address of school that children (the suspect's) currently attend: very valuable if a suspect on the run takes his children with him. Sooner or later they will attend some school. The new school will request records from the prior school attended by the children, and this can provide the address where the suspect has relocated.

20. Previous addresses: suspect may return to city or area where he used to live.

21. Barber or beauty shop: suspect may return there.

22. Parole or probation officer has much valid information.

23. Clubs, organizations, hobbies: provide persons to interview for leads and addresses where suspect may be located.

24. Hangouts: names of locations where suspect may be found.

25. Arrestee's vehicle and updated aka/moniker information: provides valuable information that may not be contained in other files.

26. Page two (reverse side of Form 5.10): provides military service information, *modus operandi*, narcotic use, oddity information, demeanor of suspect at time of arrest and during investigation. Also, a narrative by the investigator outlining the reason for the arrest, the arrestee's *modus operandi*, and the investigator's opinion or facts known about the arrestee's criminal background is placed on page two. If the arrestee was armed, information on how the weapon was obtained and used is given, along with descriptions of any other violent acts or threats on the part of the arrestee. In conclusion, it is important to provide information on any other criminal cases pending on the arrestee.

## SUMMARY

Police records assist law enforcement agencies in gathering information on crimes, arrests, and complete modus operandi data. Unless needed information can be readily retrieved from the records, it is often useless. Therefore, this information is indexed and systematically filed or stored via computers for future retrieval. Police planning relies heavily on statistics and other data provided by its records system. Records are the heart of a police department, as well as a permanent record of activities.

Information contained in police records is confidential, and requires controls by means of a General Access Police. A police records division is generally organized by sections. It can consist of simply a few files or be a large, computerized system, depending on the needs of the particular agency.

A plan of a records division organized by sections, each with specific functions is outlined here: (a) Crime and Miscellaneous Reports Section, (b) Criminal Records Section, (c) Warrant and Teletype Unit, and (d) Automated Criminal Record and Information Systems.

This last includes: (FIS) Field Identification System, County Warrant System, (NECS) Network Communication System, which allows basic inquiries to AWWS to be interfaced with the state's Law Enforcement Telecommunications System and (NCIC) the National Crime Information Center of the FBI. The investigator's Final Report, completed by investigators on all suspects requiring a follow-up investigation, provides useful leads with which to locate a suspect at a later date.

## DISCUSSION QUESTIONS

1. What are the purposes of police records?
2. Why are police records confidential?
3. What is the general access policy to police records?
4. Describe the organization of a police records division.
5. What individual record files are maintained in a crime and miscellaneous reports section?
6. What individual record files are maintained in a criminal records section?
7. Discuss the use of the oddity file by an investigator.
8. Name the duties performed by the warrant and teletype unit.
9. What is a "rap sheet?"
10. Describe the following: (a) the Automated Field Interview System, (b) the County Warrant System, (c) the Law Enforcement Telecommunications System, (d) the National Crime Information Center and (e) the Investigator's Final Report and their uses by an investigator.

# SOURCES OF INFORMATION

8

## KEY TERMS AND CONCEPTS

Methods of acquiring sources of information
Procedural guidelines
Informants (definition of)
Confidentiality
Hearsay
Evaluation of information
Sources of information (non-police)

*Information* is acquired knowledge that may be obtained through study, communication, search, research and observation. It is generally accepted that we all have our limitations on the quantity of detailed information we can retain and readily recall. The more sources of information an investigator develops, cultivates and maintains, the easier his or her work will be, particularly in those cases where the solution is primarily dependent on information. Thus, in a murder case where there is no physical evidence, no known witnesses, no apparent motive, etc., an informant who can provide a solid clue would be a tremendous asset.

## METHODS OF ACQUIRING INFORMATION

### Study

Study may be through formal education or a training program in a school, college, university, or academy. It may also be through independent or group study of books, computer programs, magazines, journals, digests and other publications. Even television quiz shows and professional talk shows can be very informative and educational in a variety of fields of study.

## Communication

Victims and witnesses, when properly interviewed, are often a prime source of information. Tips, theories and advice from other investigators can also be productive if offered, accepted and checked out with objectivity. An objective critique or view of a case by a competent investigator, one not assigned to the investigation, can prove helpful to the overall effort. Another investigator may note an item that was overlooked by the investigators working the case, which may prove to be the key to the solution.

Sometimes, it is possible to be "so close to the forest that you cannot see the trees." For instance, an item of information in a case file indicates that one, Dr. John Beauregard, who claimed to be a marriage counselor from a major city in another state, was the person last seen with the murder victim prior to her death. Dr. Beauregard has since disappeared and all record checks reveal no information whatsoever. However, there is no indication in the case file that the local or other city telephone directories or city directories were checked for "Beauregard." Surprisingly enough, the name and address desired may be in a telephone book or in the city directory. Some major city libraries maintain city directories of other major cities in their states and of other states as well.

The personal informants of the criminal investigator, whether they are paid for information or provide information for other reasons, are imperative to the lasting, continuing effectiveness of the investigator. The development, cultivation and maintenance of productive personal informants often requires the investigator to deal with a wide range of people from the various socioeconomic levels in society. Informants may be anyone: from a public spirited "pillar of the community," to someone representing the depths of the criminal element. Each informant in this broad spectrum can, on occasion, provide the investigator with useful information. The information will usually be within the scope of the informant's individual environment, yet will often dovetail with other information that has been obtained.

## Search and Research

Searching and researching records for information is a tedious, time consuming, and probably the most unglamorous chore in the investigator's overall activities. Nonetheless, experienced investigators attest to the value of records, other than police files, as sources of information that often uncover personal facts about an individual. Such information may reveal a motive for the crime in question, clarify critical questions, and facilitate a clearer picture of what the person is actually like. Most people who are motivated to get along with others in their work, school and social activities, expend some effort to do so. They develop and express verbal and nonverbal sensitivity for others; they are cooperative, polite, etc. Yet investigative experience will document the wisdom of the old cliches, "Don't judge a book by its cover," and "You don't know someone until you live with them." Even living with or near someone may, one day, serve to dramatize another cliche, "He or she is always the last to know." The news media frequently covers stories wherein families, friends and neighbors are shocked to learn that a person in their midst is a murderer or an embezzler or a suicide when he or she ostensibly had everything to live for.

It is important at this point to dispel a most unfortunate fallacy that many labor under—persons with police arrest records are probably bad, and persons that have never been arrested are probably good. Experience indicates that literally thousands of people violate laws on a day-to-day basis, yet escape arrest for a great variety of reasons—the crime was not reported, not detected, lack of enforcement, etc. The fact that a person has never been arrested does not spell "Mr. Clean" to an experienced investigator, because a careful background investigation may establish otherwise.

Records, other than police files, can furnish leads to relatives, associates, organizations, agencies, banks, employers, ex-employers, ex-wives, ex-husbands, civil court cases, creditors, etc., which may establish past frauds, embezzlements, or other criminal activity on the part of the individual. These leads are often more productive than those contained in police files, due to the fact that persons seeking to qualify give valid information when initially applying for employment, credit, marriage licenses, public utility services, etc.

## Observation

A good investigator develops the ability to take accurate notice of, and pay attention to people, objects, events and their attendant circumstances. He or she utilizes the five senses, i.e., sight, hearing, smell, touch and taste. The observations of other investigators, particularly those working the same category of crime, are often very valuable. The great value of collaboration in investigations, and of a free exchange of observations and information between investigators, was recognized many years ago by law enforcement worldwide.

Investigators' associations that are organized at county and state levels according to specialty of assignments are common. Many agencies and associations maintain an exchange of investigative information with other states and foreign countries.

## Physical Properties

The potential for valuable information from the physical aspects of evidence rests in the proper collection, handling and preservation of physical evidence from crime scenes and other pertinent areas. This is followed by the invaluable technical and scientific services of the criminalistics laboratory.

# PROCEDURAL GUIDELINES

## Sources of Information

The investigator must first determine what sources of information exist in general and concentrate this effort within the areas of information that are, or may be, most useful to his assignment. For example, all investigators should know the general locations of recorded sources of information and the kinds of records contained in various record files, both public and private.

The investigator should learn how to gain access to public records through their custodians, and learn how (or through whom) to obtain needed information from private records. This knowledge is usually learned from senior investigators. With regard to the investigator's individual assignment(s), he or she must concentrate personal contacts and rapport-building efforts on those persons through whom he/she may have access to select information from both public and private records. An example of the benefit of this general and select access to recorded information is illustrated here:

Three investigators in a particular agency work individual assignments. One works homicide, the other two work burglary and
frauds, respectively. All three know and use the general sources of
recorded public information. The homicide investigator has developed
personal contacts with autopsy surgeons, psychiatrists and custodians
of certain records that the other investigators do not know exist. The
burglary investigator has contacts in the garment industry and can,
through the records found there, identify the manufacturers of a garment (i.e., a sport jacket) even if all the labels have been removed. The
frauds investigator has a contact that can trace the assets of an individual through private records throughout the United States and into
foreign countries without causing a stir or requiring governmental intervention.

The case may occur when each of these investigators requires the
personal and private sources of the other to obtain information. The
homicide investigator may have a sport jacket with all labels removed
that was left at the scene of a murder. The burglary investigator's garment manufacturing contacts may, through examining the material,
type of stitching, buttons, etc., identify the manufacturer. The manufacturer's records may indicate the wholesale or retail outlet(s) that
jackets of this model and size were sold to. It may be an exclusive
number for one outlet, nevertheless the investigator can run down the
lead to its ending and, with some luck, locate a sales slip with a name
and address on it that will pay off with a suspect.

On the other hand, the burglary investigator may have a case in
which he suspects the alleged victim has falsely reported assets taken
in a burglary. He may need the services of the frauds investigator's
contact to trace the victim's assets, which effort may possibly uncover
assets concealed in another state or country. Either the burglary or
frauds investigator may have the occasion to need an expert opinion or
information from the homicide investigator's contacts regarding a suspect, victim, or witness.

Investigators must also develop and cultivate contacts with public officials, business persons, school officials and the clergy within
the area of their assignment. Almost any person may be of assistance
to in investigator at one time or another, depending on the assignment.
It is most valuable to cultivate sources of various types before they are
needed. Many investigators maintain an indexed card file of sources
of information, the kinds of information available, the reliability of the
sources, whether they are unpaid or paid, and their police record number (if applicable). If a source is a member of the criminal element, it is

also necessary to update the card as to addresses, hangout, personal habits, etc.—any information that will facilitate locating the source when needed.

# HOW SOURCES ARE DEVELOPED AND MAINTAINED

## Public Records

The investigator must exercise tact and courtesy in dealing with a custodian of records. No matter how highly authorized the investigator may be to obtain information from public records, there is no excuse for a demanding air on his or her part. Many investigators owe a good portion of their accomplishments to the tenacious and cooperative efforts of custodians of records. This fact, coupled with productive personal informants, has lead to the old adage in investigative circles, "You're only as good as your sources of information." This saying, while not completely true, does point up the importance and value which experience dictates should be placed on sources of information.

## Private Records

By cultivating and maintaining rapport and friendship with the custodians of records, by cooperating with and being on friendly terms with other investigators who may already have access to them, certain private records that are highly secret or confidential in nature can often be made available to an investigator. The custodian may be dealing with several investigators or agencies, yet will not normally reveal the involvement of the one to the other.

Integrity is a must if contacts of this nature are to be maintained. The investigator must be ever mindful of the fact that generally private persons do not have to divulge information or produce records except by court order. There are exceptions. In some states a physician who treats a person with a gunshot wound or a battered child must report the incident. One must consider that many custodians of private records could suffer serious embarrassment or be discharged from their jobs if their dissemination of information were made known.

## Informants—Definition

An *informant* is any individual who provides information relevant to an investigation or to some matter of police interest.

## Public Apathy

Public apathy towards crime varies with communities. Communities that have long experienced a high crime rate, with much violence inflicted on victims and reprisals to those that cooperate with the police, display the greatest apathy. It is not uncommon to read of a case where people stood by and watched while a victim was robbed, raped or killed. The reality which police face in these communities is that self-preservation is a great motivator. Many potential informants place a higher value on their physical well-being than whatever degree of satisfaction they might derive from performing their civic duty by giving information to the police and testifying in court.

Communities that are not conditioned to high crime rates and violence and have not known criminal reprisals, in general tend to be more receptive to police appeals for cooperation. Many persons are aware that they cannot be punished for not reporting a crime or for withholding information from the police. An exception to this is the offense of *compounding a crime*, a felony in most states. Any person is guilty of compounding a crime who has knowledge of the actual commission of a crime and takes money or any gratuity or reward, etc., to conceal such a crime or withhold evidence or refuse prosecution. The only exceptions are those cases which can be compromised by approval of a court.

The above facts have been related to emphasize the difficulties that may be encountered by investigators in developing, cultivating and maintaining productive informants.

## Privacy

When an investigator selects or is approached by a potential informant, the first, and all future meetings, must be in private. There must be no witnesses as to how and from whom the information was obtained. An exception to this rule can occur when investigators work as a team. By prior agreement, the informant may agree and feel comfortable working with the team. If he or she does not, the indicated investigator must meet with the person privately.

## Confidentiality

The confidentiality of a source of information must never be violated, unless the urgency of the circumstances dictates its necessity and the source agrees. The investigator must insure that the information received in confidence is not used in any way that will make it possible for the suspect in the investigation to guess the source. Informants who have not been protected in this manner have lost their jobs, have been the victim of violent reprisals or have lost their lives. The informant must be reassured that the confidentiality will be maintained. The best way to effect this reassurance is to keep the promise.

## Ethics

Although the investigator should develop and cultivate a productive relationship with an informant based on trust and a mutual need, the relationship must not involve illegal or unethical practices. For example, investigators who are using prostitutes, drug addicts, or burglars as informants cannot cultivate their relationships to the stage where they engage in sexual contact with prostitutes, use drugs with or furnish drugs to the addicts or fence stolen property for the burglars. This may sound bizarre, but it has happened, and there are ex-policemen around (some in prison) to prove it.

Forgetting the unethical aspects of the above practices for a moment and concentrating on the practical issues, here is what usually happens to the productiveness of these relationships as a result of such practices. Deterioration sets in. The informant rather than the investigator starts running the case, because he or she has lost respect for, or fear of, the investigator. The investigator has lowered himself to the informant's level; the informant feels the investigator is no better than he. This admonishment as to illegal or unethical practices naturally extends to relationships with all informants.

## Identity Protection

As already mentioned, the identity of the informant must be protected; it can be a matter of life or death. The investigator should generally never meet with an informant at the police station. Locations for meetings should be different for each occasion, so as not to set a pattern that can be detected and followed. Code names or symbols can be used for contacting informants by telephone or in person.

Normally, a confidential informant is never used as a witness in court. Many jurisdictions would rather have the case dismissed than risk their informant's cover or life. The informant should be continuously admonished not to carry any items that would suggest a confidential involvement with law enforcement.

## Human Relations

Proper human relations practices are always necessary. All sane human beings regardless of their character, economic status, education, social status or occupation have feelings. Some are resigned to, or satisfied with, their lot in life. Others would like to feel they are on the way up and trying to achieve a goal.

Regardless of which category informants fit into, they all have a need for feeling worthwhile—dignity or status—if you will. The investigator cannot afford to forget this important factor in dealing with informants. Treat all informants in a fair manner, and never make promises you cannot keep. No one enjoys being played for a "patsy."

### *Making Promises*

Normally, investigators have no authority of their own to make promises to an informant who is liable for or is awaiting prosecution. Investigators can ethically tell the informant that they will advise the prosecutor or the court of any cooperation; however, this is not to be construed to indicate that if an informant possesses critical information needed to resolve a major case and requests some compensation or personal benefit, that such a request must be ignored. The informant's offer can be relayed through the appropriate channels of the justice system (i.e., police, prosecution, courts, corrections, etc., for consideration).

With appropriate authority in advance, the investigator may agree to provide the informant with money or some other personal benefit for the information. In cases of this type, the value of the information must be tested first, then the payment made. In other words, this prevents buying "a pig in a poke."

Authorized arrangements with informants where information was offered that identified murderers, robbers, locations of money and jewelry stashes, as well as testimony as state witnesses in exchange for money, a definite parole date from prison, a transfer from one prison to another, the expediting of the immigration of a loved one, etc. have been made. The criminal justice authorities involved performed with integrity, once the informants delivered.

It is important to realize that the above activities are neither mysterious nor unusual. It is a common practice in the United States and in foreign countries for police agencies to pay money for information. This is provided for in their operational budgets.

## Plea Bargaining

*Plea bargaining* involves an agreement between the prosecution and the defense that is advantageous to a defendant (i.e., a reduction of a charge or a lesser sentence) in exchange for a plea of guilty. This saves the expense of trials and helps clear crowded court calendars. In regard to defendants turning state's witnesses and testifying against codefendants in exchange for personal acquittal, this practice is also authorized by law.

It is necessary that the criminal justice systems recognize the importance of critical information in the fight against crime, and make every effort to treat informants fairly and maintain trust. In conclusion, it is poor human relations for the informant to become aware that the investigator may refer to him as a "stool pigeon," "stoolie," snitch," etc.

# INFORMANT MOTIVATION

## Public Spirit

This may include any member of a community who feels it a public duty to give information to the police. Unfortunately, not all public-spirited people have information that is of value to police investigations. Investigators may at times have to check out information that amounts to no more than busy work, because the source wants to help but does not know anything of value. One category of public spirited persons that often do possess valuable information are the aforementioned custodians of private records. Common sense will dictate how closely the investigator must observe the confidentiality rule with those sources that create busy work.

## Appreciation

Desire to express appreciation for past treatment by police is a common motivation. Many persons, however, are apprehensive about dealing with law enforcement officials, some with good cause, because of an abrasive police experience in their past. However, positive experiences with police officers leave most people with a desire to cooperate, particularly with the individual officer or investigator involved in the positive experience. It is not unusual for such a person to call an officer or investigator and provide information.

The value of the information will vary with the degree of exposure the informant has to crime. Thus, a bartender in a high crime frequency area will have access to more criminal information than will a housewife in a law abiding household in the same neighborhood.

## The Acceptance Seeker

This type of informant includes those persons from any walk of life who are perhaps in need of acceptance to bolster their wobbly, if not negative, self-image. The spectrum ranges from a law abiding person who attempts to know all that is going on in the neighborhood and frequently calls a police contact with information, to the petty criminal who operates on the fringes of the heavy criminal action. This latter type may provide valuable information to the investigator if the relationship between them is properly developed. Both types in these examples derive a self-benefiting reassurance that they are accepted when the police listen to their information.

## The Paid Informant

This "mercenary" is of a breed all his or her own. As mentioned in an earlier paragraph, law enforcement worldwide is engaged in paying money for information. This practice has long been recognized as a necessary and productive aid to law enforcement. Some agencies (usually federal) budget large sums for continuing sources of paid information. Others pay the informant a percentage of the amounts recovered as a reward.

Regardless of the investigator's assignment, there are two cardinal principles he or she must keep in mind when dealing with paid informants. First, the investigator must remember that the usual prime motivation of the informant for providing information is money. A paid informant can be lured away by another agency that can pay more for information—a close relationship between informant and the investigator notwithstanding. Second, some paid informants make their entire livelihood selling information. This, at times, requires their living with and gaining the trust of the criminal element then betraying that same element for money. The conclusion of this is obvious. If a paid informant will betray others to obtain information, he is certainly capable of betraying the investigator when the price is right.

## Fear as a Motive

Sometimes, persons (generally of the criminal element) may offer information to police in exchange for seclusion or protection from others in the criminal element. The degree to which agencies will get involved in such arrangements will depend on the importance of the case and the resources available to provide the necessary services. Some federal agencies have arranged for changes in identity of an informant and family, relocations to other areas or countries, or an isolated, secure cell in a prison.

## Revenge as a Motive

The revenge motive has probably imprisoned as many persons as any other behavioral product of our human emotions. A desire for revenge can become an obsession. Some persons will seek to destroy the object of their revenge, even at the risk or certainty of self-destruction. One case involved the wives of a very financially successful gang of male supermarket bandits. The wives called the police and laid out the entire case because their husbands were out partying with other females. In the end, the wives were sentenced to jail along with their husbands because they had been drivers of the getaway cars.

In another case, a suspect became outraged when he learned that he had been cheated by his two crime partners on the division of the take in several armed robberies. He gave information freely to the police that brought about his conviction and that of his two partners. But unfortunately for him the sweet taste of his revenge did not last long; he was stabbed to death four months after he arrived in the state prison.

## Repentance as a Motive

On occasion, a conscience-stricken or frightened criminal seeks to give information concerning his own criminal violations or those of others. Such persons may simply turn themselves in to the police.

## Mental Illness

Every community has its share of mentally ill persons who periodically confess to crimes they have not committed or who make nuisances of themselves by offering worthless information. While time consuming to investigate, such reports cannot be dismissed without checking on them.

## Zeal for Investigation

Many non-police persons from all walks of life have a great desire to investigate and to know what is going on. If their investigative interests lie in the criminal area, the cultivation of their friendship would be a wise move for the investigator to make. This writer has found examples of criminal investigative interests and talent among news reporters, crime writers, insurance underwriters, political writers and social workers. Many have been most helpful in cases.

## Elimination of Competition

Sometimes a criminal may inform on another to eliminate competition. In one case, a professional burglar did not want "junkies" hanging around and provided information to the narcotics investigator to get rid of them.

*Note:* It is not uncommon for an informant from the criminal element to be providing information to one specialized investigator while avoiding arrest by another. For example, a bookmaker might provide information to a robbery investigator regarding strangers who display sudden wealth, while at the same time a vice investigator is trying to make a case against the bookmaker. Sometimes an informant for one investigator is arrested by another investigator and calls for help. How much assistance the informant gets will normally depend on the case against him and on how productive he has been to the police in the past.

# HEARSAY INFORMATION

Hearsay information was defined in Chapter 4; therefore, it will suffice to say, at this point, that in dealing with informants, the investigator must seek out the source that has personal knowledge of the information. He or she must get all the information possible on the first contact with the source, as a subsequent contact may not materialize. Also, it must be remembered that just because the information is hearsay is no reason to disregard it—at least not initially.

## EVALUATION OF INFORMATION

Evaluation of the information received from an informant is always important. If the informant has proven reliable in the past, then the evaluation task may not be laborious. It may merely require that the investigator determine if it is probable that the informant has provided valid information before taking action. If the informant is not a known reliable source, the investigator must expend the necessary effort to check out all parts of the information and if possible verify it, thus avoiding premature action.

For instance, if the investigator receives information from a reliable private detective (who traces assets) that a suspected member of an organized crime group has deposited a large sum of money in the personal bank account of a local zoning commissioner, it is probable that this informant has acquired valid information. It would be reasonable for the investigator to seek to determine a connection between the commissioner's zoning decisions and the suspected organized crime member. However, if a streetwalker, who is not a known reliable informant, relates to an investigator that one of her "tricks" who works at City Hall, says the zoning commissioner is taking payoffs from organized crime, it is possible—but not especially probable—that this informant has acquired valid information. The investigator should check all aspects of the information before taking any action.

## LANGUAGE AND OTHER FACTORS

Communication with an informant can be frustrated at times by a language barrier. The use of an interpreter may be necessary and can be very productive. Sometimes it is advantageous for an investigator to be able to speak a second language, depending on the area and needs of the assignment. However, research has failed to establish that being monolingual stifles development of investigative ability, or that cultural or ethnic differences present insurmountable problems. Law enforcement should have no language, ethnic, or cultural boundaries.

# NON-POLICE SOURCES OF INFORMATION

The following is a list of those non-police sources of recorded information that are most commonly useful to criminal investigators. To attempt to list all sources in this category that might at one time or another be used by an investigator would be redundant and not in keeping with the objectives of this chapter.

## Municipal and County Levels

1.  City or County Clerk: business licenses, marriage license applications.

2.  City or County Assessor: plots, maps of real property, addresses, owner, taxable value and improvements.

3.  Tax Collector: taxpayers of property and all background information on the property

4.  Public Works Department: city maps, streets, addresses, alleys, tunnels, sewers, etc.

5.  Building and Safety Department: building permits, building inspectors and blueprints for constructions

6.  Health Department: communicable diseases

7.  Personnel Department: employment and background information on civil service employees

8.  Credit Union: savings and loan information on employee participants

9.  City or County Recorder: marriage licenses, birth certificates, death certificates, recorded deeds on properties, etc.

10. Welfare Department: records on welfare recipients

11. School District: current and past records on students

12. City or County Court Records: Civil files: files on actions concerning liens, damages, divorces, changes of name, insanity and probate. Criminal files: files on all criminal actions, complaints (crime/crimes charged), arraignments, transcripts of preliminary hearings with testimony of all witnesses, identification of defense counsel, prosecutors, and subpoenas served. Superior Court

records of civil and criminal actions may be included or separated, depending on the size of the court district

13. Controller: records of all civil service employees and their payroll records

14. Registrar of Voters:

    a.   Name of registrant, address including cross streets

    b.   Occupation of registrant

    c.   Political party affiliation

    d.   State of birth

    e.   If naturalized, all information pertaining thereto

    f.   Disability that prevents registrant from marking ballot

    g.   Last place of registration

    h.   Date and reason for cancellation of registration

    i.   Registered voters listed according to precinct

    j.   Roster of voters: signature and addresses from polling places

    k.   Nomination papers of candidates for public office

15. Coroner or Medical Examiner

    a.   Files including full identification and/or description (John or Jane Does) of deceased; date and report of autopsy, if conducted; date and report of inquest, if held; list of property found on deceased and its disposition; notes left by the deceased; cause of death, if determined; and disposition of body on all coroner/medical examiner cases.

    b.   Typical types of death requiring Coroner/Medical Examiner:

        (1)   Homicides

        (2)   Suicides

        (3)   Poisonings

        (4)   Violent deaths by accidents, where there is a probability of a criminal charge rising from the case

        (5)   Suspicious deaths

(6)   Deaths from unknown causes

(7)   Sudden deaths—doctor not in recent attendance

16. Public Administrator: files on estates of deceased persons where there is no will and heirs are unknown, or where a will is left but no executor is named. Also, those estates referred to the administrator by the court.

17. Public Utilities: records of subscribers, applications for service, toll and long distance calls, kind of residence or business, numbers of instruments and meters at location, etc.

   a. Telephone companies

   b. Gas companies

   c. Electric companies

   d.  Water companies

   e.  Telegraph companies

18. Other Sources:

   a.   Taxicab companies: drivers and records of trips

   b.   Auto rental agencies: records of renters

   c.   Travel agencies: records of trips made by clients

   d.   Railroads, steamship lines and airlines: same as above

   e.   Express companies: records of shipments

   f.   Moving companies: records of moves by clients

19. Directories:

   a.   Telephone Directory: published numbers, listed by name, address and telephone number

   b.   Street address Telephone Directory: published and non-published numbers, listed by address, name and telephone number (issued to police)

   c.   Telephone Number Directory: published and non-published numbers listed by telephone number, address and name (only the telephone company has this directory)

20. City Directory: name, address and occupation

21. Professional Directories: medical, bar association, etc.

22. Who's Who: biographies of prominent people

23. Baird's Manual of American College Fraternities: men's and women's fraternities and sororities, histories, location of chapters, publications, etc.

## State and Federal Levels

Almost every profession, technical occupation requiring a license, consumer item (e.g., food, drugs, clothing, cars, etc.), and income is either licensed, regulated or taxed by state and federal agencies. The records of these agencies contain much information that can be valuable to the investigator. Some of these records are not generally accessible, but the type and circumstances of the investigation will determine their availability. On occasion, a court order is required to gain access to such records.

1. State Agencies:

   a. Secretary of State: all articles of incorporation in the state, changes of names by persons recorded by county clerks, records of candidates and election returns

   b. Controller: records of all state employees including their payroll records

   c. Department of Consumer Affairs: records of the boards and bureaus that license and regulate professions, vocations, manufacturers and businesses

   d. State Tax Board: tax records.

2. Federal agencies:

   a. Postal Service: Postal laws and regulations prohibit dissemination of information by any employee; investigators should contact the U.S. Postal Service Inspectors for assistance when information is needed. A federal search warrant may be required

   b. U.S. Immigration and Naturalization Service: records on alien registrations, deportations, naturalizations, visas and manifests of passengers arriving at ports of entry.

    c.  U.S. Civil Service Commission: employment and background information on civil service employees

    d.  State Department: passport information and foreign agents registration act

    e.  U.S. Department of Treasury: Customs service, Internal Revenue Service, Secret Service

    f.  Department of Transportation: Coast Guard, Federal Aviation Administration

    g.  Departments of the Air Force, Army, Marine Corps and Navy: military records

    h.  Veterans Administration: records of benefits, hospitals and outpatient clinics

3.  Miscellaneous:

    1.  National Auto Theft Bureau: files on professional auto thieves and theft rings. This valuable organization is maintained by insurance companies

    2.  Private Investigation Agencies: variety of valuable information

    3.  Laundry and Dry Cleaners Association: maintains files on laundry and cleaners marks

    4.  Drugstores — prescription records

    5.  Telephone and mail services: much personal information on clients

    6.  Doctors, attorneys and accountants: much personal information on clients

    7.  Clergymen: in touch with community

    8.  Hospitals: files on patients

    9.  Newspapers: circulation, want ad and morgue files

    10.  Consumer credit bureaus: credit information nationwide

    11.  Credit card companies: oil companies, International Diners Club, American Express, etc.; credit and personal information

12. Banks, savings and loan associations: financial and personal information on clients

13. Better Business Bureaus: information on reputations of businesses

14. Chambers of Commerce: city directories and information on businesses

## SUMMARY

*Information* is acquired knowledge that may be obtained through study, communication, search, research and observation. It is impossible for any one person to know everything, yet it is possible for a person to know where to obtain information on almost all subjects. The more sources of information an investigator develops and maintains, the easier his or her work will be.

Study may be obtained through formal education or training programs or a variety of self-study methods. Communication with victims, witnesses and informants can provide valuable information. The search and researching of records is tedious but often very productive to the investigator. By developing the ability to use the five senses accurately, investigators can become trained observers. This ability can make valuable contributions to the success of their own investigations, as well as other investigations wherein their collaboration may be requested. The proper collection, handling and preservation of physical evidence, followed by the services of the criminalistics laboratory, is a prime contributing factor to a successful criminal investigation. The practice of sound human relations principles and the careful establishment of the necessary trust and cooperation of the custodians of public and private records can be vital to obtaining necessary information. These records systems contain much valid and useful information not found in police record systems.

An investigator should develop and maintain personal informants. A relationship between an investigator and a personal informant is usually based on trust and a mutual need. The investigator needs information, and the informant may have a need to display public spirit, express appreciation for past treatment by the police, or may seek acceptance to bolster a negative self-image. The informant may also be motivated by a desire for money, fear, revenge, repentance, a zeal for investigation, a desire to eliminate competition, or mental illness.

In all cases, dealings with informants must be private, confidential and ethical. The informant must be protected and treated fairly. Information received by investigators must be evaluated before action is taken. The use of an interpreter may, on occasion, be required to overcome a language barrier.

Recorded sources of information other than police agencies are available on municipal, county, state, and federal levels. These records systems contain numerous items of personal information on individuals in all walks of life and can furnish many productive investigative leads.

## DISCUSSION QUESTIONS

1.  What are the various sources of information acquired through communication? List several examples.

2.  What are the various sources of information acquired through search and research? Discuss several examples.

3.  Name the various sources of information acquired through observation? Discuss several examples.

4.  What are the various sources of information acquired through study?

5.  What are the various sources of information acquired through physical properties? Discuss several examples.

6.  Explain how sources of information are developed.

    a.  Public records

    b.  Private records

    c.  informants

7.  Why is confidentiality important in dealing with an informant?

8.  How is an informant protected? Discuss.

9.  Discuss human relations in dealing with an informant.

10. Define and discuss the various motivators of informants.

11. Define and discuss several examples of recorded sources of information other than police agencies.

# SURVEILLANCE AND UNDERCOVER INVESTIGATION

## KEY TERMS AND CONCEPTS

Surveillance (definition of)
Surveillance (types of)
Undercover (definition of)
Undercover (purpose of)
Communication while undercover
Types of undercover assignments

Some criminals develop a skill or jungle-like ability to conduct their illegal activities in ways that defy detection through the use of standard overt techniques of investigation. In an effort to combat this type of criminal, police engage in surveillances and undercover operations.

A *surveillance* is the clandestine (secret) observation of persons, places or objects. Undercover work involves the dropping of one's real identity and assuming another that blends into the area and circumstances under investigation. The purpose of surveillance and undercover operations is to obtain information as to the identities and activities of persons, or more specifically, to obtain evidence of crimes (e.g., locate contraband or stolen property, to apprehend a suspect during the commission of a crime, following its commission, or to prevent a crime).

Several types of surveillance techniques and undercover operations are discussed in detail in this chapter. Surveillance techniques and undercover operations differ considerably from one another. As stated above, the purpose of surveillance is to observe—usually from some distance—while carefully avoiding direct contact with the suspect(s). The undercover operator, on the other hand, seeks out and makes direct contact with the suspect(s); however, the undercover operator makes this contact under an assumed identity. Surveillance usually involves more than one officer; the undercover investigator generally works alone. In both types of police operations, a standard operating procedure is established to make or maintain periodic or regular contact with headquarters. Both surveillance and undercover work require considerable training and experience; both, also, require certain personality traits. All these aspects are thoroughly explained in the material which follows.

## TYPES OF SURVEILLANCE

### Fixed Post or Stakeout

The fixed post or stakeout may be in a residence, apartment, building, vehicle, rooftop, fire escape, street or other location. Observation is normally by visual means, perhaps aided by binoculars, a telescope, motion picture or videotape photography.

On occasion, the fixed post may also be equipped with listening and recording devices to pick up conversations and the sound of activities from within an office or residence wherein an electronic transmitter has been secreted. This kind of surveillance is conducted under authority of a search warrant obtained prior to the surveillance. The type of case and the attendant circumstances will dictate where the fixed post is located, what personnel and equipment will be used and the duration of the surveillance. If the location is to be continuously under surveillance for an extended period of time, an indoor location such as a residence, apartment or office is desirable for the post. Observation can be made through curtained windows or other vantage points aided by binoculars. A motion picture or videotape camera may be used to record significant activities. The advantage of the investigators being concealed in the location is obvious.

It is not uncommon for police to rent or make arrangements to use unusual locations for surveillances. If so, the numbers, physical appearances, language and actions of the investigators must blend into the area of the location, so as not to arouse suspicion. It is safe to assume that three neatly groomed white investigators carrying binoculars and photographic equipment, moving into a one bedroom apartment located in the minority skid-row area would arouse suspicion. It is not uncommon for criminals, particularly those who have grown up in the ghettos, to develop a sixth-sense which alerts them to the possibility that anyone unlike themselves is likely to be a peace officer.

If the location to be under surveillance is such that an outdoor fixed post is required, a specially equipped surveillance van may be used; however, an exchange of vehicles and locations may be needed if the surveillance continues for a prolonged period. The choice of vehicles is not limited to the above and may include telephone and electric company trucks or whatever is suitable or available.

## The Moving Surveillance or "Tail"

This type of surveillance is by visual means and may be conducted on foot or by vehicle, aircraft, or a combination thereof. Methods are dependent on the number of suspects, the area within which the surveillance is to take place (rural or urban, business or residential, vehicle or pedestrian traffic) and the suspect(s) mode of transportation. There must be enough flexibility to insure that the suspect's activities are maintained in view throughout the surveillance. The degree of difficulty in conducting moving surveillances will generally vary with the cunning, experience and resources of the suspect(s).

Some large agencies support full-time surveillance squads equipped with a variety of investigators (male, female, different ethnic groups, various sizes and body-builds), vehicles, helicopters, electronic and photographic equipment. The amount of personnel and equipment resources expended on surveillance will normally depend on need and on the enforcement priorities of the agency.

### *One-on-One Foot Surveillance*

This method is extremely difficult under the best of circumstances. The physical nature of the area and the amount of pedestrian traffic must be such as to provide some shelter for the investigator. The investigator must stay close enough to keep the suspect in view at all times, particularly if the suspect turns corners, enters doorways, etc. If the investigator is covering the suspect by walking on the opposite side of the street, he or she must stay nearly abreast of the suspect so that if it is necessary to move across the street behind the suspect, the investigator can do it quickly (hopefully unnoticed) and not be too far behind.

### Two-Officer Foot Surveillance

This method is generally more successful than the one-on-one technique. If pedestrian and vehicular traffic is heavy, then two investigators will generally stay on the same side of the street as the suspect. When such traffic is moderate, the investigators can alternate their positions from one side of the street to the other, as well as their positions relative to the suspect (see Figures 9-1, 9-2, and 9-3 for Two-Officer Foot Surveillance techniques with alternate positions).

### Three-Officer Foot Surveillance

This method is even more effective than the preceding ones. It allows more flexibility for the investigators and reduces the chance that the suspect will detect the "tail" (see Figures 9-4 and 9-5).

### Foot and Automobile Surveillance

This method involves one, two or three investigators on foot with others following in an automobile. It provides transportation for the investigators on foot in case the suspect enters a cab, bus or other vehicle. It further provides for alternating the investigators on foot with those in the automobile, thus minimizing chances of detection. Naturally, the amount and speed of the vehicular traffic on the surveillance route will affect how tightly or loosely the vehicle will follow the investigators on foot. A slow moving vehicle or one that is frequently parked or double-parked, then driven again may well cause suspicion.

### One-on-One Automobile Surveillance

This method is used when only one surveillance automobile is available. The investigator's car normally follows at the right rear of the suspect's car, to reduce the chance of attracting the suspect's attention via his rear view mirror. The distance maintained behind the suspect's car will vary with the area and the vehicular traffic, that is, whether it is urban or rural traffic.

Generally, in urban traffic, the investigators try to maintain a two-vehicle distance between the suspect's car and the surveillance vehicle. Caution must be exercised to remain in the same lane as the suspect, particularly in heavy traffic on freeways. A sudden turn or the use of an off-ramp by the suspect may result in no alternative for the surveillance vehicle but to keep going straight with the traffic, thus losing the suspect.

**Figure 9-1**   Two-officer foot surveillance. Dotted line shows alternate position of second officer.

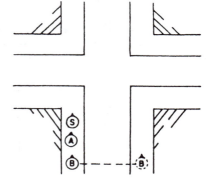

**Figure 9-2**   Two-officer foot surveillance. Suspect makes left turn. Officer "A" crosses street and Officer "B" assumes former position of "A".

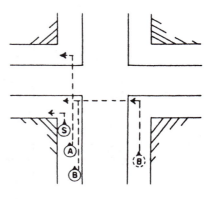

**Figure 9-3**   Two-officer foot surveillance. Suspect turns toward Officer "B" while "B" is operating across street from Officer "A".

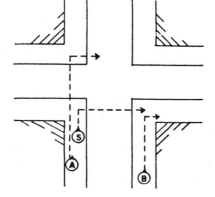

LEGEND

S   SUSPECT
A   SURVEILLANT IN LEAD
B   SURVEILLANT FOLLOWING LEAD

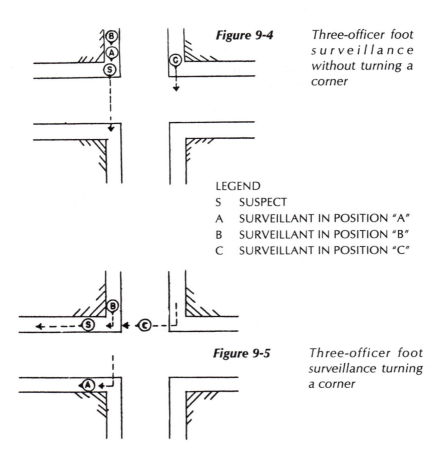

**Figure 9-4**

*Three-officer foot surveillance without turning a corner*

LEGEND

S   SUSPECT
A   SURVEILLANT IN POSITION "A"
B   SURVEILLANT IN POSITION "B"
C   SURVEILLANT IN POSITION "C"

**Figure 9-5**

*Three-officer foot surveillance turning a corner*

If the surveillance route is in a rural area, the characteristics of the road as to straightaways, hills, cross roads and the amount of vehicular traffic will determine how tight or loose the "tail" should be, and if any vehicles can be maintained between the surveillance car and that of the suspect. When conducting a surveillance at night, the surveillance vehicle should not use the high beam on the headlights as this would attract attention.

### Multi-Automobile Surveillance

This involves three or four radio-equipped surveillance vehicles on the ground, possibly augmented with a radio-equipped helicopter in the air. The increased number of surveillance vehicles provides for some of the vehicles to use known parallel routes and to alternate positions with those vehicles traveling closest to the suspect's car. A helicopter, if available, can be a tremendous plus to a surveillance. Especially during daylight hours, a supervisor can direct and coordinate a multi-automobile surveillance from the helicopter and maintain the suspect's car in view, even when it makes sudden, unexpected turns, changes routes or travels at high speeds.

An example of a multi-automobile surveillance is shown in Figure 9-6: one car is leading the suspect's vehicle and observing through the rear view mirror, another surveillance car "tails" the suspect's, while two other surveillance cars travel on parallel routes.

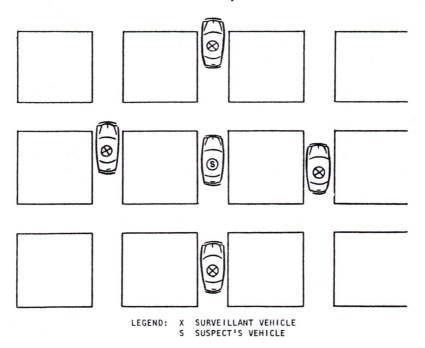

LEGEND:   X   SURVEILLANT VEHICLE
          S   SUSPECT'S VEHICLE

*Figure 9-6  Multi-automobile surveillance*

## Electronic Surveillance

This form of surveillance involves the use of electronic transmitters, induction coils, amplifiers, microphones and recorders of varying degrees of sophistication. The art of electronic surveillance and technical countermeasures is practiced much more extensively in the private sector than in law enforcement. Those in the industrial world, with billions of dollars to be made or lost via patenting or marketing products, or by winning contracts with the government and foreign countries, find it constantly necessary to protect their industrial secrets from competitors.

Industrial espionage is very big business, and consequently electronic surveillance and countermeasures have reached a high level of sophistication. For instance, the "Infinity Transmitter" or "Harmonica Bug," which is easily planted in a telephone, is activated by dialing the numbers of the telephone it is installed in without letting the phone ring. The "bug" then operates as a transmitter for all conversations or sounds of action within that room and possible adjoining rooms. The surveillant can listen on the telephone at the other end of the line. This item is sold to police and other agencies as a surveillance instrument; however, it is also available to private citizens as an audio intruder alarm. The advertisement may read, "Phone your home and listen for intruders." It is also common for manufacturers to advertise easily operated "Bug Detectors," that can locate eavesdropping installations in buildings and telephones.

If the above mentioned instruments are so easily available to almost anyone who can afford the price, it is logical to assume that other more highly sophisticated electronic equipment is available and may be used for police surveillance when authorized by a court order. A court order can be obtained from a local or federal court, based on a strong probability that such surveillance will provide evidence of a specified crime or crimes.

## Selection of Personnel for Surveillance

Investigators selected for a surveillance assignment must blend into the area of surveillance (i.e., they must resemble members of that community as to ethnic group, language and dialect, accent, if applicable), dress and general physical appearance, demeanor, etc. They must also remain particularly alert, resourceful and persevering.

# PREPARATION FOR SURVEILLANCE

Investigators must be thoroughly briefed on all facts, descriptions of suspect and vehicle, license numbers, habits and hangouts of the suspect(s) if known, known addresses the suspects may visit, associates, and the geography and background of the area where the surveillance will take place. Each investigator must be prepared to readily relate a good, plausible reason for being at the location or in an area of surveillance, if challenged.

A reliable and secure method of communication between the investigators, the lead investigator, and the supervisor in charge must be provided. The overall objective of the investigation and the specific objective of the surveillance must be clear (e.g., to obtain evidence of a crime and to observe all the activities of person(s) in order to obtain probable cause for a search warrant). Funds must be provided to investigators to cover all expected expenses. Provisions should be made for possible emergency expenditures and for a relief shift for the investigators at given intervals.

## Equipment Considerations

Vehicles must blend into the area of surveillance and be equipped with radios, extra gasoline, emergency repair equipment, food, extra license plates, disguises, etc. Binoculars and motion picture, still or video camera equipment with telescopic lenses capable of night photography may be required, and perhaps an electronic recorder. Portable transmitter/receivers and special weapons as are deemed necessary should be included in the inventory.

# SPECIAL TECHNIQUES

The special techniques and "tricks of the trade" employed by surveillance investigators, as well as by the subjects (suspects) of the surveillances, are varied and numerous. Investigators working the wide range of specialized assignments, such as robbery, burglary, shoplifting, narcotics, vice, etc., develop techniques to counteract the cunning of the kind of suspects they surveil. It is not the purpose of this section to attempt an in-depth treatment of this subject; therefore, only a selection of such techniques that are commonly used are listed:

## The Fixed Post or Stakeout

Investigators should arrive at the post one at a time (police generally travel in pairs) via public transportation or private vehicle. If a vehicle is used, it should be parked as inconspicuously as possible. Investigators must disguise any weapons or equipment brought to the post.

Vantage points from which to observe must be inconspicuous. A suspect may scan the area with binoculars in an effort to detect anything different or suspicious.

If the suspect is living at the location and the investigators are to stakeout inside and wait for him, care must be taken to check the space between the sides of the door and the door frame. A paper match stick, or similar object, can be held in place by the pressure of the closed door; then, when the door is opened, the object will fall to the floor. If the suspect placed the object in the space when he left the location, upon returning all he has to do is see the object on the floor and know the door was opened in his absence. He can well surmise that the police may be inside waiting. Many suspects have just walked away and never returned when thus alerted.

Care must also be taken when using windows to observe from, in a location where a suspect lives. A suspect may set a roll-up window blind a precise number of inches from the bottom, or reverse two blades at the top of a Venetian blind before he leaves. If the investigators inside adjust either blind in order to facilitate their observation of the suspect's approach to the location, they may sit there a long while for nothing. Suspects have been known to check the blinds on the windows of their residence when they return—some even carry opera-size binoculars for the purpose. If the blinds have been moved, they assume the probability of police being inside exists.

An old trick suspects use when staying in hotels is to call the switchboard operator of their hotel from some distance and ask for Mr. "X" (whatever name used to register). If the investigator answers the phone, good-bye suspect.

If it will be necessary for a supervisor to contact the investigators on a stakeout of this latter type, special arrangements should be made with the switchboard operator. The supervisor will use a code name when calling the switchboard, and the operator will ring the room phone two times and stop. This is a signal to the investigators that the supervisor is calling. If anyone not using the code name calls, the operator will ring the room numerous times, then tell the caller, "Sorry, Mr. `X' is out." This technique has worked often; however, its success depends on the reliability of the hotel.

## One-on-One Surveillance

A seasoned and cunning suspect can make it very difficult for a lone investigator to tail him on foot, particularly where pedestrian traffic is light and the physical structure of the area offers little protection such as doorways, shopping areas, etc. Some of the common tricks suspects use are:

- Abruptly reversing their direction on the sidewalk when entering a store, crossing a street or turning a corner to observe who is walking behind them. In this situation the investigator should not make eye contact with the suspect, but keep walking, not changing direction. He must quickly find a store front, lobby or newsstand where he can stop, pause, and look casually around to see where the suspect is. If possible, he should continue the surveillance.

- Using a decoy, an associate or crime partner— someone who would normally be a likely subject to surveil—is sent ahead of the actual suspect as bait for the surveillants. The suspect lags behind to observe if the investigators "take the bait" and tail the decoy. If they do, the suspect will then go in another direction.

- Boarding buses and streetcars, then getting off before they start to see if anyone follows them off, is a common trick. If the investigator falls into this trap, it may be best to stay on the bus or streetcar, get off at the next stop and return to the location. This will probably be a futile effort and certainly demonstrates the advantage of using two or more investigators on foot surveillance.

## Two- and Three-Officer Foot Surveillance

When entering department stores or other buildings that have several exits, several levels, elevators and are crowded with people, all investigators should follow the suspect. Although the crowd and the alternatives as to exits, floors and elevators work to the advantage of the suspect, he should not know how many investigators are tailing him or that he is being followed at all. He has only one set of eyes, as opposed to the combined visual capabilities of the surveillance team.

If the suspect upon entering a multistory building heads for the elevator, one investigator should remain in the lobby and the other(s) should enter the elevator with him. When the suspect selects his floor, the investigator(s) should choose one floor above or below that selected by the suspect. When the investigators reach their floor, they can alight and use the stairs to get to the suspect's floor and attempt to locate him and resume surveillance. In the meantime, the investigator who remained in the lobby watches for the suspect who may have gotten off the elevator on the floor he selected and taken another elevator back down to the lobby. If this has happened, the investigator must carry on the surveillance alone and trust that the other surveillants will catch up and join him.

When entering theaters, sports arenas, etc., all investigators must follow by paying admission and remain close to the suspect; otherwise, he disappears in the crowd. Exits and restrooms must be covered. This may require some alternating of positions by the investigators.

## Foot and Automobile Surveillance

The advantages of having an automobile to augment a foot surveillance are particularly evident when a suspect boards and stays on a streetcar, bus, or taxicab. In the case of the streetcar or bus, one investigator can board with him and sit behind him, while the other investigators follow in the automobile until the suspect gets off. The foot-auto surveillance can then be resumed. If the suspect enters a taxicab, all investigators follow in the automobile. When the suspect alights from the cab, the foot-auto surveillance is resumed.

## Automobile Surveillance

The suspect may send a decoy vehicle in advance with the same purpose and in the same manner as the decoy is used in the foot surveillance. If the investigators in the surveillance vehicles take the bait, the suspect's suspicions are confirmed that there is a surveillance in progress, and he or she will proceed in another direction.

The suspect may turn a corner, pull over and park, or pull into a business location through the entry driveway and exit through the other. It is common for suspects when testing for an automobile tail to jump traffic signals, drive on the wrong side of one-way streets and alternate the speed of their vehicle from fast to slow. Such maneuvers are for the purpose of observing if vehicles behind them attempt to follow. They can at times be countered by having the surveillance vehicle, which is immediately following the suspect's vehicle, continue on a normal course while the tail is taken up by another vehicle of the surveillance team. The advantage of having surveillance vehicles traveling on parallel streets, or having a helicopter in the air, is obvious.

*Note:* If investigators on a fixed-post, foot or vehicle surveillance are clearly detected by the suspect(s), an arrest should be made only if it is in order; otherwise, the investigator(s) should drop out of the surveillance.

## UNDERCOVER ASSIGNMENTS

An undercover assignment is uniquely different from a surveillance assignment in that the undercover investigator is operating under an assumed identity and seeks out and makes direct contact with the suspect(s). The investigator generally works alone, and his or her assumed identity (that is, appearance, actions, language, assumed habits and cover story) must be convincing enough to withstand the cunning scrutiny and checks of the criminal element he or she is investigating. Investigators must be able to gain the confidence and good graces of the suspect(s) to such a degree that the criminal activity being investigated will occur in the investigator's presence.

### Selection of Personnel for Undercover

Not every investigator can work undercover successfully. Undercover work requires that the investigator be able to step out of real life and fully assume a different role, much as an actor does in a theatrical production. He or she must become part of the suspect's world, taking on the personal characteristics appropriate to it: ethnic group, language (dialects, accent, colloquialisms used), physical appearance, dress, body odors (personal hygiene), finances, vehicle, personal habits and other identifying traits. In addition, he or she must possess an excellent memory and complete self-confidence, and remain constantly alert.

Alertness may prove to be the greatest asset the undercover investigator has because forgetting the undercover role even for a few seconds (perhaps by using certain words or other speech that is betraying) can destroy the cover and may cost the investigator his or her life.

Sometimes the undercover role calls for knowledge and prior experience in a particular profession, trade, occupation or sport. Knowledge of the cultural background of the suspect(s) and the area should be considered a "must" as well.

Learning to speak, think and dress like the suspect(s) and effectively circulate in the environment of the investigation can be difficult; however, if an investigator has the aptitude, the special attributes, the ability, and most of all, the desire, he or she can be successful in an undercover assignment. Undercover investigators are working effectively throughout the world today.

## Preparation for Undercover Assignments—Background Story

It is imperative that the investigator have as much background information as possible on the suspect(s) and the area in which he or she is going to operate. From this information a compatible assumed background for the investigator can be fabricated. This may include an occupation, profession, former residence, police record, associates, driver's license and other identification, vehicle, license plates, etc. Care must be taken not to select a former residence or occupation in an area where the suspect(s) is well connected. This increases the possibility that the suspect(s) may detect the investigator's cover. The investigator must be familiar with his or her background city or locale. Provision must also be made for persons acceptable to the suspect(s), such as a bartender, prostitute, bookmaker, who are prepared to vouch for the undercover investigator.

Most police and licensing agencies will cooperate with law enforcement undercover operations and provide undercover license plates (out of state if needed), drivers licenses, police records in the name of the investigator, etc. It is also important for the investigator to have in his possession personal articles (such as clothing or luggage) purchased in the background city or locale that has been chosen. Letters addressed to the assumed name, mailed from that location are helpful, too. It is obvious that the investigator cannot have in his possession or control any item that could betray his true identity (e.g., service gun, identification card, rings, phone numbers, family or other photos, etc.).

### *Faking Physical Handicaps*

The faking of physical handicaps is risky under the best of conditions. Physical handicaps, such as deafness, poor eyesight, a limp combined with the use of a cane, and other disabilities have been assumed by investigators on undercover assignments. The primary consideration before assuming a handicap must be whether it is necessary. If faking a physical handicap is deemed necessary or even desirable, the next consideration is, can the investigator maintain the infirmity while operating in the assumed role? It is possible to do so with a great deal of careful, precise practice in advance, followed up with much practical experience. This is a true test of the acting ability and continuing alertness of the investigator. Some basic tests which suspicious suspects might put to the investigator follow.

If the investigator is faking poor eyesight, the suspect could throw an object directly at his or her face to see if he or she flinches, dodges, or wards off the object. Or the suspect may put a burning cigarette lighter near the investigator's eyes to observe any reactions. It is important to remember human reflex action. If our eyes sense danger, an instantaneous message is sent to the brain, which normally calls for an immediate reaction to close the eyes or withdraw. Try standing perfectly calm while someone puts a flame to your eyes or throws something in your face. It is most difficult to avoid flinching, even with much practice.

If the investigator is faking deafness, the suspects may make a loud noise or scream behind the investigator to watch for flinching or other reaction. The investigator may be "set-up," by being allowed to hear information or a plan for a certain operation, solely for the purpose of determining what the investigator will do with the information if he or she heard it.

If the investigator is faking a limp, it is easy to place him or her in a physically dangerous situation to see whether or not he or she forgets to limp. The suspect may even try to run the investigator down with an automobile. Members of the criminal element know that self-preservation is a prime motivator in human behavior and they will not hesitate to use fear or loss of life to test any situation.

### Communications With Headquarters

Investigators must assume that suspects are as clever and cunning as they are. Never underestimate your adversary! Great care must be exercised in planning and effecting communications with the office. A cover person and address must be arranged to which any written reports are mailed. This individual could be a friend, an assumed crime associate, or other appropriate person. Reports can be made by phone to a prearranged person (supervisor) at a location not connected with law enforcement.

Depending on the assignment, it is possible to meet with the recipient of the report at various locations periodically to effect communications. It is imperative that the investigator always have a plausible reason ready for leaving the suspect(s) presence temporarily, going out of the area, making phone calls, etc., in case he or she is challenged.

## Types of Undercover Assignments

The types of undercover assignments are as varied as the investigations undertaken by law enforcement agencies. Some are conducted for the purpose of obtaining information and evidence of crimes such as conspiracy, prostitution, gambling, narcotics, robbery, and burglary. Other assignments may be for the sole purpose of gathering information on persons or groups involved in, or suspected of being involved in, criminal activities (organized crime) or disorderly conduct. It is not the purpose of this section to attempt a full treatment of such assignments, but rather, in the interests of space, to discuss a limited number of typical examples.

### *Employment, Membership and Special Assignments*

An assignment may require the investigator to obtain employment as a factory worker where an employee theft ring is operating. He will attempt to determine who is involved in the thefts, how the merchandise is being removed from the factory and where it is going. He will have to become friendly with the suspects and gain their confidence. This may require associating with the suspects and at times faking interest and participation in their criminal activities.

The investigator may join a subversive organization and become sufficiently active to attain recognition, perhaps even becoming an office holder. He or she must gain the friendship and trust of the leadership, thus facilitating the monitoring of all plans and activities. In order to investigate alleged drug or narcotic traffic, the investigator may enroll in a high school or college. He or she will become friends with the "in-group" who knows what is going on, and when the connections are right, will make buys of drugs or narcotics from the pushers and prepare cases for future prosecution.

## *Major Investigations*

A major investigation against organized crime (i.e., an extortion gang, gambling syndicate, major receivers of stolen property or securities, etc.) may require an investigator to take up residence in a particular locale for an extended period of time. Gaining the friendship and confidence of the criminal and other elements that reside in or hang around the area will put all his or her talents, training and experience to the test. Both performance and alertness must be flawless if the investigator is to obtain the desired information and evidence. Normally investigators will relay information to their supervisors by methods previously discussed under communication with headquarters.

Some large agencies will transfer in an investigator who is not known to any of the local law enforcement personnel. This is intended as "insurance" against the investigator being recognized by some officer he or she has worked with before. A mere greeting from a fellow-officer at the wrong time or place can destroy an investigator's cover.

## *Vice Assignments*

Perhaps the investigator will be assigned to work prostitution. The younger male investigator usually works female bar prostitutes who are encouraged to hang around bars as bait in order to lure male trade and to solicit drinks from them. The investigator soon learns from experience how to spot this type of woman—one who usually dresses provocatively, sits alone, chats with the bartender and eyes the men who enter. When the investigator buys a drink, his flashing a roll of money will generally attract the attention of the female prostitute and the bartender.

Before long the prostitute or bartender will suggest buying a drink for the lady. After the investigator buys a drink or two, he may suggest he is out for a good time. If in fact the woman is hustling sex, she will probably solicit the investigator to have sex for money. Generally the prostitute will ask the investigator to follow her casually to a motel or hotel nearby. When the fee is paid prior to the agreed upon sexual act, an arrest can be made.

## *Special Considerations*

There are a number of special considerations the undercover investigator must be cognizant of at all times. It is particularly precarious in that suspects can devise diabolically clever methods with which to test the investigator as to his or her identity, courage and stability.

Prostitution and Sex Crimes

Drugs

Bribes to Public Officials

Gambling

Obscene Material

Shylocking

Illegal Liquor

Vice Offenses

The investigator cannot afford to provide the suspects with the means for his or her own undoing. Although some drinking may be in order on certain undercover assignments, excessive drinking can be disastrous. The investigator cannot afford to dull his or her senses with alcohol or any other drug.

Great care must be taken by the investigator against becoming involved in any romantic, personal relationship with a member of the opposite sex while undercover. It is the oldest trap around and is particularly easy to implement when the undercover investigator is on a long, lonely assignment. It is not difficult for the suspects to procure an attractive, desirable person to tempt the investigator. The purpose of such a scheme is to involve the investigator emotionally and obtain information. There are many dead investigators throughout the world who would attest to the dangers of such an involvement, if they could speak. Male and female investigators have been working undercover assignments for decades. This is particularly true in vice and narcotic assignments. Whether or not a male and female undercover team is used for a case will depend on the nature of the investigation. In this regard, it is important to consider whether or not a female operating in a male gang will attract the amorous attentions of the suspects, when it does not serve the interests of the investigation. The safety of an undercover investigator must always remain an important consideration.

The undercover investigator must also take care not to draw excessive attention to himself or herself by claiming to be the "Head Honcho" or "Big Operator" from the background city or location which has been chosen. There are only a "few chiefs but many Indians" in any criminal element. Therefore, the top echelon is easier to check out if the suspects wish to verify the investigator's claim. A claim of this nature when found to be false may destroy the investigator's cover. It is best to keep a low to medium profile. Investigators should display only those resources (money, jewelry, clothing, etc.) that are in keeping with the assumed identity.

Suspects may sometimes run a bluff on an undercover investigator when they feel nervous or suspicious in an effort to test the investigator's courage, loyalty or identity. The caliber of the bluff will generally be in keeping with the caliber of the suspect(s)—whether tacky, average or first-class. The bluff, no matter how convincing, does not mean the suspect(s) know anything that has revealed the investigator's identity; therefore, the investigator must counter-bluff if necessary and not admit his or her identity. If the investigator's identity has in fact been detected, the nature and caliber of the case and those involved will usually determine the action to be taken. The investigator may be set up for a "hit" (death), a beating and exile, or the suspect(s) themselves may just disappear. Make no mistake, undercover work can be, and often is, extremely dangerous.

Last, but not least, of the special considerations, the investigator must not engage in entrapment. The key word in the definition of entrapment is inducement. When an officer of the law induces an otherwise innocent person to commit a crime, he or she would not otherwise have committed, the accused can raise the defense of entrapment. Notice the two key elements of entrapment: namely, (1) inducement of a person (2) by a law enforcement officer. If the accused, without outside assistance or pressure, forms the intent to commit a crime, he or she cannot raise the defense of entrapment.

# SUMMARY

The fact that some criminals develop a skill or jungle-like ability to conduct their criminal activities in ways that defy detection by routine and overt techniques of investigation, requires police to engage in surveillances and undercover operations. A surveillance is the clandestine observation of persons, places or objects. Undercover means the dropping of one's real identity and assuming another that blends into the area and the circumstances of the investigation. The purposes of both techniques of investigation is to obtain information and evidence regarding suspects and their criminal activities.

There are several types of surveillances used by law enforcement agencies. The fixed post or stakeout may be in a residence, business or other location where observation is by visual means. It may be aided by binoculars, photography, and electronic listening and recording devices. Moving surveillances ("tails") may be conducted on foot or by vehicle or aircraft or a combination thereof. These types of surveillances may involve one or more investigators, vehicles and aircraft. It depends on the number of suspects, the area within which the surveillances are to take place and the suspect's mode of transportation.

Another type of surveillance is electronic surveillance, which involves the use of electronic transmitters, induction coils, amplifiers, microphones and recorders of varying degrees of sophistication. The use of these instruments in a criminal surveillance is normally authorized by and based on a court order.

Investigators selected for surveillance assignments must blend into the area of the surveillance, remaining particularly alert, resourceful and persevering. They must be apprised of all facts regarding the investigation and the suspects involved and must be provided with the necessary equipment, communication facilities and relief personnel as required. Surveillance investigators must be briefed so they can cope with, and counteract, the cunning tricks practiced by suspects when they are protecting themselves against police surveillance.

An undercover assignment is different from a surveillance assignment, primarily in that the undercover investigator is operating under an assumed identity and seeks out and makes direct contact with the suspect(s). Investigators assigned to undercover work must be able to gain the confidence of the suspect(s) to such a degree that the criminal activities being investigated will occur in the investigator's presence. The investigator must be able not only to blend into the area and take on many of the suspect's personal characteristics, but in addition must possess an excellent memory, complete self-confidence, and remain constantly alert.

Preparation for an undercover assignment will include learning everything possible about the suspect(s) and the area to be operated. Based on this information, a compatible assumed background for the investigator can be fabricated. The preparation may include the faking of a physical handicap by the investigator, which is always risky at best. Great care must be taken in planning and executing clandestine communications between the undercover investigator and the office or headquarters. Such assignments may require the investigator to obtain certain employment, membership in particular organizations, enrollment in schools, working on vice details or infiltrating organized crime groups.

The investigator must be careful not to drink excessively, although some drinking may be required for the assignment. He or she must avoid emotional involvements with suspects of the opposite sex and not draw excessive attention from the suspects by playing the role of "Big Operator." Such a person's background is the easiest of all for suspects to check out and possibly disprove, thus destroying the investigator's cover.

# DISCUSSION QUESTIONS

1. Why do police engage in surveillances and undercover operations?
2. What are the purposes of surveillance?
3. Discuss the fixed post or stakeout in surveillance. What kind of equipment may investigator's use? What are the precautions to be taken as to the investigators and their actions?
4. Discuss the various moving surveillances, i.e., one-on-one foot, two-officer foot, three-officer foot, foot-automobile, one-on-one automobile, multi-automobile.
5. Define electronic surveillance.
6. What are the main considerations in preparing for surveillance?
7. What equipment, supplies, and other objects or materials are or may be needed for a surveillance?
8. Discuss the special techniques and "tricks of the trade" in surveillance.

9. What are the purposes of undercover work and how does it differ from surveillance?

10. Discuss selection of personnel and preparation for undercover assignments.

11. Discuss communications with the office or headquarters.

12. Explain the various types of undercover assignments and their special considerations.

# INTERROGATION PRINCIPLES

## KEY TERMS AND CONCEPTS

Interrogation (objectives of)
Admissions
Confessions
*Miranda* admonition
Interrogation (location of)
Interrogation (approaches of)
Interrogator

*Interrogation* means a formal and systematic questioning of a suspect under the assumption that a suspect will resist the interrogator's efforts to obtain the information desired. It is an adversarial relationship from beginning to end. The objective of an interrogation is to ascertain facts (truth) in a lawful, professional manner.

An admission differs from a confession primarily in the content or extent of the statement made by the suspect acknowledging guilt. An *admission* is the acknowledgment that a fact, action or circumstance is true. The acknowledgment may strongly infer or directly admit guilt; however, it will lack the details as to the elements of the crime. For example, the following are brief but meaningful admissions: "Yes, I stole the car," "I stabbed him," "I just killed a man," "I didn't mean to hurt her," and so on. A *confession* is a more complete statement admitting each element of the crime. The following is an example of a brief confession to a murder: "When I found out Joe crossed me, I went home and thought about it for a couple of days, then I decided to kill him. I bought the gun and ammunition, loaded the gun and went over to Joe's office and shot him three times in the head while he was talking on the phone."

# SPECIAL CONSIDERATIONS

## Legal Constraints

Statements given voluntarily without any compelling influences, such as promises or hope of reward, coercion or judicial compulsion, are admissible in evidence. The basic issue is *voluntariness*. Involuntary confessions are basically untrustworthy and violative of the Fifth Amendment privilege against self-incrimination. The U.S. Supreme Court's decision in the *Miranda* case [*Miranda v. Arizona*, 384 U.S. 436 (1966)] established standards for police interrogators, requiring that an accused be informed of his or her constitutional right to remain silent (Fifth Amendment) and of the right to legal counsel (Sixth Amendment).

### *The Miranda Admonition*

If a suspect in custody is to be interrogated regarding his or her involvement in a criminal offense, the suspect must be admonished (warned) that (1) he or she has the right to remain silent, (2) that any statement he or she makes may be used against him or her in a court of law, (3) that he or she has the right to speak to an attorney and to have the attorney present during questioning, and (4) that an attorney will be appointed if the suspect cannot afford one. The suspect must demonstrate understanding of these rights and must waive them before being questioned regarding the crime.

*Note:* The *Miranda* admonition is required only if the suspect is to be questioned. Voluntary declarations by suspects not under admonishment, whether in custody or not, are admissible as evidence; for instance, if Mr. Smith calls the police and says, "You better come over—I just killed my wife."

### *Public Safety Exception*

On June 12, 1984, the U.S. Supreme Court held that police are *not* required to advise suspects of their constitutional rights under *Miranda* when public safety is at stake. Specifically, the court reinstated as evidence a gun taken by New York officers prior to informing the suspect (a suspected armed rapist) of his *Miranda* rights. The officers found an empty shoulder holster while frisking the suspect in a store after a foot chase. Following a legal arrest, they asked, "Where is the gun?" The suspect replied, "The gun is over there," and pointed to a nearby carton. The officers retrieved a loaded .38 caliber revolver from the carton, then read the suspect his *Miranda* rights from a printed card. The Supreme Court, in overturning the lower court rulings, held that both the gun and the suspect's statement were admissible as evidence. The Court ruled that since the gun was concealed in the store, it posed a danger to public safety and could have been used by an accomplice.

### Voluntariness

A statement made by a suspect is deemed to be *voluntary* only if it is obtained under conditions which can not be considered as rendering it untrustworthy. Conditions which will render a statement untrustworthy are:

1. Direct physical force or abuse (e.g., physical beatings or threat of physical beatings or other abuse).

2. Indirect physical force or abuse (i.e., threat of such force or abuse directed at members of the suspect's family or friends).

3. Coercion (i.e., compelling the suspect to make a statement under fear for his or her welfare or the welfare of others close to the suspect).

4. Promises or hope of reward. Promises of lesser punishment or even stating, "It would be better for you if you confess," have been held by the courts as representing a hope of reward.

Tricks and bluff devices are valid interrogation techniques; however, they must not be of such a nature as to produce an untrustworthy statement of confession. For example, placing a suspect in such a state of fear for his or her safety (or that of a loved one) that the suspect admits or confesses a crime just to relieve the situation, would make the confession inadmissible in court. A plea of guilty to a charge in a court of law under circumstances that bear evidence of fear, hope or leniency, ignorance or misunderstanding on the part of the accused, is likewise invalid.

### Where to Interrogate

Ideally, an interrogation should be conducted in an interrogation room at the police agency. This will provide, first of all, privacy which is very important. Secondly, the location provides a psychological advantage for the interrogator. The least desirable place to interrogate a

suspect is in his or her office, home or some other personal environment. These latter surroundings bolster a suspect's ability to resist.
Just sitting behind one's own desk and bracing one's legs underneath
gives great emotional strength to resist—not to mention the overall
psychological advantage one has because the investigator is on strange
"turf."

Another advantage to the police location is that distractions can
be kept to a minimum. Simple furniture, which includes a plain chair
for the suspect to sit on, is assured. Appropriate lighting is available,
as is stenographic assistance and/or electronic recording devices. As a
practical matter, the interrogation of suspects can occur wherever and
whenever the time and location presents the greatest potential for deriving admissions or confessions. The location may be at or near the
crime scene, in a police car en route to the police station, etc.

### When to Interrogate

It is important to preface this section with a reminder that many
police cases go to trial with the only statements from the accused being those obtained by the arresting officers. This may be the only time
a suspect will talk, because following incarceration, he or she has time
to react, think over the situation, talk to fellow prisoners or a lawyer,
and thereafter remain silent.

Ideally, an interrogation should be free of time constraints on the
part of both suspect and interrogator. If there is insufficient time for a
complete interrogation, its success is in jeopardy.

### Who Should Conduct Interrogation

If the arrest of the suspect occurs shortly after the commission of
the crime, the arresting officer(s) may be the most productive
interrogator(s). If a period of time and follow-up has ensued between
the occurrence of the crime and the arrest, it may be totally improper
for any person to interrogate the suspect except the investigator who is
directly working the case.

As previously mentioned in Chapter One, investigators working
the case are generally the only persons having intimate knowledge of
all known details of the crime and the *modus operandi*. They know
what specific questions to ask and can recognize whether the information that is elicited or volunteered during the interrogation is relevant
material or reveals some otherwise important factors to the investiga-

tion. For this reason, it is not uncommon for agencies to request in a wanted suspect broadcast, "Arrest, hold and notify; do not interrogate."

There are types of suspects and cases wherein it is preferable that only one interrogator be present with the suspect. For example, in a case where one investigator has established a rapport with the suspect during the present case or in a past investigation, the suspect may feel more comfortable and talk more freely if alone with the investigator. Caution must be taken to protect the case and the lone investigator. It is desirable to have another investigator or a secretary listen to and record the interrogation. This method provides other witnesses with information on what occurs and what is said in the interrogation room. This procedure has particular importance when the suspect is a member of the opposite sex, is emotionally unstable, mentally retarded, or has any potential for creating various kinds of problems.

The use of two interrogators working as a team in conducting interrogations is a common practice. The advantages of the two-person team outweigh the disadvantages. Some of the advantages are: (1) two interrogators provide physical protection for one another, as well as protection against allegations of misconduct; (2) a two-person team can better prepare and act out trick and bluff devices (this technique will be covered in a later section); (3) if one interrogator is absent at the time of the trial due to illness, assignment, etc., the other can testify with equal force and effect.

On the other hand, there is always a potential for problems in controlling an interrogation with two interrogators present. One interrogator may become impatient with, or doubt the wisdom of the route being taken by the partner in the questioning. The one may interrupt with questions or take over the interrogation completely, thus possibly breaking the mood or emotional tension purposely created by the other interrogator. This could completely negate the interrogation.

It takes investigative partners some time and experience together before they develop a mutual respect and confidence in each other and know each other's methods of employing various techniques of interrogation. When this stage is reached, many successful interrogations will follow. When two interrogators are not seasoned partners, they may experience conflicting impressions of what occurred in the interrogation room. While one interrogator is questioning the suspect, the other may be concentrating on his or her own approach and be waiting for the chance to ask questions—rather than paying careful attention to the partner and the suspect. The suspect may crack, become emotional and confess, but later allege harassment or coercion.

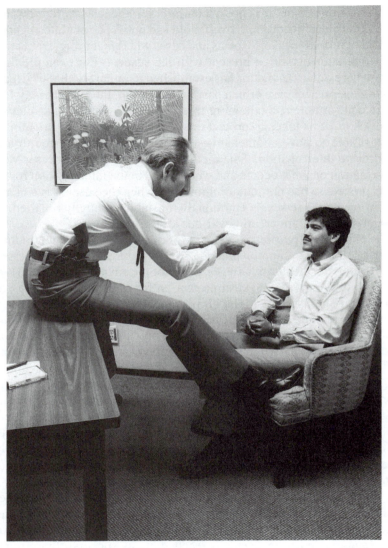

*Figure 10-1 Example of interrogation where interrogator is taking
a confrontational approach. Note the aggresive body position of
interrogator and suspect still in restraints.*

A problem of credibility will arise if the interrogator who was not paying close attention to the proceedings during the interrogation describes
the activities materially different than his or her partner.

To have more than two interrogators present during the interrogation of a suspect is obviously undesirable. The potential for conflicts in control and allegations of coercion based on the number of interrogators "forcing" the suspect, are magnified. Likewise, to interrogate more than one suspect at a time is undesirable. One suspect may dominate the other by his or her mere presence there. It is also difficult to play one suspect against the other through a trick device if each knows what the other has said. On occasion, when a deal is made with the respective defense counsels, two or more suspects may make a joint statement. A situation like this will usually involve a complicated series of crimes, wherein each suspect accepts responsibility for his or her actions in each crime. The motives for this kind of cooperative effort are basic to both the prosecution and the defense: time and money! The prosecution, through police efforts, has a good case and the suspects' attorneys know it. To try each crime in court, with the possibility of separate trials for each suspect, is very expensive and can amount to more time in prison for the defendants. Therefore, everyone—including the suspects—agrees to a deal that benefits all.

## PRINCIPLES OF INTERROGATION

Interrogation is an art. To achieve a high level of proficiency in this art, the investigator must consistently engage in the practical application of various techniques over a period of years. It is interesting to note that although the *Miranda* decision—with its advisement of constitutional rights requirements—has in some circles diminished the zest for interrogation, in other circles the *Miranda* decision has actually caused many law enforcement officers to become more proficient interrogators. The simple fact is that those who have chosen to practice a variety of interrogation techniques have learned that it is often possible to obtain information from a suspect, a *Miranda* warning notwithstanding. Wise and seasoned defense counsels advise their clients not to tell an investigator anything, and to demand that an attorney be present if they are to be questioned. This is as it should be, because it is a constitutional right. Yet many investigators have obtained admissions or confessions from previously counseled and *Miranda* admonished suspects. It appears that a similar phenomenon such as that which compels suspects to trap themselves through a *modus operandi* arises when interrogation techniques are properly applied. Obviously, said techniques are utilized only if the suspect waives his or her rights under *Miranda*. A thorough coverage of the principles of interrogation requires a complete textbook. It is not the intent or purpose of this chapter to provide this, but rather to present an introduction to the subject. For the student who desires an in-depth study of this highly specialized area of criminal investigation, the author recommends the text by Devallis Rutledge, *Criminal Interrogation, Law and Tactics*, 3rd ed., Copperhouse Publishing Co., Incline Village, NV, 1994.

The next section includes some rules and techniques which are in common practice.

## Evaluation of the Suspect

The initial approach to a suspect who is to be interrogated will be determined by an evaluation of various factors, such as the following:

1.  Who is the suspect?

2.  What is his or her relationship to the case?

3.  Is his or her guilt fairly certain (i.e., substantiated by physical or other evidence)?

4.  Is his or her guilt doubtful or uncertain?

5.  Does the interrogator have prior experience or information on the suspect as to personality traits (egoism, emotional instability, mental deficiency, conscience stricken, etc.)?

Having carefully considered all the above factors, the interrogator can compile a profile of the suspect based on the information available and select a method of approach to begin the interrogation. For example, if the suspect's guilt is fairly certain, and he or she is an emotional weakling or a conscience-stricken confessor (a "canary"), the approach would be simple. The interrogator would talk to the suspect in an understanding, matter-of-fact and logical manner, carefully pointing out the futility of resisting. The interrogator must be careful to apply just enough emotional pressure to "turn on" the suspect, but not so much as to frighten the suspect out of talking. Once the suspect has begun to talk, the interrogator must listen without interrupting, unless it is for the purpose of carefully guiding the suspect back on the trajectory of the story. In the case of the suspect who is all egotist, the initial questions may be general in nature, gradually leading to pumping up the suspect's ego to establish rapport. The interrogator could then utilize other factors, such as certainty or uncertainty of guilt.

There are always cases where the interrogator must evaluate or "size up" the suspect as he or she proceeds through the beginning (irrelevant questions) part of the interrogation. These are situations where there is little or no valid advance information on the suspect or his or her relationship to the case. The interrogator must evaluate the suspect's

- Emotional state

- Attitude

- Relationship to the case

Is he or she a principle? What motivated the involvement—revenge, money, etc.? What is his or her intelligence level and social status? Does the suspect lie in response even to irrelevant questions? When the interrogator is confident that the evaluation is complete, it is necessary to select the approach that is best suited to the suspect and the situation, then proceed to interrogate. *Note:* Refer to Chapter 4, "Interviewing", for classification of subjects as to age, sex, etc. The information there is generally applicable to interrogation as well.

## Classification of Suspects

Consider the following categories:

### *Willing Suspect*

This suspect is willing to provide the information desired by the interrogator and needs only to be approached and interrogated properly.

### *Inadequate Suspect*

This suspect is willing to provide the information desired by the interrogator; however, he or she cannot do so because of some unknown reason. The interrogator must discover the reason, neutralize it, and convert the inadequate suspect into a willing one.

### *Unwilling Suspect*

This suspect is unwilling to provide the information desired by the interrogator; the interrogator must determine the proper approach and/or technique to use to convert an unwilling suspect into a willing one.

Specific examples of willing, inadequate and unwilling suspects will be discussed in the section, "Selected Techniques," later in this chapter.

## Standard Approaches to Suspects

The majority of interrogation approaches, including those involved in "Selected Techniques," fall into either one of two general categories: the logical approach, or the emotional approach. On occasion, a combination of both logic and emotion is required.

### *The Logical Approach*

The logical approach involves the use of reason as the basis for any appeal to the suspect.

### *The Emotional Approach*

The emotional approach involves directing the appeal in a manner intended to arouse the emotions of the suspect.

## Standard Procedures for Interrogation

Once the interrogator has selected the approach to be used on the suspect, the interrogation must be continued. The following are standard procedures for conducting interrogations.

1.  The interrogator's conduct must not go beyond the accepted pressure applicable through the logic or emotion described in "Standard Approaches" or "Selected Techniques." The use of force is never justified. There is an old adage in interrogation, "Force is a weapon of the witless." Normal comforts must be provided to the suspect.

2.  The interrogator should ask only single questions and wait for the answer before asking the next question. This prevents confusion.

3.  The interrogator should avoid questions that suggest the desired answer or call for a "yes" or "no" answer. A continued use of such questions will primarily reproduce the interrogator's questions rather than the suspect's statement (responses).

4. The interrogator should ask questions in a manner that prompts the suspect to give a narrative answer, such as, "What happened then?" It is also important that the interrogation be recorded *verbatim,* via the interrogator's notes, a stenographer or electronically. The record must reflect the interrogator's and suspect's language-colloquial or profane as it may be. This will increase the credibility afforded the statement in court, particularly if the suspect takes the witness stand, and his or her own language can be compared with those factors reflected in the statement.

5. If the suspect begins a narrative story, he or she must not be interrupted. While talking freely, a suspect may outsmart himself or herself, revealing information not intended for disclosure. Once the story has been related, a commitment is made. If the story is the truth, all well and good; if not, the untruths can be attacked by the interrogator.

6. Sometimes it is necessary for the interrogator to jog the memory of the suspect. It is possible for a suspect who is attempting to "clear the slate" to be unable to recall certain crimes or details of events that are long past. This is especially true if the suspect has been involved in the excessive use of alcohol or drugs. The "jogging" can be accomplished easily by utilizing the "association method." The suspect could be asked, "Do you recall a topless cocktail lounge on Sherman Way?" If the suspect's answer is, "I held up that bar a long time ago"; the next question might be, "Tell me what you recall about the holdup." This technique permits the interrogator to jog the memory of the suspect without revealing any known details of the crime. It is not difficult to determine if the suspect was, in fact, involved in the crime. When the suspect has related intimate details known only to the victim, the responsible suspect, and the police, the interrogator can be certain the information is valid.

7. Notetaking by an interrogator or stenographer can be, at times, a precarious situation. Many persons are reluctant to talk when it becomes apparent that what they are saying is being written down or otherwise recorded. This applies especially to interrogations wherein premature note taking can "turn off" a suspect who has begun to talk. There may be occasions when notetaking must be excluded entirely due to the suspect's attitude. In these cases, hopefully, there is an electronic recording being made or a stenographer is listening and taking shorthand notes elsewhere.

If no recording methods are available, the interrogation should continue, and, when completed, the interrogator(s) must quickly make adequate notes (*verbatim* whenever possible) of the interrogation. It is interesting that the sensitivity to note taking or electronic recording varies with suspects. Thus the egotist, once cooperative and talking, will often welcome note taking or electronic recording. Many investigators have interviewed suspects that insisted on reviewing and initialing the notes to make sure they were not misquoted.

A technique that is very effective in many cases is to draw a line below the last sentence in the notes or statement and ask the suspect to sign his name along the line—"to insure that nothing can be added to the notes or statement he has approved." Another method that has been successful for many investigators in obtaining permission to takes notes in the presence of the suspect is as follows: During the preliminaries the interrogator has the case file open on the desk. When the suspect appears ready to talk, the interrogator closes the file and pushes it aside. This is ostensibly an "off the record" move. When the suspect has talked for a few minutes, the interrogator embarrassingly confesses to the suspect that he or she is on the spot—his or her memory is not that good. Perhaps in fairness to the suspect, so that his or her side of the story will not be twisted by someone later in recall, a few notes should be taken. If the suspect agrees, the investigator takes notes.

Relative to intentional omissions, lies and qualifications by the suspect, it is imperative that the interrogator remember that most humans experience difficulty in admitting errors or guilt. When people tell their side of a story, or describe an incident wherein the conclusion requires acceptance of fault by one or all of the participants, they often omit certain details, qualify their answers or even lie as to particular points. Thus a suspect may relate that while he or she was holding a gun on the victim of a robbery-murder, "The gun just went off." The suspect may find it difficult or even impossible to say, "I fired two shots at the victim and he dropped dead."

Many experienced investigators would agree that it would be unwise for the interrogator to accuse the suspect of lying or to pressure the suspect into admitting that he or she pulled the trigger, stabbed the victim, etc. Such pressure may place too heavy a burden on the suspect, and the interrogation could end immediately. It would be more productive for the investigator to go along with the suspect's omission and keep the suspect talking. The investigator may, if the gun is in evidence, be able to point out to the suspect at a later time that the gun is incapable of being fired without someone pulling the trigger, that the gun was in his or her hand when it went off, and so on. Then again, the suspect may never admit to pulling the trigger, that the gun is not in evidence, and there are no witnesses that can refute the suspect's version. So be it! Other facts revealed by the suspect in the continuing interrogation may solidify the case, or the case may go to trial with the suspect's statement as is.

On occasion a suspect may admit being at the crime scene, yet will lie as to the intent: "I didn't know my buddy was there to steal the jewelry; he said we were going to visit a friend." The suspect's prior knowledge of the reason (intent) for going to the victim's location may have to be established through other evidence. Many suspects will want to qualify incriminating answers and generally should be allowed to do so the first time around, since an unequivocal yes or no may be too difficult to obtain at the time. Example question: "Did you swing a crow bar at the officer when he went to place you under arrest?" Answer: "Well, yeah, but only because I thought he was going to hurt me. I was protecting myself." Whether or not the officer's approach posed a physical threat to the suspect is a matter that may have to be resolved by other witnesses or the officer. As to the suspect's reason for assaulting the arresting officer, most jurisdictions prohibit the use of force or weapons to resist arrest.

### *Patience*

Truth is the objective of the interrogation. Let us compare truth to a loaf of bread. With patience, the interrogator can often obtain the whole loaf of bread (truth). But there are times when it may require taking just one slice of bread at a time. If the whole loaf is not obtained, part of a loaf is better than none.

### *Use of Terminology*

The interrogator should generally avoid certain words or police terminology in asking questions. Use of those terms may increase the incriminating atmosphere of the interrogation or unduly emphasize the penalty that may ensue to the suspect. The following are examples of words best avoided, along with appropriate substitutes.

| AVOID | BETTER TO USE |
|-------|---------------|
| murder | death |
| mayhem | injury |
| robbery | property taken |
| burglary | entered |
| rape | have sex |
| assault | scuffle |
| kidnap | move |
| conspiracy | arrangement |
| embezzle | use |
| life imprisonment | some time |

### Empathy and Understanding

The interrogator can facilitate the establishment of rapport with the suspect through empathy and understanding. *Empathy* merely means placing oneself in another's position and sharing that person's feelings. Suspects often respond favorably to the interrogator who demonstrates understanding of the suspect's point of view or position. The interrogator can also be understanding regarding whatever behavior is involved in the crime. Doing so is neither condoning nor condemning, just understanding. Most persons want to feel they are worth something to themselves and, they hope, to others. When trouble comes their way, it is usually easier to cope with the problem if they can rationalize their own behavior and place at least a part of the blame for their predicament on someone or something else. To *rationalize* means "to provide plausible but untrue reasons for conduct."

In the case of crimes of passion, the rationalization route is easier for the suspect, and easier for the interrogator to empathize with and understand. For example, a suspect is accused of killing his wife and her lover, whom he found together in his own home. Without engaging in histrionics, the interrogator could say: "I can understand how any man would get upset over a situation like that. I hope it never happens to me because I don't know what I would do." The interrogator is empathetic and understanding but not condoning or condemning. The empathy and understanding technique is also useful in dealing with suspects under a variety of emotional conflicts. Perhaps a suspect places a high moral value on loyalty to peers, crime partners or others. A full confession will involve these persons, therefore the suspect may choose to limit the statement to his or her own actions in the crime. Similarly, a child molester does not want to be condemned as a "creep." The interrogator must not embarrass or belittle such a suspect, but rather encourage discussion about his misfortunes in life and help him find a rationalization for his conduct.

### Minimizing the Seriousness of the Crime

An interrogation can often be facilitated by minimizing the seriousness of the crime to the suspect. Thus, if a suspect is charged with burglary of a residence, the interrogator may reduce the suspect's apprehension by showing him the case file and complaining, "I get thirty of these 'crappy' reports every month. I don't know why we have to bother with them—a lousy TV set and some junk jewelry." If a suspect is charged with an assault to commit murder, resulting from a fight, the interrogator might loosen up the suspect by saying, "I see you and George had yourselves a scuffle. Tell me what he did to you."

### Spontaneous Remarks by a Suspect

The interrogator must be constantly alert for spontaneous remarks by the suspect that indicate guilt. These remarks may be made almost anywhere and at any time (i.e., after the interrogation is complete or en route to the station or to court). Such remarks as, "How much time off can I get if I return the money?" or "Would it make any difference if I prove that he threatened my life?" are not that unusual.

### Terminating the Interrogation

The investigator must terminate the interrogation in a manner that permits reopening the session at a later time. It must be clear to the suspect that he or she can call the investigator at any time in the future. Many investigators have found it very useful to offer to do something personal for a suspect—furnish cigarettes, make a notification to a family member, or refer family members to service agencies—whether or not the suspect has cooperated. The following case serves as an example.

The suspect was charged with several armed robberies and a murder, resulting from a series of cocktail lounge "heists." He was an ex-con, having served ten years for robbery, seven of which were in solitary confinement. The suspect was a real hard-nose who would not even admit that he was alive. When the interrogation was completed, he was asked if anything could be done for him. He pondered awhile, then asked if the investigator would call his sister in New Jersey and relay a message. The investigator offered to let him call her himself from the office, which he did while the investigator monitored the conversation. As it turned out, the suspect had a pregnant fifteen-year old runaway girl from New Jersey hidden out in Los Angeles. An arrangement was made, through Travelers Aid, for her transportation back to New Jersey to the home of the suspect's sister. The suspect confessed, and helped recover two shotguns used on the robberies and murder.

*Note:* One question an interrogator can ask a suspect who refuses to cooperate, due to the advice received from other prisoners ("jailhouse lawyers") is, "If the jail house lawyers are so smart, what are they doing in jail?"

# SELECTED SUSPECTS AND TECHNIQUES

## Willing Suspects

The classic willing suspect is the remorseful or conscience-stricken one who feels anguish or distress caused by the sense of guilt for the crime he or she has committed. Usually this type is not a hard-core criminal, but rather a first, or accidental, offender. The first offender may have gotten deeply into debt by living beyond his or her means and stolen money from an employer to stave off creditors. The accidental offender may have lost self control in an altercation and killed someone.

In either case, the interrogator must demonstrate an understanding, empathetic attitude; however, an air of assurance and control of the situation must be maintained. The interrogator may help the suspect to rationalize the action, without condoning it or condemning or embarrassing the suspect, by saying something like: "Business today makes credit so easy to get, it's no wonder people get in over their heads;" or, "Sometimes other people can really get on your nerves and drive you right up the wall." Suspects will frequently display fear of punishment or condemnation by their family and friends. Normally, a minimizing of the moral seriousness of their actions will help, for instance, "Situations like this happen every day in the very best of families." The above are examples of a combination of approaches, both emotional and logical.

## Inadequate Suspects

The term *inadequate* is a standard term used in interrogation to describe a certain category of suspects. Some interrogators will refer to these suspects as emotionally below par or deficient. There are a number of reasons why a suspect at the time of interrogation is emotionally inadequate or, if preferred, below par or deficient. Here are a few such reasons: a suspect may be suffering an emotional conflict involving a mental struggle resulting from incompatible or opposing needs, drives, wishes, or external or internal demands. Emotional conflicts can be brought on by fear of punishment or social condemnation versus the need to confess and clear the conscience. The willing suspect, previously discussed, can easily become an inadequate suspect (emotional conflict) if the interrogator applies too much pressure.

An emotional conflict may also occur if the suspect is torn between two loyalties; a loyalty to loved ones versus a loyalty to crime partners. At times, a disloyalty to crime partners can mean death. In the first instance, the interrogator should ease the suspect's fears by rationalizing and minimizing the offense. In the second, the interrogator should base his appeal on how the suspect can best serve his or her loved ones. These approaches, as with the willing suspects, are based on the use of both logic and emotion.

Other inadequate suspects are those that are obviously emotionally unstable or mentally deficient. It is a policy with many police agencies not to engage in pseudo-professional evaluations of the mental health of a suspect. Generally, if a suspect is rational enough to be processed through the normal arrest and booking procedures, this will be done. Most jurisdictions have prerequisites in human behavior, mandated by law, that must be met before any person can be admitted to a psychiatric ward for observation. In the interests of the rights of any person suspected of mental illness, these prerequisites are very demanding. As a result, it is not uncommon to encounter persons on the street or in jail that may appear emotionally unstable or mentally deficient, yet are not disturbed or deficient enough to be in a psychopathic ward.

Interrogation of suspects in this category is possible, and can be productive if the suspect can make accurate observations of persons, heights, weights, colors, etc., and relate these observations in an understandable manner. The interrogator must be considerate, calm and empathetic. He or she must be prepared for verbal abuse, as this category often includes persons who are antiestablishment or "cop haters." Unfortunately, many suspects in this category have experienced real or imagined prejudices, deprivations and other abuses in life. Usually, with careful, patient prompting, these suspects can be encouraged to relate their life's problems, and often rationalize their criminal conduct (e.g., "Why should I care about them, they don't care about me?") Again, this example illustrates the use of both logical and emotional appeals.

## Unwilling Suspects

This category of suspects encompasses the majority of those encountered by the interrogator. A suspect may refuse to cooperate or relate information for one or more of a variety of reasons. The first objective in such instances is for the interrogator to determine, if possible, the reason for the suspect's refusal to relate the information desired. Identifying the obstacles to be overcome, so that the suspect can be converted from an unwilling to a willing one, can be somewhat difficult. The suspect may be experiencing a tremendous feeling of guilt, fear of punishment, fear for the safety of a loved one, or be exhibiting a variety of defense mechanisms to shield personal inadequacies or other emotions.

It would be most naive to state that a logical approach always works on one type of suspect and that an emotional approach works on another. An experienced and successful interrogator will readily concede that most really challenging interrogations require that the interrogator be thoroughly flexible. He or she must be able to detect when to switch from the use of logic and reason to emotions, and vice-versa, at a moment's notice. For example, the interrogator must be able to appreciate that an outward display of hostility or defiance may be caused by fear, love, hate, jealousy or revenge or a combination thereof. The initial approach to such a suspect may be logical, but at the point where it is recognized that the hostility and defiance displayed by the suspect is not all that "hard-nosed" but, rather, emotionally based, indicates change is in order.

The interrogator must gracefully switch and attempt to help the suspect unload his or her emotional hostility, and in the interim, relate the desired information. It is true that many hard-core, confirmed criminals must be convinced by logic that cooperation is the way to go. These types are usually not hostile or defiant, but logical in their thinking (i.e., what is the easiest and most painless way to get out of their problem). These situations must be handled delicately so as not to stretch an appeal to logic into a promise of lesser punishment or some similar reward.

Most hard-core and confirmed criminals know the laws and the criminal justice system. They know the seriousness of the crime(s) they commit and how judges and juries react to these situations. If they are ex-convicts, they are also very aware of prison life, the power of parole boards, etc. Many experienced investigators agree that the logic that works best with these suspects is a clear description of the hopeless, habitual criminal profile they depict to the courts, juries, probation offices, prison officials and parole boards. Without making promises, the interrogator must leave the choice to the suspect: "Is this how you want to be regarded? As hopeless?"

## The Egotist

This type of suspect has an exaggerated sense of self-importance, perhaps seeing himself or herself as a "professional" in some criminal specialty—robbery, burglary, and the like—and acting accordingly. It is a person who frequently enjoys boasting about past accomplishments. By comparison with contemporaries, such suspects are often only petty criminals, yet they have a very strong need to feel important. Naturally, it is a distinct advantage for the interrogator to have knowledge of this personality type and its various traits before any interrogation.

On occasion, information as to personality type is available in police files if the suspect has a prior record. If not, the suspect's egotism may be revealed during the preliminary questioning period in the interrogation. Obviously, this type of suspect can be induced to talk of criminal exploits by a carefully, consistent and convincing flow of flattery from the interrogator. The flattery can be disguised by the interrogator as frustration or relief that the suspect has been captured or admiration for—and astonishment at—the suspect's accomplishments in the face of the tremendous odds.

An excellent example of the egotist type of suspect is revealed in the following market robbery case. The suspect would select three or four average-size markets near a freeway, then hold them up in sequence—shooting up at the ceiling of each market and terrorizing everyone present. He then hid out for the rest of the evening. He spaced these holdups with just enough time between each one to allow for an "all units" broadcast to the first robbery. As soon as all available police units arrived at the first location, he would commit the subsequent robberies at the other locations.

The suspect's method of operation was detected, and several markets fitting his MO were covered by stakeouts. He was eventually captured, but was not upset about being caught. Rather, he was amused and cocky over the thought that his capture required the services of an entire special squad of investigators. A seasoned investigator, who was supervising the case, recognized the personality type. He also noted that the suspect was very careful not to hurt anyone—just terrorize them. The interrogator's approach was a statement to the suspect pointing out the great relief felt by the entire city since his capture, the many sleepless nights suffered by investigators searching for him, and the suspect's strategic brilliance. The suspect responded with hilarious laughter. He enjoyed being held in awe, even if in jail. He responded to the interrogator's flattery by telling the interrogator just how clever he was in committing all the robberies.

## The Defiant Type

The suspect of this type may seem unmovable and unemotional. Actually, the defiance is usually a defense mechanism. The basis for the underlying problem may be a deep-rooted fear of appearing perverted or immoral if he or she confesses. Sigmund Freud defines *defense mechanisms* as the methods that an individual develops to handle conflict or anxiety. If the conventional, logical, and/or emotional approach has failed to break down a suspect's defiance, a trick-and-bluff technique may be in order.

An example of a trick-and-bluff technique that often works with a defiant suspect is the "good guy/bad guy" routine. This requires two interrogators and is most effective when they are used to working together. The interrogator that is to assume the role of the "bad guy" gives the other a cue—e.g., by raising his or her voice and closing the case file—that it is time for heavy histrionics. The interrogator becomes sarcastic, belligerent and even insulting to the suspect, perhaps ridiculing the suspect's inability to face up to reality, or saying something like, "You don't have the guts it takes to tell the truth." The other interrogator moves in with words, tone of voice, and an apparent attitude of disapproval towards the behavior of the first interrogator, and openly shows consideration for the suspect. This routine is accelerated to a point where there is an argument between both interrogators over the "bad guy's" unprofessional conduct. The climax is reached when the "good guy" reprimands the other, who storms out of the interrogating room repeating that the suspect has not told the truth.

Now that the "good guy" interrogator is alone with the suspect, tremendous consideration for the suspect must be shown. This interrogator must very carefully avoid expressing any belief in the suspect's innocence, yet indicate convincingly that he or she can understand that there must be powerful, underlying reasons for the reluctance of the suspect to discuss certain problems. If the suspect becomes convinced that this interrogator is a sensitive, understanding person, he or she may overcome the fear that is demonstrated as defiance, and confess.

## Oral and Recorded Statements and Confessions

An oral statement or confession is competent legal evidence, providing it was given voluntarily and can be so proven in court. Recorded, sound motion picture or videotaped statements or confessions are also competent legal evidence if given voluntarily. The testimony of a witness who can authenticate that the recording, motion picture or videotape is an accurate reproduction of what occurred is required.

## SUMMARY

An *interrogation* is a formal and systematic questioning of a suspect under the assumption that the suspect will resist efforts to gain the information desired. The objective of an interrogation is the discovery of facts.

An *admission* is the acknowledgment that a fact, action or circumstance is true. A *confession* is a complete statement admitting each element of the crime. Statements given voluntarily, without any compelling influences (such as promises or hope of reward, coercion, or judicial compulsion) are admissible in evidence. If a suspect in custody is to be interrogated regarding involvement in a criminal offense, he or she must be fully advised of the constitutional rights against self-incrimination (*Miranda* warning).

Ideally, an interrogation should be conducted in an interrogation room at a police agency where there is privacy and a minimum of distractions. If desired, secretarial or electronic recording facilities should also be available. Ideally, an interrogation should be free of time constraints on the part of the suspect and the interrogator. In some instances, it may be totally improper for any person to interrogate the suspect other than the investigators working the case. This is because no one else may have the necessary intimate knowledge of all known details in the investigation.

Interrogation is an art at which a high level of proficiency is attained through practical application of various techniques. The initial approach to a suspect will be determined by a careful evaluation of the suspect and his or her relationship to the case. The majority of the interrogation approaches fall under either the *logical approach,* the *emotional approach,* or a combination thereof. The interrogator's conduct must not go beyond accepted legal limits.

Questions asked by the interrogator should not suggest or call for, a "yes" or "no" answer. If the suspect begins a narrative story, he or she must not be interrupted. Premature notetaking can "turnoff" a suspect who has begun to talk. On occasion, it may be necessary to allow the suspect a face-saving device. The interrogator should usually avoid the use of terminology that may increase the incriminating atmosphere of the interrogation or emphasize the penalty that may ensue to the suspect. A display of empathy and understanding can facilitate the establishment of rapport with the suspect.

An effective interrogation can often be facilitated by minimizing the seriousness of the crime to the suspect. The interrogator must be alert for spontaneous remarks by the suspect that indicate guilt and can be admitted as evidence. The interrogator should terminate the interrogation in a manner that permits reopening the session at a later date.

A willing suspect is usually the remorseful or conscience-stricken one, who feels anguish or distress from a sense of guilt for the crime committed. The inadequate suspect is usually unable to render information because of an emotional conflict resulting from incompatible, or opposing, psychological needs. An unwilling suspect may refuse to cooperate for one or more of a variety of reasons, such as feelings of guilt, fear, love, hate, jealousy or revenge, or a combination of these. This type of suspect may be an egotist who needs to be encouraged with flattery by the interrogator.

The suspect may also be a defiant type, the defiance caused by a deep-rooted fear of appearing perverted or immoral if he or she confesses. If the conventional, logical or emotional approaches fail to break down the suspect's defiance, a trick and bluff technique may be in order.

A voice-recorded oral confession or statement, sound motion picture or videotape is competent legal evidence if given voluntarily by the suspect.

# DISCUSSION QUESTIONS

1. List the objectives of an interrogation.
2. Define an admission and a statement.
3. Identify the legal constraints regarding statements made by suspects.
4. What is the *Miranda* admonition and when is it required?
5. Discuss the issues of voluntariness relative to statements.
6. Where should an interrogation take place, and who should interrogate?
7. Discuss the principles of evaluating a suspect.
8. Contrast the logical and emotional approaches to interrogation.
9. Discuss intentional omissions, lies, and qualifications by a suspect.

# WRITTEN STATEMENTS AND CONFESSIONS

**11**

## KEY TERMS AND CONCEPTS

Written statements (purpose of)
Confessions (purpose of)
Statements (format)
Dying declaration

Criminal investigation requires the interviewing of victims and witnesses and the interrogation of suspects. Although the recording of all pertinent information via notetaking is a standard practice by investigators, the taking of written statements and confessions is also required. Care must be exercised in this process to insure the validity of all information obtained and to preserve its evidentiary value. This admonition is of particular importance in regard to admissions and confessions because the constitutional rights of the accused are directly at stake.

## GUIDELINES FOR WRITTEN STATEMENTS AND CONFESSIONS

Following a "standard" format (discussed below) is very helpful in assuring that a logical sequence is followed and that critical steps are not omitted.

### Purpose of Written Statements

*   To provide a written record of all pertinent information

- To provide a written statement with which to refresh the memory of witnesses and to curtail attempts to change testimony at a later date

- To provide both the prosecution and defense with the testimony that may be expected at the trial

## Suggested Format for Written Statements

### Heading

The heading should include the date, time and location where the statement was made. It should also include a complete identification of the person(s) making the statement, the person(s) taking down the statement, and any other persons present.

### Body

It is important to realize that a statement may be taken in any form that suits the occasion. The acceptability of the statement as evidence in a court of law is not affected by its form. The statement may be either oral, written in question-and-answer form, totally narrative, or a combination of any of these.

### Phraseology

The phraseology of the statement must reflect that of the person who is making it (i.e., intelligence, colloquial expressions, profanity, self-serving comments, half-truths, omissions, lies, etc.). If the statement is completely, or more than half, a narrative telling of events and circumstances by the person making it, maintaining the phraseology of the maker is no problem. However, if it is totally, or more than half, a question-and-answer statement, care must be taken to avoid questions that call for yes or no answers. Questions should be framed in a manner that encourages narrative answers by the suspect, such as, "What did you do then?"

### Chronological Order

The interrogator must guide the person making the statement using questions or prompting remarks to cover all the pertinent activities related to the crime in a chronological (time sequence) order.

### Corpus Delicti

The interrogator must be intimately familiar with all the elements of the crime under investigation and the manner and degree of proof required for each. It is imperative that all the above elements, the *corpus delicti,* be included in the statement. This may at times require guiding the person making the statement back to a given point in it, or into a review of certain portions of it, to assure the desired coverage. In the end, the interrogator must recall the aforementioned admonition, namely, that some persons may be incapable of making a complete statement for any number of reasons. It is better to settle for part of the facts than none at all.

### *Methods*

Sometimes the person making the statement will request to write it out or dictate it to a stenographer or tape recorder. Either of these methods has an advantage as to the weight (credibility) the statement will be given in court. A statement in the maker's own handwriting would be difficult to refute, as would his or her dictation or voice on a tape. However, there are basic disadvantages inherent in these methods. The person making the statement may omit elements of the crime and other pertinent details, include extraneous or irrelevant matter, and fail to maintain a chronological order in covering various events.

Normally, interrogators prefer to take statements in a combination of question-and-answer and narrative style. The statement may be written down by the interrogator, taken by a stenographer, or recorded by electronic tape, videotape or motion picture.

### *Reviewing the Statement*

When the statement has been completed and recorded in one manner or another and is ready for a signature, it must be reviewed with the maker. The person making the statement must read the complete text; or, if illiterate, it must be read to him or her. The maker must be allowed to make and initial any corrections or deletions he or she desires and to number and initial each page of the statement as a protection against deletions or additions of pages. If the statement is an admission or confession, one or more witnesses besides the interrogator should be present when the statement is reviewed.

### *End of Statement Paragraph*

When the statement has been reviewed and corrected, the interrogator should add a concluding paragraph. This paragraph should state that the maker has read (or has had read to him or her) the entire text consisting of x-number of pages, and that he or she has initialed all corrections, additions, deletions and pages.

In the case where the statement is an admission or confession, the concluding paragraph must also state that the suspect made the statement freely, voluntarily, without coercion, and without promises or hope of reward.

### Signing the Statement

The maker should sign the statement just below the last paragraph, in the presence of the interrogator and witnesses, if possible. The interrogator should then sign the statement as a witness, as would anyone else acting as a witness.

# DYING DECLARATIONS

There are times when an investigator will be required to take a statement from a dying victim in a homicide case. Such a statement is commonly known as a dying declaration, and is admissible in court as evidence against an accused if the statement is based on the victim's personal knowledge, and is made under a belief of immediate, impending death. Therefore, the victim must know the circumstances under which he or she received the injury, and must be convinced that he or she is dying from it. The courts permit an investigator or person who hears the dying declaration to testify to such a statement (this is an exception to the "hearsay rule"), because it is believed that a person who knows that death is near will not lie.

It is imperative that the investigator fashion any questions asked of the dying victim in a manner that will require answers or physical acts from which it can be concluded that the dying victim knows the circumstances of the injury and truly believes he or she is then dying.

It is obvious that the detailed who, what, where, when, how, and why of the circumstances may, in many instances, be impossible to obtain from a dying victim. The investigator may have to settle for limited responses to the basic questions: "Do you believe you are dying now?" Answer: "Yes." "What happened to you?" Answer: "Beauregard Throckmorton shot me."

*Note:* If the victim does not die, his or her dying declaration cannot be testified to by the investigator; it is inadmissible hearsay. In future court proceedings, the victim must testify personally as to any injury inflicted by the accused.

# SUMMARY

Criminal investigation requires the taking of written statements and confessions, and care must be exercised to ensure the validity of the information obtained and to preserve its possible evidentiary value. The purpose of such statements and confessions is to provide a written record of testimony that can be expected at a trial, and to provide material with which to refresh the memories of the makers, as well as to curtail attempts to change testimony.

The heading of the statement should include the date, time, and location where the statement was made, as well as the full identity of the person making it and the person(s) taking it down. The statement may be oral or written, in question-and-answer format, or totally narrative, or a combination of all of these. The words and phraseology of the statement should reflect that of the person making it, and questions calling for a yes or no answer should be generally avoided. All pertinent activities relating to the crime should be covered in chronological order, and it is imperative that all the elements of the crime (corpus delicti) be included in the statement if at all possible.

The statement may be written by the suspect, the interrogator, taken by a stenographer, or recorded by electronic tape, videotape, or motion picture.

When the statement is completed, it should be reviewed with the maker, who should initial any corrections or deletions, and number each page in the presence of a witness(es). The ending paragraph should confirm that the maker has read, or has had read to him or her, the entire statement and that he or she has initialed all corrections or deletions. In the case of an admission or confession, the final paragraph must also indicate that the statement "was made freely and voluntarily." The maker should sign the statement just below the last paragraph. The interrogator and other witnesses should also affix their signatures to the document.

Sometimes an investigator may take a dying declaration from a victim. A statement of this type is admissible as evidence (this is an exception to the "hearsay rule"). The wording of the statement must indicate that the victim knows the circumstances under which he or she received the injury and must have a hopeless belief that death is imminent. Admissibility of a dying declaration is based on the belief that a person who knows death is near is not likely to lie. If the victim recovers, the dying declaration cannot be admitted in evidence.

# DISCUSSION QUESTIONS

1. Explain the purposes for written statements and confessions.
2. What information should be included in the heading of a statement?
3. What information should be included in the body of a statement?
4. Explain the importance of phraseology in a statement.
5. Why is it important to follow a chronological order in a statement?
6. Discuss the importance of corpus delicti as it applies to a statement.
7. Discuss the various methods of taking and recording statements.
8. Evaluate the procedure for reviewing a statement.
9. List the required contents of the ending paragraph of a statement.

# INVESTIGATIVE GUIDELINES FOR SELECTED CRIMES AND SCENES

12

## KEY TERMS AND CONCEPTS

Signs of death
Cause of death (determination of)
Autopsy
Wound identification
Adipocere
Mummification
Post-mortem protocol
Robbery investigation
Burglary investigation
Vehicle theft
Forcible rape
Abused children (indicators of)
Arson laws

    The investigative guidelines discussed below are intended to demonstrate that each type of crime or investigative scene is, in one sense or another, a special situation requiring certain techniques and treatments that are in some way unique to that scene or crime. Seasoned criminal investigators have learned through experience to understand and appreciate the value of utilizing what may be called programmed techniques when conducting investigations. The guidelines are based on practical experience and "investigative hindsight," and are designed to lead the investigator through several selected scenes in an appropriate and orderly step-by-step sequence. A coverage of all possible situations in this manner would be a task beyond the scope of this text, so it must be realized that these guidelines are to serve as "reminders for the investigator." Any section of a guideline can be modified to include whatever action the circumstances of the scene require, in keeping with the investigative techniques covered in other chapters.

# DEATH SCENES

It has been estimated that approximately 25 percent of all deaths require investigative services by law enforcement agencies. An officer or investigator responding to a scene where a death is alleged to have occurred must not take this allegation for granted; rather, one should exercise investigative judgment in reaching a determination that the victim is, in fact, dead. Normally, a physician or coroner determines if death has occurred at a scene, yet many jurisdictions permit paramedic and rescue units to make this finding.

## Has Death Occurred?

It is important that the peace officer or investigator know those body conditions that must be checked to determine if death has occurred. If there are any signs of life, the investigator's first action is to attempt to preserve it. Svensson and Wendel in their book, *Techniques of Crime Scene Investigation,* state: "As a rule, it is reckoned that death occurs when the breathing ceases, the heart no longer beats, and the pulse cannot be detected. These changes in vital functions cannot, however, be considered as certain signs of death, but the following are unquestionable signs of death:

- Changes in the eyes
- Coldness of the body
- Rigidity of the body
- Livid stains on the body
- Signs of putrefaction

### Changes in the Eyes

After death, the cornea will lose its luster and its sensitivity and reaction when touched by a foreign object. The pupils generally lose their symmetry and appear egg-shaped. If these conditions exist, death has probably occurred.

### Coldness of the Body

This is indicated by a drop in the body temperature; and the body feels cold after eight to twelve hours. Under average circumstances, a body will lose 1.5°F of body temperature per hour following death, and will attain the temperature of the surrounding air, water, or other material after eight to twelve hours. The speed of cooling, also depends on the amount of flesh and covering on the body. A police officer can best estimate the temperature of a body by checking the armpit.

### Rigidity of the Body (Rigor Mortis)

*Rigor mortis* is the stiffening of muscles in the body after death caused by chemical changes in the muscle tissues. The onset and speed at which rigor mortis will set in varies according to a number of circumstances. For example, the physical build and muscular development of the deceased may well affect the time. It has been noted that in deaths occurring under violent muscular strain, rigor mortis appears more quickly than usual. It is well established that heat accelerates rigor mortis rather than retarding it. The combinations of variables that affect the phenomenon are numerous, but some acceptable rules of thumb to work with are given below. On the average the rigor mortis cycle is:

1. The jaws and neck—2 to 4 hours

2. The mid-torso and legs—4 to 8 hours

3. The arms and remainder of the body—8 to 12 hours

4. Body will remain in rigor mortis—12 hours

5. Rigor mortis will leave the body in the same sequence as it began

6. Cycle completed—36 hours

### Livid Stains on the Body (Post-mortem Lividity)

When death occurs and the heart is no longer active, the blood in the body will drain to the lowest parts of the body nearest the floor or whatever base the body is resting on. Only constrictions or pressure will prevent this settling of blood caused by force of gravity. Thus a body lying on its back during this blood-settling period will not develop lividity in those parts of the body that are pressed directly to the floor, because the pressure at those points will prevent the blood from draining any lower (see Figure 12-1).

In the case of a hanging, where the body has remained in that position for a sufficient period of time, some lividity will appear above the constriction (noose) as well as in the legs and hands. Post-mortem lividity is usually violet-reddish in color, except that where carbon monoxide or cyanide poisoning is involved, in which case the markings are decidedly reddish. This lividity is normally noticeable in two hours after death and will generally be well developed in four to eight hours.

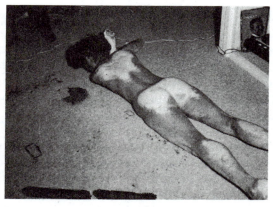

*Figure 12-1 Post-mortem lividity on body of victim who died on her back and was subsequently rolled over approximately eight hours after death occurred.*

Once the lividity has settled in, it will not change if the body is moved. The position of the lividity on a body in relation to the position in which the body is found can indicate to the investigator if the body was moved sometime after death. Suspects have often moved the clotted bodies of their victims hours after death occurred, being unaware of the post-mortem lividity factor. They have thus left a valuable clue for investigators.

The investigator can be certain that death has occurred if the body shows signs of putrefaction (decay). If putrefaction is somewhat advanced, the odor from the body is unmistakable. Normally, the first signs of putrefaction are a greenish discoloration of the skin on the abdomen and a softening of the eyeballs. Heat, cold, dryness and water all affect the speed at which body tissues decompose, bacteria will multiply and putrefaction will develop.

Oxygen and moisture will enhance putrefaction and extreme cold will deter it, yet a body in cold water will remain outwardly normal in appearance for some time. In one case, a small boy drowned and lay at the bottom of a swimming pool where his body was concealed by algae for 23 days. When the gas formation in the body caused it to rise to the surface, there were no external signs of putrefaction. The 32°F temperature of the water at the bottom of the pool and the lack of oxygen present, prevented outward putrefaction.

*Note:* If the investigator determines, by preliminary observations and interviews of witnesses at the scene, that death has occurred or if death has been pronounced by qualified medical personnel—the next concern must be, if the death was due to natural causes. If the death was natural, the investigator will be guided by the reporting procedures of the jurisdiction involved. If the death was not natural, the investigator should proceed with the crime scene investigation techniques covered in Chapter 5.

The importance of complete crime scene coverage is obvious in a homicide, yet is sometimes overlooked in apparent suicides and accidental deaths. A complete investigation of an apparent suicide may prove the death was, instead, an accident or even a murder. On occasion, a suicide will have the outward appearance of a homicide, which may be coincidental or by design on the part of the deceased for insurance or some other reason. Accidental deaths require a complete investigation, because negligence may be the prime cause of death and a reason for criminal prosecution. It is not uncommon today to find criminal prosecutions of employers arising from the accidental deaths (at work) of their employees, wherein the employer has been grossly negligent in providing safe working conditions. The guidelines that follow are offered with the reminder that nothing should be touched, moved, or altered until it has been identified, measured, printed and photographed.

# DETERMINING CAUSE OF DEATH

In some cases the cause of death may appear obvious to the investigator (e.g., the deceased's throat cut from ear to ear, the head blown off by a rifle blast through the mouth, or the deceased may be hanging with his or her neck in a noose). In other cases, the cause of death may not appear obvious and will require a detailed examination (including an autopsy) by the coroner or medical examiner.

In any case, the coroner has a responsibility for inquiring into, and determining the circumstances, manner and cause of death, in all cases where there are reasonable grounds to suspect that the death was caused by an act of another person through criminal means. The interview of witnesses may reveal the cause of death. Regardless of whether or not the death was witnessed, an examination of the body must be made.

## Examination of the Body

A detailed examination of the body will be made after measurements for the sketch, applicable fingerprints and photographs have been taken as described in Chapter 5. The external appearance of the body must be carefully observed and described in the investigator's notes, and necessary close-up photos must be taken to cover:

1. Cause of death, if apparent

2. Weapons or means used, if apparent

3. Condition of the body: coldness, bloodiness, degree of decomposition, state of rigor mortis, lividity, position, etc.

4. Clothing: kind, condition (e.g., torn, disarrayed, etc.). Describe jewelry, if any

5. Location and appearance of wounds or signs of violence: close-up photos (in color, if possible) are a must

6. Presence of blood: size, shape and degree of coagulation of spot(s) or pool(s)

7. Condition of the eyes, mouth (opened or closed). If mucous, saliva, blood or vomit are present, note the amount, direction and flow

8. Color of skin

9. Hands and fingernails: hands may be enclosed in paper bags to preserve evidence potentials (e.g., fingernail scrapings)

10. Shoes should be examined for debris and other substances

11. Has the body been moved? If so, by whom: relatives, ambulance crew, etc.

12. Before moving body, if possible (e.g., it is on a hard surface) draw an outline of the body on the surface with chalk

13. When the body is moved, check the underside and the surface the body was lying on for possible evidence

An investigator should generally not search the deceased for the purpose of learning his or her identity. This information can be obtained from the coroner when it is available. *Note:* On homicides, prior to the removal of the body by the coroner, the investigator should make arrangements for color and black and white photos of the body and a later undressing and cleaning of wounds. In addition, he or she should request fingerprints, hair samples from the head, eyebrows and pubic area and fingernail scrapings from the body. All clothing and other property on the body should be carefully preserved for laboratory examination. The collecting, handling and preservation of all other evidence found at the scene should be done in keeping with the techniques discussed in Chapter 5.

## Hangings or Strangulations

In a hanging, the method or object used may be obvious (e.g., the body is still hanging). A careful search of the premises will determine if the object used (rope or other ligature) came from the premises or was brought there. This may indicate planning on the part of the suspect in a homicide or the victim in a suicide. In any event, the body should not be cut down until all necessary examinations, photos, etc. are completed. Never cut a rope or other ligature at the knot. Leave the noose on the neck for examination and removal by the pathologist or coroner.

In strangulation cases, the procedure is very similar except that the body will not be hanging and the method and/or object used may be much less obvious if it is not left on the body. Never cut or remove a ligature from a body; leave it for examination and removal by the pathologist or coroner.

# AUTOPSY BY CORONER OR MEDICAL EXAMINER

The coroner may be an elected or appointed official who maintains a quasi-judicial function. The medical examiner is usually an appointed forensic pathologist. Some jurisdictions have combined the two positions into one office known as the medical examiner-coroner. The coroner is (or will usually have on his or her staff) a forensic pathologist. This combined office is attained either through the election or appointment process.

In years past, the autopsy was often the only means of determining the cause of death. Today the forensic pathologist utilizes the services of the anesthesiologist, radiologist, odontologist, toxicologist, psychologist and psychiatrist. In addition, modern instrumentation (such as the scanning electron microscope and the transmission electron microscope) are enabling the discovery of details heretofore not possible.

The forensic pathologist is an important component of the investigation and can render great assistance to the investigator. Many coroners allow investigators to attend the autopsies. It is recommended that the investigator attend, if possible, (particularly in questionable or sensitive cases) when the cause of death is complicated and very difficult to detect, or the case is part of a series of deaths.

In addition to answering a number of questions imperative to the investigation, the pathologist can, on a one-to-one basis, discuss the following important events with the investigator if the latter attends the autopsy:

- Discuss the methodology and the reasons for its use during the autopsy.

- Each finding of the autopsy can be pointed out and explained while in progress.

- The investigator can witness the comparison of the weapon in custody with the wound made on the body.

# IDENTIFICATION OF THE DECEASED

In many cases the identification of the deceased may be made at the scene by relatives or friends or determined from personal identification and other belongings. On occasion fingerprints, photographs, tattoos, and identifiable moles or scars can be utilized in this process if the body is not decomposed. If the body is somewhat decomposed, visual identification may not be possible even by the deceased's family. In this event, positive identification is often made by an odontologist from a study of the various defects and irregularities in the teeth (i.e., dental work—fillings, crowns, bridges), the amount of wear of the teeth or evidence of disease. The odontologist can compare his or her findings with existing past dental records and X-rays of the deceased.

Very extreme cases of decomposition or skeletons present a more difficult problem for identification. This study by a scientist is called *forensic anthropology*. It is not the intent of the writer to treat this subject in great detail here, but rather to point out some of the questions the scientist seeks to answer in his or her study to establish identity.

When the case involves an attempt to identify the remains of a known person that are almost skeletal, the task is easier than in the case where the remains are those of an unknown person. The known individual may have existing medical and dental records. Information as to sex, age, race, and other physical characteristics is also available. This data is obviously lacking in the case of an unknown person.

## Unknown Remains

The scientist is faced with the following questions in establishing the identity of an unknown person:

1. Are the remains human? Usually this is not difficult to determine by tissue tests.

2. If the remains are human, how long has the person been dead? The greater the amount of tissue still present, the easier it is to determine the amount of time evolved in decomposition. If all that remains is a skeleton, the study is much more complex. Charles E. O'Hara in his text, *Fundamentals of Criminal Investigation* states: "Considerable number of years are required for the disappearance of tissue in a buried body. If only bones are discovered, it may be said that they have been buried for a very long time."

3. Are the remains those of a male or female? Although the skull and long-bones of the male are generally larger and heavier and

contain other characteristics that mark the difference, the most commonly referred to difference is found in the pelvis. Harrison C. Allison in his book, *Personal Identification*, states: "In general the ilia (hip bones) in the female may be said to have a dish-like shape, while those of a male are more bowl shaped. The opening from the upper pelvis in the female tends to be larger and more rounded than in the male."

4.   What was the approximate age of the person at the time of death? The transformation of hyalin cartilage into bone progresses from birth through the preadolescent and postadolescent stages and into maturity. An estimate as to age can be made from a study of this transformation. An examination of the pelvis will also provide a reliable estimate as to the age of the person at the time of death.

     According to Harrison C. Allison: "The *symphysis pubis* is the point or near contact of pubic bones. These two bones do not fuse, but are separated by a disc of fibrocartilage. Changes in shape and surfaces take place with advancing age. In youth the surfaces are rigid, much like the wind waves of sand on the desert. By age 20, these ridges begin to be reduced and the outer rim becomes more oval in shape. By the late thirties and early forties the surface will become smooth. Above age 50 a breakdown is noted which continues on throughout the remainder of life." An estimate of age can also be made from the study of the teeth (e.g., the wear on chewing surfaces, transparency of the roots, loosening of the teeth and closed root openings).

5.   What was the race of the deceased? There is a tremendous variability of characteristics in bones within a given racial group. Moreover, many of the characteristics found in one racial group are also found in others. Thus, it is not surprising that any discussion of race differences that may be identifiable from bones is highly controversial.

     In the light of the evident mixtures of races in the world today, it is reasonable to say that there are really no pure races. It is further apparent that it is impossible to do no more than deal in limited probabilities when attempting to identify the race of the deceased from bones.

# IDENTIFICATION OF WOUNDS, BRUISES AND MARKS

The identification by the pathologist of wounds, bruises and other indications of trauma on a body is a part of the autopsy. The source or cause of the wounds may also be determined. During this process it can be determined whether the wounds are defense wounds, mutilations, or self-inflicted (suicide). It can also be determined whether or not any bullet wounds are the contact type.

## Lacerations

A *laceration* is a tear in the tissue caused by a direct or indirect blunt force. The tear may be of the skin or of the internal tissue, such as the wall of the stomach. When the skin is attached to bone, the wound has ragged edges.

## Incised Wounds

An *incised wound* is a cut produced by a sharp edge being drawn across tissue under pressure. For examples of incised (defense) wounds on the inside of the hand of a murder victim (see Figure 12-2).

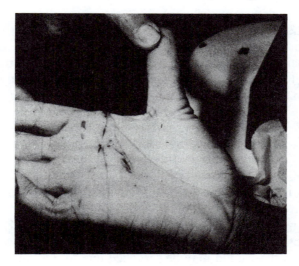

*Figure 12-2 Incised defense wounds on murder victim. (Courtesy of Los Angeles Police Dept.)*

## Stab or Puncture Wounds

A stab or puncture wound is produced by the penetration of tissue with a sharp, rigid, usually slender weapon with a point. However, the weapon need not have a sharp edge (see Figure 12-3).

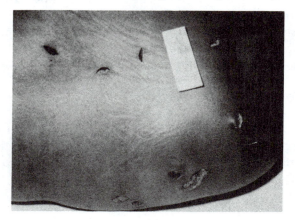

*Figure 12-3 Stab wounds produced by a small kitchen knife.*

## Gunshot Wounds

"When a bullet strikes the body, the skin is first pushed in and then perforated while in the stretched state. After the bullet has passed, the skin partially returns to its original position, and the entry opening is drawn together and is smaller than the diameter of the bullet." (Svensson and Wendel, *Fundamentals of Criminal Investigation*, pp. 337.)

## Contact or Near-Contact Wounds

A *contact wound* is one where the muzzle of the gun is placed against or near the body and the gun is fired. Normally the wound is larger than the diameter of the bullet due to the additional force of the expanding gas that has not escaped and enters the wound. The edge of the contact wound may invert and powder will be in the wound. The skin around the wound may be scorched due to the flame from the muzzle. A near-contact wound may also be surrounded by a ring (tattooing) caused by unburned powder.

## Entrance Wound From a Distance

This wound appears as described under "Gunshot Wounds." In addition, the wound contains no powder, tattooing or scorched skin.

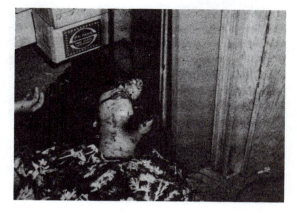

*Figure 12-4 Near-contact wound under the chin with a shotgun.*

## Exit Wound

If the shot was fired from a distance it may appear the same as the entrance wound. However, it may be larger than the diameter of the bullet if the bullet has been deflected in going through the body or has shattered a bone.

In cases of contact or near-contact wounds in the head, the bullet will not always exit. Bullets fired from small-caliber guns into the head may not shatter when striking bone and scatter throughout the brain, or may not shatter and not exit due to lack of velocity. However, a near-contact wound under the chin from a high velocity weapon will cause a large exit wound.

## Ligature Marks and Bruises

Some ligatures used in strangulations (i.e., towels, tablecloths, etc.) may not leave very distinctive marks on the victim's neck. In the following figure, the victim was beaten with fists, stabbed with a small pocket knife, and strangled with a leather boot-lace. The bruises, stab wounds and ligature marks are apparent in Figure 12-5.

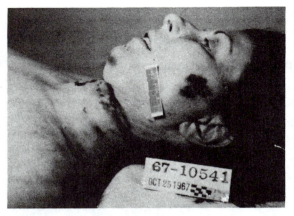

Figure 12-5 Bruises from fists, stab wounds from pocket knife, and ligature marks from bootlace on murder victim.

# HOMICIDE, SUICIDE OR ACCIDENT INVESTIGATION

Some cases of sudden death present unique problems for the investigator. At times it is not readily apparent whether the death is a homicide, suicide or an accident. There are several questions that should be answered expediently when examining the death scene.

1.  What is the cause of death?

2.  Could the victim have produced the injuries or brought about the effect which caused death?

3.  Are there signs of struggle?

4.  Where is the weapon, instrument or object which caused the injuries, or traces of the medium which caused death?

The causes of death may be obvious, such as gun shot wounds, stab wounds, strangulation, etc., or there may be no externally visible sign that indicates an obvious cause of death. In cases where the cause of death is obvious, it is important to determine if the deceased could have produced the injuries himself or herself, or could have brought about the effect which caused death. In cases of suspected suicide wherein the wound from a firearm was believed self-inflicted, the gun would have been fired from a short distance. If the firearm is a rifle or shotgun, it will usually be a direct contact wound. It should be evident whether or not the deceased could physically have accomplished the firing, considering the length of weapon, position and arm reach, entrance wound and how the trigger was depressed. The firearm will usually be near the body.

If the deceased could not have physically accomplished the above, a homicide should be suspected. Other cases of suicide are quite obvious whether the act was accomplished by hanging, poison, gunshot, pills, etc. Many victims leave notes. Others have made threats of suicide to friends and relatives or have previously attempted suicide. In suicides by knife wounds, the wounds are usually within easy reach of the victim's arm, neck, wrists or thighs or at an artery that will cause rapid bleeding. On occasion, "hesitation wounds" (cuts) will be present around the area of the fatal wound, indicating the victim experimented before completing the act.

Occasionally, an ostensibly normal, happy, successful (i.e., everything to live for) person commits suicide and his or her death puts family and friends into a state of shock and disbelief. The natural reaction of loved ones is to maintain that the death was an accident. On occasion, someone will even move the death weapon found at the scene or try to explain away ropes, chains or other ligatures used for hanging as part of an "experiment" or "research." In the case of a shooting, the family may claim the deceased was "cleaning his gun."

The most common alleged accident is the overdose of pills. Many suicides have been attributed to an "accidental" overdose. It is the policy of experienced investigators to search for the truth, and often a background investigation of the victim will reveal the motive for the suicide. Common motives may include: teenage pregnancy, a homosexual life of many years standing unknown to family and friends, a well-concealed drug addiction, embezzlement, a youngster's failure to meet the success demands of parents, a warped sibling rivalry, undetected mental illness, etc.

It is understandable that a family may not want to, or ever accept, suicide as the cause of death. The investigator, however, has the legal responsibility of establishing fact. The above is not to be construed as to indicate that accidental deaths do not occur; they do. Generally a thorough coverage of the death scene and background investigation of the victim can resolve the question of homicide, suicide or accident.

# ESTIMATING THE TIME OF DEATH

When the investigator does not have a reliable witness to the decedent's death, it is imperative to the case that an estimate as to the time of death be determined. There is, at present, no single independent method for the determination of the post-mortem interval, i.e., the time interval between death and the discovery of the body. However, the forensic pathologist may arrive at an estimate as to the time of death, by examination of the body and the use of supportive autopsy findings as follows:

1.  Changes in the eyes

2.  Coldness of the body

3.  Rigidity of the body (rigor mortis)

4.  Livid stains on the body (post-mortem lividity)

5.  Signs of putrefaction (decay)

6.  Rectal and liver temperature

7.  Amount of urine in the bladder

8.  The stomach contents (i.e., type of food ingested and degree of digestion)

Notwithstanding all the above scientific evaluation, the importance of the evidence and information obtained at the death scene by the investigator cannot he overemphasized. The time the deceased was last seen alive, the condition of the location where the body was found (if at home check newspapers for dates, mail in the mailbox, utensils, dishes and food in the kitchen, lights or TV on or off) and a detailed account of the victim's last hours alive, must all be determined.

## Adipocere

This is a condition that replaces putrefaction (decay) in a dead body. It is useful to the pathologist in estimating the time of death. Adipocere occurs when the fats in the body undergo hydrogenation (to add hydrogen to the molecule of an unsaturated organic compound). This hydrogenation occurs when a body is continuously exposed to moisture, not necessarily immersed in water. During this process the fats on the outer surface of the body turn into fatty acids and the outer tissues are converted into a yellowish-white waxy substance. In a moderate climate it will take up to a year for a major portion of the body to display adipocere. In a tropical climate, signs of adipocere may appear much sooner.

## Mummification

This is a condition that is not found frequently. It occurs where a body lies in a warm, dry place exposed to a circulation of air. The flesh of the body dehydrates or dries up thus inhibiting putrefaction. Gradually the body becomes hard and dry and leather-like. Research revealed one mummified body found in a California murder. The victim's body was dumped and lay in a warm, dry cover in a canyon for months. The time of death was established by the murderer.

## Post-Mortem Protocol

A post-mortem protocol is an official report of the medical-legal investigation conducted by the office of the medical examiner or coroner. On occasion, the cause of death in a case may be obviously visible to the investigator, as well as to the pathologist, and confirmed by the autopsy (e.g., shootings, stabbings). The "official" cause of death, however, is a determination only the pathologist can make. Some cases require extensive examination and the specialized services of the other scientists previously mentioned before the coroner may certify a cause of death. The following is a synopsis of a post-mortem protocol of an autopsy on a strangulation murder victim (taken from an actual case).

# ANATOMICAL SUMMARY

Death ascribed to: Asphyxia

Due to: Strangulation

Fatal Wounds:

1. Fractures of the thyroid cartilage.
2. Hemorrhage of the esophagus and the thyroid.
3. Cyanosis of the face.
4. Protrusion of the tongue through the mouth.

Respiratory System:    Pulmonary condition marked.

Urogenital System:    Fluid material in the vaginal canal.

External Examination: The body is that of a well-developed, well nourished female of fair complexion weighing 125 pounds, measuring 65 inches in length. The scalp is covered by black hair. The eyes are blue. There is no evidence of trauma on the chest, abdominal wall, upper arms, elbows, forearms, hands and legs.

Fatal Wound: There is a rectangular, small, dark red abrasion on the left side of the neck, just above the left clavicle. It measures 1/2 inch in length and 3/8 inch in width. The abrasion is noted 1 1/2 inches above the clavicle and 2 inches to the left of the midline. There is subcutaneous hemorrhage in the neck just beneath the above abrasion. The neck strap muscles are removed and there is dark red hemorrhage on the right side of the corner of the hyoid bone.

There is a fracture of the hyoid bone noted as well as hemorrhage and fracture of the right corner. There is considerable hemorrhage and a fracture noted at the left thyroid corner. There is also hemorrhage in the posterior wall of the esophagus at the level of the thyroid.

Findings Associated With the Fatal Wound: There are multiple petechial hemorrhages in the conjunctival of both cues, and the right upper eyelid. There are petechial hemorrhages in the epicardium and pleural surfaces of both lungs.

Body Cavities: The pleural and abdominal cavities contain no excess fluid. The lower edge of the liver is 2 cm. below the costal margin the midclavicular line.

Cardio-Vascular System: The heart weighs 240 grams and the normal contour and the pericardial cavity contain no excess fluid. The right ventricle is dilated. The left ventricle is not dilated. The leaflets are normal in number and condition. The aorta and the coronary arteries are normal: there is no evidence of heart disease.

Respiratory System: The right lung weighs 750 grams, and the left, 550 grams. Both lungs are congested and edematous. The trochesbronchial tree contains no obstructive material.

Liver and Biliary System: The liver weighs 1,540 grams, is dark red and congested. The gallbladder contains dark mucoid fluid and the bile ducts are widely patent.

Hemic and Lymphatic System: The spleen weighs 230 grams, is congested; and the bone marrow is dark red.

Endocrine stem: The adrenals, the thyroid gland and the pituitary gland are normal.

Urinary System: The kidneys weigh 395 grams and are normal. The urinary bladder is normal.

Genital System: The external genitalia show no abrasion or contusion. The orifice of the vagina is traumatized, there is injury in the vaginal wall and fluid material; a smear is taken from the vaginal wall. The uterus is normal as is the anal area.

Digestive System: The esophagus has a longitudinally folded mucosa. The stomach contains 95 cc. of masticated food that appears to be toast. The intestines are normal as is the pancreas.

Skeletomuscular System: The clavicles, ribs, vertebrae and pelvic bones are not fractured. The bones of the extremities are not fractured.

Head and Central Nervous System: The brain weighs 1,300 grams. There is no evidence of contusion of the temporal muscles or the subcutaneous tissues of the scalp. There is no blood in the epidural, subdural or subarachnoid spaces of the calvarium. There are no cortical contusions or hemorrhage of the basal ganglia. The cerebellum and brainstem show no abnormalities. There is no skull fracture.

Specimens: Blood was taken for alcohol determination. Representative sections are taken for the hold jar; vaginal smear taken. Results of laboratory examinations of specimens are forthcoming.

The preceding coverage of an autopsy by the coroner has been a basic example. Deaths by poison, sexual perversion, criminal abortion, fire, and dismemberment will require other specialized services by the coroner.

Some deaths may not require extensive follow-up investigation. For example, a clear-cut suicide with all conclusive evidence at the scene, or a shooting with the suspect in custody and all necessary evidence obtained during the crime scene coverage, will not require extensive follow-up. On occasion, the investigator is confronted with a real puzzle requiring the utilization of all the investigative techniques and services thus far discussed to arrive at a solution.

A killing that occurs during the commission of another crime (such as robbery, burglary or rape) is usually coincidental to the other crime. Thus, the investigator who is attempting to identify and apprehend a suspect in a robbery-murder is actually looking for a hold-up man, and so on. The question of motive for the killing in these cases is generally conceded to be that of the basic crime (i.e., robbery, burglary, or rape). In cases where no other crime is involved other than the killing, determining the motive may require a complete background investigation of the victim, including retracing his or her actions from the time he or she was last seen alive up to the time of death. Determination of the motive may narrow down the search for the suspect.

## ROBBERY INVESTIGATION

Robbery is a very common crime in most cities. The suspects range from teenage novices to the strung-out hype, to the professional. The victims range from a drunk in an alley, to a liquor store or bank, to the supermarket or armored truck.

During the past 35 years, the number of "professional" holdup men and gangs has dropped. Many of these "pros" have gone into more lucrative and less violent activities such as dealing in drugs. Robbery crime rates are still high because it is still a fast way to obtain ready cash; it continues to be attractive, especially to the young criminal.

The following outline of investigative guidelines for robbery investigation is offered as a supplement to general techniques previously covered:

*Type:*
1. Business:        Bank
                    Market
                    Liquor Store
                    Street (strong-arm)
                    Bar

Gas Station
Armored Truck, etc.

2. Residence:     Single Family
Apartment (Manager?)
Hotel
Office
Business at Residence

3. Person:        Strong Arm

### Location:
On or close to main streets, freeways or near residential area?
(Complete address)

### Date and Time:
Also day of the week.

### Date and Time Reported to Police:
This can be highly significant. If the clerk telephoned the owner before calling the police, he or she may have been instructed to report a loss higher than actually occurred, in an attempt to defraud the insurance company. Insurance companies keep statistics on robberies. Make use of their information. (They usually know the "professional victims.")

### Type of Property Taken, Value:
Be specific. Many suspects will ask for a particular item just prior to the actual commission of the robbery. A pattern such as this can be extremely helpful.

### Weapons or Force Used:
Excessive force used? Obtain a detailed description of the weapon.

### Trademarks of Suspects:
1.   Actions

2.   Conversations (accents, particular inflections, etc.)

### Vehicle Used by Suspects:
Year, make, body style, color (unusual shades), license number. (*Note:* Body damage, unusual paint, any distinguishing marks, stickers, muffler noise, etc.)

***Suspects:***

1. Name and address if known.

2. You want a "word picture" as well as a listing of routine items such as sex, descent, age, height, weight, hair, eyes, complexion, clothing, etc. Begin at the top of the head and work down. Draw your witness out. He probably remembers more than he thinks he does. Include all distinguishing or unusual features (scars, marks, tattoos, physical defects, etc.) Booking number, if arrested.

***Victim:***

Name, address, phone numbers (residence and business). Double check the phone numbers; an incorrect or omitted phone number may result in much lost time. Also include victim's sex, descent, and age (need complete identification).

***Witnesses:***

Name, address, phone numbers (residence and business), occupation, sex, descent, and age. Where can they be reached during the day? Reconstruct occurrence from statements of victims and witnesses. *Note:* Past experience indicates that the best results are obtained when the victim and witnesses are interviewed separately and out of earshot of one another.

Canvass the neighborhood for witnesses. *Note:* Don't overlook this. A recent string of bank holdups was solved when a witness walking some distance from the scene, observed two men change vehicles. He became suspicious and wrote down the license number of the departing vehicle. This information resulted in the arrest and conviction of two suspects. Crime scene search as per basic techniques. Check stolen cars statewide (may be used by suspects).

***Mug Books of Robbery Suspects:***

Check recent prison releases (obtain descriptions and match against wanted suspects). Check teletypes of other robberies for MO pattern or other information that may fit.

***Hypes:***

Gang files, flyers on wanted criminals, field interrogation cards regarding cars and suspects.

### Information:
From informants in criminal element: bars, hypes, poolrooms and other hangouts.

Criminals with money usually spend it. They generally like to spend it on "booze" and women and in familiar surroundings. Check hangouts of this type. You would not expect to find a poorly dressed, unkempt stickup man in a fashionable night spot, etc.

### Traffic Citations:
Statewide check that may fit the vehicle used in the job. Check MO files in patterns (both local and regional).

### Stakeouts:
See stakeout coverage.

### Response to a Robbery Call:
1. Officers should be alert when responding to a robbery call.

   a. Suspect may have traveled but a short distance from scene.

   b. Search should begin when officers approach the vicinity of the crime.

2. If crime location is adequately covered, other assigned units should concentrate search to surrounding areas (first unit should broadcast that the scene is covered).

3. First unit to arrive should obtain sufficient preliminary working information.

   a. Description of suspects

   b. Description of vehicle used

   c. Time and direction of flight

   d. Weapon used

4. This preliminary data should be transmitted to headquarters for broadcasting.

   a. Permits other units to conduct a more efficient search of the surrounding area

   b. The assigned officers can then return to the victim and obtain more detailed information

    c.   Supplemental information will narrow the field of search to specific individuals, vehicles or areas

5.   Deployment for search of suspects who have just left the scene

    a.   If robbers are to be captured, they must be outguessed and their actions anticipated by investigating officers

    b.   Methods employed will depend upon certain factors

       (1) Method of escape (airlines, bus depots, train depots)

       (2) Time elapsed since commission of the crime

       (3) Distance suspect would be able to travel since the crime as committed, as determined by:

          (a)   Density of vehicular or pedestrian traffic

          (b)   Weather conditions

          (c)   Street construction in the district

          (d)   Any other unusual circumstances which might affect suspect's rate and direction of traffic

    c.   Lobbies and waiting rooms

       (1)   Some suspects seek concealment by sitting in lobbies and waiting rooms.

       (2)   Hope to remain unnoticed by mingling with large groups of people.

       (3)   A transportation waiting room provides access to a means of transportation.

    d.   Bus and streetcar zones

    e.   Business establishments

       (1)   May be near scene of robbery

       (2)   May enter establishments under pretense of transacting business

       (3)   Officers cannot search all business premises, but they can be on the alert for suspects entering or leaving

       (4)   Suspect may have two sets of clothes on, or may have changed clothes

f.  Bars and restaurants

   (1)   Dimly-lit interiors

   (2)   Groups of persons usually present

   (3)   In restaurants suspect will be found

   (a)   In booth

   (b)   At the counter farthest from the door

## Robbers are Dangerous

All robbers should be considered armed and dangerous. Some will kill just for the sake of killing, even when the victim does not resist. We read frequently of a robbery victim being executed by a bandit just before the thief left the scene. Some bandits, high on narcotics or drugs, may panic at the slightest resistance or other provocation. This frequently spells death for the victim.

A lone officer should not enter a location being robbed by more than one suspect. He or she should call for assistance and assume a position of advantage, and should be aware that a getaway car and driver may be nearby. In any case, this action and that of any officers assisting must be designed to minimize danger to the victim and other innocent persons (e.g., customers) present at the scene. It may be necessary to wait for the suspect(s) to emerge from the location before attempting an arrest. Many officers have been killed or taken hostage, or have led suspects into taking victims and witnesses hostage and embarking in wild shootings, by taking premature action. It is difficult, if not impossible, to provide more than general guidelines to follow in responding to a robbery-in-progress scene. Each robbery scene will differ; no one can predict what suspects, victims and witnesses will do under pressure. The officer must rely on training, common sense and a cool head, and must play his or her role according to the circumstances of each case.

# BURGLARY INVESTIGATION

Burglary is another very common crime in both rural and urban communities. It is basically a crime against property rather than people. Notwithstanding this fact, many persons have been injured or killed by burglars. Burglary is a crime of opportunity and will occur as often as the opportunity is presented to the burglar within his area of operation. It is not surprising that burglary continues to be the fastest growing crime. The majority of suspects are young, as indicated by statistics attributing 75 percent of known burglaries to persons under 25 years of age. Many of these young or casual burglars are drug users who support their habits with the proceeds from burglaries, while others burglarize to augment their income or for the thrill derived from stealing. The "professional" burglar, who is motivated by the challenge of planning and carrying out a high class residential or commercial burglary wherein the proceeds are much greater, is generally not a youngster nor a drug addict.

With regard to burglary rates, it is a fact that residential burglaries occur much more frequently than do nonresidential burglaries. Residential burglaries are also increasing faster than nonresidential burglaries, particularly in suburban areas undergoing rapid population growth.

Traditionally, the main target of the typical residential burglar is movable property that can be easily converted to cash (e.g., jewelry, TVs, stereos, furs, etc., and money). Most residential burglaries occur during the day when the residences are unoccupied. This is especially true on weekends. Nonresidential burglaries are more likely to occur at night and on weekends when the business or other premises are closed.

The type of property stolen by the commercial burglar is likely to be that which can be readily converted to cash (e.g., electronic equipment, business machines, typewriters, TV's), and money. However, the availability of good "fences" (receivers of stolen property) will dictate how often the casual and the professional burglar will steal artifacts, large volumes of machinery, clothing, jewelry, etc. Excellent examples of this fact are the phony stolen property receiver fronts ("sting" operations) set up in several major cities in the United States by undercover agents of various city, county, state and federal law enforcement agencies. These fronts (ostensibly retail and wholesale businesses) have received (purchased at much below wholesale prices) millions of dollars in stolen property from burglars.

## The Fence

The *fence* (receiver of stolen property), in many cases, is ostensibly a legitimate business person. As such, he or she is frequently in a position not only to convert stolen goods into cash, but often can function as a source of information to the burglars, as to low risk or lucrative opportunities. Many fences function as a "bank" for burglars, by providing bail money, hideout money, etc. Without fences the majority of the casual burglary system would quickly disappear; it is obvious burglars cannot eat, wear or use all their loot.

Some professionals have their own very private connections (fences) in the United States and foreign countries who convert highly valuable and difficult to dispose of artifacts, jewelry, rare coins, etc., into money. It is not uncommon for this caliber of fence to receive large quantities of valuable jewelry or art and ship it out to other states or countries to prearranged receivers. The receivers will place the items on the market for sale or remove the precious stones from their mountings, recycle the metals in the mountings, and place the stones back into the wholesale market. Art objects are sold to private collectors.

On occasion, a burglar will steal artifacts that are too "hot" for a fence or collector to handle. A case reviewed in research involved the recovery of $1,000,000 in Indian artifacts stolen from a museum. The items were so well-known, their value being primarily historical, that no fence or collector contacted by the burglar would touch them. The burglar was left holding a large quantity of artifacts that he could not convert into the price of a steak dinner. This burglar lacked the organization and planning characteristic of the true professional, otherwise he would have known in advance the lack of fencing potentials of his valuable loot.

## Residential Burglary

Studies by various police agencies indicate that carelessness by citizens in leaving their residences and garages unlocked, or otherwise inadequately secured, perpetuates the opportunity for the burglar to steal. Residences should appear occupied at all times, particularly during the weekend absences of the occupants (i.e., some lights should be left on, both inside and out). Bolt locks on doors and windows can diminish opportunity, and engraved identification on easily pawned entertainment equipment can lessen the ease of conversion of the loot into money.

Unfortunately, burglary and receiving stolen property are not considered serious enough crimes to warrant severe and deterrent sentences by the justice system. One must consider that the confirmed burglar may commit 20 to 30 jobs before being caught. If the suspect is a juvenile, he is apt to be back on the street before the arresting officer ends that day's tour of duty. In the case of the adult burglar, it is not uncommon for the suspect at the time of arrest to be out on bail on three or four previous burglaries. When the sentences are finally determined, they are likely to be light unless the victim was injured by the burglar or the burglar has a long history of convictions. Couple the above circumstances with the ever-ready and available fences and increasing drug addiction among young people, and we have the climate for a perpetual residential burglary problem.

## Non-Residential Burglary

It is often very difficult, if not impossible, for nonresidential premises to appear occupied during nights and weekends when closed. Private patrols to augment police patrols are useful as deterrents; however, the professional burglar (usually a male), who is most likely to be involved as a suspect in a first-class nonresidential burglary, will rarely be caught on his first job. When he is caught he will have enjoyed the proceeds of numerous, often lucrative, burglaries and will face the low risk of heavy punishment. These odds make burglary a gratifying profession for the person who prefers to steal for a living.

## Police Personnel

Police personnel in most cities are necessarily thinly spread to cover all responsibilities to the community served. No city can afford the tax burden of a twenty-four hour police guard at every residence, nor can the owners of nonresidential premises afford private patrol on that basis. If such coverage were possible, it is very doubtful that any community would want to live under such conditions, even if all burglaries were prevented. It is, therefore, logical that many police forces are sponsoring burglary prevention programs within their communities which encourage citizen participation. With a reduction of casual burglaries (by eliminating the obvious opportunities), police could concentrate their available personnel on the professional burglar.

## Investigative Guidelines

The following outline of investigative guidelines for burglary is offered as a supplement to the techniques previously covered.

### Type:
1.  Residence, house, single family, apartment, mobile home, etc.

2.  Nonresidence: store, office, factory, warehouse, gas station, etc.

3.  Occupants: Any present at time of burglary?

### Location:
Complete address with nearest cross street. Description of the residence or building (e.g., size, number of stories, color, etc). Complete identification of resident or occupant.

### Date and Time:
(Day of week) reported. When did occupants last leave location? Were all doors and windows locked? If so, by whom? Where were the keys?

### Visitors:
Were there any recent visitors to premises: relatives, business associates, salesmen, utilities servicemen, poll takers, etc.?

### Entry:
Means and point of entry: evidence of forcible entry on doors, window locks, possible tool marks. If no evidence of forcible entry, check possibility of pass key or lock-trip device (e.g., plastic strip). *Note:* The photography and sketching techniques covered in Chapter Five are used with emphasis on building, point of entry and tool marks.

### Prints:
Fingerprints, footprints, and tire tracks inside and outside (as per Chapter 5).

### Property Taken:
A complete listing of all property taken as per Chapter 3, "Investigator's Notes and Reports." Special attention is given to when the missing property was last seen by the victim. If the property has not been seen for a period of time prior to the break-in, it may have been misplaced or taken on a prior occasion by a relative or visitor. It is important to note what property that would normally be attractive to a burglar was not taken. Why would the burglar limit himself or herself to one type of property only (i.e., drugs, furs, etc.)? This information could furnish a lead as to the suspect.

### Modus Operandi:

1. Type of property attacked: Description.

2. Point of entry: Door, window, roof or transom on front, side or rear of building; on first floor, second or other floor.

3. Means of attack: Tool (e.g., screwdriver, crow bar, key, lock pick, ladder used, ropes, brace-and-bit, chisel, glass cutter, etc). *Note:* On a burglary of a safe, was an explosive used, burning torch, combination and lock punched out, box ripped open with a bar or the combination manipulated?

4. Date, time and day of the week property was attacked.

5. Object of attack (e.g., anything that was available or selected items).

6. Trademark: Assaulted victim, committed nuisance (e.g., urinated, defecated, cut telephone wires, left obscene or other notes, poisoned pets, posed as peddler or handicapped person, looking for employment, used moving van or truck or other vehicle). Did burglar hide-in until business closed? Is burglar a ransacker who leaves a mess (e.g., drawers, doors opened with property scattered, or is he methodical and neat)? Did the burglar help himself to food or drink, or is there evidence that he was familiar with the premises? Did he use matches or leave cigarette butts?

7. Are there other burglaries in the area with the same *modus operandi*?

### Crime Scene Coverage:

The burglary crime scene is covered with the same basic techniques treated in Chapter 5. Special attention should be given to the neighborhood coverage for witnesses and information.

### Follow-Up Investigation:

The follow-up investigation will utilize many of the techniques and services treated in previous chapters (e.g., the *modus operandi* files, arrest records, fingerprint files and field interview card files in the police records system). Informants and other sources of information may furnish leads, as will the analysis and examination of recovered physical evidence by the laboratory.

# VEHICLE THEFT INVESTIGATION

Vehicle thefts are most prevalent in urban cities; so common that some major cities may have one hundred or more vehicles stolen daily. While the total vehicle recovery rates reported by some cities (80% plus) are impressive, many of the vehicles recovered have been stripped to a non-operative condition or wrecked. The non-recovered vehicles are usually processed by commercial vehicle theft rings. The high cost of new vehicles, auto repairs, miscellaneous parts and high performance engines, maintains commercial vehicle theft as a tremendously profitable "business." Commercial thieves will either dismantle vehicles locally for sale as parts, or alter the ownership documents and vehicle for local sale or take the vehicles out of state for disposal. Many stolen vehicles, particularly luxury models, are shipped to foreign countries for sale.

## Registration Counterfeiting

Some vehicle thieves have access to counterfeit registration and ownership document blanks. They prepare them with the false registration and owner information and a false vehicle identification number (VIN). Many states have confidential methods of identifying counterfeit paper from the genuine. This information is furnished to investigators by their respective agencies.

A common method used in altering genuine documents is by using ink eradicator or a caustic solution. The laboratory can identify those alterations that are not otherwise readily apparent to the investigator.

## Vehicle Alterations

Many vehicle thieves will change the VIN plates of motor vehicles. Every domestic motor vehicle manufacturer is required by federal regulation to have a VIN plate attached to the dashboard of each vehicle. The locations of those VIN plates will vary as to the make and model of the vehicle. The method of attaching the VIN plate will be individual with the manufacturer, i.e., two spot welds, round head rivets, rosette head rivets, etc. Any variation in the manner in which the plate is secured to a vehicle is an indication that the vehicle may be stolen.

There are also secret vehicle identification numbers placed by individual manufacturers in very inconspicuous locations on components (e.g., engines, etc.) that vary by make and model. The above information is furnished to law enforcement agencies by the manufacturers. The sophisticated auto thief may attempt to alter, remove, or destroy VIN plates and secret numbers when located (refer to "Numbers Restoration," Chapter Six).

## License Plate Change or Alteration

Changing license plates or altering existing plates is not a difficult task for the commercial thief. The change or alteration in plates may be as simple as the labor involved in removing and securing several metal screws or using a little tape. On the other hand, it may involve re-registering a well-altered vehicle. The author was present in a South American country when a criminalist there identified a luxury vehicle which had been stolen in California, re-registered in Florida, shipped to one South American country, then sold in the other where the author made the observation.

## National Auto Theft Bureau

The National Auto Theft Bureau (NATB) is a private organization, funded by a group of insurance companies. It provides current stolen-vehicle information on a nationwide basis, assists law enforcement agencies in the investigation of commercial motor vehicle theft rings, identification of altered and obliterated identification numbers, and provides training in vehicle theft investigation. The services of the NATB agents are available through various field offices in the United States.

## Motorcycle Thefts

Motorcycle thefts constitute about 15 to 20 percent of the vehicle theft problem. A motorcycle is very vulnerable to theft; it can be picked up and put into a truck, and a protective chain can be cut with bolt cutters. A motorcycle is easy to hot-wire or just roll away, once free from a chain or lock. The recovery rates reported for motorcycles are much less than that for other motor vehicles. This is primarily due to extensive stripping of bikes by thieves, who often leave only an abandoned frame. There is also the alteration of numbers, re-registration and sale of stolen bikes that account for part of the unrecovered numbers.

It is not uncommon for one stolen bike to contain parts from several other stolen bikes and to have been put together and painted in a bike shop or backyard garage. The location of serial numbers on motorcycles vary according to make and model; the frame number is usually the vehicle identification number (VIN) rather than the engine number.

## Suspects in Vehicle Thefts

The "joyrider" is generally a teenager in need of transportation or just getting some kicks out of stealing a vehicle and driving it awhile. This suspect will normally not strip the vehicle and will often abandon it within walking distance of the suspect's home or other destination. The joyrider commits most vehicle thefts.

The commercial vehicle thief may be, and often is, very sophisticated in his or her operation, as previously indicated.

## Investigative Guidelines:

The following outline of investigative guidelines for auto theft is offered as a supplement to previously covered techniques:

### Type:
1. Motor vehicle: year, make, model, body type, color, VIN, license number, state, year

2. Motorcycle: year, make, model, frame type, color, VIN, license number, state, year

3. Present owner (full identification)

### Location of Occurrence:
Complete address, type of premises. Was ignition locked, doors locked, keys in vehicle?

### Date and Time of Occurrence:
Condition of vehicle; stripped or damaged; date and time reported stolen.

### *Person Last Seen Driving Vehicle:*
Name, address and phone number.

### *Suspects:*
Suspects and circumstances surrounding theft and any information connecting vehicle with another crime (e.g., robbery, etc. MO used in theft.

### *Appearance and Actions of Drivers:*
The appearance and actions of the driver of a vehicle may often provide the officer with cause to investigate.

1.  A very young teenager or adult whose appearance and dress does not fit a luxury vehicle, or who seems unfamiliar with the operation of the vehicle (e.g., location of keys, jerky starts and stops, etc).

2.  The driver who slows down and avoids passing a police vehicle, then turns on the first available street.

3.  The driver who attempts to drive away from the scene of a minor traffic accident.

4.  The driver who quickly alights from the vehicle and hurries back to the police car when pulled over. He may also be nervous and give evasive answers to questions by the officer.

### *Appearance of Vehicles:*
The appearance of vehicles may often provide the officer with cause to investigate.

1.  License plates poorly attached to the license plate frame on an otherwise sharp appearing vehicle, i.e., screws loose, attached with wire, etc. Bugs on a rear plate would indicate it came from the front of a vehicle. Out-of-state plates on an in-state plate frame would be cause for suspicion. Investigators should be familiar with the beginning numbers of temporary paper plates in their jurisdiction. The beginning numbers assigned to new cars differ from those assigned to used cars (e.g., "O" or "1," etc). Altered license plates are a good indication the vehicle is stolen.

2.  Vehicles parked overtime in restricted zones, or parked (abandoned) in isolated areas. Vehicles with broken windows or

windwings, or where there is evidence of debris under the vehicles indicating they have been parked at the location for a period of time.

3. The vehicle is stripped, or displays evidence of tampering with the VIN plate, or evidence of hot-wiring (e.g., loose wires near the ignition).

4. Vehicles without registration papers may be stolen. *Note:* There is an obvious irregularity with which motorcycle manufacturers stamp serial numbers on their products. This is causing some measure of difficulty in the identification of valid serial numbers. It is, therefore, advantageous to become familiar with the current practices of the individual manufacturers, i.e., B.S.A., B.M.W., Triumph, Harley Davidson, Honda, Yamaha, etc.

5. Stakeout of Stolen Vehicles: When a vehicle is identified as a stolen vehicle some consideration should be given to the question: has it been totally abandoned, or may the thief return to use it again? If the vehicle has been identified as being used in a series of current crimes, or in even one serious crime, it may be worthwhile to expend some time on surveilling the vehicle. The following circumstances may justify a surveillance:

   a. The vehicle is parked near an entertainment location the suspect may be attending. He may return for the vehicle.

   b. The vehicle's motor is running (i.e., possible getaway car).

   c. The engine, radiator, and exhaust pipe are hot or warm, indicating it was driven recently.

6. Latent Prints and Photography: Recovered stolen vehicles that are identified as being used in connection with other crimes like homicide, robbery, rape, burglary, kidnapping, hit-and-run, etc., are generally examined by a technician for latent prints and photographed expeditiously. The condition of the vehicle (stripped, etc.), availability of field officers or technicians trained in photography and developing and lifting prints, and the agency policy will determine when other recovered vehicles are processed in this manner.

7. Follow-up Investigation: The investigator will utilize the techniques and services treated in previous chapters, in the follow-up investigation of vehicle thefts.

# FORCIBLE RAPE INVESTIGATION

Forcible rape is a very painful, humiliating and traumatic experience for any woman. Many victims cannot believe this violent and degrading experience has happened to them. Some have nightmares and difficulty sleeping afterwards. Many respectable members of society, and a good portion of the criminal element, regard the rapist as scum, yet in some minds the crime of rape is a paradox. Thirty-five years ago, many police officers would believe an alleged rape victim's story only if her body bore marked evidence of violence, i.e., bruises, cuts, etc.

*Rape* is generally defined as a carnal knowledge of the human female against her will or by force and violence. In recent years, community pressures (principally from feminist groups) have brought about a much more sensitive and realistic investigative and judicial approach to the handling of rape cases.

## Attitudes Towards Victims

It is unfortunate that although the police, the judiciary, and the community have to some degree taken a more sensitive and serious interest in the crime of rape, some attitudes still reflect a misunderstanding of the nature of the crime. Forcible rape is a crime of violence rather than a sex crime. It is not uncommon for one to hear that the incidence of rape will continue to increase as long as women feel free to go out alone at night to bars, to work at odd hours and dress provocatively. Such an attitude is extremely provincial and uninformed. If one is to believe that the only way to deter rape is to keep women locked up at home under guard, society is in bad shape indeed!

Some positive community-based programs have been initiated, in cooperation with police agencies, to assist rape victims. Rape victims, especially those who are reluctant to call the police, may contact a rape assistance center and receive counseling and direction regarding important medical procedures to be followed in connection with the police report. These centers also offer follow-up counseling to assist the victim in coping with the emotional and physical trauma suffered.

Some states have enacted legislation designed to increase the sensitivity and proficiency with which public servants handle sexual assaults. In 1976 California, for example, amended its Penal Code and

Health and Safety Code, imposing requirements on the Department of Justice, the Department of Health, and the Commission on Peace Officers Standards and Training, concerning training of personnel regarding protocol, medical examinations, and investigative procedures in connection with sexual assaults.

## Effects on Victims

The effects of rape on victims may vary according to the violence or threat of violence involved in the assault, the age of the victim, her cultural background and prior sexual experience. Most feel degraded, angry, guilty, or in fear of dying, or a combination thereof. Others may go into a state of depression following the assault that can result in suicide if not properly treated. Still other victims go through a gradual emotional breakdown resulting in erosion of their social life and a negative attitude towards sex. It is also obvious that the risk of pregnancy and venereal disease is always present.

## Suspects and Their Motivations

Forcible rape suspects can be found in any ethnic, socioeconomic and intelligence group. Statistics indicate that the age may range from early teens to sixty years of age and over. The majority of forcible rapes are committed by males between the ages of fifteen and thirty. Studies further indicate that rapists commit the majority of their assaults within their own ethnic group, i.e., white suspect, white victim; brown suspect, brown victim; black suspect, black victim. The prime question that remains in the minds of police, the community and behavioral scientists is "why does a man commit forcible rape?" The following information hopefully sheds some light on this question.

## Motivations

One authority on the sexual offender, Dr. B. Karpman in his book, *The Sexual Offender and His Offenses*, states, "In some men only the resistance of the women makes them potent. This is probably the mechanism of rape." A respected criminologist, Vernon Fox states, "Forcible rape is a sex crime according to official crime statistics, however, it is not seen as sex crime by rapists, but rather as a crime of violence and aggression that releases pent-up anger."

In a recent rape awareness seminar presented by the District Attorney of Santa Barbara County in California, sexual assault was studied from the viewpoint of the victim, the police, and the rapist. The statements of Karpman and Fox are reinforced by the interviews of police, victims and rapists in connection with the seminar, which revealed no experience that bore any relation to sexual passion. "The actual feelings experienced by the victims and rapists were those associated with other acts of violence and terror."

Some examples are: "I felt much more a victim of violence than sexual intent," reported Kathy, who was raped while hitchhiking, "His entire attitude was hostile, bitter and angry." Kim, who accepted a stranger's invitation for a cup of coffee and was subsequently raped, states, "He couldn't maintain an erection, but took pleasure in observing my helplessness. I begged him for my safety, and he laughed at me, while threatening to gouge out my eyes and dislocate every bone in my body."

The validity of the above victims' perception was corroborated in the interviews of eight convicted rapists who are inmates at Atascadero State Hospital. For example, Bobby, a sex offender since age twelve, assessed his motivation as follows: "I was trying to get fear from my victims because I was full of fear of women myself. The goal was to completely control a woman and the satisfaction is in the humiliation of women against whom I felt envy and hatred." Verne, an inmate for several years, describes his motive: "It wasn't sex I was looking for, I was angry about something else and I was gonna rape something." *Note:* The use of the word "something," rather than "someone," in reference to the victim.

## The Rape Murder

The ultimate violent unleashing of pent-up anger, revenge and fear within the rapist may result in a rape murder or a series of such crimes. Karpman states, "Rape murders result from aggressive sexual reaction to inner fear. Rapists who murder their victims are motivated by fear of social consequences and by fear of the strength of their own social aggression."

## The Judiciary and Rape

It is apparent that the momentum of the anti-rape efforts primarily of the feminist organizations is being felt in the judiciary. The opinions of a few jurists in various parts of the country, that females wearing tight blouses are inviting rape, has caused a noticeable backlash. At least one judge lost his job, others have been censured or have had their decision on such reasoning reversed. Some states have reacted by enacting legislation that mandates prison terms for first offenders in cases of rape by force or violence. The vast majority of our judges have a very enlightened view of the violent motives behind the crime of rape.

## Investigative Guidelines

The following outline of investigative guidelines for forcible rape is offered as a supplement to previous general techniques covered:

### Location:
Complete address

### Date and Time:
Note time of arrival, also time and date of occurrence

### Victim:
Determine condition; obtain identification. If victim requires ambulance, summon. One officer should accompany victim to hospital.
### Suspect:
If suspect is still at scene, follow arrest procedures (see medical report for physical evidence check).

### Isolate and Protect:
The crime scene, according to procedures in Chapter 5, must be isolated and protected.

### Obtain Identification:
Identify all witnesses; separate for interviews; be certain to identify witness who discovered victim or received first complaint.

### Female Officers:
If practical, a female should be present when victim is interviewed. Interview the victim in privacy; rapport with victim is a must. This is the prime reason for the desirability of a female investigator being present, when at all possible (in the case of female victims). Often the

state of shock and anxiety of the victim will greatly increase the difficulty of relaxing the victim and establishing rapport. The investigator(s) must carefully explain to the victim the necessity for asking piercing personal questions. A detailed account of the entire incident must be obtained, including activities prior to, during and after the crime.

### *Obtain All Information:*
Regarding the suspect's activity; his actions, statements, complete physical description, modus operandi and unusual characteristics.

### *Determine:*
If the scene has been altered or contaminated, i.e., has the victim changed clothing or bathed, discarded any clothing or bedding or cleaned up the crime scene. Collect and preserve bedding, towels, etc.

### *Utilize Crime Scene Techniques:*
(i.e., physical evidence, fingerprints, photos, etc.)

### *Document Victim's Condition:*
Photos of injuries (consent required), condition of clothing, hair, etc.

### *Reconstruct the Crime Scene:*
With victim (verbally), without any physical disturbance of evidence potentials.

### *Collect and Preserve All Evidence:*
(e.g., weapons, ligatures used to tie the victim, etc.) Use techniques previously covered in Chapters 5 and 6. Make appropriate notifications to supervisors and juvenile division, in the case of a minor. Parental or guardian consent is required for medical treatment and/or specimens)

### *Medical Treatment and Specimens:*
1. If practical, a change of clothing should be obtained for the victim, as clothes being worn may be treated as evidence.

2. Transport victim to hospital for medical treatment and collecting of evidence of sexual assault.

3.  Doctor will examine for bruises, vaginal and rectal tears or lacerations and other injuries. Only a female officer may be present in an examination room, and only with victim's permission.

4.  Investigator should request the following slides and check for physical evidence whether or not the victim has bathed or douched since the assault.

    a.  Vaginal slides (rape)

    b.  Rectal slides (sodomy: both male and female victims)

    c.  Oral slides (Oral copulation: both male and female victims)

    d. Loose hairs

5.  Additional samples for further laboratory comparison:

    a.  Sample of victim's blood for typing, properly preserved and refrigerated

    b.  Sample of victim's saliva for blood typing

    c.  Adequate number of hair samples from various parts of victim's head and pubic area

### *Photos:*

Photos of injuries are taken in the presence of the doctor and/or nurse.

### *Medical Report:*

These should reflect the injuries, the treatment given and the specimens taken.

### *Suspect(s) Arrested:*

1.  If more than one, separate the suspects immediately.

2.  Make note of any spontaneous remarks by suspect(s).

3.  If arrested at the crime scene, remove from the scene immediately.

4.  Do not permit suspect(s) on or to reenter the crime scene for any purpose. The defense can later claim that evidence incriminating the suspect(s) was left on the scene when the suspect(s) was there with the officer and not during the commission of the crime.

5.  Do not allow the suspect(s) to communicate with the victim or witnesses unless absolutely necessary.

6.  Photograph all evidence of injuries, and/or damaged or stained clothing on suspect(s).

7.  Collect and preserve all evidence potentials on suspect(s), e.g., semen or blood stains, hair, etc.

8.  Obtain blood and urine samples from suspect for typing and analysis for alcohol and/or drugs.

9.  If suspect(s) left crime scene, check escape route for discarded evidence.

### *Follow-Up Investigation:*

The follow-up investigation will utilize many of the techniques and services treated in previous chapters. Again, the investigator will re-interview the victim and witnesses, check modus operandi, reexamine the crime scene and utilize sources of information, etc. It is important to clarify that the initial call at the crime scene is the preliminary investigation. All subsequent investigation is follow-up, therefore, the same techniques and sources apply to the follow-up investigation of many crimes.

# ABUSED CHILD INVESTIGATION

Children have been subjected to maltreatment for centuries under the belief that physical punishment is primarily necessary to maintain discipline or train and educate. Some centuries ago, such punishment was used as a means by which to please a certain god or to drive the evil spirits from a child. Beatings to drive out the devil were considered a form of acceptable psychiatric treatment, especially in the case of children. The mutilation of children as part of a religious rite, or by traffickers in children for purposes of using them as professional beggars, dates back to the days of Caesar. Children subjected to having their eyes gouged, the amputation of arms and legs or castration were not uncommon in that period.

Slavery provided another means through which children were abused by being sold as chattel. Urbanization and the machine age in the United States led to still other forms of child abuse. Children as young as five years of age were worked 16 hours a day and many were shackled with chains to prevent them from running away. The mortality rate of these children during this period was astronomical due to pulmonary consumption and other diseases.

It is most unfortunate that child abuse still prevails today. Whipping a child is still a prerogative of parents, and in many jurisdictions a like prerogative of teachers. The age-old dictum, "Spare the rod and spoil the child," is still believed and practiced by many.

## Magnitude of the Problem

Child abuse is a national problem, the scope of which is indeed alarming. The National Institute of Mental Health recently released statistics indicating that between one and a half and two million children are kicked, punched, burned or bitten every year by their own parents. Nearly 50,000 youngsters are actually attacked by parents wielding knives and guns. State authorities in California relate that there were more than 100,000 suspected cases of child maltreatment reported in California in 1992. The magnitude of the problem is generally accepted as being much greater since many cases go unreported.

It is clear that child abuse and neglect occurs in all cultural, ethnic, occupational, and socioeconomic groups. It is a problem which requires cooperation between the various involved agencies and the community in prevention, education, reporting, training and treatment.

The California Attorney General's Office does not favor steps towards decriminalization of child abuse as propounded by some social service agencies. It points out that although the right of parents to control and raise their own children is accepted as a fundamental right in our society, intervention is justified by a paramount social interest, namely, protection of the child. The Fourteenth Amendment of the United States Constitution states that everyone is entitled to equal protection under the law. The willful breaking of a child's leg by a parent or guardian is a physical assault by one human being upon another and clearly a crime.

The agencies of government dealing with crime must be involved, although it may not always be appropriate to handle this type of crime with traditional crime and punishment approaches. All segments of the system must work together, pooling their expertise in arriving at the best disposition for each case. The disposition may be filing of criminal charges, removal of the child from the control and custody of the parent, appointing a guardian for the child, or counseling and treatment for the child abuser.

The magnitude of the child abuse and neglect problem in Los Angeles County has brought about the development of a Legal Child Protection System. For example, recent figures indicate an average of 25,000 families containing over 50,000 children are referred yearly by various law enforcement and social agencies to the Children's Services (DCS) for protective services in Los Angeles County alone.

The Legal Child Protection System involves the cooperative efforts of the schools, medical professionals, law enforcement, health services, treatment services, self-help groups, city attorneys, district attorneys, courts, correctional institutions, mental health facilities, parents, guardians, and relatives. The great need for this system and more preventive action as well as community education, is emphasized by research studies confirming that the above figures represent a conservative estimate of less than one-third of the actual child abuse and neglect incidents occurring in Los Angeles County every year.

## What Constitutes Child Abuse

In most states, *child abuse* is any act of omission or commission that endangers or impairs a child's physical or emotional health and development. This includes physical and corporal punishment, emotional assault, emotional deprivation, physical neglect and/or inadequate supervision, sexual assault and exploitation.

The elements of specific offenses falling within the above mentioned general categories are contained in penal and civil codes of each state. It is not the intent of this section to treat the numerous penal and civil code sections in the United States pertaining to child abuse, therefore, it will suffice to state that the offenses are categorized as felonies and misdemeanors. The punishments prescribed range from imprisonment in a state prison, to imprisonment in a county jail. It is important to note that laws pertaining to homicide are equally applicable in child abuse cases that result in the death of the victim.

### *Some Indicators That a Child May Need Protection*

1. The child bears bruises, welts and contusions which may indicate that the parent or caretaker has begun inflicting minor injuries, and may go on to cause future permanent injury or death.

2. The child is overly aggressive, disruptive, destructive and hostile. He or she may be emulating parental destructive behavior.

3.  Evidence of poor supervision, signs of physical neglect or appears in need of medical attention, dental work or glasses.

4.  The child complains of beatings and maltreatment.

5.  The parents are aggressive, abusive or apathetic and unresponsive when approached about problems concerning the child.

6.  Any indication of sexual assault.

### *Specific Indicators of Suspected Child Abuse*

#### *Burns*
Burns are often difficult to evaluate, yet some are characteristic. For example, a recognizable object like the grill of a heater or the element of an electric stove evenly burned into the skin of a child indicating a prolonged contact is an indicator of abuse. An indicator that a child was forcibly held down sitting in a tub of hot water would be a doughnut shape burn of the buttocks. In forcibly holding the child in the tub, the center part of the buttocks would be pressed tightly against the bottom of the tub, thus not burning that area. Another indicator of abuse would be burns that are pointed or deeper in the middle, suggesting that a hot liquid was poured on, or a hot object pressed in.

#### *Strappings*
Lash and belt buckle marks are indicators of abuse. Straps or other flexible objects create a wraparound appearance. An ironing cord is a particularly common source of trauma and lacerations to the abused child.

#### *Deep Muscular Bruises or Hemorrhage*
This trauma is caused by blows from blunt objects on soft tissue. The trauma rarely discolors; however, the blood collection can be detected by X-ray.

#### *Head Injuries*
When a small child receives an accidental blow to the head, part of the impact is usually absorbed by the shoulders. A blow of this type will rarely cause more than one crack in the skull; however, if the child is slammed against a wall, the back of the head may shatter.

An interesting case reviewed in research, involved a one year old male child who had died, according to the parents' story, as a result of a fall from a high-chair while eating his breakfast. The external examination of the child's body, with particular attention to the head area, revealed no marked evidence of trauma. The autopsy revealed four fractures of the skull with evident subdural hematomas, as the cause of death. Subdural hematoma is a hemorraghic collection under a fibrous membrane (dura) that envelops the brain.

The fractures were all on the top of the child's skull, and the underlying hematomas gave strong indication that the fractures did not occur at one time, but rather over a period of months. A close examination of the high-chair revealed it was physically impossible for the child to have dropped himself repeatedly on top of his head and survived to the date of his death. It was obvious that someone else, probably the parents, were responsible for the child's death. Interrogation of the parents revealed that the father, who was somewhat impatient, had been thumping the child on the top of the head with his fist, when the child balked at eating his mush in the morning.

### Whiplash/Shaken-Infant Syndrome
The California Attorney General's Office states that the essential element in the whiplash/shaken-infant syndrome presents an extraordinary diagnostic contradiction. There are no signs of external injury to the infant's head, yet there are intracranial and intraocular (behind the eyes) hemorrhages. Prolonged shakings of the infant may result in motor defects, mild retardation and permanent vision impairments that are not noticeable until the child reaches school age.

### Bruises, Abrasions, Lacerations and Scars
These signs of injury, found in varying colors (indicating various stages of healing) should be suspect. The primary places to look are the rear surfaces of the body, from the neck to the knees.

### Fractures
Long-bone fractures that are the result of twisting have a spiral characteristic. X-rays may reveal multiple healing or already healed fractures.

### Emotional Assaults
Emotional abuse is inflicted on a child by parents or caretakers through excessive belittling, sarcasm and negative moods. Another

source of emotional assault is parents making completely unreasonable demands of a child. Obviously, every child cannot be a scientist, a doctor, another Joe Namath or Michael Jordan. Some parents use children to satisfy their own ego needs. Many parents who fail to accomplish some goal try to force their child to do so.

An interesting case of continuing emotional assault that was reviewed in research relates the following: A disturbed mother would purchase a toy for her little girl, then allow the child to learn to love the toy. At the point where the child loved the toy and enjoyed playing with it continuously, the mother would break it into little pieces in the presence of the child. A prolonged repetition of this routine caused serious emotional damage to the child.

### *Emotional Starvation*
Emotional starvation, where parents or caretakers do not provide an atmosphere in which the child feels loved, wanted, secure and worthy, is as damaging as emotional assault.

### *Physical Neglect*
The failure of the parent or caretaker to provide adequate food, shelter, clothing, protection, medical and dental care.

# SEXUAL ASSAULT AND EXPLOITATION

## Incest

Incest is a much more common problem than most realize. It crosses every walk of life. This form of child abuse is often hidden within the family; therefore, the problem is likely to be much more extensive than that which is reported to authorities. Parents who become involved in incest often make the child believe that sex is a game that is a necessary part of being loved. In most cases, the father is the initiator of incest, usually with a daughter, several daughters, or step children. Sexual abuse occurs to infants and children of both sexes and all ages, however, it is most frequent with girls. Children that seek help are often accused of making up stories, and mothers who may know the facts may "look the other way," to avoid problems. National figures on incest are somewhat incomplete; however, the National Center on Child Abuse and Neglect suggests that over 100,000 children are abused sexually in this country each year.

## Child Pornography

Child pornography is, conservatively speaking, a multimillion dollar business that is nationwide in scope. The Los Angeles Police Department estimates that in Los Angeles alone, as many as 30,000 juveniles are sexually exploited annually, and that more than 3,000 of that number are under 14 years of age. Thousands of films, magazines, and photographs have been seized which depict children (some as young as four years old) involved in sexual activity.

It has been difficult for police to state exact figures on children involved in pornography, because much of this activity goes unreported. California has become a haven for the runaway juvenile, who, when alone and without funds, is an excellent target as a "model" for pornography.

## Child Molesters and "Chicken Hawks"

The Los Angeles Police Department Unit defines the *child molester* as a male or female (but primarily an older adult heterosexual male ) who receives sexual gratification from young girls. A *chicken hawk* is defined as a male (homosexual adult ) or female who receives sexual gratification from young boys. The child molesters and chicken hawks usually have a specific age preference.

Many of these suspects are financially secure persons who provide good food, spending money, lodging, even elaborate gifts to their victims. In essence, the wants and needs of the child (who is often a runaway) are catered to in return for willing participation in sexual activity. These suspects often use pornographic materials to stimulate both themselves and the victims. Publications are available that list hundreds of locations throughout the United States where the young can be found.

## Affects of Abuse on the Child

The combination of physical punishment and rage can cripple, handicap or kill a child. Emotional cruelty can similarly cripple and handicap a child emotionally, behaviorally and intellectually.

The following information was briefed from the reports on the recent hearings before the Subcommittee on Children and Youth of the Committee on Labor and Public Welfare, United States Senate. These hearings were conducted in support of the National Center on

Child Abuse and Neglect, which provides financial assistance for demonstration programs for the prevention, identification and treatment of child abuse and neglect.

An unpublished study by a doctor in Philadelphia of 100 juvenile offenders revealed that eighty percent of the offenders had a history of being neglected or abused as children. In addition, 40 percent of the offenders remembered being knocked unconscious. A study of 150 convicted rapists, at Rahway State Prison in New Jersey, revealed that 75 percent of the rapists had been sexually abused as children, often so brutally that they repress the memories of the experiences. A study of six convicted first-degree murderers (parents were also available for study) in Minnesota, by G. Dungan, M.D., et al, revealed that three of the murderers had been seriously abused and beaten by their parents in very early infancy and childhood.

## Child Abuser Profile

What kind of people vent their fury, frustration and disappointments in life on small children? This question has troubled medical and social research workers, as well as law enforcement and social agency personnel, for many years. The awareness of the extent of child abuse has widened to the extent that many states have enacted laws requiring doctors to report cases of child injury that may have been caused by assault. Doctors have coined the phrase, "battered child syndrome," to describe newly recognized cases of child abuse. To date, the majority of the abusers (suspects) in these cases are the child's parents or caretakers.

It is most interesting that few child abusers have been found to be psychotic or psychopathic, yet authorities caution that psychotic abusers are the most dangerous. Researchers tend to agree that many abusers (usually parents) are merely using the same destructive techniques on their children that their parents practiced on them. It is clear that without appropriate intervention, treatment, and education these destructive patterns of behavior may be transmitted for generations.

It is important to note that child abuse is rarely the result of any one factor. It is a combination of circumstances coupled with the personality types. For example, and if a parent who is under emotional stress has a predisposition towards maltreatment and the child triggers the parent's contempt or resentment, if the parent has no other outlet for his or her aggression, the results will likely be child abuse.

The following are some of the characteristics, including childhood experiences and adult life-styles of child abusers:

### As Children:

a.  As children, they experienced a deep loss of a sense of worth (i.e., a very negative self-image).

b.  An abiding feeling that regardless of their efforts, they could never do enough at the right time for their parents.

c.  An abiding feeling that they were a source of disappointment and/or disgrace to their parents.

d.  They experienced physical, sexual and emotional abuse—usually from their parents or caretakers.

### As Adults:

a.  They have perpetuated the above childhood feelings.

b.  They are immature, have poor impulse control and often have sexual difficulties.

c.  As a family they tend to become socially isolated, are lonely and friendless.

d.  They are often apathetic and neglect their own physical health.

e.  They are competitive with their own children and play to win, rather than to instruct the child.

f.  They are overly defensive towards authority.

g.  They have a negative attitude towards community participation (e.g., school, church, etc).

h.  The use of infants and children to satisfy their love needs.

i.  The use of drugs and alcohol to flee from reality.

j.  Little concern or remorse over the child's battered condition.

k.  Display cooperation with authorities based on fear for themselves, rather than a concern for the child.

l.  Usually have a failing family due to poor communication and understanding among family members and a vulnerability to any and all stresses.

m.  Child abusers are recidivists (repeat offenders), who continue their behavior until the child is removed from their custody and/or they are successfully treated.

## Treatment of Child Abusers

Most experts in the field dealing with child abuse agree that prison sentences or fines alone are not likely to rehabilitate the child abuser. Treatment facilities for abusing parents are being developed and implemented nationwide in universities and public service agencies. The growing trend is primarily due to the realization on behalf of professionals in the field that parental problems that cause child abuse may be successfully treated by group therapy and home visits.

The essence of the therapy treatment involves assisting the parents in improving their self-image, controlling their destructive impulses, learning to set limits on their behavior. It is believed that when they feel better about themselves and satisfy their emotional needs for love and self-respect, they will be less likely to abuse their own children. Abusive parents are very sensitive and even antagonistic towards authority figures, therefore, the home visitation process is provided to parents participating in the therapy group only upon request.

The home visits by trained professionals (often nurses) involve the process of reparenting. These parents need mothering, they need someone to help them manage their own lives, to understand their children's needs and behavior and to advise and guide them when faced with even the simplest crisis. For example, a child may be testing his own independence by responding "No" to a request from a parent. This behavior is very common and normal, yet it can trigger an abusing parent into a fit of rage and serious abuse of the child. The visiting professional, if present when it occurs, can explain the behavior to the parent and provide appropriate guidance in coping with the situation.

## Police Role Increases

In recent years law enforcement agencies throughout the United States have been re-examining their responsibilities in the area of child protection. In most jurisdictions more children with problems are known to the police than any other agency. This is primarily due to the fact that police are often the only community agency with 24-hour field service, thus many dependent, neglected and abused children come to

their attention. Police have recognized that they have specialized duties in this area and that the recognition, evaluation and investigation
of neglect and child abuse cases is difficult, complex and time-consuming.

The victims are often too young or too frightened to give comprehensive testimony. Coupled with the lack of reliable witnesses and
uncooperative parents (usually suspects), likens these cases to other
crimes wherein physical evidence plays a major role. In a homicide,
the degree of physical evidence often determines whether or not a prosecution will occur. It is often the same in child abuse cases. The degree
of training required for the child abuse investigator is very extensive.

Law enforcement's growing concern for the problem of child
abuse is reflected by the National Association of Chiefs of Police and
many other agencies providing specialized training in child abuse and
neglect. Many agencies include this training in their police recruit
courses as well as advanced and in-service refresher courses for investigators. In 1974 the Los Angeles Police Department created the nation's
first specialized child abuse unit in a police agency.

### Child Protection Section

The Los Angeles Police Department (and many other police agencies) has for many years utilized juvenile investigators in child abuse
cases.

The Child Protection Section has city-wide jurisdiction with offices in Parker Center and the San Fernando Valley. The investigative
responsibilities of the unit are:

- To receive, verify, evaluate, properly investigate, and complete
  all complaints involving children suspected of being physically
  or sexually abused by their parents or guardians.

- To investigate all coroner's cases involving children under 18
  years of age, where parents or guardians are suspected perpetrators, except for deaths resulting from traffic or aircraft accidents.

- To prepare the necessary reports and evidence for the case
  presentation to social service agencies, prosecuting officials, and
  the juvenile and criminal courts.

Some investigators believe that improved reporting procedures
and greater public awareness and interest in child abuse cases may
account, in a large part, for the rising statistics reflected nationwide. It

is also apparent that specialized training has raised the level of expertise for child abuse investigators. A review of the files of this unit revealed some frightening examples of child abuse up to and including the dismembering of a child's body. As in the above figure, the victim, a 4-year old female, was severely burned in the lower portion of her back and buttocks, when forced to lay on a floor furnace by her parents, for not responding promptly.

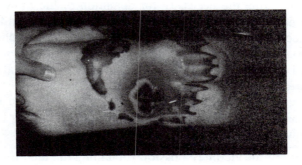

*Figure 12-6 Floor furnace burns on a child's back*

## Investigative Guidelines—Child Abuse

The following investigative guidelines are offered as a supplement to the general investigative techniques previously covered, with a reminder that a death of a child is handled in the same manner as that of an adult. When an investigator or officer responds to a call where a minor is reported to have sustained physical injuries which appear to have been caused by other than an accident, or the minor has been sexually molested, or has been willfully abused physically or emotionally or the child's health is endangered, the investigator or officer should:

1. Interview the person reporting the incident or requesting the service. Record the date, time, place and location of the interview and full identification of the party.

2. Determine if the victim is in need of immediate medical attention, request medical assistance if not already provided for. NOTE: Whether medical treatment is provided for at the scene or later at a hospital, the interview of the attending physician and the following information is imperative.

3. Full identification of the physician, his or her medical diagnosis and the doctor's professional opinion, whether or not the release of the minor would be detrimental to his health or welfare. This information is needed as a basis for making a decision as to whether or not the minor should be placed in temporary custody pending a full investigation. If the physician refuses to offer such an opinion the investigator must evaluate the entire circumstances to determine the necessity for detention of the minor. NOTE: The decisions the investigator/officer makes and the information collected may save the minor's life. Experienced child abuse investigators state that in many cases, where a previously battered child is returned to its parents, that child will later be permanently disabled or even killed. Abusing parents who have caused the death of one of their children have been known to move to another state and continue the abuse of their remaining children.

4. Interview the victim (if possible) obtaining full identification and all information regarding the circumstances of the situation.

5. Interview the parents or caretaker obtaining full identification and all information regarding the circumstances of the situation.

6. Determine if there are other children in the family, their whereabouts, and condition. Interview in above manner (if possible).

7. Crime Scene: Use crime scene techniques that may be applicable to the situation (e.g., photos, collection, handling and preservation of physical evidence, etc).

8. Have color and black and white photos taken of visible injuries to the victim.

9. In case of death an autopsy is in order.

10. It is also important that bruises, welts, cuts or abrasions be carefully described as to shape, size, color and location on the body. Doctors who are experts in child abuse cases can often, based on this information, refute false stories told by the abusers as to the causes of the injuries.

11. In sexual assault cases, follow the same procedures for examination, medical treatment, slides, etc. as covered in Forcible Rape Section. Obviously, if the victim is a male there will be a slight variation in the procedures.

12. Canvass the neighborhood for witnesses to the abuse or prior abuses or prior hospitalizations of the victim.

13. If a determination has been made to take the victim into protective custody the investigator should:

  a.  Notify the parents or caretakers (if available).

  b. Make notification to or obtain approval from the appropriate social agency in the jurisdiction.

  c.  If the victim requires continued hospitalization, make appropriate arrangements with the medical facility for police protective custody.

  d.  Make appropriate written reports that include justification for protective custody of the victim.

### *Follow-up Investigation*

This will involve the use of various techniques previously treated. Particular attention should be given to interviews of school teachers and nurses as to the victims prior behavior and physical condition. Friends and relatives may be excellent sources of information as to prior abuses.

*Note:* It is important to state that a juvenile court proceeding wherein the question of future custody of a child is in issue, is a different situation than a criminal trial of a parent for child abuse. The rules of evidence differ in each proceeding. Evidence that may not be admissible in a criminal trial, may be admissible in a juvenile court proceeding. The intent of the juvenile proceeding is to protect the child. Courts have held that illegally obtained evidence can therefore be used for this purpose, since it is more important to protect a child than to deter alleged unlawful police conduct. Guilt in a criminal case must be proven beyond a reasonable doubt, while a dependency petition in Juvenile Court is proven by a preponderance of evidence.

### *Combined Community Effort*

There is evidence that a variety of communities in the United States have formed interagency councils composed of police, prosecutors, schools, social and health agencies to prevent, investigate, prosecute or treat child abusers. Training programs have been developed in schools for students and teachers, specifically including training for students on the responsibilities of parenthood, and identification and referral training for teachers in recognition of child abuse and how to provide needed services within their agencies. Police and prosecuting agencies have introduced specialized training programs for recruits, advanced officers, investigators and prosecutors. These programs are updated regularly with seminars on child abuse and deaths of children, including the latest information available in the behavioral science area.

These interagency councils sponsor and actively lobby for needed legislation dealing with child abuse problems. Notwithstanding the growing awareness, concern and effort nationwide, the battle against child abuse will be uphill for some time.

## ARSON INVESTIGATION

*Arson* is a crime against either persons or property. It may be defined as the willful and malicious burning of another's property or the burning of one's own property with intent to injure or defraud the insurer of that property. Arson may include the burning of all kinds of buildings, structures, aircraft, watercraft, crops, forest land and personal property. Arson laws will vary as to details throughout the United States, however, most will contain as the core of the *corpus delicti*:

1.  That the fire was ignited willfully and maliciously to destroy buildings or property (of human origin, by incendiary means, not natural or accidental).

2.  That burning actually occurred (property need not be destroyed, scorching is sufficient).

3.  That the property is of another, or in the case of one's own property the intent was to injure or defraud the insurer.

4.  That any person who caused the fire to be set, aided, counseled or procured the burning is equally responsible as the actual fire setter.

In 1978, Congress directed the F.B.I. to include arson as a Part I crime on the index of crime in its Uniform Crime Reporting (UCR) program. This measure was dictated due to the alarming rise of the crime of arson in the United States.

A most recent study by John Hall, of the National Fire Protection Association, indicates that in 1995 the direct cost of arson was $1.9

billion. It is impossible to estimate the cost to the public in terms of higher insurance rates, medical expenses, and other related costs.

## Motive for Arson

Although the motive for arson is not one of the elements of the crime (*corpus delicti*) it is important to determine the motive, if at all possible. Development of motive will often determine the direction the investigation will take, and it can assist the prosecutor presenting the case in court by showing why the defendant was involved in the arson. The two most common motives are (1) concealment of other crimes and (2) defrauding an insurance carrier.

### *Concealment of Other Crimes*

The investigation may encounter an arson that was committed to conceal a murder, burglary or an embezzlement. The arsonist intends that the fire will destroy all evidence of his or her identity, as well as the evidence of the original crime.

### *Defrauding the Insurance Company*

In most insurance fraud cases the fire setter (arsonist), or the one who procures the fire to be set, knows that the fire insurance monies collected will equal or exceed the amount obtained by selling or otherwise disposing of the property. The fire is usually set so as to appear accidental. There are many individual types of insurance fraud arsons; some of the most common are offered as examples:

### *Quick Profit*

This type of arson often starts with the purchase of rundown inner-city real estate for the purpose of a rental property investment. Most inner-city real estate investors can completely retrieve their initial investment in a few years, besides having the advantage of a tax write-off. The catch is to make such an investment profitable, the building must be maintained in livable condition. If the investor can stay one step ahead of building inspectors, without any major expenditures for upkeep, the investment can be profitable. However, once the investor is required to bring the building up to acceptable standards, the inner-city real estate investment is no longer profitable. At this time the property owner may decide to "sell" the property to an insurance company. In order to obtain the highest insurance possible, the owner will manipulate the paper value of the property, by selling it to an accomplice for an inflated price (no money changes hands) and the original owner will retain title.

Insurance is often obtained just before the fire is set in order to reduce the amount of insurance premium and to limit the time the insurance company has to inspect the property. Some owners, bent on this type of arson, will obtain a bank mortgage on the property at the inflated value, and then name the bank as the beneficiary on the insurance policy. In this way the arsonist attempts to disguise the motive and to obtain his or her money up front in the form of mortgage money.

A property owner may also be motivated to burn insured property because of a need for ready cash. Failure of a business may motivate its owner to commit arson to collect the insurance money. On occasion, racial, labor and political conflicts give rise to acts of arson for the purpose of intimidating the opposition or to accentuate a protest issue.

### Revenge, Spite or Anger

Many domestic quarrels, conflicts between groups and personal grudges have resulted in arson, as an attempt to finalize the existing differences.

### Mental Illness as a Motive

There are several types of mentally ill suspects that have been encountered by arson investigators over the years. Some examples are as follows: (1) The simple schizophrenic who has accomplished very little in life and blames the world for his or her failures; setting fires is a means of "getting even.," (2) The paranoid schizophrenic who suffers from delusions of persecution and strikes back at his or her "persecutors" with arson, (3) The psycho-neurotic which includes the pyromaniac, who, when the urge arises, is seized by an uncontrollable compulsion to set a fire, (4) The sociopath which includes the sex psychopath who is the most dangerous type of compulsive fire setter. This type of suspect may masturbate while watching the fire or may reach an ejaculation just by viewing the fire, hearing the sirens and enjoying the excitement of the fire scene.

### Vandalism

Fires set in public buildings, particularly in schools, are rapidly increasing. The suspects in these cases are apparently demonstrating their hostility toward the establishment and a desire to destroy for the sake of destruction.

## The Fire Triangle

The so-called "fire triangle" consists of three basic elements, all of which must be present for a fire to occur; oxygen, fuel, and heat. Oxygen makes up approximately 21 percent of the earth's atmosphere and supports combustion. Fuels usually exist in liquid, gas or solid states, such as gasoline, natural gas or wood. Heat sufficient to ignite the fuel may originate from matches, cigarette lighters, candles, electrical devices, chemical reactions, mechanical devices and explosives.

## Classes of Fires

The most important use of the classification of fires is for selection and application of the proper extinguishing agent. It is also necessary for the investigator to be familiar with these classifications so that he or she may communicate with fire department personnel.

Class A — Fires in ordinary combustible materials such as wood, cloth, and paper.

Class B — Fires in flammable petroleum products or other flammable liquids, gases or greases.

Class C — Fires involving energized electrical equipment.

Class D — Fires in combustible metals, such as magnesium, titanium and sodium.

## Determining the Point of Origin

Where did the fire originate? Information can be obtained by questioning firefighters about the location of hot spots, which direction the fire was moving, how fast, etc. The most information will be gained by going through the scene and noting what areas suffered the most fire damage and exposure to heat. The origin is evidenced by the depth of char on burned items, degree of destruction, spalling, metal or glass bent or melted by exposure to heat for a longer time than other areas, and burning or heat fading of paint. Be alert to multiple sources or the entire structure as the origin. (See Figure 12-7).

## What Caused the Fire?

All possibilities of accidental or natural causes of a fire must be investigated and eliminated before the investigator can concentrate on the assumption that arson is involved. Proof that all accidental causes were eliminated by investigation is usually required before a basis for a charge of arson is established. Some of the common accidental or natural causes of fires are as follows:

Accidental fires are frequently caused by faulty electrical systems (e.g. overloaded circuits, defective switches, deteriorated insulation on wiring and pennies inserted in fuse boxes). Electrical appliances with short circuits, gas leaks in pipes, stoves and heaters or clothing being dried too close to fireplaces are also common causes of accidental fires. The careless use of matches and careless disposal of cigarettes, cigars and pipe ashes must be included as accidental causes of fires, as are those incidents where a person falls asleep while smoking in bed or on the couch.

Heating of material to its ignition temperature results in spontaneous ignition or combustion. There are many and varied conditions under which spontaneous combustion can occur. Some of the more common types of this combustion are as follows.

Fermentation, which occurs in vegetable matter such as hay, straw or grain can cause fires. When the moisture level in the fermenting matter reaches a critical point, combustion may occur. Another type of

*Figure 12-7 Arson via flammable liquid with point of origin at window. Note both sides of window barely touched by flames (Courtesy of East Los Angeles College).*

spontaneous combustion occurs in "oxidation heating" of vegetable oils or materials containing vegetable oils. Large oil-soaked mops stored in a small closet where heat (created by oxidation) is contained until combustion occurs, is an example. Spontaneous combustion by chemicals added to such hazardous materials as sodium, sodium peroxide, potassium peroxide, and phosphorus, are not uncommon.

An incendiary fire is intentionally set. The means used to start the fire will vary from a hand-held source of heat, such as a match or cigarette lighter, to a delay device such as a burning candle placed on top of combustibles, a lighted cigarette with matches around or a more sophisticated electrical device. By using a delay device, such as an igniter, the arsonist has time to leave the scene before the fire starts. In any case, the choice of igniter used will usually depend on the skill of the arsonist and the motivation for setting the fire. Although most arsonists plan that the igniter will be destroyed in the fire, on occasion this does not happen and evidence of the igniter is found at the scene.

### *Indications of an Incendiary Fire*

1. A fire that has more than one point of origin (e.g., separate tires burning in different locations simultaneously). A relatively new scientific understanding of "flashover" is a phenomenon in which a fire, even an innocent one, can virtually explode in a small room to temperatures of 2,000 degrees caused by fire gases that gather near the ceiling. The igniting of items on the floor, with multiple points of origin caused by flashover, can mimic arson.

2. A fire where normal ventilation from existing vents has been altered. A fire will burn upwards and will be drawn toward ventilation; an arsonist may have opened doors, windows, punched a hole in a wall or ceiling to increase the draft and the spread of the fire.

3. A fire scene may have evidence of the use of accelerants such as gasoline, kerosine, paint thinner, lacquer and others. The odors of accelerants may be recognizable; however, the portable catalytic combustion detector (Sniffer) is frequently used to detect accelerants. This detector operates on a basic heated-vapor principle. Vapor samples are heated and any combustible gas present will oxidize and can be electronically analyzed as to the accelerant present.

4.  A fire that produces smoke of a color that is not in keeping with the building or materials stored there. Black smoke usually indicates the burning of petroleum products; white smoke the burning of vegetable compounds, hay and phosphorus; and yellow or brownish-yellow smoke, the burning of film, nitric acid, sulfur, hydrochloric acid or smokeless gunpowder.

5.  A fire that generates heat not in keeping with the building or materials stored there may be an indication that flammable substances were added.

6.  A fire scene may have evidence of incendiary igniters or timed explosives.

## Investigative Guidelines

The following outline of investigative guidelines for arson is offered as a supplement to previous techniques covered.

*Type:*
1.  Residence — house, single family, apartment, mobile home, trailer, etc.

2.  Nonresident — store, office, school, factory, warehouse, aircraft, boat, etc.

3.  Open field — wild land, etc.

4.  Occupants or anyone present at the time of or prior to the fire.

*Location:*
complete address, and nearest cross street (if applicable). Description of the residence, building, aircraft, boat or area of fire. Complete identification of the resident, occupant or owner of the area involved.

*Date and time (day of week) reported:*
Who reported fire and was this person present when the firefighters arrived? Did this person remain at or near the scene during the fire fighting activities?

A fire scene can be a crime scene, evidence of arson may be present, so this requires an effort to preserve the scene. It is appreciated that fire fighters must secure the fire, yet every effort must be made to avoid tramping through the building since an incendiary device may be trampled or destroyed.

### Point of origin:

First attention is given to determining the point of origin of the fire (charring pattern).

### Conditions that indicate an arson may be involved:

1. Separate and uncontrolled fires

2. Odors of accelerants

3. Incendiary devices (candles, electrical and mechanical devices)

4. Disconnected oil or gas lines

5. Unexplained holes in walls (drafts)

6. Evidence of trailers used to spread the fire (accelerants)

### Isolation:

If the scene is complicated, it may be necessary to require a complete isolation of the scene by police order. Too often the necessary mopping up required of firefighters to completely extinguish all possibilities of fire leaves a difficult scene for the investigator.

### Searching a fire scene:

This is similar to searching any crime scene; the investigator looks for means and points of ignition and any evidence that may connect a suspect to the scene.

Any items suspected of containing accelerants (gasoline, etc.) are collected and transported to the laboratory in airtight containers, other evidence collection should follow crime scene techniques.

### Interview:

All victims and witnesses should be interviewed including all possible witnesses discovered through a thorough neighborhood canvass.

### Photography of a fire scene:

This should follow crime scene photography techniques. The burning should be photographed from the point of origin through the path of the fire.

*Motive:*

If the fire scene reveals evidence that an incendiary fire has occurred, the investigator should then attempt to determine the motive for the fire and who would have an opportunity to set the fire. A complete evaluation of all available background information on the property owners, with regard to all the motives for arson, must be made. All parties to the insurance coverage on the property must be included in this check as well.

Some states utilize what is termed the "Arson Pattern Recognition System." This is a computerized intelligence analysis tool which detects and predicts incendiary crimes by pattern recognition. Data taken from investigators' reports is programmed to recognize trends in arson cases that form distinctive patterns. Using these predictions of where and when future incendiary fire will occur, investigators can identify arson suspects.

*Other follow-up investigation techniques:*

Techniques utilized by the investigator in identifying and apprehending the arsonist, are much like the techniques previously treated in this text. The laboratory services available for the examination and analysis of physical evidence are similar to those previously discussed in Chapter 6. (For evidence of an incendiary fire (see Figure 12-7).

# COMPUTER CRIMES

The continuous growth of computer crimes in recent years has compelled many law enforcement agencies to become more conversant in the high-technology and sophistication of techniques involved in many of these offenses. Law enforcement, private computer security consultants and prosecutors throughout the U.S., are banding together to combat the problem. These crimes include using a stolen card to make fraudulent withdrawals from an automatic teller, changing school grade records, the sabotaging of intelligence files, stealing trade secrets, and manipulating a bank's central computer to embezzle large sums of money.

All fifty states and the federal government have laws that criminalize the invasion of another's computer. It appears that there is no specific type of common computer crime and the problem can be as varied as the suspects involved. The equipment needed for electronic crime, i.e., a personal computer and a modem to link the computer with telephone lines, can be purchased by anyone. The magnitude of losses on a nationwide basis which can be attributed to computer crime is staggering. Some experts estimate annual losses in excess of one billion dollars. Some police agencies have created computer fraud investigative units, staffed by fraud investigators, additionally trained in computer technology.

The U.S. Government has two training centers for computer crime investigators. One is located at the FBI Academy, in Quantico, Virginia, and the other at the Federal Law Enforcement Training Center in Glynco, Georgia. Both centers report that police departments throughout the U.S. are enrolling officers in their courses. It is quite clear that the general investigative techniques treated in the preceding chapters of this text are applicable to the investigation of computer crimes. In addition, the investigator should acquire an adequate familiarization with computer technology so that he or she feels comfortable with and can visualize what is going on, when a consultant explains how the computer was used in a fraud.

## SUMMARY

It has been estimated that approximately twenty-five percent of all deaths require investigative services by law enforcement agencies. When an officer or investigator responds to an alleged death scene he or she must know the body conditions that must be checked to determine if death has occurred. The cause of death may appear more obvious in one case than in others. Determining the cause of death may require a detailed examination of the body including an autopsy by the coroner or medical examiner. The identification of an unknown deceased may require the services of specialists other than an autopsy surgeon (e.g., odontologist and the forensic anthropologist).

All robbers should be considered armed and dangerous. Some will kill just for the sake of killing, even when the victim does not resist. In most robbery cases victims and witnesses will have seen the suspect(s), thus requiring the use of in-depth interviewing techniques. This includes "word picture" descriptions of suspects, weapons, and vehicles, neighborhood canvasses for witnesses and other information as well as the use of informants. The investigator will also need to utilize modus operandi files and other recorded sources of information and laboratory techniques for handling physical evidence.

Burglary is a crime against property rather than people, yet many persons have been killed or injured by burglars for being present when the suspect arrived or otherwise interrupting the burglary. Residential burglaries occur much more frequently than others. Without the existence of receivers of stolen property (fences), the casual burglar would disappear. The investigator will utilize laboratory techniques for physical evidence potentials at the crime scenes, trace stolen property, utilize modus operandi information and other sources of recorded information and informants.

Vehicle and motorcycle thefts are most prevalent in urban cities; some reporting 100 or more stolen daily. Some cities report 80%+ recovered vehicles, however, may of these have been stripped. The prime challenge to the investigator is the commercial vehicle theft rings who dismantle vehicles, alter the ownership document, registrations and vehicles for local or out of state sale. A great ally to the investigator is the National Auto Theft Bureau, as are laboratory services for physical evidence potential and the identification of altered stolen vehicles, the modus operandi files, other recorded sources of information and informants.

Forcible rape is a crime of violence, rather than a sex crime per se. Many rapes still go unreported; however, the rate of reported rapes is increasing. The rape crime scene should be treated with the same caution and care as to physical evidence potentials, laboratory services utilized, search for and interview of witnesses and the use of recorded sources of information as other major crime scenes. If practical, a female investigator should be present when a female victim is interviewed. The rape victim must receive medical examination and treatment and a search for evidence of sexual assault must be made as soon as possible. The follow-up investigation will utilize the techniques previously discussed under other crimes.

Children have been subjected to maltreatment for centuries under the belief that physical punishment is primarily necessary to maintain discipline or train and educate. Children have been abused as part of psychiatric treatment, religious rites, slavery, child labor and at the hands of their parents, caretakers or others. Child abuse is at an epidemic level nationwide and it occurs in all cultural, ethnic, occupational and socioeconomic groups. In most states, child abuse is any act of omission or commission that endangers or impairs a child's physical or emotional heath and development. A child abuse case may require the use of any or all of the investigation techniques, laboratory and recorded services previously discussed (including homicide techniques when a child dies from the abuse).

Arson is a crime against both persons and property and is defined as the willful and malicious burning of another's property or the burning of one's own property with intent to injure or defraud the insurer. The overall cost of arson may total more than $10 billion annually. It is important for the investigator to determine the motive for the arson if possible, because this will often set the direction the investigation will take. The investigator will utilize any or all of the techniques and services previously discussed in addition to specific crime scene considerations and instrumentation relating to arson cases.

Computer crime is growing to the extent that states have now enacted legislation making it a crime to invade another's computer program. Annual computer crime losses are now estimated at one billion dollars.

Most of the techniques applicable to other frauds are applicable to computer crimes, except that the investigator must be familiar with computers.

## DISCUSSION QUESTIONS

1. Discuss the methods of determining if death has occurred, i.e., body changes.
2. Discuss the methods of determining the cause of death.
3. Discuss the external examination of a dead body.
4. Name the reasons for investigators attending autopsies.
5. Discuss the various methods of identifying the deceased.
6. Describe the various types of wounds.
7. How is the time of death estimated?
8. Discuss the deployment for search of suspects who have just left the scene of a robbery.
9. Why is the burglary crime rate so high?
10. Discuss the various methods of altering vehicles.
11. List the motives of rapists.
12. What laboratory tests are required in rape cases?
13. Discuss the history of child abuse.

14. Discuss the magnitude of the child abuse problem.
15. List the various kinds of child abuse.
16. Discuss the effects of various kinds of child abuse on the child.
17. Discuss the child abuser, as a child and as an adult.
18. Discuss the treatment for child abusers.
19. Define arson.
20. Discuss the motives for arson.
21. Identify the components of the fire triangle, give examples.
22. Explain the classes of fires.
23. How is the point of origin of a fire determined?
24. Discuss the various causes of fires.
25. Discuss the types of crimes being committed with the use of computers.

# NARCOTICS AND DANGEROUS DRUGS

13

## KEY TERMS AND CONCEPTS

Narcotics and dangerous drugs (definition of)
Depressants
Tranquilizers
Stimulants
Cocaine and crack
Hallucinogens
Marijuana
Drug informants
Investigation guidelines
Model Forfeiture Law
Posse Comitatus

The term *narcotic* usually refers to opium and pain-relieving drugs made from opium, such as morphine, paregoric and codeine. These and other opiates are obtained from the juice of the opium poppy, papaver sonniferum. Heroin, Percodan and Dilaudid are derivatives of morphine. Also classed as narcotics are cocaine, ecgonine, coca leaves and several synthetic drugs such as demoral and methadone. Narcotics are indispensable in the practice of medicine as analgesics which relieve pain and induce sleep.

Under medical supervision narcotics are administered orally or by intramuscular injection. As drugs of abuse, they may be sniffed, smoked or self-administered by subcutaneous (skin-popping) and intravenous (mainlining) injection. It can generally be stated that users of narcotics in the non-medical sense are attracted to its use by the feeling of euphoria it produces. The term *dangerous drugs* refers to a variety of non-narcotic substances classified as depressants, stimulants, hallucinogens and cannabis.

Depressants, when taken as prescribed by a physician, may relieve anxiety, tension and assist in the treatment of hyperkinesis, narcolepsy and weight control. Cocaine, which is classified as a narcotic and is also a stimulant, is used as a local anesthetic. Of the various hallucinogens only phencyclidine (PCP) has a medical use as a veterinary anesthetic. In the cannabis classification, marijuana and tetrahydrocannabinol are under investigation as useful in the relief of the after-affects of chemotherapy and the relief of intraocular (eye) pressure in the treatment of glaucoma. Excessive use of depressants induces a state of intoxication. Users of stimulants depend on them to feel stronger, more decisive and self-possessed. Hallucinogenic drugs distort the perception of objective reality. With regard to the cannabis classification, users may experience euphoria and relaxed inhibitions with small doses, with paranoia and possible psychosis as the result of overdoses.

The legal foundation for the United States government's strategy of reducing the consumption of illicit drugs is the Comprehensive Drug Abuse Prevention and Controlled Substances Act (CSA).

## THE EXTENT OF THE PROBLEM

The overall extent of drug abuse is difficult to assess, yet it is clearly evident that it is a major problem in our country. According to the most recent U.S. Government conducted National Household Survey on Drug Abuse, marijuana is the most commonly abused illicit drug—used by more than nine million Americans. Furthermore, only 44.9 percent of those surveyed believed that occasional use of marijuana involved great risk of harm. In the workplace, almost 10 percent of U.S. workers reported that they were current users of marijuana. It is estimated that over 32 million people in the United States will pay over $18 billion each year for the drug.

The traffic in cocaine is spiraling upward continuously. It is impossible to estimate the dollar value of the cocaine traffic in the United States at this time; however, intelligence sources suggest that South American countries export over $125 billion (street value) annually, much of which is smuggled into the United States.

"White Heroin," of Southeast Asian origin, has become increasingly available. Phencyclidine (PCP) use is more prevalent, with hospitals reporting a significant increase in PCP related admissions. Drug dependency in the United States continues to escalate and presents a difficult challenge to the criminal investigator. The street value of drugs sold in the U.S. was over $205 billion in 1995.

People of all ages are aware of the dangers of drugs. Communities recognize the need to educate their young about the dangers of drug use. In addition, people support the fight against drugs. They advocate police taking an active role in reducing drug trafficking and stopping the importation of drugs into the United States. Drug use and trafficking arrests continue to climb. Police and sheriff's agencies made an estimated 1.1 million arrests for drug law violations during 1995, according to the Uniform Crime Reports (UCR) of the FBI. Excluding traffic violations, one of every thirteen arrests was for a drug-related offense.

| Table 13.1 Percent of violent offenders under the influence of drugs or alcohol, as perceived by victims | | | | |
|---|---|---|---|---|
| Type of Crime | Alcohol Only | Drugs Only | Both | Not Sure Which Substance |
| Crimes of Violence | 21 | 7.6 | 5.6 | 1.8 |
| Rape | 21.2 | 7.2 | 9 | 0* |
| Robbery | 8.9 | 12.2 | 4.5 | 1.8 |
| Aggravated Assault | 23.4 | 9.6 | 6.4 | 1.8 |
| Simple Assault | 24 | 4.8 | 5.3 | 1.9 |

*Estimate is based on 10 or fewer sample cases.
Source:Criminal Victimization in the United States, 1989

Control of illicit drug use and trafficking is considered crucial to reducing crime, thus the majority of law enforcement agencies are operating special drug enforcement units. These units are found primarily in large metropolitan communities. Of the smaller departments serving 2,250—9,999 people, 19 percent had special drug enforcement units.

Drug abuse has a direct correlation to crime. Most violent offenders are under the influence of some type of drug when committing a crime. See Table 13.1. These statistics tend to hold true for youthful offenders as well. Nearly 40 percent of incarcerated youth in long-term, state operated facilities have admitted to being under the influence of some drug at the time of their offense. Therefore, we can see how drugs play a major role in crime today.

Law enforcement agencies take this problem so seriously that they have also implemented internal drug testing programs. A majority of state police departments and approximately half of all local police and sheriff's departments serving a population of 25,000 or more require that all applicants for sworn positions take a test for illegal drugs. In approximately two-thirds of the local police and sheriff's departments non-probationary officers can be dismissed with one positive test.

## OPIUM

Opium poppies (papaver sonniferum) were grown in the Mediterranean region as early as 300 B.C. At various times it has been produced in Hungary, Yugoslavia, Turkey, India, Burma, China, Pakistan, Afghanistan, Iran, Laos, Thailand and Mexico. At least twenty-five organic substances can be extracted from opium. The first derivatives of opium were morphine and codeine, both used as analgesics and cough suppressants. Other derivatives are papaverine, an intestinal relaxant, and noscapine, a cough suppressant, neither being regulated by the controlled substance act. A small amount of opium is processed by U.S. pharmaceutical and chemical firms for the manufacture of paregoric, an antidiarrheal preparation.

The traditional method of collecting raw opium is by incising (cutting) the seed capsules that are left after the petals have fallen—horizontally in Turkey, vertically in Southeast Asia. The opium, which appears in white droplets, hardens and turns brown before it is harvested (see Figures 13-1 and 13-2).

*Figure 13-1 Incised opium poppies, note sap on pod.*

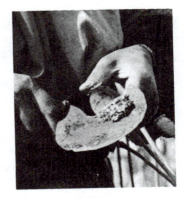

*Figure 13-2 Hardened opium being scraped from pod.*

## Opium, How Used

The use of opium in the United States, at present, is not prevalent. However, its use is not uncommon in eastern countries. The most common method of using opium is by smoking it in a long-stemmed pipe. The method is quite simple. A small ball of opium is held by a needlelike instrument over a flame until it is fuming. The ball is then placed in the bowl of the pipe and the user inhales the fumes.

## Effects

The effect resulting from smoking opium may include a feeling of euphoria, drowsiness, respiratory depression, constricted pupils and nausea. Almost always the user develops a tolerance, as well as a physical and psychological dependence, on the narcotic, which results in addiction. The slang terms for opium are "mud" and "tar."

# MORPHINE

Morphine is the principle constituent of opium, ranging in concentration from four to twenty-one percent. In the medical profession it is one of the most widely used drugs for the relief of pain. It is produced as white crystals, tablets and injectable preparations.

## Morphine, How Used

Medically, morphine is injected subcutaneously, intramuscularly or intravenously. The user will generally inject morphine directly into the bloodstream with a regular hypodermic needle or a homemade variety called an "outfit."

## Effects

The effects resulting from the use of morphine are similar to those experienced by opium users. The probabilities of developing a tolerance (as well as the physical and psychological dependence) are high, thus addiction usually occurs quickly.

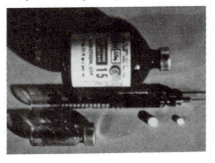

*Figure 13-3 Morphine is often an injectable liquid. (Courtesy D.E.A.)*

# CODEINE

Codeine is an alkaloid that is found in raw opium. It is legally distributed widely in tablets, white crystals and injectable preparations.

## Codeine, How Used

Codeine is used singularly, in tablet form, or combined with other products such as Emperin Compound or APC for the moderate relief of pain. It is used in liquid form in preparations for the relief of coughs and is also used in the injectable form for the relief of pain.

## Effects

The effects resulting from the use of codeine, as compared with morphine, are much less as to analgesia, sedation and respiration depression. However, there is a potential for a user of codeine to develop a moderate physical and psychological dependence on the drug as well as a tolerance. Heavy use of codeine may cause dilated pupils and nausea.

# HEROIN

Heroin was first synthesized from morphine in 1874, and was first produced as a pain remedy in Germany in 1898. Heroin was widely accepted as a pain remedy for years without recognition of its addictive potential until 1914 when the United States legislated the Harrison Narcotic Act.

Pure heroin is a white powder with a bitter taste. Illicit heroin may vary in color from white to brown because of impurities left from the manufacturing process or the presence of diluents such as food coloring, cocoa or brown sugar. Pure heroin is rarely sold on the street to an addict. It is generally diluted with sugar, starch, powdered milk, or quinine in rations ranging from nine to one, to as much as ninety-nine to one. The dilution accounts for the enormous profit to the seller, who buys it pure and dilutes it for sale to the addict. In street slang heroin is referred to as "H," "Smack," or "Horse" and a variety of other names.

## Heroin, How Used

Heroin is injected subcutaneously, intramuscularly or intravenously, and, on occasion, is used by sniffing. An addict will usually inject heroin directly into the bloodstream with a standard hypodermic needle or a homemade variety called an "outfit." Sometimes, the addict will copy the new user by subcutaneous (under skin) injections to hide the puncture wounds that are characteristic of intravenous injections.

The user may inject subcutaneously anywhere on his or her body. With regard to intravenous injections, there is a large variety of locations on the body used by addicts such as veins in all parts of the arms, wrists, legs and feet. Some addicts inject heroin into the veins on the inside of the lower lip or even inside the nose. It is a common practice for a user to inject (fix) into a tattoo already on the body or to be tattooed over scar tissue from old hypodermic marks in an effort to conceal present or past use.

*Figure 13-4 Heroin varies in color from white to dark brown (Courtesy of D.E.A.).*

## Effects

The effects resulting from the use of heroin are similar to those experienced by the opium user. Because heroin is much more potent in its pharmacological effects than morphine, and the tolerance for this drug builds much faster than other opiates, it is considered the most dangerous of all drugs. The physical and psychological dependency potential of this drug is also high; therefore, continued use ultimately leads to addiction. When an addict, whose body has become accustomed to heroin that has been diluted ninety-nine to one by the peddler receives a fix containing a much higher percentage of pure heroin, he or she may suffer an overdose or even death.

# METHADONE

Methadone was synthesized by German scientists during World War II, due to the shortage of morphine. Methadone is chemically different than morphine or heroin; however, it produces many of the same effects. It was introduced into the United States in 1947 as an analgesic and distributed under the trade names of Amidone, Dolophine and Methadone.

During the 1960s, it became widely used in the treatment of narcotic addicts. Essentially, methadone differs in effects from morphine based drugs in that it lasts up to twenty-four hours, thus permitting a once-a-day administration in heroin detoxification program. Additionally, methadone is almost equally effective whether administered orally or by injection.

Although methadone treatment develops tolerance and dependence, the withdrawal symptoms are less severe than when an addict ceases to use heroin. The use of methadone in detoxification programs for heroin addicts remains a controversial issue, i.e., the use of one drug to replace another. Specifically, addicts seem to miss the "tremendous high" produced by heroin that is not provided by methadone. This may account for many addicts returning to the use of heroin or fatally overdosing on methadone.

A substitute for methadone, currently under investigation for heroin detoxification programs, is levo-alpha-acetylmethodol (LAAM). This closely related synthetic compound lasts from forty-eight to seventy-two hours, and would reduce the necessary clinic visits by the addict from once a day to a maximum of three times per week.

*Figure 13-5 Methadone is an opioid, or synthetic substitute for opiates (Courtesy D.E.A.).*

# DEPRESSANTS

Substances regulated under the Controlled Substances Act (CSA) as depressants have a high potential for abuse associated with both physical and psychological dependence. Taken as prescribed by a physician, depressants may be beneficial for the relief of anxiety, irritability, tension and insomnia. The most commonly used depressants are chloral hydrate, a variety of barbiturates, glutethimide, methaqualone and the benzodiazepines. The abuse of depressants may cause effects that range from a state of intoxication, from a moderate overdose, to coma, a cold and clammy skin, a weak and rapid pulse and a slow or rapid but shallow respiration, from a severe overdose. Death will follow if the reduced respiration and low blood pressure are not counteracted by proper medical treatment. A mixture of depressants and alcohol is not an uncommon cause of death.

## Chloral Hydrate

Chloral hydrate is the oldest of sleep inducing drugs. It was first synthesized in 1862, and supplanted alcohol, opium and cannabis preparations to induce sedation and sleep. Its popularity declined after the introduction of barbiturates, but chloral hydrate is still widely used and is sold under the brand names of Notec and Somnos.

## Barbiturates

Barbiturates are derivatives of barbituric acid, the result of the condensation of malonic acid and urea. Adolph Von Baeyer first prepared barbituric acid in 1864 in Ghent, Belgium. Barbital, first discovered in 1903 by German scientist Emil Fisher, was the first derivative of barbituric acid which showed strong sleep-inducing effects.

To date, approximately 2,500 derivatives of barbituric acid have been synthesized; however, only about fifteen remain in widespread use. Small therapeutic doses tend to relieve nervous conditions and larger amounts can induce sleep. Accidental overdoses of barbiturates, due to drug automation, are not uncommon. Drug automation is defined as, "the state of mental confusion in which the barbiturate user forgets how much he or she has already taken and unwittingly ingests an overdose." The amount that would constitute a lethal dose of barbiturates will vary with the individual user; however, severe poisoning or death may occur which more than ten times the full hypnotic dose (1,000 to 2,000 mg.) is reached.

Barbiturates have a high potential for developing a physical and psychological dependence as well as tolerance in the user. Addictions to the user of barbiturates are common, as are the devastating withdrawal symptoms that many in the medical profession describe as more severe and dangerous than the withdrawals from heroin addiction.

Barbiturates are classified into three categories. Each classification is based on the duration of their effects and the speed with which they take effect.

### Long Acting

Slow in taking effect. Lasts up to twenty-four hours. These barbiturates are used as minor tranquilizers or anticonvulsants in the treatment of epilepsy and are widely abused.

### Short To Intermediate Acting

Faster in taking effect. Do not last as long as the long-acting barbiturates. They are the most widely prescribed and frequently abused of the barbiturates. The best known are the red capsules containing sodium secobarbital, which are known on the street as "reds" or "red devils." Also common is the trade name Seconal that one manufacturer uses for this barbiturate.

### Ultra-short Acting

Fast in taking effect when injected intravenously, produce sleep in approximately 15 minutes. These barbiturates are not frequently abused and are used primarily prior to surgery in connection with an inhaled anesthetic.

Other barbiturates that are commonly abused are Tuinal, in red and blue capsules, which contain sodium secobarbital/amobarbital and are known on the street as "rainbows" or "tooies" and Nembutal, a yellow capsule containing pentobarbital, is known on the street as "yellows" or "yellow jackets."

## GLUTETHIMIDE

Glutethimide was first introduced in 1954, and was believed to be a safe, non-addicting substitute for barbiturates. However, glutethimide has proven to have no particular advantage over the barbiturates, in that, following oral administration, effects begin in about thirty minutes and last for four to eight hours. It is very difficult to reverse overdoses of this drug due to the long duration of its effects;

said overdoses often resulting in death. The trade name for glutethimide is Doriden.

## METHAQUALONE

Methaqualone is a synthetic sedative that has been widely abused in the belief that it is non-addictive and an aphrodisiac. This drug has a high potential for physical and psychological dependence as well as tolerance. Large doses can cause serious poisoning accompanied by coma or convulsions. It is taken orally and bears the trade names of Optimil, Parest, Quaalude, Somnafact and Sopor.

## TRANQUILIZERS

There are several tranquilizers marketed in the United States, that fall under the scope of the C.S.A., because their continued use leads to tolerance and they have a moderate potential for physical and psychological dependence. These tranquilizers bear the trade names Equanil, Miltown, Serax, Tranxene and Valium. They are administered orally and prescribed for the relief of anxiety, muscle spasms or as sedatives. Their effects may include slurred speech and intoxication, which may last from four to eight hours. An overdose will cause shallow respiration, cold and clammy skin, dilated pupils, weak and rapid pulse, coma and possible death.

## STIMULANTS

The two most prevalent stimulants are nicotine in tobacco and caffeine in coffee, tea and some bottled beverages. When these stimulants are used in moderation, they tend to relieve fatigue and increase alertness; however, there are more potent stimulants, that because of their psychological dependence, and tolerance producing potential, are controlled by the C.S.A. These drugs stimulate the central nervous system, which may result in increased alertness, excitation, euphoria, dilated pupils, increased pulse rate and blood pressure, insomnia and a loss of appetite. An overdose of stimulants may cause agitation, increased body temperature, hallucinations, convulsions and possible death.

Users tend to rely on stimulants to feel stronger, more decisive and self-possessed. Because of the cumulative effects of the drugs, chronic users often follow a pattern of taking "uppers" in the morning and "downers," such as alcohol or sleeping pills, at night. Stimulants are administered orally, by injection, or sniffed. The principal stimulants controlled by the C.S.A. are cocaine, amphetamines, pheumatrazine and methylphenidate.

## COCAINE

Cocaine is the most potent stimulant of natural origin. It is extracted from the leaves of the coca plant (erythroxylon coca) which has been cultivated in the Andean highlands of South America since prehistoric times. The leaves of this plant are chewed in this region for refreshment and relief from fatigue. Pure cocaine, the principle psychoactive ingredient, was first isolated in the 1880s. First used as an anesthetic in eye surgery, it soon became useful in nose and throat surgery because of its ability to constrict blood vessels and limit bleeding. In recent years its legal use has been enhanced by the introduction of a morphine/cocainebased elixir, which relieves suffering associated with terminal illness.

Coca plant          Coca processing          Cocaine

*Figure13-6 The coca plant, coca processing, and cocaine (Courtesy of the Drug Enforcement Administration, U.S. Department of Justice)*

Cocaine is made by putting dried coca leaves in a plastic container with water and sulfuric acid. The mixture is stirred periodically. After several days, the liquid is removed, leaving a grayish coca paste.

To this paste is added gasoline, potassium permanganate and ammonia. The reddish brown liquid, which results, is then filtered.

Filtered and dried cocaine base is then dissolved in a solution of hydrochloric acid and acetone or ethanol. The white solid which forms is cocaine hydrochloride. Cocaine hydrochloride is filtered and dried under heat lamps to form a white crystalline powder. The cocaine is now ready for distribution, usually in one kilogram (approximately two pound) packages. Before reaching the street, cocaine is diluted with sugars, such as mannitol (a baby laxative) or anesthetics, such as lidocaine. It is usually sold in this form in 1-gram packages.

Cocaine is converted into "crack" by heating it with baking soda and water. The resulting shavings or chips are smoked in a cigarette or pipe and is ten times as addictive as cocaine taken in other forms.

## AMPHETAMINES

Amphetamine was first synthesized in 1887 and first used clinically in the mid-1930s to treat narcolepsy, a rare disorder resulting in the uncontrollable desire to sleep. Amphetamines stimulate the central nervous system, which accounts for their street name as "pep pills." Following the introduction of the amphetamines into the medical field, the number of conditions for which they were prescribed multiplied, as did the quantities made available. They are marketed under the trade names Benzedrine, Biphetamine, Desoxyn and Dexadrine.

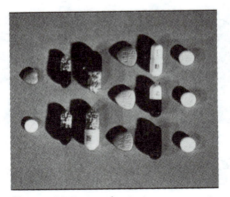

*Figure 13-7 Amphetimines come in the form of capsules, pills, or tablets (Courtesy of D.E.A.).*

The medical use of amphetamine has expanded from the treatment of narcolepsy to the treatment of hyperkinesis and weight control. Amphetamines have a high potential for psychological dependence and their use does develop a high tolerance. They are administered orally and by injection and may cause increased alertness, excitation, euphoria, insomnia and loss of appetite. An overdose of amphetamines can cause hallucinations, convulsions and death. Amphetamines are manufactured in a variety of forms.

## ICE (Smokable Speed)

Ice is a freebase form of powdered methamphetamine (speed). Ice is called by many names: glass, L.A. glass, hot ice, super ice, and L.A. ice. Ice is usually smoked in a glass pipe or cigarette. Ice is made by washing speed in illegal chemicals, available on the black market, producing the solid ice. The most popular form of ice looks like a piece of ice from the freezer. It is water-based and burns quickly. Another type of ice is oil-based. It is yellowish, burns slower and longer and leaves a dark brown residue. A high from ice lasts from 8 to 30 hours as compared to a crack high which lasts 8 to 20 minutes.

Ice is much cheaper to make than crack and is deadlier and more addictive than crack. Drug addicts who already smoke crack are the heaviest users of ice.

*Figure 13-8 Ice, a rock form of methamphetamine, is smoked. (Courtesy of D.E.A.).*

The psychological effect of ice is primarily a toxic psychosis with delusions of grandeur. The physical effects are a skyrocketing heart rate and blood pressure, extreme energy, not sleeping, euphoria, and seizures that can occur within 6 seconds after one hit of ice. Pupils of the eyes become very small, fevers may mount to 106 degrees, causing brain damage, leading to violent behavior and paranoia. Extended use can be fatal.

## PHENMETRAZINE AND METHYLPHENIDATE

The medical indications, effects and patterns of abuse of Phenmetrazine, marketed as Predulin and Methylphenidate, marketed as Ritalin, compare closely with those of other stimulants. Phenmetrazine is primarily used as an appetite depressant. Methylphenidate is used in the treatment of hyperkinetic (overactive) behavioral disorders in children. These drugs are available in a variety of tablet forms.

## HALLUCINOGENS

The hallucinogenic drugs, as their name implies, cause hallucinations wherein the user experiences sensory illusions and perceives unreal sights and sounds. Under the influence, the user may speak of "seeing sounds" and "hearing colors" and his or her senses of direction, distance and time become disoriented. Continued use of hallucinogenic drugs produces tolerance, thus resulting in greater doses.

The principle hazard of the hallucinogens is that their effects are unpredictable each time they are taken. Toxic reactions that precipitate psychotic reactions and even death can occur. The drugs have not been shown to produce physical dependence. The most widely known hallucinogens in the illicit traffic are LSD, Mescaline, Psilocybin-Bilocin, MDA and PCP. They are administered orally, by injection or sniffed.

## LSD (LSD-25, Lysergide)

Doctor Albert Hoffman, a Swiss biochemist, is credited with the first synthesis of LSD in 1938. He had been working with lysergic acid derived from ergot, a black fungus that develops in rye grains. In the course of trying different chemical combinations, he added molecules that created a new compound D-Lysergic Acid Diethylimide Tartrate (LSD-25). The hallucinogenic effects of this drug were discovered in 1943 when he accidentally swallowed or absorbed through his skin, some of the chemical and experienced a state of "pleasant drunkenness," which was characterized by an "extremely stimulating fantasy."

Recognizing the perception-altering properties of the drug, he later returned to his laboratory and swallowed 250 micro-grams of LSD and experienced the same results. LSD is probably one of the most potent hallucinogens now known to man. There are medical claims that LSD is useful in producing valuable changes in chronic alcoholics, and others with serious personality disorders. However, LSD remains a subject for debate and a concern to law enforcement because it is not clear what degree of danger the drug presents to the psychological health of any persons who use it and the resultant effect to the user and those around him.

Even though LSD is not physically addicting, there is an onset to tolerance. For example, a user taking a normal dosage (of 100-250 micro-grams) may have to increase his or her dosage the following day to obtain the original experience. The tolerance diminishes as rapidly as it builds, and in a lapse of a few days it may be lost. Some experts believe that repeated use of this drug may develop a psychological dependence and that a serious overdose can cause psychosis and possibly death. The drug is odorless, tasteless, and clear of color unless mixed with another substance.

## LSD, How Used

LSD may be found in liquid, tablet or powder form. It is usually sold in the form of tablets, thin squares of gelatin ("window panes") or impregnated paper ("blotter acid"). The most common way of administering LSD is orally (i.e., tablets, capsules, liquid impregnated substances, such as sugar cubes or dissolved in beverages).

A user may also inject LSD intravenously; however, there is no apparent increase in effect and this method is infrequently used. Some users saturate tobacco with LSD and smoke it, but the drug induced state is not as intense as when taken orally. LSD is readily absorbed from the intestinal tract; therefore, there is little advantage in intravenous injection of the drug.

## Effects

LSD will normally take effect in forty-five to sixty minutes, yet symptoms may appear in fifteen minutes in sensitive individuals. The effects may last from four to twelve hours, or may reoccur as long as one year after the last dose. Auditory and visual hallucinations occur, time and depth perception are distorted, subjective time stands still, music may have "scent" and sound may have "color."

Illusory phenomena are common. One high school girl cut all the flexor tendons in her wrist when she looked in the mirror and imagined she saw her face begin to dissolve. The user will also experience a loss of appetite, nausea, headaches and dilated pupils.

## MESCALINE (Peyote)

Mescaline is derived from the buttons of the peyote cactus. The buttons are dried, ground into powder and usually taken orally. The use of mescaline has been traditional by Indians in Northern Mexico for centuries to induce trances necessary for tribal dances. The Native American Church, which uses peyote in religious ceremonies, has been exempted from certain C.S.A. provisions.

Hallucinations and illusions that last from five to twelve hours can be attained from a dose of 350 to 500 mg. of mescaline. Mescaline is not known to develop a physical dependence, and its potential for developing a psychological dependence is not certain. Continued use of mescaline can develop tolerance. An illustration of the peyote cactus is offered in Figure 13-9.

## PSILOCYBIN-PSILOCYN (Mushrooms)

Like peyote cactus, psilocybe mushrooms have been used for centuries in traditional Indian rites. When they are eaten, these "sacred" or "magic" mushrooms affect mood and perception much like mescaline and LSD. Users are not known to develop a physical dependence nor is there evidence for a psychological dependence; however, continued use will develop tolerance. For an illustration of the psilocybe mushrooms, see Figure 13-10.

Figure 13-9  Peyote cactus (Courtesy of D.E.A.)

Figure 13-10  Psilocybe mushrooms ("shrooms")
(Courtesy of D.E.A.)

## MDA (3.4 Methylenedioxyamphetamine)

Chemically, MDA is related to the amphetamines and mescaline, and it is one of the many chemical variations of those drugs that have been illicitly synthesized in laboratories. This drug is sold in powder, tablet or liquid form. It is usually administered orally and may be "snorted" or injected intravenously.

This drug does not produce a physical dependence and its potential for developing a psychological dependence is unknown, however, continued use will develop a tolerance. MDA produces a feeling of well-being but is not known to cause the visual and auditory distortions like LSD.

## PCP (Phencyclidine)

Phencyclidine was investigated in the 1950s as a human anesthetic, but because of side effects of confusion and delirium, its development for human use was discontinued. It became commercially available for use in veterinary medicine in the 1960s under the trade name Sernylan.

Since 1967, phencyclidine has been produced in clandestine laboratories, which provide the majority, if not all of the PCP on the United States' illicit market. More commonly known as PCP, phencyclidine is sold under at least fifty other names, including "Angel Dust," "Crystal," "Supergrass," "Killer Weed," "Embalming Fluid" and "Rocket Fuel." It is also frequently misrepresented as Mescaline and LSD. Phencyclidine, in its pure form, is a white crystalline powder that quickly dissolves in water. Due to poor manufacturing conditions, much of the illicit PCP contains contaminants, causing the color to range from tan to brown to a gummy mess. It is sold in tablets, capsules, powder and liquid form and administered orally, injected or smoked.

A common method of use is by spraying or dusting the drug on mint leaves, parsley or marijuana and smoking the substance. Researchers agree that PCP probably produces more violent behavior changes than any other illegal substance. It is apparent that the violence producing potential of the drug is unpredictable, whether the person is on his or her first experience or is a habitual user.

Many police agencies are encountering persons under the influence of PCP, who display an incredibly high pain threshold and super strength. For example, one department reported that a medium-sized man under the influence of PCP walked through a plate glass window in a store. When the two officers, responding to the police call, attempted to apprehend this suspect they were thrown about, bitten, and kicked. They found the usual police equipment and restraints useless. It took eight officers, several of whom were injured, to finally control the subject.

Aside from the possible violent behavior, PCP may cause convulsions, stupor or coma followed a psychosis resembling paranoid schizophrenia. Illicit PCP laboratories are increasing, since a few hundred dollars can equip a ramshackle operation and provide the readily available chemicals that easily convert into hundreds of thousands of dollars on the illicit market.

The use of PCP is growing, particularly among juveniles in Southern California. One major department reported an increase of 137% in PCP arrests, over a one-year period.

# MARIJUANA (Cannabis Sativa L)

Marijuana, the popular name of the cannabis plant, is a drug that is prepared by drying the leaves and flowering tops of the plant to make a tobacco-like material. Marijuana grows in many parts of the world, including the United States, without much care. The botanical term for marijuana is Cannabis Sativa L, which is the name of an Indian hemp plant. The potency of the end product (euphoric high) varies widely and depends not only on where the plant is grown but also on the parts of it that are used and the amount of the main intoxicant chemical, delta-9-tetrahydrocannibol, (THC) present.

There are a variety of cannabis plants with origins in different parts of the world. Cannabis Americana and Cannabis Mexicans, are grown in the Western Hemisphere and are the most commonly used in the United States. Cannabis Indica is found in Asia, Africa and the Middle East and is one major source of hashish, a resin extracted from the very top of the plant, that is reported to be much stronger than marijuana.

## Appearance

The cannabis is a leafy plant which grows for the season, dies down, then springs up again the following years from its own seed. The plants are of the male and female variety, which is necessary for reproduction. Cannabis grows to a height of four to twenty feet with flowers composed of irregular clusters of seeds, light yellowish-green in color.

The leaves are composed of five to eleven (always an uneven number) leaflets or fingers which are from two to six inches long. These leaves are a deep green color on the upper side and a lighter green on the under side. The plant is odorous, sticky and is covered with fine hairs. Although both the male and female plants have flowering tops and produce the resin that has THC, the male plant has so little resin that it is essentially useless in supplying the psychoactive (euphoric "high") effects.

Figure 13-11 The marijuana plant has an odd number of leaflets per stem. (Courtesy of D.E.A.)

No one really knows where the plant came from. The Chinese first recorded the existence of cannabis in 273 B.C. For centuries cannabis hemp was the principal source of clothing fibers for the Chinese. Its use for the psychoactive effect was first limited, then altogether forbidden. For centuries, every system of philosophy and religion in India was entwined with the use of cannabis. In recent years the Chinese government has sponsored programs to phase out the use of the drug.

The use of cannabis in the Americas as a euphoria producing agent dates back to the 1920s. Prior to that period it was principally used as a commercial product, hemp. It is estimated that approximately five to ten percent of the marijuana used in the United States is grown here; the remainder comes mostly from Mexico and Columbia.

Mexican marijuana is usually smuggled in one-kilo (2.2 lbs.) bricks, then cut and sold in pounds, half-pounds, ounce bags (known as "tins" or "cans") or cigarettes known as "reefers," "joints," or "sticks." Despite the fact that the U.S. Congress declared marijuana illegal in 1937, the Drug Enforcement Administration of the U.S. Department of Justice recently reported that 43 million Americans have tried marijuana and 16 million used it during the month before the survey.

## Marijuana, How Used

In the United States marijuana users will generally smoke the substance in the form of a cigarette or in a pipe; however, it is occasionally sprinkled on food and eaten. In smoking marijuana the experienced user will inhale the smoke deeply and hold it in his or her lungs as long as possible in order to effect a rapid and full transfer of the THC, via the air cells of the lungs, into the bloodstream.

## Effects

When marijuana enters the bloodstream, it causes several psychological effects which may vary with the user, the potency of the drug and the length of the ingestion period. The significant actions of the drug are manifested in changes referable to the central nervous system. Shortly after inhaling marijuana smoke, the user may experience a feeling of euphoria (a "high") and a relaxing of inhibitions. His or her awareness, sense of touch and perception may be considerably altered, particularly as they relate to time and space.

# HASHISH

The Middle East is the main source of hashish. It consists of the drug-rich resinous secretions of the cannabis plant, which are collected, dried, and then compressed into a variety of forms, such as balls, cakes or cookie-like sheets. Hashish in the United States varies in potency and in appearance, ranging in THC content from trace amounts up to ten percent. The average is reported to be 1.8 percent. The most common method of using hashish is by smoking it in a "hash" pipe, and it is generally much more potent than marijuana.

# HASHISH OIL

The name *hashish oil* comes from the drug culture and is a misnomer in suggesting any resemblance to hashish other than its further concentration. Hashish oil is produced by a process of repeated extractions of cannabis plant materials to yield a dark, viscous liquid, current samples of which average about 20 percent THC. In terms of psychoactive effect, a drop or two of this liquid on a cigarette is equal to a single "joint" of marijuana.

Coordination is usually altered, although the user may fail to recognize this, and intellectual capacities are impaired, particularly those which govern judgment of speed and accuracy. It is obvious that driving a vehicle while under the influence of marijuana is dangerous. Habitual use can lead to a psychological dependency on the drug, and withdrawal symptoms after stopping heavy use.

# DRUG INVESTIGATION TECHNIQUES

Investigations of narcotics and dangerous drugs utilize many of the techniques discussed in previous chapters of this text. However, successful investigations in this area require concentration on determining that narcotics or dangerous drug abuse exists (users), the immediate sources of supply (peddlers) and the sources of production (laboratories, traffic, dealers). To develop the expertise necessary to accomplish these objectives, the investigator is first required to know about and be able to recognize the drugs, drug addicts, users and suspected peddlers. He or she must learn the general *modus operandi* of these individuals, including the slang terms used in the drug culture. Total knowledge of, and the use of appropriate slang terms, are musts in the development of rapport with contacts (overt or undercover), and can lead to fruitful sources of information.

With regard to determining the main producers of illicit drugs, it is generally accepted that these sources are in foreign countries, such as Colombia, Mexico, Asia, Turkey and South America. The FBI and Drug Enforcement Administration, often in collaboration with foreign police and American agencies such as the U.S. Coast Guard, U.S. Customs, state, county and municipal law enforcement, expends continuous effort and resources to control the entry of these drugs into the United States. Although the prime producers of most controlled depressant and stimulant drugs are legitimate pharmaceutical firms, investigations throughout the United States frequently uncover clandestine laboratories producing hallucinogens for the illicit market. It is also apparent that much of the supply of the legally manufactured drugs on the street arrive there by way of theft at the point of manufacture, during shipment or at pharmacies or medical facilities. Additionally, the investigator can expect that the ever increasing market for marijuana in the United States will encourage American production far beyond the backyard patch for private use.

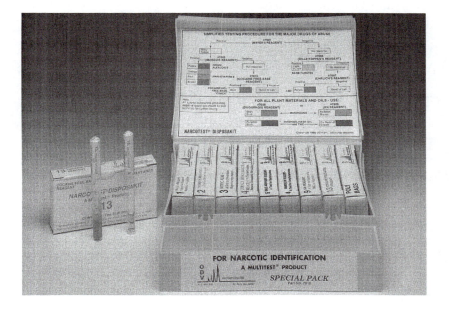

*Figure 13-12 Example of one of many different types of field I.D. kits for drugs (Courtesy of ODV, Inc.).*

Successful narcotics and dangerous drugs investigation will necessarily make prime use of sources of information. Of the many sources available, the informant will play a dominant role in the success or failure of the investigations. At times, it will be necessary to utilize information just to achieve the first determination that "a narcotics or dangerous drugs abuse exists." Follow-up observation by the investigator can validate or negate the information. It is, therefore, important that the investigator utilize a realistic guideline in dealing with informants related to the drug scene.

Generally, there are four types of informants in the drug area: (1) law enforcement agencies whose investigative efforts and expertise can be relied upon, and can save much time and effort for the investigator in selecting the persons or area he will concentrate on; (2) the citizen informer who has observed narcotic and drug activity and has no axe to grind other than a desire for a clean community; (3) the tested or reliable informer, whose reliability is based on the fact that he or she has on several prior occasions given information which has led to valid arrests and convictions; and (4) the untested, or sometimes anonymous informer, who relates information for a variety of reasons. Regardless of the source of information, the investigator must, through observation, investigation and analysis of evidence, establish legal grounds for a search warrant or probable cause for an arrest.

# INVESTIGATIVE GUIDELINES

   A.   The First Determination: Does Drug Abuse Exist? (Users)

        1.   It is important to be able to recognize the outward signs and symptoms of drug abuse; however, it is also important to realize that even experts have difficulty making accurate diagnoses. Unusual or odd behavior may not always be connected with drug abuse. A diabetic may have a valid reason for possessing a syringe and needle or having tablets or capsules. The investigator should seek professional advice when in doubt.

        2.   Common Signs of Drug Abuse

            a.  Changes in attendance or capabilities at work or school

            b.  Poor physical appearance, including lack of attention to dress and personal hygiene

            c.  Wearing sunglasses constantly indoors or at night in order to hide dilated or constricted pupils and to compensate for the eyes' inability to adjust to sunlight. Marijuana causes bloodshot eyes

            d.  Unusual efforts made to cover arms, in order to hide needle marks

            e.  Association with drug users

            f.  Stealing items which can be readily sold for cash (to support a drug habit)

        3.   Indications of Possible Misuse

a. Depressants (Barbiturates)

1) Symptoms of alcohol intoxication, but without the odor of alcohol on breath

2) Staggering, stumbling, or apparent drunkenness, with out odor or use of alcohol

3) Falling asleep while at work or school

4) Appearing disoriented; slurred speech; pupils dilated; difficulty concentrating

b. Stimulants (Amphetamines)

1) The person may be excessively active

2) Excitation, euphoria, and talkativeness; pupils dilated

3) Long periods without eating or sleeping

4) Increased blood pressure or pulse rates

c. Narcotics

1) Scars ("tracks") on the arms or backs of hands, caused by injecting drugs

2) Pupils constricted and fixed; possibly dilated during withdrawal

3) Scratches self frequently

4) Loss of appetite. Frequently eats candy or cookies, and drinks sweet liquids

5) May have sniffles; red, watering eyes and a cough which disappears when he gets a "fix"

6) Users often leave syringes, bent spoons, cotton, needles, metal bottle caps, medicine droppers, and glassine bags in locker or desk drawers

7) The user is lethargic, drowsy, and may go "on the nod"    (i.e., an alternating cycle of dozing and awakening)

8)  During withdrawal, the addict may be nauseated and vomit. Flushed skin, frequent yawning, and muscular twitching are common

d.  Marijuana

1)  In the early stages of marijuana usage, the user may appear animated with rapid, loud talking and bursts of laughter. In later stages he or she may be sleepy

2)  Pupils may be dilated and the eyes bloodshot

3)  May have distortions of perception and hallucinations

4)  The marijuana user is difficult to recognize unless he or she is actually under the influence of the drug, and even then may be able to work reasonably well

5)  The drug may distort depth and time perception, making driving or the operation of machinery hazardous

e.  Other Hallucinogens

1)  Behavior and mood vary widely. The user may sit or recline quietly in a trance-like state, or may appear fearful or even terrified

2)  In some cases, dilated pupils

3)  Increase in blood pressure, heart rate, and blood sugar

4)  May experience nausea, chills, flushes, irregular breathing, sweating and trembling of hands

5)  There may be changes in sense of sight, hearing, touch, smell and time

6)  It is unlikely that a person who uses LSD or PCP, for example, would do so at work, since a controlled environment, often involving a friend to provide care and supervision of the user, is generally desired

B. Second Determination: (Immediate Sources of Supply Peddlers)

    1.  Obtain leads on peddlers, their area of operation and possible locations of drug caches, by use of informants

    2.  Conduct surveillances of suspected peddlers to determine the working patterns of their drug operations, establish a basis for search warrants, and other leads that may lead to a raid and/or arrests

C. Third Determination: Sources of Production

    1.  The use of informants and surveillance techniques can lead to sources of production, particularly clandestine laboratories, that are popping up throughout the United States

    2.  The illicit use of PCP is growing so rapidly, it is estimated seven million people, many of whom are of school age, have used this drug. As to the main producers of illicit drugs (foreign countries), the investigator can collaborate with other agencies at all levels to contribute to the control of this traffic

D. Searches

    1.  Arrest-Based Searches: In each case in which there is a search for evidence at the time of arrest, the circumstances must indicate both a bona fide arrest and a search incidental to the apprehension

    2.  When a valid arrest is made, the scope of the search is now limited to the person of the arrestee and the area within the immediate control of the prisoner at the time of arrest, from which he or she might gain possession of a weapon, or of destructible evidence

    3.  Consent Searches: The courts have held that a constitutional right may be surrendered, if it is surrendered knowingly and voluntarily

    4.  The Fourth Amendment is no exception to this rule, and officers may request consent to search a person, a car or a dwelling place

5. Before approving a consent search, the court will examine the circumstances in which consent was granted

E. Search Warrant: A search warrant may be issued by a magistrate, based on an application supported by an affidavit, setting forth probable cause for believing that:

1. The property was stolen or embezzled

2. The property or things were used as the means of committing a felony.

3. The property or things are in the possession of a person with the intent to use it as a means of committing an offense, or the property or things have been delivered to another party for concealment.

4. The property or things constitute evidence that tends to show a felony has been committed or that a particular person has committed a felony.

## Search Warrant Affidavit

The affidavit must specifically name or describe the person, and particularly describe the property and the place to be searched. The facts that are the basis for the probable cause may be known by the investigator or based on information from an informant. If the information has come from an informant, his or her past reliability will be of considerable importance for a search warrant to be issued based solely on the informant's word, a magistrate will probably require the investigator to cite past incidents of reliable information, arrests and seizures of contraband. A demonstration of the informant's knowledge of the particular drug involved, the method of trafficking and abuse, can also be significant.

## Search of Persons

The investigator must take for granted that a suspect will make every effort to carefully conceal illicit drugs. Therefore, the search must be methodical, intensive and imaginative. Drugs may be found concealed in cigarette holders, fountain pens, cigarette lighters, pinned

$\begin{array}{c}\text{13}\end{array}$

inside of trouser linings at the waistband, pinned inside of a necktie, a trouser fly, a pants leg, secured to a leg or arm or in a hairdo, or secreted in rubber fingers or balloons in body cavities, in hatbands, cigarette packages, linings of clothing or in false heels on shoes or boots. Actually, no part of a person's body or clothing should be overlooked, and for obvious reasons, a policewoman should conduct the search of female suspects.

## Search of Vehicles

It is a common practice to use vehicles to transport illicit drugs. The locations are limited only by the imaginative capabilities of the offender. Some of the common locations are in the spare tires, false gas tanks, behind headlights or taillights, under dashboards, in glove compartments, in headliners, under fenders, in steering wheels, window compartments, behind hubcaps, etc.

Although a search warrant is usually required for a search of a house, the courts have developed the doctrine of "probable cause to search a motor vehicle," without an arrest or search warrant, when there is probable cause to believe that the car contains stolen property, contraband, evidence or fruits of a crime.

In *Carroll vs. United States*, the issue was the admissibility in evidence of contraband liquor seized in a warrantless search of a car on the highway, where it was not practicable to secure a warrant because the vehicle could be quickly moved out of the location or jurisdiction in which the warrant would be sought. The court noted that the search of an automobile on probable cause proceeds on a theory wholly different from that satisfying the search incident to an arrest. The right to search and the validity of the seizure are not dependent on the right to arrest. They are dependent on the reasonable cause the seizing officer has for belief that the contents of the automobile offend the law.

## Search of Premises

The lawful search of a premises must be as methodical and thorough as in a crime scene. Some of the common places used to hide illicit drugs are; (1) bathrooms: within the furniture, baseboards, cabinets, hampers, water tanks, and under washbowls; (2) bedrooms: within mattresses, wastebaskets, bedposts, facial tissue boxes, compartments in the floor covered with a rug, and ceiling light fixtures; (3) kitchens: between walls and built-in cabinets, in trash cans, freezers, ice cube trays in refrigerators, and pinned to backs or bottoms of drawers; (4) living rooms: behind paintings, in seams of stuffed furniture and behind light plates or ceiling light fixtures; (5) walls or windows: compartments built in walls or around windows; (6) clotheslines: clothing or bags hung on lines may contain drugs.

The collection, handling and preservation of narcotic and dangerous drug evidence follows the same principles for handling evidence that are discussed in Chapter 5. The follow-up investigation can be accomplished by utilizing the techniques and services available that are previously covered in this text.

# MODEL FORFEITURE OF DRUG PROFITS ACT

While all states arrest drug dealers and seize drugs, fewer than ten states seize drug profits. Most states have neglected to pass laws attacking the finances of drug dealers.

To help correct this oversight, DEA has developed a "Model Act" based on the 1978 Federal Forfeiture Law. It consists of an amendment to the Civil Forfeiture Section of the Uniform Controlled Substances Act, now enforced in forty-seven states. Those states adopting this provision would be authorized to seize and deposit in their treasury the following:

1. All money and property which was used to buy drugs

2. All property purchased with profits from drug dealing

3. All funds used to facilitate any drug law violation

Federal Bureau of Investigation and Drug Enforcement Administration agents have captured over $500 million just in the past four years. It is possible that the cost to taxpayers for drug enforcement could be considerably offset by the large sums being seized, if all states would adopt and vigorously enforce this provision in the law. No doubt, the taxpayer would welcome drug enforcement paying its own way.

# *POSSE COMITATUS*

A new law has now lifted the previous ban on military participation in antidrug smuggling operations. The Latin term, *posse comitatus,* literally means "power of the county," and traditionally encompasses every able-bodied person 18 years of age or older, in a county which the sheriff may summon for assistance if needed. Since 1878, Title 18, U.S. Code, Section 1385 (Posse Comitatus Act) has prohibited the use of the military as a *posse comitatus.*

On December 1, 1985, President Reagan signed into law a Department of Defense Authorization Act, which amended the Posse Comitatus Act. The Secretary of Defense may now authorize law enforcement agencies to use the following in antidrug smuggling operations:

1.  Relevant information collected during military operations

2.  Military equipment and facilities

3.  Training and advisory services

4.  Department of Defense personnel

## DESIGNER DRUGS

The Drug Enforcement Administration (DEA) of the U.S. Department of Justice, on September 11, 1985, released a report on "Controlled Substances Analogs," which refers to substances of abuse that are "designed" by clandestine chemists. The aim of these chemists is to manufacture compounds that produce the "high" and the euphoria of controlled substances (such as narcotic stimulants, depressants or hallucinogens), but that are chemically different, and thus not subject to the provisions of the Controlled Substances Act. By selling these chemical variants, ("designer drugs"), the clandestine manufacturer can meet the needs of drug addicts and still avoid criminal sanctions.

This practice was first noticed in the 1960s, on a limited basis for some tranquilizers. However, the current wave involves the manufacture of synthetic narcotics. For example, synthetic heroin is up to one thousand times more potent than "natural" heroin.

There were more than ninety overdose deaths in California alone in 1985 attributed to synthetics. Designer drugs are much less expensive than the real thing, leading many addicts to ignore the danger factor for a "cheap high." The DEA is expediting the listing of these analogs in Schedule 1 of the Controlled Substances Act, which will make them illegal to manufacture, possess, etc.

## SUMMARY

The term *narcotic* usually refers to opium and to pain relieving drugs made from opium. Also classed as narcotics are cocaine, ecgonine, coca leaves and several synthetic drugs. The term *dangerous drugs* refers to a variety of non-narcotic substances classified as depressants, stimulants, hallucinogens and cannabis. It is estimated over 32 million people in the United States will pay over $18 billion each year for cannabis and over $125 billion for cocaine.

The use of PCP and ice continues to escalate as do other drug abuses. Narcotics and dangerous drug investigations generally utilize the techniques previously discussed; however, success also requires determining the extent to which users, peddlers, illicit laboratories and dealers may exist. It is also necessary that the investigator become a trained observer with regard to narcotics, drugs, abusers, and peddlers and learn the *modus operandi* and slang terms of the drug culture.

## DISCUSSION QUESTIONS

1. Define the term *narcotic*, and list the various drugs within this classification.
2. Define the term *dangerous drugs*, and discuss the various non-narcotic substances within this classification.
3. What is opium, its source, and how is it used?
4. Discuss and compare morphine, codeine and methadone, their sources, how they are used and their effects.
5. List the various depressants.
6. What is a stimulant? Give some examples.
7. Define hallucinogen.
8. Explain the effects of marijuana and hashish.
9. Discuss the new, so-called "designer drugs."
10. What can be seized under the Forfeiture of Drug Profits Act?
11. How has the posse comitatus law been changed to provide more effective drug enforcement?
12. What are crack and ice? How are they different?

# TERRORISM, BOMBINGS, HOSTAGE INCIDENTS

14

## KEY TERMS AND CONCEPTS

Terrorism (definition of)
Terrorist (profile of)
Explosives (types of)
Bombs (types of)
Bomb disposal
Bomb threat evacuation
Crisis Negotiation Team (components of)

## TERRORISM

In researching the highly sensitive area of terrorism and terrorist activities, this author found that the most enlightening and updated studies have been conducted by the U.S. Department of State. Much of the following information was provided to this author by that agency.

*Terrorism* has no fixed or precise definition. Generally, the term is used to describe "any activity which involves the threat or use of violence for the psychological effects it has on the people or group against which it is directed.*"*

In a manner of speaking, terrorism, whether domestic or international, is a "hate crime" or crime of revenge. Often the perpetrator, or the group he represents, is suffering from some real or imagined injustices and is seeking this cowardly type of "revenge." Fear is generated by the crime's very nature, which is often senseless, wanton killing, and callous indifference to human life. This fear is the source of the terrorist's power and exemplifies his challenge to government and to organized society.

Ninety-five percent of all terrorists use one or more of the following six basic tactics:

1. Bombings

2. Assassinations

3. Armed assaults

4. Kidnappings

5. Barricade and hostage situations

6. Aircraft hijackings

The newest tactic, fortunately not often used as yet, is the deployment of poison gas in confined areas, such as subways.

## Hijacking

Hijackings, alone, account for almost half of all international attacks on commercial aviation. More than 30 percent of all international hijacking is against American, French, Israeli and United Kingdom interests.

## Hostage Taking

The taking of hostages often results from a situation where the perpetrator's escape from the scene of a terrorist act is interrupted by the police. The suspect(s) may take hostages to avoid an immediate arrest. Once they have enhanced their position by taking hostages, they will use the hostages to bargain for freedom, money or the means of escape. Resolving a hostage situation requires prudent, patient, expert application of proper police tactics.

## Recent Statistics

There were 273 international terrorist attacks during 1998, a drop from the 304 attacks recorded the previous year and the lowest annual total since 1971. The total number of persons killed or wounded in terrorist attacks, however, was the highest on record—741 persons died and 5,952 persons suffered injuries.

- Most of these casualties resulted from the devastating bombings in August of the U.S. Embassies in Nairobi, Kenya, and Dar es Salaam, Tanzania. In Nairobi, where the United States Embassy was located in a congested downtown area, 291 persons were killed in the attack, and about 5,000 were wounded. In Dar es Salaam, 10 persons were killed and 77 were wounded.

- About 40 percent of the attacks in 1998 (111) were directed against U.S. targets. The majority of these (77) were bombings of a multinational oil pipeline in Colombia that terrorists regard as a U.S. target.

- Twelve U.S. citizens died in terrorist attacks last year, all in the Nairobi bombings. Each was an Embassy employee or dependent.

- Eleven other U.S. citizens were wounded in terrorist attacks in 1998, including six in Nairobi and one in Dar es Salaam.

- Three-fifths of the toal attacks were bombings (166). The foremost type of target was business related.

## Transnational Terrorism

Individual and group-sponsored terrorist acts have overshadowed state-sponsored terrorism more recently. Many of these terrorists–some loosely organized and some representing groups–claim to act for Islam and operate increasingly on a global scale. These transnational terrorists benefit from modem communications and transportation and have global sources of funding. They are knowledgeable about modern explosives and weapons, and are more difficult to track and apprehend than members of the old established groups or those sponsored by states. Many of these transnational terrorists were trained in militant camps in Afghanistan or are veterans of the Afghan war.

In 1995, a conspiracy to bomb U.S. airliners over the Pacific was uncovered in the Philippines. This group was led by the mastermind of the World Trade Center bombing, Ramzi Ahmed Yousef, and exemplifies this kind of transnational terrorism.

Terrorism by extremist individuals or groups claiming to act for religious motives continued to dominate terrorism in 1995. In Israel, new suicide bombings by radical Islamic Palestinians and the assassination of Prime Minister Rabin by a Jewish Israeli extremist, are examples of continued efforts by terrorists to derail the Israeli-Palestinian peace process. Islamic extremists also waged a series of terrorist acts in Egypt, France, Algeria, and Pakistan.

## Ethnic Terrorism

Ethnic-based terrorism also continued in 1995. The Kurdish group, calling itself the "Kurdistan Worker Party, pressed its terrorist campaign in Turkey and Western Europe. Terrorist attacks or threats erupted in the Caucasus, and Tamil separatists used terrorism to advance their cause in Sri Lanka (formerly Ceylon).

## Hostage Taking

Hostage taking continued to be a major form of terrorist activity, especially in countries like Colombia, where terrorists often have been able to extort ransom payments. This is a common technique used by the illicit drug lords in Columbia. Even high ranking police officials and judges have not been immune from this form of terrorist activity.

## International Efforts to Combat Terrorism

Nations around the world are  increasingly working together to fight terrorism through law enforcement cooperation. Several governments turned over major terrorists to U.S. authorities for prosecution in 1995, including the reputed mastermind of the World Trade Center bombings, Ramzi Ahmed Yousef. Some of Yousef's suspected gang members also were apprehended by other governments and extradited or rendered (similar to extradition) to U.S. authorities.

Another major victory for the rule of law occurred in October, 1995 when a U.S. court convicted Umar Abd al-Rahman and nine co-defendants of conspiring to wage a war of urban terrorism against the United States.

Several multilateral conferences on counter-terrorism in 1995 are a sign of recognition that international cooperation against terrorists is critical. Argentina, for example, convened a regional ministerial meeting on counter-terrorism in August in the wake of two major car bombings in Buenos Aires in 1992 and 1994. Senior officials from Chile, Brazil, Paraguay, Uruguay, the United States, and Argentina, the host nation, discussed practical measures against the terrorist threat posed in the region.

The "group of seven" (G-7) plus Russia also held an unprecedented counter-terrorist conference at the ministerial level in Ottawa in December. In their Declaration, the ministers of the G-7 and Russia pledged to take action in the following areas:

- Strengthening the sharing of intelligence on terrorism
- Pursuing measures to prevent the terrorist use of nuclear, chemical, and biological materials
- Inhibiting the movement of terrorists
- Enhancing measures to prevent the falsification of documents
- Depriving terrorists of funds
- Increasing mutual legal assistance
- Strengthening protection of aviation, maritime, and other transportation systems against terrorism
- Working toward universal adherence to international treaties and conventions on terrorism by the year 2000

The United States, for its part, has made progress in many of these areas. For example, the White House has sought to increase the use of extradition as a counter-terrorist tool. The U.S. is engaged in an active program of negotiating new and updated extradition and rendition treaties with nations around the world. At year's end, five new extradition treaties were pending before the U.S. senate for advice and consent to ratification. Twenty other treaties were at various stages of negotiation at this writing.

In addition, the President signed an Executive Order in January 1995 blocking the assets in the United States of terrorists and terrorist groups who threaten to disrupt the Middle East peace process and prohibiting financial transactions with these groups.

Last year, at the dedication of a memorial in Arlington National Cemetery to commemorate those killed in 1988 in the Pan Am 103 bombing, the President said: "Today, America is more determined than ever to stand against terrorism, to fight it, to bring terrorists to answer for their crimes." More and more nations are demonstrating that same determination as the international battle against terrorism gets stronger each year.

## Political Terrorism

Political terrorism may be defined as violent criminal behavior designed primarily to generate fear in the community, or a substantial segment of it, for political purposes. The deliberate killing of a public official, unconnected with any other crime, for the purpose of intimidating other public officials, would be characterized as an act of political terrorism.

## Non-Political Terrorism

There is a vast area of true terrorist activity that clearly cannot be termed political; notably that frequently ascribed to the present-day operations of organized crime. This is true terrorism, exhibiting conscious design to create and maintain a high degree of fear for coercive purposes. The end product is individual or collective gain, rather than the achievement of a political objective. Unquestionably, such terror may affect society and its patterns of behavior on a considerable scale. Teenage gang activities, that often include murders of rival gang members and innocent bystanders, designed to terrorize a community, also fall within the definition of non-political terrorism.

Other types of non-political terrorism are the acts of mentally disturbed persons such as "mad bombers" and "snipers" who kill indiscriminately, presumably in obedience to some internal demand of a psychopathological nature.

## Profile of a Terrorist

There currently are numerous types of terrorist groups, each made up of a variety of individuals with widely divergent national and sociocultural backgrounds. Women as well as men, are actively involved in terrorist activity. This makes it extremely difficult to develop an overall "terrorist profile" of the "average" terrorist.

For some, becoming a terrorist is an act of retaliation against society for some real or imagined injustice. For others, terrorism constitutes a type of religious or nationalistic crusade. This latter type is often willing to die for their cause in suicide missions, as many news stories will verify. Many terrorists share a common hatred for the U.S. government and the governments of most of the free world. Many claim allegiance to various Third World liberation movements.

# BOMBINGS

According to the U.S. Department of State, there were 273 international terrorist incidents in 1998, a drop from 304 attacks recorded the previous year.

## Government Sponsored Terrorism

Another disturbing trend is state sponsored terrorism (supported by foreign governments). Seven nations are designated as states that sponsor international terrorism. They are: Cuba, Iran, Iraq, Libya, North Korea, Sudan, and Syria. If one examines international terrorism by itself, the picture is getting bloodier.

In 1993 the one international terrorist "spectacular" was the February 26 bombing of the World Trade Center in New York City. This massive explosion left a 100 foot by 100 foot opening in the underground parking garage. The blast scattered debris throughout an adjacent subway station and filled all 110 floors of the north tower with smoke. The effects of the blast and the ensuing fire and smoke caused six deaths and over 1,000 injuries.

The World Trade Center bombing is considered an act of international terrorism because of the political motivations that spurred the attack and because most of the suspects who have been arrested are foreign nationals. However, the FBI has not found evidence clearly indicating which foreign government was responsible for the bombing.

## Terrorism Becoming More Violent

There are several explanations why terrorism has grown bloodier. The terrorists themselves have become brutalized by long struggles. The public has become numbed by the senseless slaughter. In order to gain worldwide attention and stay in the headlines, terrorists increasingly resort to acts of greater and greater violence.

Terrorists also have become more proficient, they can now build bigger bombs. At the same time, the composition of terrorist groups has changed as more brutal men have replaced the older generations of terrorists who debated the morality and utility of actions against selected individuals.

## Types of Explosives

In broad terms, an *explosive* is any material capable of rapid conversion from either a solid or a liquid to a gas with resultant heat, pressure and loud noise. Many chemicals, alone or in mixture, possess the necessary properties for an explosion.

## Low Explosives

A low explosive is usually that which is used to propel bullets from guns, such as black powder and rifle powder. Gun powder is not made to explode violently, yet will detonate and explode violently under certain conditions if confined properly and will ignite with a spark or flame.

## Primary High Explosives

High explosives are very sensitive to heat, friction and shock and detonate violently. They are used in small quantities in blasting caps, primers and detonators to set off secondary high explosives.

## Secondary High Explosives

These explosives are relatively insensitive to heat, friction and shock. They are primarily used as booster charges and main bursting charges, such as TNT and dynamite.

## High and Low Order Detonations

An explosive that has detonated to its maximum velocity is referred to as a *high order detonation*. An explosion that has detonated at a rate lower than its maximum, is referred to as a *low order detonation*. This type of detonation can be caused by improper ignition, a separation between the blasting cap and the main charge, an intentional arrangement by an explosives expert (bomb disposal) or old explosives.

## Ignition of Explosion

Bombs (explosives) can be ignited in many ways including: (1) Ignition by flame from a fuse, like a fire cracker fuse; (2) Ignition by an electrically heated wire, much like a spark plug which ignites gasoline fumes; (3) Ignition by a percussion cap or primer which in turn ignites the main charge (i.e., firing pin on a gun strikes the percussion cap and ignites the charge [propellant]); (4) Ignition by friction very similar to striking a match on an abrasive surface; (5) Ignition by using a blasting cap to detonate dynamite to its maximum rate; or (6) Ignition by the sudden release of high voltage into thin wires, causing them to explode and detonate the explosives.

The field of explosives is highly specialized and deals with home-made, commercial and military varieties. The bomb disposal instrumentation and techniques are equally specialized. It is not the intent of this coverage to offer an in-depth treatment in this area but rather a look at some common or disguised bombs that may be encountered by police.

## Types of Bombs

There are several basic types of bombs and incendiary devices with which the police must deal. Some of the more common are discussed below.

### *"Molotov Cocktail"*

This device is a bottle filled with a flammable liquid, usually gasoline and has a saturated wick which is ignited before throwing. This crude hand-thrown incendiary dates back to the biblical days and derived its present nickname during World War II due to its use by the Russians.

### *Pipe Bomb*

This bomb is commonly used because the materials required are easily obtained and construction is relatively simple. The ordinary pipe bomb is a short piece of pipe that is capped at both ends and has a small hole drilled either on one of the capped ends or on the side of the pipe, for insertion of the fuse. The pipe is frequently filled with smoke-less powder and on occasion, with a stick of dynamite to shatter the metal (shrapnel effect). If desired, the shrapnel effect of a pipe bomb can be augmented by wiring spikes on the outside. In addition, the detonation time can be delayed by taping matches and a cigarette to the end of the fuse. In such instances, the bomber lights the cigarette and has ample time to leave the scene (see Figure 14-1).

Another type of homemade pipe bomb, was used by a militant organization in Los Angeles, to booby trap the windows of their offices. The bomb is equipped with dry cell batteries (electricity), electrical blasting cap, clothes pin (switch) with copper contacts on jaws and a piece of string with an insulated wedge. When the window is opened, the string pulls the wedge out of the clothes pin, the contacts on the jaws snap closed, the circuit is complete and the blasting cap detonates, setting off the main charge in the bomb (see Figure 14-2).

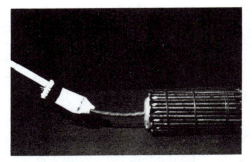

Figure 14-1 Pipe bomb with spikes wired on the outside and delayed fuse (cigarette, matches) (Courtesy of Los Angeles Police Department)

Figure 14-2 Pipe bomb equipped with batteries, blasting cap, clothespin switch with insulated wedge (Courtesy of New York Police Department)

### Letter Bomb

The letter bomb often comes in a regular size envelope. It may be somewhat stiffer than the usual letter, particularly near the edges. This type of bomb is detonated by a pressure-release mechanism, which is activated when the cover sheet is removed and the cardboard container is unfolded, releasing the cocked firing pin (see Figure 14-3).

### Book Bomb

This type of bomb is constructed by hollowing out a book and enclosing a device with an electrical firing pin. The bomb is activated when the book is opened. It is not uncommon for the bomber to select a book with an attractive title, to lure the curious one to open it and take a look.

## Search Aids

The use of highly-trained dogs, who by use of their keen sense of smell, alert police to the presence of explosives has proven to be a very valuable aid to police. In addition, portable X-ray mini-equipment that operates from a power supply or battery pack is available to examine a suspected package, suitcase, etc., and to determine if it is a bomb and if so, its construction and method of activation.

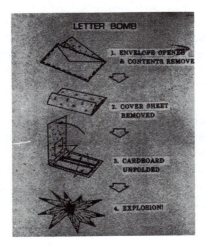

*Figure 14-3  Typical letter bomb*

# BOMB DISPOSAL

Many police agencies have bomb disposal units or squads which are highly trained in the recognition, evaluation, disarming, detonation and disposal of explosive materials. Other police agencies, depending on size and need, may have one bomb disposal technician or rely on the use of technicians from a larger agency or the military. Many of these technicians have been trained by the Department of the Army Explosive Ordnance Disposal Detachments which are located at various locations in the United States.

It is highly desirable that all agencies develop procedures for re-sponding to bomb incidents in advance, including evacuation proce-dures, search procedures, damage control measure and the service of a bomb technician. This coverage of bombings has been limited to home-made bombs; in that light the following is offered:

## Recognition

A homemade explosive may be as small as a cigarette lighter or as large as an automobile. There is no special type of package for an explosive device. High explosives, like dynamite and military type plastics, need no confinement to achieve their explosive potential and may be found without a container. Common containers used for home-made bombs include flashlights, lunchboxes, portable radios, thermos bottles, or packages delivered by mail or left at a location.

## Ignition Mechanisms

Ignition mechanisms for homemade bombs vary from the ultra simple safety fuse (light it and run) to very complicated and sophisti-cated triggering devices. Common types of time delays utilized in the construction of homemade bombs include wrist and pocket watches or clocks. More modern activists may be found using chemical delay fuses which do away with mechanical breakdowns and the ticking sound which seems so dear to the hearts of motion picture special effects personnel.

Many homemade bombs are fitted with secondary ignition de-vices which are designed to detonate the bomb in the face of anyone trying to take it apart or tamper with it. The inclusion of mercury switches in the simplest homemade bomb insures detonation if the device is lifted no more than one-tenth of an inch. Collapsing circuits, found in some homemade bombs, require that all the wiring of the device be visually traced by disposal personnel prior to any wires be-ing cut or disconnected.

### *Homemade Bombs*

The most common type of explosive in use by amateur bomb makers is gunpowder. Since homemade bombs can vary so greatly in size, sophistication and explosive potential, no one set of rules govern-ing disposal methods for homemade bombs would be valid in all cases.

*Figure14-4 New state-of-the-art bomb disrupter stand and laser sight. A technician can remove endcap from a pipe bomb at ten feet, versus two or three inches with the old disrupters (Courtesy Los Angeles Police Department).*

In any instance, where a person has reason to believe that they are confronted with a possible homemade explosive device, the device should be treated as the "real thing." The person finding such a device should immediately take whatever steps are necessary for his or her protection and the protection of those nearby.

### *Evaluation and Damage Control*

The only persons who should ever be called upon to examine, transport, or dispose of a homemade explosive device are those with the specialized training, experience and equipment for the safeguarding of the human lives and property involved. A non-expert person should not try to open the object, cut holes into the object, or lift and transport it to a "safer" place. Opening lids, cutting strings, lifting, shaking, tilting, cutting wires, or cutting through the outer or inner wrappings of homemade explosive devices are some of the most common methods of causing a detonation of the device.

*Figure 14-5 A bomb robot (top photo) is remotely controlled by a technician via closed-circuit television (Courtesy of the Los Angeles Police Dept.)*

Just because a person hand-carries a suspicious package or brief-case into a building and sets it down, does not mean that someone else can pick it up and carry it out of the building with impunity. The common theatrical method of disposing of a homemade bomb, that of dousing it in a pail of water, serves no good purpose whatsoever. Water will not put out a blackpowder safety fuse. If the device functions electrically, the water may complete all of the circuits present, thus resulting in detonation.

It is not advisable to place objects on top of a suspected device or to ring it with filing cabinets or other office furniture. Anyone touching or moving objects near a suspected homemade device is placing themselves in grave physical danger. The "blast channeling" effect achieved by moving filing cabinets around the bomb, or by placing desks over it, is generally more than negated by the additional shrapnel created by those objects in the event of an explosion.

Experienced personnel can take advantage of their training and equipment to reduce some of the danger inherent in the handling and disposal of homemade bombs. Well-equipped bomb disposal units may utilize armored suits and shields to examine, move and penetrate suspected devices.

Portable X-ray units may be employed to look through and examine the electrical circuitry present in the bomb. Cryogenics may be employed to cool or freeze the device, reducing the electrical potential of any batteries present and the explosive potential of the device overall.

### Search Procedures

Procedures should be developed in advance by the individual agency for conducting bomb searches within buildings. The basic search plan may be modified at the time of the incident, taking into account the type of structure to be searched, building area, availability of personnel and supposed time of explosion, if known. The persons searching for possible explosive devices must be thoroughly familiar with the area to be searched, the personnel and the items normally found therein.

What are some of the more obvious areas to search? In public buildings certain areas lend themselves to the aims of the radical bomber. Public waiting rooms, restrooms and stairwells have been prime targets for homemade explosive devices. Those locations are favored due to their ease of direct access. Outside stairways, low awnings and low accessible roofs are favored targets for a bomb to be tossed upon while passing. Any critical areas such as power transformers, telephone and computer banks should be checked on a routine basis. Also, consider increased security measures for these type of areas.

## Bomb Threats

If a bomb threat is received or a bomb is located should police evacuate the premises? The decision to evacuate should be made by the person in charge of the premises, if evacuation is not automatically required by law. Evacuation procedures that will produce the least amount of confusion should be followed. Evacuation may be carried out as a fire drill or by notifying occupants and visitors via the public address system, switchboard and telephone to evacuate as a civil defense drill.

Factors such as undue alarm, morale, cost of disruption to business, protection of property from theft during evacuation, number of persons involved, size of building, location of the possible bomb in the building, and evacuation area should be considered in determining if a building is evacuated. It is most important that police agencies develop a search plan and an evacuation plan. These plans should include who to contact in their organization and what governmental agency has jurisdiction for responding to potential bomb situations in their particular area.

The inexperienced person, when confronted by a possible or confirmed explosive device, must avoid panic. Panic can kill and injure as equally well as a bomb. The person confronted with a possible explosive device should immediately take whatever precautions are necessary for his or her personal safety and the safety of those persons nearby. The only persons qualified to examine, dismantle, or transport homemade explosive devices, are those with experience, specialized training and equipment normally found in a qualified law enforcement bomb disposal unit. No unqualified persons should attempt to neutralize, move or in any way manipulate a confirmed or possible explosive device, either remotely or directly.

## Exploded Bomb

The investigator will utilize the crime scene techniques previously covered, augmented by the services of the bomb unit (technicians) and other laboratory services required by the situation. The follow-up investigation and case preparation will utilize the general investigation techniques previously covered.

# HOSTAGE INCIDENTS

The taking of hostages by traditional criminals, psychopaths, or terrorists, are very sensitive incidents which cause difficult problems and require crucial decisions by the responding law enforcement agencies. The success of the police response can be enhanced greatly by a well-trained Crisis Negotiation Team. Law enforcement agencies and colleges offer hostage crisis negotiation courses designed for law enforcement personnel who already possess a basic knowledge of hostage situations. Because much of the tactical information in these courses is and should be restricted, this author will not delve into great detail here. However, the above resources are highly recommended for concerned criminal justice personnel.

## Personality Characteristics of Hostage Takers

This treatment will cover the basics relative to the personality characteristics of hostage takers, the psychological aspects of hostage incidents and the Crisis Negotiation Team concept. The following materials were furnished by the Supervising Negotiator of the Los Angeles Police Department, Metropolitan Division, Special Weapons and Tactics (SWAT), Crisis Negotiation Teams.

### *Traditional Criminal*

The traditional criminal is usually rational and in control of the situation while committing the crime. The arrival of the police during the commission of the crime, thwarts the planned escape, therefore, hostages are taken to avoid arrest and bargain for freedom. This type is accustomed to having complete control and thus experiences great frustration and conflict through the loss of control to the police and the inability to obtain what he or she wants.

Since these criminals are usually rational, their prime interest and demands will deal with a means of escape and safety. They are considered the easiest type of hostage taker to negotiate with. While the initial confrontation with the police may be explosive, the passing of time will permit a reduction in anxiety and tension. Time is an ally in these situations; the longer the suspects can be contained in the initial locations, the less likelihood there is of a hostage being killed.

### *Sociopath*

The sociopath does not have self-control and has a deep resentment for society as a whole, particularly authority figures. He or she is often one who has had little or no success in life. They lack guilt feelings, have no real conscience or regard for others and have an incapacity for love. Sociopaths have an unconscious need for punishment, coupled with a need to prove their self-worth.

A hostage situation may well represent more than a means of escape; it may be the sociopath's last effort to prove that he or she can be successful at something. It is not uncommon for this type to be suicidal and to manipulate the situation to a point where they are killed by the police. The appropriate police response is to maintain, but minimize, the presence of police officers from the offender's view.

### Psychotic

The psychotic harbors a great inner frustration and conflict. He or she experiences delusions, most commonly those of persecution and has a basic lack of trust in interpersonal relationships. The psychotic expects to be deceived or attacked or to be held in contempt. His or her inner pressures are projected outward at the external prosecutors. This type may experience pleasure from the predicament of the hostage situation by being the center of attention. As time wears on and energy runs low, he or she may consider murder or suicide as a means of solving his/her problems.

### Paranoid Schizophrenic

The paranoid schizophrenic experiences bizarre delusions, loses contact with the environment and may have auditory hallucinations (hear voices). He or she is generally a "loner" who has lost all basic security, is estranged from society and is in great need of a protective and reassuring figure.

### Terrorist

The terrorist channels hate and rage into a cause, which is often political or religious in nature. Terrorists often have a deep conviction and belief that their cause is right, that they must seize control and overturn the enemy (the establishment) and increase public support for the goal; thus publicity via the media becomes a tool of the terrorist.

As the struggle for the cause continues, the terrorist's need for recognition grows. This will require more publicity and propaganda and the terrorist knows that violence will bring both. The typical terrorist leader is charismatic, strong, and exhibits an all-out commitment to the cause. He or she will use violence and philosophy to formulate the desired new moral code. Others who join the cause are followers who have dependency conflicts and identify with a strong leader.

# Psychological Aspects of Hostage Incidents

Negotiating in hostage incidents involves understanding the psychology of both the suspect and the incident. To develop an understanding of those psychological aspects, and to assist the negotiator in the intervention of the crisis, the following concepts are defined.

### *Frustration and Conflict*

A motivated individual is one with a need or a drive; a goal. When an obstacle or barrier is placed in the way and frustrates the attainment of a goal, it becomes a source for conflict. These sources of frustration and conflict are generally classified into three categories: (1) Environmental—caused by obstacles such as physical barriers. (2) Personal—caused by an inadequacy in reaching a goal. This criminal is experiencing personal frustrations due to his or her inadequacy in conducting everyday life. He or she can generally be classified as failing in social relationships. (3) Conflict—caused by motivational conflict within the person. Because two motives somehow conflict, the satisfaction of one means the frustration of the other.

### *Anxiety*

Frustration, hostility, and anxiety are so interwoven that it is difficult to tell which produces which. Anxiety is the constant companion of frustration, particularly conflict-induced frustration. Severe anxiety causes discomfort, and consequently, it motivates a person to get rid of it. The frustrated person will bend his or her efforts to do away with anxiety. In fact, the reduction of anxiety often becomes so important that the person neglects the frustration linked with it. Psychological defenses against anxiety are called defense mechanisms. Defense mechanisms cannot be dealt with as such, they only tend to identify behavior.

## Defense Mechanisms

A comprehension of some of our basic defense mechanisms will help one to understand the rather complex psychological aspects of a hostage incident. The following is offered for that purpose.

### *Rationalization*

Rationalization depends upon the fact that any of several different motives may produce a given action. When rationalizing, a person explains his or her behavior as being due, not to the true motive (of which he or she is ashamed), but rather to another motive which sounds better. The person is not deliberately lying, but fools themselves into believing that what he or she says is really true.

### Reaction Formation

In reaction formation, rather than deny and make verbal excuses for unconscious feelings (as in rationalization), the individual behaves completely opposite to these feelings. In a sense, they act out the lie. An example would be a mother who rejects her child, but does it by smothering the child with attention so that the mother can hide her true feelings from herself.

Many of the "cranks" who bother police agencies demonstrate reaction formation by their single-mindedness of purpose. An example might be the citizen who sees "threats to decency" on every side and spends every available waking moment plowing through smutty material to prove their point.

### Projection

This defense is less desirable than rationalization or reaction formation, in that it involves a greater degree of distortion of fact. Furthermore, it involves a judgment of the other person's motives rather than denial of one's own. When a person dare not recognize shortcomings and unsocial tendencies in themselves, but sees them in others when there is no justification for it, they may be said to be projecting. Such a person sees only flaws in the other person. A mild example would be a person who consistently "out-fumbles" other people in picking up the check, but who frequently criticizes others for being stingy. A far more serious example of projection is found in the severely mentally ill person who attributes to others their own deep feelings of hostility and may wind up harming some complete stranger in order to "protect" themselves.

### Displacement

Sometimes people dare not give the type of reaction they would like to give in a specific situation. They sometimes carry the tendency to give this reaction to a second setting which seems safer. In the second setting they appear to others to react very strongly to a very mild cue, and the reason for this is that they are actually displacing feelings of aggression or a similar emotion stemming from the first situation.

### Examples

An officer who has been criticized by his superior may over-react to any hint of criticism from a motorist. A male motorist may displace his own frustrations with his wife onto another motorist who frustrates him slightly while he is driving. This defense is less desirable than those previously mentioned because usually innocent people are the recipients of the individual's aggression.

### Fantasy

Day dreams are a common defense mechanism. In some persons these fantasies become quite strong. Occasionally, when some kind of peculiar behavior is observed, it is to the person's fantasy that one must turn for explanation. If the person's fantasy life were understood, his or her actions would be quite predictable.

Quite often, individuals utilize daydreams to release tension by fantasizing what they'd like to do rather than actually carry out inappropriate behavior. For this reason, it is not an unhealthy defense unless one begins to substitute fantasy for reality and then operates in keeping with his or her wishful thinking. At that point, he or she would be considered mentally ill.

### Repression

This mechanism refers to motivated forgetting. Everyone possesses many memories of which he or she is unaware. These memories are held down because it might be too embarrassing or threatening to a person if he or she recognized them. In psychotherapy, these memories may be brought to the surface and used in the person's treatment. The chief point to be remembered here is that people can honestly forget things very rapidly when it is to their advantage to do so. The fact that repressions operate in all of us makes it all the more necessary that detailed records be kept whenever the necessity for accurate recalling of events may arise.

### Emotional Insulation

When people have their feelings hurt frequently, they sometimes decide to protect themselves by refusing to "stick their necks out" any longer. By erecting a strong shell and living alone inside of it, they save themselves from future hurt. At the same time, this cuts them off from pleasant contact with others. This mechanism is most apt to be demonstrated by a person with considerable experience in law enforcement work who gradually becomes disappointed with his or her life and disgusted with people in general, because of the ones he or she encounters in the line of duty.

Unfortunately, they tend to mar their relationship with others and usually become very lonely persons. All people need the stabilizing influence of friends to maintain their own balance and realistic viewpoints.

The most healthy of all defense mechanisms are the following three. These involve an active attempt to deal with reality and still attain some satisfaction of one's motives or goals.

### Compensation

Compensation is the device where, when one avenue of satisfaction is blocked, another avenue is taken which will bring a roughly equivalent reward to the individual. For example, a high school boy is most apt to get recognition through athletic ability. If he does not have this ability, he can get a somewhat similar degree of satisfaction through managing a team or writing sports for the school paper. In most cases compensation is a healthful device. In some cases, however, the alternative road picked for satisfaction is not a good one, and here compensation becomes unhealthy.

### Identification

The mechanism of identification consists of attaching ourselves to other persons or things and making their strong points and successes our own. We might be said to be "ego" involved with the organization, team, or person with whom we identify. This is quite a normal mechanism and children learn much by identifying with their parents. We also see parents identifying with children, as in the case of the mother who through her daughter, tries to realize her own frustrated ambition to be a stage star. People who identify with their children resent any criticism of them since it becomes personal.

Identification can be a very positive force, as when the normal child does identify with his or her parents and gets some feeling of what it is like to be a grown-up by wearing grown-up clothing and acting out grown-up roles. Sometimes the process of identification can create trouble, as when juveniles pick the wrong kind of person to identify with and attempt to model themselves after some criminal.

### Sublimation

This defense mechanism is employed by all individuals and is probably the most desirable as it enables one to function in society.

Sublimation involves finding a suitable socially acceptable release from one's tensions and frustrations. The boy who releases his frustration and anger in competitive contact sports, such as football, is utilizing sublimation. Similarly, the officer who has been in a tense, stressful situation all day and goes "jogging" for a few miles after work is releasing his or her tension through physical activity. In each situation, the individual's basic drive has not been denied, instead he or she chooses a constructive rather than destructive mode of expression.

The above, of course, is not a complete listing of all defense mechanisms, but serves to present a fairly broad sample of them. Frequently, a person will demonstrate the use of several mechanisms at one time. It should be remembered that these are basically protective devices and that a direct attack on them usually does more harm than good.

# THE CRISIS NEGOTIATION TEAM

The success rate of law enforcement in defusing potentially dangerous spontaneous situations is excellent. Training, experience and natural skills, which most officers possess, lend themselves to the proper handling of various routine incidents most effectively. Hostage situations, on the other hand, require considerably different methods of resolution. For example, time is the officer's greatest ally in hostage situations. The success of any counter-hostage plan is also dependent upon sound decision-making, flexibility, good communications and close coordination of verbal and physical tactics.

The Crisis Negotiation Team (CNT) within the typical metropolitan police department, is designed to support tactical activity with verbal intervention in crisis or hostage incidents. Communications or "negotiations" with criminals is designed to gain time for the safe release or rescue of hostages and gain the tactical advantage over the incident. Negotiations also provide decision makers with the opportunity to objectively evaluate complex problems presented and arrive at well-planned solutions.

Typical large police departments' CNT teams consist of the following personnel:

- Supervisor
- Primary negotiator
- Secondary negotiator

- Investigator
- Psychologist

There are three key objectives that Crisis Negotiation Team personnel strive to achieve:

- Safety for all people involved
- Safe release or rescue of hostages
- Apprehension and prosecution of suspects involved

The CNT's purpose is to provide verbal and tactical support to the Special Weapons and Tactics (SWAT) team responsible for controlling a barricaded suspect or hostage situation. Negotiations with potentially dangerous persons are considered "verbal tactics" and fall within the preview of SWAT. Therefore, the supervisor and primary and secondary negotiators of the CNT should be selected from personnel assigned to the department's SWAT team.

Investigative personnel are usually selected from specialized groups within the department and provide criminal profiles of perpetrators. They also subsequently handle the prosecution of suspects involved. If the department has a Behavioral Services Section, they are utilized in evaluating motives, types of criminals and predictability of behavior. Investigative and psychological personnel do not negotiate with criminals involved. The purpose of having the CNT negotiators with the SWAT team is to provide for a continuity of events should negotiations fail to secure the release of hostages and it becomes necessary to implement a physical rescue of the hostages.

## NEGOTIATOR SELECTION CRITERIA

In medium to larger sized police agencies the Behavioral Science Services section selects persons for hostage negotiations who meet certain psychological criteria. They must be able to perform objectively and efficiently during high-stress situations and over prolonged periods of time.

Personnel being considered for primary and secondary negotiator positions are typically administered several psychological tests. These tests are then evaluated to determine individual intellectual achievement, independence, flexibility, tolerance, well-being, cooperation, responsibility and patience.

The qualifications and personal attributes for SWAT team members are equal or more stringent than those indicated for CNT members. SWAT personnel are evaluated under actual field conditions, in addition to the tests administered within a clinical environment. Investigative and alternate negotiation personnel are typically selected on the basis of experience, expertise, gender, and language capabilities. There is usually no psychological testing administered to investigative personnel.

# CRISIS NEGOTIATION TEAM RESPONSIBILITIES

As indicated previously, the Crisis Negotiation Team's main purpose is to "defuse" critical situations where hostages are involved. It is also this group's purpose to gain time, which very often results in release of hostages and surrender of the suspect(s) responsible. It is imperative that the CNT coordinate closely with the SWAT team. In order to accomplish this close coordination, the role and function of each member of the CNT must be clearly understood by all. The following is a summary of the CNT's basic responsibilities.

## Team Supervisor

The CNT supervisor is (1) responsible for negotiation team operation; (2) coordinates and delegates activities within the team; (3) maintains close liaison with the tactical commander and SWAT team leader, keeping them informed of negotiations; (4) provides the primary negotiator with tactically significant information; (5) delegates procurement of resources and logistics as necessary and (6) conducts hostage debriefings.

## Primary Negotiator

The primary negotiator is a SWAT team member who (1) establishes and maintains an open line of communication with the suspect(s); (2) attempts to establish a working rapport with the suspect(s); (3) attempts to negotiate the release of the hostage(s) and (4) conducts hostage debriefing sessions.

## Secondary Negotiator

The secondary negotiator is also a SWAT element member. His or her role is to (1) provide relief for the primary negotiator; (2) maintain a log and advisory notes for the primary negotiator; (3) monitor tape recordings of the negotiations; (4) organize logistics and (5) maintain an open line of communication with the tactical commander. The secondary negotiator must remain with the primary negotiator and have firsthand knowledge of all that has transpired. He or she also conducts hostage debriefings.

### Team Investigator

The CNT investigator (1) provides investigative resource intelligence and serves as advisor on militant groups, (2) establishes criminal profiles and collects evidence for prosecution purposes, and (3) must have a thorough concept of negotiation and tactical team operation. The investigator does not negotiate with the hostage taker(s).

### Psychologist

The psychologist (1) serves as advisor to the negotiation team supervisor; (2) advises regarding psychological identification and predictability of suspect and hostage behavior; (3) provides suggestions to avoid reaching a negotiation impasse and (4) conducts hostage debriefings. He or she does not negotiate with the hostage taker(s).

## THE INTELLIGENCE SECTION

Terrorists do not plan their operations openly. Going underground and engaging in clandestine activities are essential to a terrorist movement. Law enforcement cannot merely respond to violent acts after they have occurred, therefore, police intelligence is the first line of defense against terrorism.

Preventative intelligence via a collaboration of federal, state, county and municipal law enforcement agencies is imperative. This would include the regular and effective collection, processing, storage, retrieval and exchange of information relating to persons and organizations reasonably suspected of engaging in specified violent, intimidating or subversive conduct.

All legal standards must be observed before engaging in and during a preventive intelligence operation. This activity may include the use of paid and unpaid informants and a variety of surveillance and undercover techniques. The investigator may be able to develop a conspiracy case before a terrorist act occurs. If an act is not prevented, the investigator is then responsible for identifying and apprehending all persons responsible for the act. The crime scene, follow-up investigation and case preparation will utilize the general investigation techniques previously covered.

## SUMMARY

Terrorism is coercive and designed to manipulate the will of its victims. A great degree of fear is generated by the terrorist's callous indifference to human life. This fear is the source of the terrorist's power. International terrorism will continue as an extreme expression of nationalistic, ethnic, and political discontents. Political terrorism is violent criminal behavior designed to intimidate a community, or segment of it, for political purposes.

Non-political terrorism, on the other hand, is designed to coerce its victims for individual or collective gain. There is no hard evidence that indicates that there are "born terrorists." Thousands of individuals may suffer from political and social frustrations and may go through radicalizing experiences, but only a handful become terrorists. According to the U.S. State Department, there has been over 8,000 international terrorist incidents from 1968 to 1986, causing in excess of 3,000 deaths.

Some of the common and disguised bombs that may be encountered by police are molotov cocktails, pipe bombs, letter and book bombs. Police use highly-trained dogs to alert them to the presence of explosives and portable X-ray equipment is available to examine a suspected container to determine if it is a bomb and if so, its construction and method of activation. A bomb technician is always used for disarmament and disposal of explosives.

The taking of hostages by traditional criminals, psychopaths or terrorists creates difficult problems that require crucial decisions by the responding law enforcement agencies. The personality characteristics of hostage takers will differ. Traditional criminals are usually rational and their prime interest and demands will deal with a means of escape and safety. The sociopath has a deep resentment for society as a whole, frequently does not have self control and may be suicidal. The psychotic harbors a great inner frustration and conflict, often has delusions of persecution and may consider murder or suicide as a solution to the problem. The paranoid schizophrenic experiences bizarre delusions and hallucinations, has lost all basic security and needs protection and reassurance.

The terrorist has channeled hate and rage into a political or religious cause and has a fanatical conviction that the establishment must be seized or overthrown. The terrorist thrives on publicity and propaganda and knows that violence will bring both. Negotiating in hostage incidents involves understanding and dealing with the psychology of both the hostage taker(s) and the incident. Some understanding of frustration, conflict and anxiety and the various defense mechanisms employed to relieve anxiety is necessary.

The Crisis Negotiation Team is designed to support tactical concepts by verbal intervention into crisis or hostage incidents. Communications or negotiations with hostage takers attempt to "buy" time for the safe release or rescue of the hostages and gain tactical advantage over the incident. Personnel involved in hostage negotiation should be able to perform objectively and efficiently during high stress situations and over prolonged periods of time. Therefore, the selection and training of these personnel is of prime importance.

# DISCUSSION QUESTIONS

1. What is terrorism?
2. Discuss the difference between political terrorism and nonpolitical terrorism.
3. Are there "born" terrorists? Discuss the research information on this question.
4. Define the following: low explosive, primary high explosive, secondary high explosive, high order detonation and low order detonation.
5. Describe the various methods of igniting explosives.
6. Describe the types of bombs treated in this chapter.
7. Discuss the personality characteristics of hostage takers (i.e., the traditional criminal, the sociopath, the psychotic, the paranoid schizophrenic and the terrorist).
8. Explain the Crisis Negotiation Team concept.
9. List the negotiation team selection criteria.
10. Discuss the Crisis Negotiation Team's responsibilities.

# CASE
# PREPARATION

15

## KEY TERMS AND CONCEPTS

Preparation of the case for the prosecutor
    Synopsis
    Guidelines
    Special considerations
Grand jury indictment
Statute of limitations
Specialized investigators
Plea bargaining
Adjudication

Case preparation involves a systematic organization of all the information, evidence and documents related to a case. From the inception of the investigation, categories must be designated for all information and materials involved in the case. Some examples are: the crime scene, the follow-up of investigative leads, laboratory services and outside agency collaboration and assistance, etc. By maintaining the information and materials in these categories, it will be easier to correlate and coordinate the coverage and progress in the case.

Experience indicates that it is easy to say, "No stone will be left unturned in this investigation," but it is extremely difficult to accomplish without a well-organized method of handling paperwork. In major cases involving a series of crimes, whether they are murders, robberies or major frauds; investigative leads, information, anonymous tips or even crank calls can be lost in the shuffle, without good administration. For this reason many police departments have initiated the "Major Investigation Task Force" concept. This concept involves basic short-range, mid-range and long-range planning. This provides necessary personnel from a skeleton staff to the full-fledged crew required for various types of major investigations.

The names and specialized experience or talents of investigators, technical personnel, supervisors and administrators are maintained in special files or in a computer. When a major crime or series of crimes calls for task force action, a team of the desired specialty and size can be put together promptly. For example, the assassination of the late Senator Robert F. Kennedy required the formation of a special 40-person investigative unit. The unit was organized in several categories including: (1) Administrative Section, charged with records and evidence control; (2) Screening Section, charged with screening and correlation of all incoming information, leads and documents including depositions; (3) Case Preparation Section, charged with preparation of the case for trial, medical and personal background investigations of Sirhan Sirhan and his family and investigations of conspiracy allegations; (4) Specialized Interviewing Teams Section, charged with interviews not specifically handled by other sections; (5) Polygraph Section, charged with all polygraph examinations conducted during the investigation.

The unit was dramatically named Special Unit Senator (SUS) and was staffed by the Chief of Detectives, a captain, three lieutenants, 32 investigators and three stenographers. The variety of expertise represented by the staff included homicide, conspiracy, intelligence, polygraph, foreign languages, etc. The services of special prosecutors, psychiatrists and other county, state and federal agencies were utilized regularly.

Every investigative technique and service covered in this text was used to one extent or another. It was this author's privilege to assist in the organization of the unit and to serve as supervisor of the Case Preparation Section. The organization, correlation and control of all information, documents and exhibits is the key to good case preparation; as was true in the case mentioned.

# PREPARING THE CASE TO PRESENT TO THE PROSECUTOR

The investigator first prepares a synopsis (review) of all the pertinent information, evidence, documents and exhibits in the case. The synopsis must include all material which establishes the existence of the *corpus delicti* and the identity of the person or persons to be charged. It will also include a list of witnesses and exhibits, with a brief summary of the facts and identifications each witness (including investigators) can testify to. Additionally, the synopsis will contain any allegations of innocence expected from the defense. These allegations may be in the form of alibi witnesses, lack of intent, insanity, mistaken identity, self-defense or accident.

## Seizure of Evidence and Voluntariness of Statements

The synopsis will include a brief statement of fact relating to each item of evidence setting forth the exact circumstances under which all evidence was seized in order to evaluate its admissibility in court. The nature and circumstances under which admissions or confessions were obtained must also be stated, so that the voluntariness of the statements may be evaluated by the prosecutor.

## Witness Information

The synopsis will include any negative information concerning any witnesses. This would include criminal records, physical or emotional instabilities, handicaps or any factor that could affect the witnesses' performance in the court room. The investigator should also include information on those witnesses that will require review of their testimony before trial. In some sensitive or complicated cases the prosecutor may review testimony with all witnesses including investigators, laboratory personnel, psychiatrists, etc., before trial. All information regarding potential or actual hostile prosecution witnesses must be included in the synopsis.

## Special Considerations

On occasion the investigator may learn of defense strategy plans that are of prime importance for the prosecutor to know. For example, it is not uncommon for the defense counsel in a major case to acquire personal information regarding the prosecutor or the judge that are expected to be involved in the case. Information that the prosecutor or the judge is short-tempered or is offended by defense counsels who engage in theatrics or badger witnesses, can be used advantageously by the defense. Defense attorneys sometimes capitalize on certain characteristics of the prosecutor or the judge, via their general deportment or method of cross-examination of witnesses. This maneuver can reach the point where the prosecutor and the judge are both angry at defense counsel and can culminate with the judge overruling a proper defense motion. This will provide the defense with a prejudicial error on which to base an appeal, in the event the defendant is convicted.

## Case Folder for the Prosecutor

The completed synopsis and copies of all official reports and statements referred to therein are placed in a case folder for the prosecutor. The folder will include the reports on all evidence mentioned, its examination, its location (official custody) and its availability to the prosecutor and the court. The prosecutor may represent either a city, county, state or federal government depending on the specified crime and jurisdiction involved.

The prosecutor may file a complaint charging the suspect(s) with a specific offense(s) if, in his or her opinion, the charges are substantiated. He or she may also deny the complaint for reasons of insufficient evidence or may request further investigation of the case by the investigator or the prosecutor's office. It is not uncommon in many jurisdictions for felony cases to be referred by district (county) attorney's offices to city attorney's offices, for reduction to misdemeanors. In the final analysis, when a prosecutor files a complaint, the respective court in that jurisdiction will issue a warrant of arrest for the suspect.

## Presentation of the Case to the Grand Jury

In highly sensitive and other selected felony cases, the prosecutor may proceed by grand jury indictment, instead of the complaint process. Some examples of the kinds of circumstances which may cause the prosecutor to utilize this procedure are as follows:

### Statute of Limitations

The statute of limitations may be running out on a case and the suspect(s) is not in custody. This means that criminal action via the courts against the suspect has not been initiated. The *statute of limitations* is the time within which the suspect must be charged and it is computed from the date of the commission of the crime or the date the crime is discovered. Examples that are applicable in many jurisdictions are as follows:

| CRIME | STATUTE OF LIMITATIONS |
|---|---|
| Murder | None |
| Embezzlement of public moneys | None |
| Kidnapping for ransom, reward or extortion | None |
| Falsification of public records | None |
| Acceptance of bribe by a public official | Within 6 years after commission |
| Grand theft | Within 3 years after discovery |
| Forgery | Within 3 years after discovery |
| Voluntary manslaughter | Within 3 years after discovery |
| Involuntary manslaughter | Within 3 years after discovery |
| Other felonies | Within 3 years after commission |
| Misdemeanors | Within 1 year after commission |

*Note:* If at the time of, or after a crime is committed, the suspect is out of the state within which the crime was committed, the statute of limitations does not start until the suspect enters the state where the crime was committed. If a jurisdiction fails to initiate criminal action within the limitation of time for the particular crime involved, the statute of limitations will have run out on that crime and the suspect is free from prosecution.

### *Reluctant Victims or Witnesses*

The case may involve reluctant victims or witnesses in, for example, a rape, homicide or organized crime situation, where threats of violence have been made against them. The grand jury hearing can be held in secret in such cases, thus protecting and reassuring the reluctant participants.

### *Frauds—Public Officials*

Rather than file a complaint, the prosecuting attorney may seek a grand jury indictment in a highly involved fraud case, where the prosecution desires to eliminate the exposure of victims and witnesses to media publicity or cross-examination by the defense. In cases where police officers or other public officials are suspected of criminal acts, the prosecuting attorney is likely to present the matter to the grand jury.

## Grand Jury Hearing

At present, lawyers are not permitted in a grand jury hearing. This rule is applicable in federal courts and most state courts. Defense lawyers are permitted to remain outside the hearing room and clients may leave the hearing to confer with them.

The grand jury hearing is not a criminal trial, primarily because the defendant cannot cross-examine the witnesses against him. However, in practice, all testimony is taken under oath and the rules of evidence are followed. Many defense counsels take issue with this factor, claiming that the absence of a lawyer during the hearing permits a zealous prosecutor to engage in improper questioning of witnesses. Other lawyers and jurists have stated that a grand jury is no more than a "rubber stamp" for the prosecutor. It is clear that the grand jury process is under examination. In California, one indicted by a grand jury has the right to a preliminary hearing, for the purpose of deciding if they must stand trial. State and federal legislation, designed to permit defense lawyers in the grand jury room and to provide for the review of indictments by a judge, is being considered.

At present, grand jurors may ask questions of the witnesses and they often do so. As a body they can request the accused to testify. Witnesses can excuse themselves to consult with a lawyer who is waiting outside the room, then return to the witness stand and refuse to testify or comply with the request. The presentation of testimony and evidence in a grand jury hearing otherwise follows the same procedure as a court hearing or trial.

## Grand Jury Indictment

When a grand jury votes to indict an accused, a "true bill" is drafted by the prosecutor and given to the foreman of the jury for the required signature. The indictment is then presented to a judge of the superior court. The judge will issue a bench warrant charging the specific offenses and indicating the bail (if the offense is bailable). The indictment has the same force and effect as a preliminary hearing, wherein the defendant is held to answer to the charges in superior court. This is followed by the filing of an "information" in the superior court by the prosecutor. Like the grand jury hearing the preliminary hearing is not a criminal trial, but rather a proceeding by which it is determined whether or not a crime was in fact committed and if there is reasonable cause to believe that the accused committed the crime.

The running of the statute of limitations on a crime is stopped by either a grand jury indictment and bench warrant or when the accused is held to answer in a preliminary hearing and the Information is filed in superior court.

## Advantages of the Grand Jury Procedure

Some of the advantages of the grand jury procedure to the prosecutor and to a community are obvious in the previous sections. Negative attitudes, expressed by some lawyers and jurists towards the grand jury notwithstanding, it cannot be ignored that many sensitive and complex cases may have never come to trial without this process. Historically, the exposure and eventual prosecution of persons involved in corrupt political machines in various major cities in this country, would not have occurred had it not been for the independent actions of grand juries.

## Disadvantages of the Grand Jury Procedure

There are disadvantages in the grand jury procedure for the prosecutor. Opinions to the effect that a grand jury is no more than a rubber stamp for the prosecutor notwithstanding, in fact, it is the exclusive province of a grand jury to render an indictment or not, as it sees fit. The prosecutor's power is limited, as he or she personally, cannot charge the accused with any crime in this process, even if the evidence substantiates it. Only the grand jury may do so. Another disadvantage of this process is that the transcript of a grand jury hearing cannot be submitted to the trial court to be used against a defendant as it can in the case of a preliminary hearing.

## Additional Investigation Requested

The prosecutor or the grand jury may request that additional investigation be conducted in a case. If this occurs, it will normally be after the prosecutor evaluates the case that is presented by the investigator. If the case is intended for the complaint and preliminary hearing process, the prosecutor is generally the sole judge of whether there is sufficient evidence to proceed with a criminal action. However, if the case is intended for the grand jury it may be first evaluated by a criminal complaints committee of that body for evidential sufficiency.

That committee, independently, or acting with the prosecutor, can request additional investigation. On occasion, a major case may require the assignment of a special prosecutor at the inception of the investigation. In this event it is not uncommon for the prosecutor to collaborate in the direction of the investigation and furnish investigators, if the office has such a staff.

Who conducts the investigation is normally determined by the nature of the case and the particular kinds and levels of investigative expertise required. For example, if the investigation thus far has been conducted by the police and the additional investigation required is within their expertise, then that agency will normally complete the case. If the additional investigation required is not within the expertise of the police, the prosecutor may furnish the investigators required from his staff (if available) or from other agencies and private sources. In a case where a special prosecutor is involved from the start, the investigation may be conducted by police or investigators from the prosecutors office, and any other specialized assistants which may be needed.

## Specialized Investigators Other Than Police

The specialized investigators that are normally not a part of many police agencies may be members of the investigative staff of the county prosecutor, the state attorney general, the United States Attorney, or other public and private agencies. Some examples of the expertise that is available and which may be required are as follows: (1) major fraud specialists (i.e., stocks, bonds, corporations, computer frauds); (2) tax specialists; (3) consumer frauds specialists (i.e., automobile and television repair, false advertising); (4) psychiatrists, psychologists, physicians and other scientific expertise needed to investigate and refute defense contentions relative to mental state, insanity or accidental causes of death in homicide cases.

## Pretrial Discovery

An important consideration during the investigation and case preparation, are the pretrial discovery rules in many jurisdictions. The defense may make a certain motion in court to require the police or the prosecutor to produce certain items of evidence against the accused or a list of witnesses. If the court grants the motion, it will order the prosecutor to produce the evidence. A motion for discovery may, of course, be denied by the court when there is evidence indicating that granting the motion will create an imbalance in the favor of the accused, or pose a serious threat to the life of a witness. For example, the accused may request the names and addresses of all witnesses, a copy of their statements to the police and the right to interview them without police interference. If the life of an eyewitness to the crime would be endangered by this process, the court may deny access to the witness and grant only the testimony expected from that witness.

## Plea Bargaining

Plea bargaining involves negotiation between the prosecutor and the defense counsel. By the means of this negotiation, an agreement is reached whereby the defendant is allowed to withdraw a plea of innocence for the purpose of entering a plea of guilty. The fact that the agreement is always to the advantage of the defendant, accounts in part, for the popularity and broad use of this procedure by defense counsels. Many prosecutors, particularly in large jurisdictions, who have overcrowded court calendars, understaffed offices, and budget problems are willing participants, as well.

A basic example that occurs regularly is as follows: The defendant is charged with five counts (separate crimes) of robbery or burglary. The prosecution has a well-prepared case that will likely result in verdict of "guilty on all counts" by the judge or jury. The defense counsel will normally (in keeping with the best interests of his client) advise the defendant that he will most probably be convicted on all charges. He will ask the defendant's permission to plea bargain with the prosecutor, that is, enter a plea of guilty to one count and request dismissal of the remaining four counts "in the interest of justice." If the defendant agrees and the defense counsel and the prosecutor come to the same terms, the court is notified and asked for its concurrence. The court can reject the agreement, but will normally not do so unless the plea of guilty violates the defendant's rights in some way.

Defendants are frequently willing to plead guilty to a lesser included offense such as theft rather than robbery. This eliminates the need for a lengthy trial and usually results in a lighter sentence; thus relieving the overcrowded prison system to some degree. Regardless of the savings in time and money, many people are opposed to plea bargaining. Alaska, in 1975, for example, banned plea bargaining. The California Supreme Court has generally upheld the constitutionality of a voter-approved initiative which practically eliminates plea bargaining.

Some critics of the process claim that the prosecutor's prime reason for participating in plea bargaining is that it offers a high conviction record he or she can talk about at election time. Some investigators resent the practice, particularly when the prosecutor does not show the courtesy of consulting with them before making an agreement with the defense. The criticisms notwithstanding, plea bargaining does provide the defense counsel with a method of insuring his client the best legal defense possible. He would be remiss in his duties if he did not make every legal effort to gain advantage for his client.

## When to Terminate an Investigation

It is obvious that in a case involving a crime that has no statute of limitations, such as murder, the investigation will remain open until it has been solved and the guilty person(s) is charged with the offense and brought within the jurisdiction of the appropriate court. Many police agencies terminate an investigation when the case is classified as "cleared." The reasons for classifying cases as cleared are varied and not as yet uniformly practiced. Case clearance policies are set for individual police agencies by their respective administrators.

Some of the reasons for classifying cases as cleared are as follows: (1) case is solved, suspect is arrested and charged; (2) case is solved, suspect is arrested in another state and extradition of the suspect has failed or is considered infeasible by the prosecutor; (3) case is solved, the victim refuses to prosecute; (4) case is unfounded by investigation; or (5) case is solved and suspect is dead.

*Note:* It is important to point out that the classification of the case as "cleared" and the termination of an investigation by a police agency does not preclude a reopening of the investigation by the prosecutor or grand jury at a county level or the attorney general at the state level. One of the important features of the criminal justice system is that it provides a method of checks and balances. Without this provision in the system, fraudulent investigations, cover-ups and other acts of malfeasance could go unchallenged by higher authorities.

## An Adjudicated Case

A case is considered *adjudicated* when it has been settled by a court. The conviction and sentencing of a defendant in a case does not always mean that the case is permanently closed, however. If a prejudicial error or other injustice was suffered by the defendant during the trial and the record so reflects, the case may be successfully appealed by the defense. If a case is appealed it is not considered adjudicated until the appeal has been denied by the highest court of jurisdiction. Because of the above factors, the investigator (particularly in major cases) should clear with the prosecutor, before making a disposition of evidence that is in police custody.

## SUMMARY

Case preparation involves a systematic organization by categories of all the information, evidence and documents related to the case. The maintenance of all information and materials in categories provides easier correlation and currency of coverage and progress of the case. Guidelines for preparing the case to present to the prosecutor first call for the investigator to prepare a synopsis of all the pertinent testimonial information, evidence, documents, and exhibits in the case. The synopsis will include expected allegations of innocence by the defense, the conditions under which evidence was seized, the voluntariness of statements by the accused, defense strategies known to the investigator and negative information concerning prosecution witnesses.

The completed synopsis and copies of all official reports and statements are presented to the prosecutor. The prosecutor may represent either a city, county, state or federal government depending on the specified crime and jurisdiction involved. The prosecutor may file a complaint charging the suspect(s) with specified offenses, deny the complaint for reason of insufficient evidence or request further investigation to substantiate the case or proceed to reduce the case to a lesser charge. In highly sensitive cases or when it is desired to stop the running of the statute of limitations (usually when the suspect is not in custody), the prosecutor may proceed by a grand jury indictment. The case prepared for the prosecutor may come under scrutiny by the defense via a pretrial discovery motion. A motion for discovery may require the police or prosecutor to provide for inspection of certain items of evidence against the accused or a list of witnesses and the right to interview the witnesses without police intervention. Such a motion may be denied by a court if granting the motion will create an imbalance in favor of the accused or pose a serious threat to the life of any witness.

It is not uncommon for a defense counsel to resort to plea bargaining, particularly when the prosecution has a strong, well prepared case. Plea bargaining is a negotiation between the prosecutor and the defense counsel, whereby if an agreement is reached, a defendant is allowed to plead guilty to a lessor number of crimes charged or a lessor and included offense within the specific crime that is charged. This arrangement is always to the benefit of the accused and also saves much money in terms of court time for the prosecuting jurisdiction. Although a criminal investigation may be terminated and cleared by a police agency, as per policy of the individual agency; such a case may be reopened by a prosecutor or a grand jury action. A case is not considered adjudicated until it has been settled by the court and all appeals have been exhausted.

## DISCUSSION QUESTIONS

1. Explain the Major Investigation Task Force concept.
2. List the contents of a synopsis of all the pertinent information in a case.
3. Define the search and seizure factors and the voluntariness of statements in the case.
4. Discuss the special considerations in the case preparation.
5. List the contents of a case folder that is prepared for the prosecutor.
6. Explain the complaint process for filing charges against the accused.
7. Discuss the grand jury process for securing an indictment against the accused.
8. What are the statute of limitations for various crimes in your state?
9. Discuss the kinds of cases that a prosecutor may present to the grand jury.

10. Contrast the advantages and disadvantages of the grand jury process.
11. Explain pretrial discovery.
12. Compare plea bargaining advantages and disadvantages.
13. Explain when to terminate an investigation.
14. Define an adjudicated case.

# COURT DEMEANOR AND TESTIMONY

**16**

## KEY TERMS AND CONCEPTS

First impressions
Court demeanor (definition of)
Objective attitude
Defense tactics
Procedures for qualifying as an expert witness
Expert testimony
Cross-examination

The courtroom demeanor of every officer or investigator, and all other witnesses involved in a case, may legally be considered as evidence in a criminal trial. The demeanor of the officer or investigator can be as important to the prosecution as the arrest of the accused and the seizure of incriminating evidence. Many prosecutors go over the pertinent "do's" and "don'ts" of courtroom demeanor with investigators and other prosecution witnesses during the review of their expected testimony. All prosecution witnesses must present their testimony in the most objective and effective manner possible.

It is important to note that there can be a difference between the attitude displayed by the prosecutor and that displayed by prosecution witnesses (especially peace officers) during a trial. For example, a prosecutor is charged with the diligent presentation of the people's case against the accused. He or she may at times be required to assume a tenacious posture in cross-examining a defense witness or arguing an issue to the judge or jury. This occasional behavior can and should be expected from any astute prosecutor. In short, tenacity and assertiveness on the part of a prosecutor is appropriate courtroom demeanor.

On the other hand, a too-assertive prosecution witness (particularly an officer or investigator) is often perceived by the jury or judge as biased against the accused. It is appreciated that in certain cases a bias against the accused on behalf of the victim or certain witnesses, may be anticipated or even accepted by a judge or jury. However, a bias displayed against the accused by the officer or investigator before a judge or jury can spell disaster to the prosecution's case.

In regard to expert witnesses, it will suffice at this point to state that a person may qualify to testify as an expert if he or she is skilled or experienced in a certain area. The witness may be an officer or investigator, a scientist, a physician or a mechanic who has been qualified by the judge as competent to testify as an expert on the particular issue. Even though the witness is qualified as an expert by the court, the amount of credibility and weight given their testimony is the sole prerogative of the judge in a court trial or the jury in a jury trial. The following material is primarily directed to the officer or investigator who is to appear as a witness in a trial.

## FIRST IMPRESSIONS

The first impression that a judge or a jury will form of an officer or investigator will be based on visual perceptions. Prior to being called to the witness stand the officer or investigator may have been identified from the stand by a prior witness or may have been observed in consultation with the prosecutor. Since first impressions (particularly of people) may be difficult to change or overcome, it is imperative that the officer's or investigator's physical appearance be non-offensive to the judge and jury. The officer or investigator should appear neat, clean and well-groomed. Consider hair, beard, mustache, clothes, shoes, hands, fingernails, etc. Care should be taken not to wear jewelry that is gaudy or identifies membership in a particular organization. If not appearing in uniform, the prospective witness should wear conservative clothing, including a shirt and tie for men. Gum chewing and the wearing of sunglasses should also be avoided, as these otherwise harmless habits may be interpreted by the judge or jury as a too-casual attitude towards a serious matter. The officer or investigator should also give the appearance of being physically fit. This recommendation is not to be interpreted as a condemnation of those who do not workout (exercise) regularly, etc. It is offered as a reminder that however freshly scrubbed and neatly attired, a "physical slob" will present a poor appearance. This appearance is not conducive to a positive impression of the officer or investigator by the judge and jury.

## Demeanor, Conduct, and Attitude

The officer's or investigator's conduct and attitude will be under scrutiny (particularly by the jury) during the entire trial. A professional and dignified impression inside and outside (halls, elevator) the court-room is important at all times. It is not difficult for one who has a heavy case load, with many court appearances, to develop a casual or routine attitude or conduct toward cases. What may be a daily routine to a peace officer can and often is a serious matter to the court, jury and the defense. A defendant's life, liberty or personal reputation may be at stake in the proceedings. It is, therefore, imperative that the officer or investigator be constantly aware of the positive and negative factors of courtroom demeanor.

## A Professional Approach

An objective attitude is attainable with concentrated effort. It re-quires a mental conditioning on the part of the officer or investigator and much practical application. Mental conditioning is required prin-cipally because we all have our opinions, likes, dislikes, certain biases and prejudices with regard to kinds or types of people, places, occur-rences and things. To control these behavioral characteristics in such a manner as to permit the officer or investigator to portray an objective and professional conduct and attitude under all circumstances, requires a realization that he or she is a professional with a duty to perform. He or she may even, on occasion, find it necessary to "play the role," thus controlling any strong emotions they might feel toward a suspect who has committed a heinous crime against an innocent victim.

Secondly, experience will confirm the wisdom of the old adage, "practice makes perfect." The more practical application given to this mental conditioning in court appearances, the more proficient the of-ficer or investigator will become in performing professionally at a trial.

Another extremely important part of the investigator's conduct and attitude involves verbal and nonverbal (body language) communi-cations. What one says, how one says it and one's body language (pos-ture, use of arms, hands, feet or eyes) and the tone or feeling reflected in the voice can be crucial to a case. These factors can be just as impor-tant as the testimony itself.

*Figure 16-1 The all important first impression is irreversible.*

## Elements of Good Courtroom Demeanor

The following points are offered as guidelines to appropriate conduct when called to testify in court. By following these basic suggestions, the police witness cannot help being more effective when on the
witness stand. Appropriate personal appearance has been previously
discussed; other important factors are:

1.  Answer only the question asked.

2.  Make sure your answer is responsive to the question.

3. Avoid volunteering information that is not requested.

4. Prepare to testify by reviewing notes and testimony with the prosecutor.

5. Avoid answering too quickly, especially on cross-examination (this gives the prosecutor time to object to a question if appropriate).

6. Be sure you clearly understand the question before answering, if not, ask for clarification.

7. When testifying as to a defendant's statements, do so verbatim as much as possible (including profanity and colloquial phrases).

8. Be sure everyone in the court understands exactly what person or exhibit you are referring to in your testimony.

9. When in the courtroom, address the Judge as "Your Honor;" outside as "Judge."

10. Determine from the prosecutor how he or she wants you to communicate with him (if necessary).

11. Avoid disrupting the prosecutor with excessive communications (notes).

12. If, after being excused from the stand, you feel the prosecutor failed to ask a pertinent question, leave the stand and tactfully advise the prosecutor so that you may be recalled, if he or she so chooses.

13. Readily answer all questions, whether they bring forth facts that are favorable or unfavorable to the accused.

14. When asked a question requiring an explanation (rather than a simple "yes" or "no") ask the court's permission to explain, then proceed based on the court's ruling.

15. When necessary to refresh your memory on the witness stand by reviewing your notes, request the court's permission before doing so (notes so used are legally open for inspection by the defense).

16. When answering complex questions, be sure to identify that portion of the question being answered.

17. If an objection is made while testifying, stop testifying, and do not continue until the court has ruled on the objection.

18. If approached by a juror during trial for any reason, tactfully explain the impropriety of such contact (mistrial) and politely leave.

19. Speak loudly enough to be heard by all jurors, both attorneys and the judge.

## Courtroom Practices to Avoid

Some of the following points might seem rather obvious and perhaps unnecessary to mention. However, they are all rather common errors which can sometimes easily occur if an effort is not made to avoid them.

1. Any display of prejudice or over-zealousness by word or actions.

2. Arguing with defense.

3. Joking with the defendant, defense counsel, the prosecutor or any witness inside or outside of the courtroom (before or during trial).

4. Failing to look directly at the person asking the question.

5. Obviously stalling in answering defense counsel's questions.

6. Overstating or exaggerating one's experience or qualifications.

7. Failing to speak clearly and distinctly and using technical police terms or slang.

8. Offering opinions and conclusions when not asked to do so.

9. Appearing to be unprepared to testify.

10. Being late to court or dozing in court (while waiting to testify).

11. Discussing the case with the defendant inside or outside the courtroom.

12. Carrying on conversations with other witnesses in the courtroom while the trial is in progress (contempt of court).

# THE DEFENSE

The criminal justice system provides that a defendant is presumed innocent until proven guilty beyond a reasonable doubt in a court of law. A defendant may admit guilt to a charge as previously covered under "Plea Bargaining." However, if the defense elects to go to trial, the presumption of innocence holds, regardless of how conclusive the evidence of guilt may be. It is important to fully appreciate that a defense counsel has the duty and responsibility for providing the defendant the best legal counsel available.

The foregoing has been offered to point out the seriousness of the defense's responsibility and to provide an understanding of the tactics that will become evident when the defense has a well-prepared case. Understanding and appreciating these factors will facilitate good courtroom demeanor on the part of the officer and other prosecution witnesses. Several of the most common defense tactics are offered below.

## Defense Tactics

A major objective of any good criminal defense is to break down prosecution witnesses by vigorous cross-examination, thus reducing, if not eliminating, their credibility and the weight given their testimony by the judge or jury. This will include taking advantage of and pursuing any uncalled for opinion, conclusion, exaggeration, untruth or otherwise prejudicial remark made by any of the witnesses. Also to be expected as a defense tactic is the methodical review on cross-examination of all the circumstances surrounding an identification of the defendant, particularly as to his or her being on the crime scene.

It is not uncommon for an astute defense counsel to question the witness' memory of the physical characteristics of the location where the identification occurred. This may include the lighting conditions, the weather, the number of persons present, the sobriety or emotional condition of the witness at the time, the condition of the witness' eyesight (glasses, etc.) the witness' hearing, etc. This line of questioning is perfectly proper and may lead to a witness answering a question: "I don't remember," or "I think so but I'm not sure now," or "I only had two drinks, but I was perfectly sober," or "I only saw him for a moment, but I'm sure it's him," or "I only use glasses for reading, my eyesight is good otherwise," etc. Any one of the above answers can provide a defense counsel with a wedge, that if pursued vigorously, can result in reducing if not eliminating the credibility of a witness.

The defense counsel may well realize that the witness being cross-examined is an honest person who is telling the truth to the best of his or her ability, yet the defense attorney has a duty to perform and must cross-examine. The honest reactions of prosecution witnesses under fire may vary. Those that hold up best on the witness stand are those that have been properly briefed and have reviewed their testimony during the case preparation process.

A case reviewed in research revealed one such witness whose testimony terminated in a comical yet effective manner. In this case the defendant was on trial for the robbery and shooting of a bartender in a tavern during the evening hours. The lighting in the tavern was adequate and there were eight other patrons present. The witness was seated two stools away from the defendant at the time of the holdup and shooting and so testified at the trial. The witness also made a positive identification of the defendant.

The defense counsel vigorously cross-examined the witness on all the aforementioned circumstances. He could not, however, break down the witness' testimony on the first round of questions. He therefore, proceeded to attack the witness' memory on the size of the tavern, the length of the bar, the number of stools and the sexes and descriptions of the other patrons present. As one might suspect, the witness became a little irritated with this line of questioning. He turned and faced the judge and asked if he could say something to him. The judge allowed him to speak and he stated, "Your Honor, I went into the tavern to have a drink. I didn't go there to inspect the place, measure the bar, count the stools or interview the customers. All I know is that a few minutes after I got there the defendant came in and held-up and shot the bartender." The judge turned to the defense counsel and asked, "Any more questions counsel?" The defense wisely declined to further question the witness.

Another common defense tactic is to ask prosecution witnesses the following question, "Have you discussed your testimony with anyone prior to taking the witness stand?" If the witness has not been properly advised during the case preparation process to expect such a question and to answer, "Yes, I discussed my testimony with the investigator and the prosecutor," he or she may become rattled or answer, "No" to what may sound like an accusation, rather than a question. A "no" answer by the witness can lead to other questions by the defense, which will possibly reduce the credibility of the witness. A "yes" answer would normally close the issue since reviewing testimony with witnesses is a proper procedure.

# THE EXPERT WITNESS

Any person who is skilled or experienced in a particular area can be qualified by a court to offer testimony as an expert. It is not necessary that this person possess a formal degree or be licensed to practice a particular profession. Law enforcement personnel who are experienced in bookmaking, narcotics and traffic investigation, frequently testify as experts in court proceedings. Criminalistics laboratory staff, composed of criminalists and chemical, firearms, fingerprint and instrument technicians must all qualify to testify as experts in court. Other members of the criminal justice system who frequently testify as experts are the pathologist and other scientists who are members of the coroner or medical examiner's staff.

A defense counsel may utilize an expert in any field of expertise (i.e., technical, investigative, medical, psychiatric, etc.) in the preparation of a defense. The defense may then seek to introduce such testimony by qualifying the witness in court as an expert. The foregoing examples of persons who commonly testify as experts are intentionally limited in the interests of space. Judy Hails Kaci states in her excellent text, *Criminal Evidence*, 3rd edition, "An expert witness is a person who is called to testify about a relevant event based on his/her special knowledge or training. Expert witnesses are called to help the jury understand the evidence. They are in court to explain things to the jury. Experts are not allowed if the facts can be understood by the jurors without their help."

## Qualifying the Witness as an Expert

A prosecution or defense witness who is to testify as an expert must first be questioned (direct examination) under oath, as to his or her qualifications in the particular area the opinion testimony will relate to. If the witness is to testify for the prosecution, the direct examination is conducted by the prosecutor; the opposite if the witness is for the defense. The purpose of this examination is to inform the trial judge of the skill, practical experience, training or education the witness has in the particular area. This would include prior appearances by the witness on courts as an expert, as well as any teaching or authorship of articles and books in the area of expertise.

When an officer or investigator is to appear as an expert witness he or she should prepare a concise summary of his or her background, including all the aforementioned factors that are applicable. They should be most careful not to exaggerate or misrepresent any part of the background and be prepared to recite the summary clearly and confidently under direct examination by the prosecutor. A good first impression made by this witness on the judge and jury may be a lasting one. It may even deter an extensive *voir dire* (preliminary) examination by the defense counsel.

The *voir dire* examination is for the purpose of challenging, disputing or discrediting the competency of an opposing witness or a juror. On occasion, when the witness is a well-known and respected expert who has testified many times before in a jurisdiction, the opposing counsel may already be satisfied with his or her qualifications and objectivity and may waive the voir dire examination. In any case, the witness must be prepared to objectively and dispassionately answer questions that may attack his or her asserted expertise. It is obvious that if this witness is ill-prepared in any way or displays a lack of confidence or makes any misrepresentation as to qualifications or is, in fact, unqualified, his or her credibility may be destroyed during the *voir dire* examination. When the *voir dire* examination is completed (not waived) the judge will rule whether or not the witness is an expert in the particular area in issue. If the ruling is in the affirmative, the witness will be allowed to testify.

## Testimony by the Expert

Like all other witnesses, the expert witnesses must testify under oath to tell the truth in the matter pending before the court. Once the oath has been administrated the direct examination can begin. The side offering the testimony is generally allowed to proceed with questions and answers that lay a foundation for the relevancy of the testimony regarding facts at issue in the trial.

For example, the witness may be a firearms identification expert who has conducted firing tests and bullet comparisons on a .38 cal. revolver recovered from the defendant at the time of arrest with a bullet recovered from the victim's body. The gun has already been introduced into evidence via the testimony of the arresting officer. The coroner or medical examiner has testified that the victim died of a gunshot wound and has identified a .38 cal. bullet, that is also in evidence, as the same bullet he or she removed from the body of the victim. The prosecutor will normally have the expert examine and identify the revolver in question and the bullet recovered from the victim's body, as the same items he or she examined in the laboratory (see Marking of Evidence, Chapter 5).

The expert will then examine and identify the test bullet(s) (packaged in a separate evidence container) he or she fired from the above mentioned revolver during the laboratory examination. The expert will describe his or her examination of the evidence in detail. This might include the test firing, microscopic comparison and forensic photography, etc. The expert will usually have enlarged photographs of the death bullet alongside of several photographs of the bullets fired from the suspect's revolver. The photographs serve as visual aids to assist the court or jury, the prosecution and the defense, in following the expert's testimony as he or she describes the lands, grooves, and striations left on the surface of the bullet by the rifling inside the barrel of the revolver. The expert will indicate the points of comparison used in examining the death bullet and the bullets test fired from the revolver. The expert will then be asked by the prosecutor if he or she has formed an opinion as a result of the examination. The expert will then state his or her opinion which may be, for example: (1) An all-conclusive opinion that the death bullet and the bullets test fired, were all fired from the same revolver; (2) A conclusive opinion as to only some of the points of comparison and inconclusive as to others; with a closing remark that all the bullets in question were probably fired from the same revolver; (3) An inconclusive opinion on all points of comparison, due to the worn out and deteriorated condition of the rifling in the barrel of the revolver. It is important to state that the opposing side (the defense in this case) may raise objections during the expert's testimony on points, that if sustained by the court, may favor the defense. Many defense counsels will research the area of expertise being testified to by the expert and be prepared for objections or piercing cross-examination. Others, depending on the expertise in issue, will employ another expert in the same field to testify for the defense and attempt to discredit the prosecution's expert. Psychiatrists frequently appear as experts in criminal trials; one for the prosecution and one for the defense; each offering psychiatric testimony in opposition to the other. This is a grave reminder that the courts view expert testimony as advisory, only.

## Cross-examination

When the direct examination of a witness is completed by the prosecution or the defense, the witness is then open for cross-examination by the opposing side. This procedure provides an opportunity for the opposing side to test the credibility of the witness. The cross-examination is normally limited in scope to the issues or evidential matters testified to in the direct examination. The opposing side, however, may ask the witness questions on cross-examination that expand upon or explore the information provided in the direct examination. A question may be directed to a positive statement made by the witness on a controversial issue. For example, a statement by a psychiatrist that a criminal's mind can be read and his or her behavior accurately predicted, would likely be the subject of some controversy in the field of psychiatry.

The cross-examination may be concentrated on discrediting the witness by a skilled review of the techniques employed by the witness in conducting the tests or examination. Pointing out that such techniques are not the latest or the most professionally accepted might be the approach used. If the witness' testimony is in variance with his or her prior testimony offered at a preliminary hearing or grand jury hearing, it is almost certain that an attempt will be made to impeach the witness.

## Redirect Examination

When the cross-examination of an expert witness is completed, the side calling the witness, may again question its witness under redirect examination. This prerogative is allowed for the sole purpose of clarifying (if needed) information offered by the expert witness under cross-examination. If the witness undergoes redirect examination, the opposing side can again cross-examine, however, the questions are normally confined to the information brought out in the redirect examination.

## Rebuttal Testimony

Rebuttal testimony, in essence, is testimony which is normally offered by the prosecution (after the defense rests) to refute evidence offered by the defense that places doubt on the defendant's guilt. This defense evidence may be in the form of witnesses who place the defendant at a location other than the scene of the crime, when it occurred. This most commonly used approach is known as the "alibi defense."

Many otherwise convincing alibis provided by honestly mistaken or dishonest eyewitnesses have been overcome by good police work in gathering physical evidence. For example, five members of a family including the defendant's wife, testified that the defendant was sitting at the wife's bedside in a hospital in another state, when the crime occurred. Only additional prosecution witnesses, placing the defendant near the scene at the time of the crime, and some important physical evidence also placing the defendant at the scene of the crime, overcame the dramatic effect of the alibi witnesses presented by the defense.

The reality one must face here, is that although a defendant's loved ones may commit perjury to save one that is dear to them, it is also possible that the alibi may be valid and the defendant is actually innocent. It is particularly important to remember this in cases where the prime evidence against the defendant consists only of personal identification by witnesses.

It is important to note that prosecution rebuttal witnesses are subject to defense cross-examination. The defense may also follow-up by presenting evidence and witnesses to refute the prosecution's rebuttal evidence or witnesses. Therefore, if the prosecution presents rebuttal testimony, the defense may counter it. The prosecution is generally not allowed to introduce evidence on rebuttal that should have properly been a part of the prosecution's "case in chief." This prevents surprises by the prosecution that would place the defense at unfair advantage with no time to prepare a response. A court will permit new evidence to be presented by the prosecution only if it can be shown that it is relevant and that the prosecution had no prior knowledge of its existence. If this occurs, the defense must be given time to prepare a response.

In the end, the deciding factor is how much credibility and weight is given to all witnesses and other evidence by the judge in a court trial or by the jury in a jury trial. The expert witness, however highly qualified, may be rebutted and the court or jury may accept or disregard the expert's testimony.

## SUMMARY

The demeanor of every officer or investigator, and all other witnesses involved in a case, is "evidence" in every criminal trial. Many prosecutors go over the pertinent "do's" and "don'ts" of courtroom demeanor with investigators and other prosecution witnesses during preparation of the case.

The first impressions that a judge or a jury will form of the officer-witness will be based on their visual perceptions. Since first impressions (particularly of people) may be difficult to change or overcome, it is imperative that the officer or investigator's courtroom demeanor be objective, impersonal, and professional throughout the trial.

All prosecution witnesses must appreciate that a defense counsel has the duty and responsibility for providing a defendant the best legal defense available, regardless of how conclusive the evidence of guilt may be. Understanding and appreciating this factor will facilitate good courtroom demeanor on the part of these witnesses; they may expect that a diligent defense counsel will vigorously cross-examine them in an effort to reduce or eliminate their credibility.

Any person who is skilled or experienced in a particular area can be qualified by a court to offer testimony as an expert. It is not necessary that this person possess a formal degree or be licensed to practice a particular profession. Both the prosecution and the defense may utilize an expert in any particular profession. Both the prosecution and the defense may utilize an expert in any particular field of expertise in the preparation of their case or as a rebuttal to evidence offered by the opposing side. The expert helps the triers of fact to understand areas not within the common knowledge of non-experts. In the end, the deciding factor is how much credibility and weight is given to the expert's testimony; the court or jury may accept or disregard it.

## DISCUSSION QUESTIONS

1.  Discuss the importance of the first impression formed by the judge or jury of the officer or investigator.
2.  Explain the general positive and negative aspects of the conduct and attitude of the officer or investigator in and around the court.
3.  Review specific elements of poor demeanor in court and on the witness stand.
4.  Discuss specific elements of good demeanor in court and on the witness stand.
5.  What is the responsibility of the defense counsel?
6.  List four various defense tactics a witness might expect.
7.  Explain the general use of expert witnesses.
8.  List the qualifications necessary for a witness to be an expert.
9.  Explain the direct examination of the expert witness.
10. Discuss the cross-examination process.
11. Review the rebuttal process.

# INNOVATIONS IN INVESTIGATIVE TECHNOLOGY

## KEY TERMS AND CONCEPTS

Psychemedics drug testing
Operation cease-fire
Lifeguard
Implications of I.D. System
Hughes' "Probeye" infrared viewers
Psychological profiling
Satellite technology
Video Image Printer
Cybercrime

Because of budgetary constraints at all levels of government, law enforcement agencies have not been (and probably will never be) able to afford the high cost of the research, design, development and adaptation of improved modern technology. Thus far, with few exceptions, most of the scientific instrumentation, physical, biological, pathological, chemical and other analytical techniques utilized today in criminalistics laboratories and coroners offices were first perfected under private auspices.

Scientific research and technological development by private industry has most fortunately been adapted to law enforcement use, wherever applicable. Until recent years, only the field of medicine was commonly associated with the law enforcement and legal fields. This association was identified by the use of the word "forensic", which Webster defines as "a science that deals with the relation and application of medical facts to legal problems." In the light of the contributions that modern technology and other sciences continue to make to the law enforcement and legal fields, it is most proper to refer to these contributions as "forensic technology," and "forensic psychology."

# PSYCHEMEDICS HAIR ANALYSIS TEST

The Psychemedics drug test is a proprietary (privately owned) drug screening process with the highly technical name of "radioimundassay of hair" or RIAII for short. More simply described, RIAII is a technique which uses a small sample of human hair to detect whether an individual has used certain illegal drugs. This test meets criminal law criteria requiring both on-site collection as well as a visible chain of evidence.

This test is highly effective and is based on the simple fact that once drugs are ingested (used), they circulate in the user's blood–often for long periods of time. Trace amounts of the drug are trapped in the core of the hair shaft. These traces cannot be washed or bleached out. A drug history can be obtained from an RIAII analysis of the individual's hair.

Psychemedics Corporation, the private company which developed the technique, has obtained a patent for the process which was pioneered by Dr. Werner C. Banngartner, the company's founder.

# LATEST GOVERNMENT ANTICRIME ACTIVITY

## FBI

The FBI is investing $520 million in a computerized system that will hold prints on 32 million criminals and suspects. This will permit local law enforcement agencies to check a suspect's prints in two hours. The system began operation in 1998 and handles up to 50,000 daily requests for verification.

## ATF

The Bureau of Alcohol, Tobacco and Firearms recently demonstrated its "Operation Cease-fire," which uses lasers and computers to "read" bullets recovered from crime scenes. The device records the markings guns leave on every bullet they fire. By comparing the read-ings from various crime scenes, a process that takes only four seconds, police can determine if the same gun was used at one or more of the crime scenes. Washington D.C. police were able to connect scores of shootings in their first month of operations.

# FORENSIC ENTOMOLOGY

A leading Orange County, California, forensic entomologist (in-sect expert) Jim Webb, is a boon to local law enforcement. Much can be determined by identifying the types and stages of development (e.g. egg, larvae, pupae, of insects found around dead bodies). Webb can help ascertain when a victim died, whether cocaine or other drugs were involved and if someone moved the body. He has helped link a suspect to a strangling by matching chigger bites on the suspect. The San Di-ego District Attorney credits Webb with destroying a killer's alibi in a serial murder case by using maggots to peg the time of death. There are approximately 20 forensic entomologists in the nation; three are in California.

# HUGHES' "PROBEYE" INFRARED VIEWERS

Hughes Aircraft Company has designed, developed and manufac-tured three models of the "Probeye" Infrared Viewer. The Model 649 for mining maintenance and safety, the Model 650 for industry and energy management and the Model 643 for fire and police agencies.

The Hughes infrared viewer is a highly sensitive, hand-held im-ager, which presents in its observer's eyepiece a detailed thermal pic-ture of the entire scene within the field of view. Probeye clearly re-veals temperature differences as little as 0.1° C between closely adja-cent objects and between objects and background, thereby quickly and accurately locating sources of heat. Moreover, it does this in total dark-ness, and through smoke and dust.

The Probeye Infrared Viewer is based on the principle that all objects, animate or otherwise, radiate infrared energy according to their temperature. As Probeye scans a scene, it detects and converts the lev-els of such radiation to corresponding levels of visible light, thereby producing on its viewing screen a display containing readily discern-ible temperature patterns of all objects in range. The thermal picture so presented is in red, to maintain its observer's night vision (see Figure 17-1). Many police agencies are using the Probeye Infrared Viewer in criminal investigations that require the search for victims or suspects, that may be in open fields or lying in bushes or weeds (kidnappings, narcotic smuggling, etc.). Probeye is equally effective from a helicopter as it is on the ground (see Figure 17-2).

The lifesaving attributes of the "Probeye" are attested to in police, fire and military files. Many incidents are cited where flood survivors, hidden by foliage and smeared with mud, and fire victims, invisible through thick smoke, were located only by use of this scanner. Along with its important lifesaving function, the device is additionally making important contributions to the criminal investigation field. For an illustration of two typical police uses of the Probeye (see Figure 17-1 and 17-2).

*Figure 17-1 Pointed in total darkness, the Probeye Infrared Viewer readily discerns a police suspect (Courtesy of Hughes Aircraft Company).*

*Figure 17-2   A 3:00 a.m. Probeye scan of this plant's parking lot clearly shows cars (Courtesy of Hughes Aircraft Company).*

# INVESTIGATIVE HYPNOSIS

On March 11, 1982 the California Supreme Court by a vote of 5 to 2, barred the use of virtually all testimony from victims or witnesses who had been hypnotized to enhance their recall of an event. Since that date, virtually every state in the country has barred or severely restricted the use of hypnosis in criminal cases. Thus, for all practical purposes, hypnosis is no longer a viable tool for use in criminal investigation.

# THE COGNITIVE INTERVIEW

As a result of severe restrictions on the use of hypnosis in criminal cases, police investigators avoid the use of hypnosis of victims and witnesses whose testimony might be needed in court.

However, with little or no fanfare, psychologists have developed a substitute memory jogging technique called the "cognitive interview." This new "witness memory retrieval" technique provides a workable alternative to investigative hypnosis. The technique is a psychologically sound method of systematically guiding a witness or victim through a four-step "witness memory retrieval interview procedure." The four steps are called:

1. Reconstructing the circumstances

2. Reporting everything

3. Recalling the events in different order

4. Changing perspectives

Memory researcher, Dr. R. Edward Geiselman, UCLA Psychology Department, and his colleagues Dr. Ronald P. Fisher, Florida International University, and David P. McKinnon, developed the procedure following considerable scientific and practical research. Ninety-one graduate student volunteer witnesses participated in a controlled experiment with the Los Angeles Police Department.

The witnesses were shown four films used by the Los Angeles Police Department to train officers in shooting techniques. The crimes depicted included a bank robbery, a liquor store robbery, a family dispute and a warehouse search. In each film at least one individual is shot and killed. The films were very realistic and produced psychological reactions in the student witnesses which would be expected in similar real life situations. The witnesses were divided into three groups. They were then interviewed by investigators from the Los Angeles police department and other local and federal agencies.

Group one was interviewed in the traditional manner. Group two was hypnotized and interviewed by trained forensic hypnotists. Group three was interviewed by investigators briefed in the use of the "cognitive interview technique," pioneered by Geiselman and his colleagues. The results were carefully tabulated and compared.

Both groups two (hypnosis) and three (cognitive interview) were able to recall significantly more valid information than group one (traditional interview method). However, group three, which used the cognitive interview or witness memory retrieval interview technique was able to recall 35 percent more critical details than did group one. Even with this substantial increase in recalling details, there was no increase in inaccurate information by the witnesses in group three.

A number of law enforcement agencies have adopted this new technique which is surprisingly uncomplicated. The technique is now taught at the Delinquency Control Institute, University of Southern California. A step-by-step tutorial videotape depicting the technique is also available.

## PSYCHOLOGICAL PROFILING

The staff of the Behavioral Science Unit, FBI Academy, provides (on a time available basis) psychological profiles of suspects in multiple rape, child molesting or motiveless murders; crimes in which there is sufficient evidence of psychopathology at the crime scenes. Typically, the more bizarre the crime, the greater the chance that the *modus operandi* will reveal rage, hatred, fear, love or ritualistic behavior; the psychological assessment of which can produce a profile indicating the possible personality type of the suspect(s). Traditionally, a crime scene is usually confined to the immediate area in which the crime was committed. For purpose of profiling, however, the term "crime scene," also includes the victim(s), and all other locations involved in the crime. Profiling is designed to enhance the work of the investigator. While the investigator searches for and collects evidence, the behavioral scientist researches and catalogs "emotional evidence" such as information relating to rage, hatred, fear, ritualistic behavior, etc., applicable to the crime. The entire basis for a good profile is a good crime scene examination and adequate interviews of victims and witnesses.

Dr. Martin Reiser, Director of Behavioral Science Services, LAPD, cautions in a recent issue of "Police Chief" magazine, that psychological profiling is not a magical or exact science. In fact, it is merely an inferential process analogous to the psychological evaluation done with patients in order to gain a deeper understanding of their psychological problems.

As an example, Reiser refers to the so-called "Skidrow Stabber Case" in Los Angeles in the early 1970's. In this series of killings, all victims were male, middle-aged derelicts, habituates of the area, who had had sexual relations just before being killed. The ritualistic M.O. repeated in each case included genital mutilation and throat slashing. This revealed explosive-compulsive behavior by a paranoid psychotic, with underlying homosexual conflicts. The psychological profile developed from factual and speculative information included a possible middle-aged white male with a psychiatric history with prior hospitalization and possible training in hand-to-hand combat. Armed with this information, investigators concentrated their attention on private and Veterans Administration hospitals. They subsequently arrested a suspect who had used a similar MO in prior years. Corroborating evidence and a confession was thereafter shortly secured. The suspect was tried and convicted. The skidrow murders ceased.

## BULLET FLIGHT TRACKING

A device that can track a bullet in flight and almost instantly identify its source has been unveiled by the Lawrence Livermore National Laboratory. This invention, called "Lifeguard," could one day protect soldiers from snipers or monitor high-crime areas. This unit acts as a sentry. It detects if a bullet is moving, the direction it is taking, and the origin of the bullet.

Project leader, Tom Karr, using a custom computer code, fashioned a sensor and a miniature computer that can be either mounted on a rifle or hand carried. The device processes signals and retraces a bullet's path back to its source.

## LASER DEVELOPMENT OF LATENT PRINTS

Laser light is now being used in many larger crime laboratories to develop fingerprints which could otherwise be invisible. Florescent chemicals, which are sensitive to lasers, are applied to areas suspected of bearing latent fingerprints. Laser light is highly intense and induces florescence in the substances used to treat the prints. This makes the glowing print visible to the naked eye so that it can be photographed or otherwise preserved.

## SATELLITE SURVEILLANCE

Satellites are now being employed to augment criminal investigations by use of real-time viewing (viewing events as they are unfolding) and historical review (events that took place in the past that were captured by this medium and archived for future use). Although governmental sources for this type of information are available, it has seldom been released to agencies. Due to this fact, a new industry is emerging which makes a business out of providing this information by accessing numerous worldwide databases that archive aerial and space photography along with satellite imagery.

An example of real-time viewing would be the use of satellites to monitor the riots that occurred in Los Angeles following the Rodney King trial as they progressed. Movements of the rioters were tracked which produced estimates on the overall scope of the problem, relative intensity of area rioting, and the spread rate and directional flow of the rioters. This information also helped to develop engagement strategies for containment and/or suppression by law enforcement.

An example of historical viewing would be the request for a specific time range and location viewing (i.e., 600 - 1600 hrs U.S. CST on 20 April 1993, Waco, Texas, for the Branch Davidians compound). The special investigation team set forth to review the events of this final day of the standoff between the Branch Davidians and the F.B.I could request the archived photographs to augment their own evidence collected at the scene to help determine the origin of the fire that destroyed the compound and wiped-out the cult. The scope of the search is virtually limitless and extends back in the 1960s with choices between aerial and space photography or satellite imagery. Resolution down to two meters can be produced in order to manifest the best clarity.

As the number of satellites increase and technological advances continue in the area of magnification resolution we should see a dramatic increase in the use of this type of evidence. With the ability to real-time view a situation like the L.A. riots, together with the ability to historically review crime scenes, the use potential for law enforcement is enormous.

## VIDEO IMAGE PRINTER

More and more crime scenes are being photographed with video recorders. Patrol cars and booking locations are being equipped with video recorders at a surprising rate. This is all due to the fact that, for example, it is much easier to prosecute a drunk driver if the jury and/or judge is able to see videotape capturing the actual traffic stop and resulting arrest. The jury is actually able to be taken back to the "scene of the crime" through a videotape which they are commonly able to relate. The same is true of crime scene depiction. Juries are now able to see "first hand" what the crime scene looked like, the position of the body, entry point, layout of the building, etc., without the need for imagination, as is the case with sketches and still photography.

Unfortunately, the investigator often needs to produce still photographs for evidence identification, suspect or victim identification, enlargements for increased scrutiny, etc., and the video tape does not satisfactorily function for this purpose. Thus the video image printer has been developed which produces "stills" from video tape via connection to a common video recorder.

Now detailed video capturing of events and crime scene can take place through the use of a video recorder whose tape later can be manipulated to produce a variety of images (i.e., videotape, Polaroids, enlargements and reduction of individual frames of the video) (see Figure 17-3).

## CRIMINAL RECORDS DATABASE

Instead of waiting more than 20 days for critical information, judges and law enforcement agencies in 15 states now can uncover a suspect's identity and criminal history before leaving the courthouse. All 50 states are expected to be connected within the next few years.

The new Integrated Automated Fingerprint Identification System, which began operating July 28, 1999, was dedicated by FBI Director Louis Freeh at the FBI's Criminal Justice Information Services Center in Clarksburg. The $640 million electronic database of fingerprints

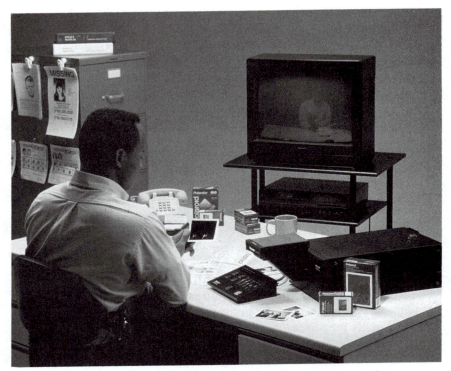

*Figure 17-3 Freezeframe Plus Video Image Printer generating evidence Polaroids (Courtesy of the Polaroid Corp.)*

will help police around the country decide within two hours whether a suspect should be freed on bail or held in custody.

It reduces to electronic data some 34 million fingerprint cards, the equivalent of 18 stacks as tall as New York's Empire State Building. It also slashes the wait for civil background checks from more than three months to just 24 hours. Before the new system was available, fugitives and repeat offenders were often released by judges who had no criminal history to peruse before the bail hearing.

The FBI receives about 50,000 fingerprints a day, about half of them are criminal matters. About 10 percent, or 5,000, are for people being arrested for the first time, so the FBI has no prior data on them.

# CRIME DNA

In a computer at a secret location, the FBI has opened a national DNA database that advocates say could significantly reduce rape and other crimes by helping to catch repeat offenders earlier. The national DNA database consists of 50 databases run by the states but unified by common test procedures and software designed by the FBI. The database, with a new generation of forensic DNA techniques, promises to be so efficient that some civil libertarians fear it will be expanded from people convicted of crimes to include almost everyone, giving the government inordinate investigative powers over citizens.

## Comparison

It will be possible to compare a DNA sample from a suspect or crime scene in one state with all others in the system. The national database has been nearly a decade in the making. The final pieces fell into place when Rhode Island became the last state to set up a DNA database. But the system still faces many unresolved issues, which are likely to play out according to reaction from the public and the courts. One such issue is the decision as to what types of offenders should be included. Another is whether the mass screening of suspects' DNA will prove constitutional.

## Criminal DNA

Criminals leave blood when breaking and entering; they shed hair and skin cells in fights, deposit saliva on glasses, and leave sweat stains in head bands. From only a few cells in such sources, enough DNA can be extracted to identify the owner. A DNA database of sufficient size could presumably help solve many crimes.

In Britain, which started a DNA database earlier and has fewer administrative and constitutional hurdles to overcome, there was considerable crossover among different kinds of offenses. "People who commit serious crime very often have convictions for petty crime in their history, so if you could get them on the database early, you may prevent serious crime," said David Werrett, manager of the DNA database for England and Wales.

New DNA technology has linked a Santa Ana sex criminal to the 1977 rape and slaying of a Bellflower woman who lived directly above his apartment.

Harry Lavon Rowley, a 45-year-old convicted rapist, was charged in Los Angeles County on charges that he strangled Pamela Sperry in December 1977, a crime that stymied investigators until samples of body fluid in storage for two decades were reexamined recently with the latest DNA technology.

Rowley, who at the time lived in Sperry's Bellflower apartment building, had been arrested in the weeks after Sperry was found strangled with a telephone cord, but a judge ruled that there was not enough evidence to try him on charges of murder, rape and burglary. The evidence was filed away and gathered dust until it was dug out by Los Angeles County Sheriff's Investigator Louie Danoff, after Sperry's family contacted him for an update on the case.

Danoff determined that Rowley was in custody on another charge and arranged for a warrant so that a body fluid sample could be taken and compared to the stored ones. If convicted, Rowley could face the death penalty. The four-time felon is also being investigated in conjunction with the 1988 slaying of Rachel Sugarman, a 37-year-old woman who was strangled and set afire in her Tustin apartment.

## CYBERCRIME

Even as you read this, cybercrime is maturing so quickly that it is difficult, if not impossible, to define it. Twenty years ago we had no cybercrime, but today we experience a myriad of sophisticated attacks on a daily basis. Most are targeted against governmental sites and large cyber-based businesses. Most computer crimes are easy to commit and difficult to detect and apprehend the culprit. Most of these crimes are committed by "insiders" and are never prosecuted. The best defense to this type of crime is prevention through better security—physical and software. Major cybercrimes tend to be investigated by the FBI because they extend beyond state jurisdiction.

In October 1994, the Computer Fraud and Abuse Act was enacted. Since then we have sought to deal with the early crimes of unauthorized access to data to the more modern malicious attacks bombarding ISPs (AOL, E*TRADE, etc.) *requests for service* that crash servers and e-mail viruses (e.g., I LOVE YOU, 2000), both of which resulted in billions of dollars worth of damage. In 2000, with electronic transfers of funds exceeding $3 trillion a day, the potential for cybercrime is enormous. The majority of these crimes are carried out by young, well-educated sophisticates who hide their trails well, and it requires enormous amounts of technical expertise and equipment to track and apprehend these individuals.

Today, the local investigator is not typically expected to solve major cybercrime, but he or she is expected to recognize that a computer crime has occurred. Once recognized, the services of special investigators from the FBI should be requested.

Other types of locally investigated computer crimes range from sex-related crimes (e.g., child pornography, indecency) to sabotage, larceny and forgery. Typically, these types of crimes are investigated on a local level and follow the same guidelines as non-cyber equivalents.

# SUMMARY

Thus far, with few exceptions, most of the scientific instrumentation, physical, biological, pathological, chemical and other analytical techniques utilized today in criminalistics laboratories and coroners' offices, were first perfected under other than public service auspices; then adopted to law enforcement use. Among the various scientific and technological developments by the private sector, that have been so adapted, the following are of particular interest to criminal investigation.

Hughes Aircraft Company's "Probeye" Infrared Viewer, Model 643, is a highly sensitive, hand-held imager, which presents in its observer's eyepiece, a detailed thermal picture of the entire scene within the field of view. It quickly and accurately locates sources of heat in total darkness, through smoke and dust, and is equally effective from a helicopter as it is on the ground. This device is based on the principle that all objects, animate or otherwise, radiate infrared energy according to their temperature. Many police agencies are using the Probeye Infrared Viewer in kidnapping and narcotic investigations, where the victims or suspects may be in open fields lying in brush or weeds. "Forensic Entomology" is the study of the ages and types of insects (larvae) in a decomposing body to assist in estimating when a person was killed.

The cognitive interview provides a reasonable alternative to investigative hypnosis. This is a welcome development in light of the severe restrictions being placed on hypnosis by the courts. Great strides are being made in the use of DNA "Fingerprints," although the procedure is expensive and time consuming. Laser light is now being used in many crime labs to make latent fingerprints visible.

Psychological profiling of suspects is possible in multiple rape, child molesting and motiveless murders; crimes in which there is sufficient evidence of psychopathology at the scenes. The more bizarre the crime scenes the greater the chance the MO will reveal rage, hatred, fear, love or ritualistic behavior, indicating the possible personality type of the suspect(s).

Use of satellite technology will greatly enhance the investigators' ability to view limitless material from photography and imagery. The saying "big brother is watching" is now more appropriate than ever before.

New technology almost certainly brings both positives and negatives to our society. Law enforcement always has to balance on the fine line between one's right to privacy and society's right to know. As new technologies provide better crime detection and solution, the courts will be asked to render judgment as to the inevitable question on limits to the use of satellite imagery, covert surveillance, hypnosis and the like along with the myriad of other potential skills and equipment that in the future will make themselves available to the investigator. The investigator's job is to use every means at his disposal to solve the crime at hand within the boundaries of the law. Therefore, it is imperative the modern investigator keep apprised of new technology and methods.

## DISCUSSION QUESTIONS

1. Describe the usefulness of the Psychemedic hair analysis testing.
2. What is the latest ATF anticrime device?
3. Discuss the application of the Probeye Infrared Viewer to criminal investigation.
4. How does the Probeye Infrared Viewer work?
5. Explain how the cognitive interview improves memory.
6. Explain psychological profiling.
7. What is "Forensic Entomology?"
8. Define cybercrime and describe a recent occurrence of it.

# GLOSSARY

**ACCELERANTS:** Substances that cause fires to burn faster and hotter.

**ACCESSORY:** Anyone except a husband, wife or member of the offender's family who knows the offender has committed a felony or is liable to arrest, yet harbors, conceals, or helps the offender avoid or escape arrest, trial, conviction, or punishment.

**ADIPOCERE:** Occurs when the fats in the body undergo hydrogenation i.e., body is continuously exposed to moisture; not necessarily immersed in water. The outer tissues turn into a yellowish white waxy substance.

**ADMISSION:** A statement containing information concerning a crime.

**ADULT:** In criminal justice usage, a person who is within the original juridiction of a criminal, rather than a juvenile, court because his or her age at the time of the alleged criminal act was above a statutorily defined limit.

**ALGAE:** Pond scums and stoneworts, non-vascular plants.

**AMPHETAMINES:** Stimulants.

**ANATOMICAL:** Having to do with the structural makeup of a body, any of its organisms or parts.

**ANESTHESIOLOGIST:** A physician who specializes in the science of anesthetics.

**ANESTHETIC:** A substance capable of producing esthesia, a loss of sensation.

**ANTHROPOLOGY:** The study of man in relation to distribution, origin, classification and relationship of races, physical character, social relations and culture.

**AORTA:** The great trunk artery that carries blood from the heart to branch arteries to be distributed throughout the body.

**ARREST:** Taking a person into custody in the manner authorized by law.

**ARREST WARRANT:** A document issued by a judicial officer which directs a law enforcement officer to arrest an identified person who has been accused of a specific offense.

**ARSON:** The malicious, willful burning of a building or property.

**ASPHYXIA:** Suffocation.

**ASSAULT:** Unlawfully threatening to harm another person, actually harming another person, or attempting to do so. Formerly referred to threats of or attempts to cause bodily harm, but now usually includes *battery*.

**ASSOCIATIVE EVIDENCE:** linking a suspect with a crime.

**AUTOMATED FINGERPRINT IDENTIFICATION SYSTEM:** A system using computers to review and map fingerprints.

**AUTOPSY:** An internal examination of the body after death.

**BAIL:** To effect the release of an accused person from custody in return for a promise that he or she will appear at a place and time specified and submit to the jurisdiction and judgement of the court,guaranteed by a pledge to pay the court a specified sum of money if the accused does not appear.

**BARBITURATES:** Depressants.

**BALLISTICS:** The science of the motion of projectiles in flight.

**BLASTING CAP:** A small thin-walled cylindrical case, filled with a sensitive high explosive; used as a detonator and can be fired by safety fuse, electrical current or chemical action.

**BOOKING:** A law enforcement or correctional administrative process officially recording an entry into detention after arrest, and identifying the person, place, time and reson for the arrest.

**BOOKMAKING:** Soliciting and accepting bets on any type of sporting events.

**BOOBY TRAP:** An explosive device that is exploded by an unsuspecting person, when performing a presumably safe action.

**BURGLARY:** The unlawful entry of a structure to commit a felony or theft.

**BURN INDICATORS:** Visible evidence of the effects of heating or partial burning.

**CANNABIS SATIVA L:** Marijuana.

**CASE LAW:** Decision by Appellate and Supreme Courts that affect a change or sustain laws in pertinent criminal codes.

**CAST:** To make an impression using plaster of Paris or a similar substance. Also the name of the physical reproduction of such an impression.

**CASTRATION:** To remove the testis (male genital glands).

**CEREBELLUM:** A part of the brain.

**CHAIN OF EVIDENCE:** Establishes each person having custody of evidence.

**CHARISMATIC:** A person who has special charm or appeal.

**CHILD MOLESTING:** Includes lewd and lascivious acts, indecent exposure, incest, and statutory rape. Usually a felony.

**CHOLINE:** A vitamin of the B complex that is very essential to the liver function.

**CHRONOLOGICAL:** Arranged in or according to the order of time or occurrence.

**CIRCUMSTANTIAL EVIDENCE:** A fact or event that tends to incriminate a person in a crime, e.g.., being seen running from a crime scene.

**CLAVICLE:** A bone in the shoulder.

**COGNITIVE INTERVIEW:** Interviewing technique that helps victims or witnesses put themselves mentally at the scene of the crime.

**COMPLAINANT:** Person requesting an investigation or that action be taken. Is often the victim of a crime.

**CONFESSION:** A statement by an accused admitting all the elements of the crime.

**CONJUNCTIVAL:** A membrane on the inside of the eyelids and over the forepart of the eyeball.

**CORONARY ARTERIES:** Arise from the aorta and supply the tissues of the heart itself.

*CORPUS DELICTI:* The necessary elements that constitute a crime.

**CORTICAL:** The outer part of an organ.

**CRACK:** Cocaine mixed with baking soda and water, heated in a pan, and then dried and split into pellet-size bits or chunks which are then smoked to produce effects ten times greater than cocaine at a tenth the cost.

**CRIME:** An act or omission forbidden by law and punishable by a fine, imprisonment, or even death. Crimes and their penalties are established and defined by state and federal statutes and local ordinances.

**CRIMINAL INVESTIGATION:** Seeking all facts associated with a crime to determine the truth: what happened and who is responsible.

**CRIMINAL STATUTE:** Legislative act relating to crime and its punishment.

**CROSS-EXAMINATION:** Questioning by the opposite side in a trial to assess the validity of testimony given under direct examination.

**CUSTODIAL INTERROGATION:** Questioning by law enforcement officers after a person has been taken into custody or otherwise deprived of freedom in a significant way.

**CYANOSIS:** A blueness of the skin caused by a deficiency in oxygenation of the blood.

**DEPRESSANTS:** Drugs that reduce restlessness, emotional tension, and induce sleep; most common are the barbiturates.

**DETONATOR:** A sensitive high-explosive, used to set off the main charge of high explosives.

**DIRECT EXAMINATION:** The initial questioning of a witness or defendant during a trial by the lawyer who is using the person's testimony to further his or her case.

**DNA:** Deoxyribonucleic acid, an organic substance found in the nucleus of living cells that provides the genetic code determining a person's individual characteristics.

**DNA FINGERPRINTING:** Analysis of blood, hair, saliva, semen, or cells from almost any part of the body to determine a person's identity.

**DRUG AUTOMATION:** The state of mental confusion in which a barbiturate user forgets how much he or she has already taken and unwittingly injects an overdose.

**DURA:** A fibrous membrane that envelopes the brain.

**EDEMATOUS:** An accumulation of fluid.

**ELECTRON:** A particle charged with negative electricity.

**ELECTRONIC SURVEILLANCE:** Using wiretapping and/ or bugging to obtain information.

**ELEMENTS OF THE CRIME:** Conditions that must occur for an act to be called a specific kind of crime.

**EMPATHY:** Placing oneself in the other's position and sharing his or her feelings.

**ENCODE:** To transpose material or a message into code.

**EPIDURAL:** Outside the dura (brain membrane).

**ERYTHROXYLON COCA:** The coca plant (cocaine extracted from the leaves).

**ESOPHAGUS:** A muscular tube that extends from the pharynx (behind the mouth cavity) to the stomach.

**EUPHORIA:** A feeling of well-being or elation.

**EVIDENCE:** Anything that helps establish the facts related to a crime.

**FACT:** Something known to be true.

**FELONY:** A major crime such as homicide, aggravated assault, or robbery. Usually carries a penalty of imprisonment in a state penitentiary or death.

**FENCE:** One who receives and disposes of stolen property, on a regular basis.

**FIELD IDENTIFICATION:** On-the-scene identification of a suspect by the victim of or witness to a crime, conducted within minutes of the commission of the crime.

**FIRE TRIANGLE:** The three major elements necessary for a substance to burn: heat, fuel, and air.

**"FIX":** To inject drugs.

**FORENSIC:** Suitable to courts of justice.

**FORENSIC SCIENCE (CRIMINALISTICS):** Applies the physical sciences and their technology to examining physical evidence.

**FORGERY:** Signing someone else's name to a document or altering the name or amount on a check or document with the intent to defraud.

**FRAUD:** Intentional deception to cause a person to give up property or some lawful right.

**FRISK:** An external search of an individual's clothing. Also called a *patdown*.

**GANGLIA:** A nerve center at the brain stem.

**GENETIC FINGERPRINTING:** Using DNA analysis to identify a person.

**HALLUCINOGEN:** Mind-expanding drugs, including LSD, DMT, and PCP or angel dust.

**"HASH":** Hashish.

**"H" "SMACK," "HORSE":** Street slang for heroin.

**HOMICIDE:** The killing of one person by another.

**HYALINE CARTILAGE:** A transparent substance with cells imbedded, that is present in joints, respiratory passages and most of the fetal skeleton.

**HYPNOSIS:** A trancelike condition psychically induced where the person loses consciousness but responds to the hypnotist's suggestions.

**HYPOTHESIS:** An assumption made for the sake of argument.

**HYOID BONE:** A bone located at the base of the tongue.

**IGNITER:** Substance or device used to start a fire.

**INFORMANT:** Any individual who provides information relative to an investigation or some matter of police interest.

**INCEST:** Sexual intercourse between persons so closely related it is forbidden by law.

**INFORMANT:** Any individual who can provide information related to a case and who is not a complainant, witness, victim, or suspect.

**INFRARED:** Thermal radiation (red) with wave lengths that are longer than those in visible light.

**INTERROGATION:** Questioning persons suspected of direct or indirect involvement in the crime being investigated.

**INTERVIEW:** Questioning persons not suspected of being involved in a crime, but who know about the crime or individual's involved in it.

**INVESTIGATE:** To observe or study closely; to inquire into something systematically, or to search for truthful information.

**LANDS:** The raised portions in a bore, which are actually the original surfaces of the bore, before the rifling is cut (see rifling).

**LARCENY (THEFT):** The unlawful taking, carrying, leading, or riding away of property from another's possession.

**LATENT PRINTS:** Fingerprint impressions caused by perspiration on the ridges of the fingers being transferred to a surface or occurring as residues of oil, dirt, or grease.

**LIGATURE:** Something that is used to bind.

**LINEUP IDENTIFICATION:** Having victims or witnesses identify suspects from among at least five individuals presented before them.

**LIVIDITY:** (see *postmortem lividity*).

**"MAINLINING":** Injecting narcotics directly into the veins.

**MATERIAL EVIDENCE:** Evidence that is relevant to a specific case and forms a substantive part of the case presented or has a legitimate and effective influence on the decision of the case.

**MATRICES:** A mathematical arrangement of elements in rows and columns.

**MINDSET:** A common perspective or point of view.

**MINUTIAE:** Small details.

*MIRANDA* **WARNING:** Informs suspects of their right to remain silent, to have counsel present, and to have the state appoint counsel if they cannot afford one. It also warns the suspects that anything they say can and will be used against them in court.

**MODE:** A form or method of arrangement.

*MODUS OPERANDI* **(M.O.):** A criminal's characteristic method of operation.

**MOLOTOV COCKTAIL:** A hand thrown bomb, i.e. bottle filled with a flammable liquid and has a saturated wick.

**MONIKERS:** Nicknames.

**"MUD" OR "TAR":** Opium.

**MUG SHOT:** Photograph of a person taken into custody and booked.

**MUMMIFICATION:** Complete dehydration of all body tissues in a cadaver left in an extremely dry, hot area.

**NARCOTIC:** Refers to drugs that are physically and psychologically addicting, including heroin, codeine, cocaine and morphine.

**NATIONAL CRIME AND INFORMATION CENTER (NCIC):** FBI files containing criminal fingerprint records and information on wanted criminals, stolen property, and vehicle information.

**NITRATES:** A pattern of burned, unburned and partially burned powder fragments, blown from the muzzle of a firearm, at the time of firing.

**ODONTOLOGIST:** One trained in the science of dealing with teeth, their structure, development and diseases.

**"OUTFIT":** Homemade paraphernalia used to inject narcotics (dropper, needle, spoon, cotton, etc.).

**PAPAVER SONNIFERUM:** The opium poppy.

**PARANOID SCHIZOPHRENIC:** A person who has a psychosis resembling paranoia, however usually displays hallucinations and a deterioration of behavior.

**PATDOWN:** (see *Frisk*).

**PATHOLOGIST (FORENSIC):** One who diagnoses and interprets the legal significance of anatomic and physiological changes that have occurred in the body.

**PCP (PHENCYCLIDINE):** Sold under numerous names, i.e. angel dust, crystal, supergrass, killer weed, embalming fluid and rocket fuel.

**"PEP PILLS":** Amphetamines.

**PERICARDIAL CAVITY:** Situated around the heart.

**PETECHIAL HEMORRHAGE:** A minute hemorrhage.

**PEYOTE CACTUS:** Mescaline derived from its buttons.

**PHYSICAL EVIDENCE:** Anything real (that has substance) and helps to establish the facts of a case.

**PLEURAL SURFACE:** A membrane on one surface of the lung.

**POLYGRAPH:** Lie detector. Scientifically measures respiration and depth of breathing, changes in the skin's electrical resistance, blood pressure and pulse.

**PORTRAIT PARLE:** A word picture description.

**POST-MORTEM:** After death.

**POST-MORTEM LIVIDITY:** Livid stains (dark blue or purple) on the body when death occurs and the heart is no longer active; caused by blood draining to the lowest parts of the body nearest the floor or base the body is resting on.

**POST-MORTEM PROTOCOL:** An official report of the medical-legal investigation conducted by a medical examiner/coroner.

**PREMEDITATION:** Considering, planning, or preparing for an act, no matter how briefly, before committing it.

**PROBABLE CAUSE:** Evidence that warrants a person of reasonable caution in the belief that a crime has been committed.

**PROCESSING EVIDENCE:** Includes discovering, recognizing and examining it; collecting, recording and identifying it; packaging, conveying and storing it; exhibiting it in court; and disposing of it when the case is closed.

**PROFILING:** Indicates the type of person most likely to have committed a crime having certain unique characteristics.

**PSYCHIATRIST:** A doctor who deals with mental, emotional or behavioral disorders.

**PSYCHOLOGIST:** One who deals in the science of mind and behavior.

**PSYCHOSIS:** A fundamental mental derangement, characterized by a loss of contact with reality.

**PSYCHOTIC:** A person who has a psychosis.

**PSYCHOPATH:** A mentally ill or unstable person.

**PUTREFACTION:** The decomposition of organic matter.

**QUASI-JUDICIAL:** As if it were judicial; approximately judicial.

**"RAINBOWS" OR "TOOLIES":** Red and blue capsules containing sodium secobarbital/amobarbital.

**RAPPORT:** An understanding between individuals created by genuine interest and concern.

**"RAP SHEET":** Record of the criminal and/or other history of an arrestee.

**RATIONALIZE:** To provide plausible, but untrue reasons 'or conduct.

**"REDS" OR "RED DEVILS":** Capsules containing sodium secobarbital.

**REGRESSION:** Going back to an earlier behavioral level.

**RIFLING:** A number of spiral grooves cut into the surface of the bore of a barrel of a weapon to provide the fired projectile with rotation, stability and direction in motion.

**RIGOR MORTIS:** A stiffening of muscles in the body after death; caused by chemical changes in the muscle tone.

**ROBBERY:** The felonious taking of another's property, either directly from the person or in the person's presence, through force or intimidation.

**ROUGH TAIL:** Moving surveillance where it does not matter if the surveillant is detected.

**SEROLOGY:** A science that deals with the study of the reactions and properties of serums (blood, body fluids, etc.).

**SOCIOPATH:** A person who is antisocial or lacks the capacity for social interaction.

**SPALLING:** To chip, splinter or flake.

**SPECTROGRAPH:** Laboratory instrument that burns minute samples of various substances to determine the elements present.

**STATEMENT:** A legal narrative description of events related to a crime.

**STATUTE OF LIMITATIONS:** Laws in most states require that a criminal action be commenced against an accused within a given number of years after the commission of the crime.

**STIMULANTS:** Drugs that pep people up; most common are the amphetamines.

**SUBCUTANEOUS:** Under the skin.

**SUBDURAL:** Under the dura (tissue covering brain).

**SUICIDE:** Intentionally taking one's own life.

**SURROGATE:** A substitute.

**SURVEILLANCE:** The observation of persons, places or objects.

**SUSPECT:** A person considered to be directly or indirectly connected with a crime, either by overt act or by planning and/or directing it. If charged and brought to trial, is called a defendant.

**SYNDROME:** A group of symptoms that indicate a particular condition or abnormality.

**TERRORISM:** The conscious exploitation of terror by coercion, designed to manipulate the will of its victims.

**"TIN" OR "CAN":** Ounce bag of marijuana.

**TOXICOLOGIST:** A specialist in the science of poisons and their effects.

**TRACE EVIDENCE:** Extremely small physical matter.

**TRAUMA:** An injury to a living tissue, as caused by an external force.

**UNDERCOVER:** The dropping of one's real identity and assuming another identity that blends into the area and circumstances under investigation to obtain information and/or evidence.

**VENTRICLE:** A chamber of the heart which receives blood from a corresponding atrium (passage) and from which blood is forced into the arteries.

**VICTIM:** The person injured by a crime.

**VICTIMLESS CRIME:** The victim is a willing participant in the illegal activity, e.g., a person who bets.

**VIN:** Vehicle Identification Number.

**_VOIR DIRE_ EXAMINATION:** An examination for the purpose of challenging, disputing or discrediting the competency of an opposing witness or a juror.

**WAIVER:** Giving up of certain rights.

**WIRETAPPING:** Intercepting and recording phone conversations by a mechanical device without the consent of either party in the conversation.

**WITNESS:** A person who saw a crime or some part of it being committed or who has relevant information.

# INDEX

use of 157
Operation Cease-Fire 388
Opium
  effects of 301
  how used 301

# P

Paint specimens
  trace analysis 118
Patience
  need for 23
PCP 316
Perceptions
  factors effecting 45
  mistakes in 46
  physical reconstruction of 48
Peyote 314
Photographing footprints 84
Photographs
  admissibility in court 105
Pipe bomb 339
Plaster casting 83
Plea bargaining 164, 367
Poisons
  toxicology 121
Police
  personnel 256
Polygraph
  basic uses 128
  components of 128
  examination 128
  factors affecting 129
  preparing subject for test 130
  use of in police work 127
Post-mortem lividity 232
Powder marks 116
Powers of observation
  training of 19
Prejudice
  effects of 22
Preliminary hearing 11
Preliminary investigation 4

Premeditation 2
Probeye Infrared Viewer 390
Property
  describing in report 37
property
  recovered 8
Prosecutor 14
  powers of 11
  presenting case to 9, 360
Psychological profiling 391,397
Public records
  use of 160

# Q

Questioned document 124

# R

Rap sheets
  use of 149
Rape
  investigation of 264
  investigative guidelines 267
  murders 266
Rapport 23
Records
  non-police 5
  private 160
  use of 158
Reporting
  principles of 33
Reports
  brevity in 34
  completeness 34
  final 150
  property description 37
  investigator's 33
Rigor mortis 231
Robbery 2, 9
  elements of 2
  investigation 248-253

Untrained observer
  problems of  46

## V

Vehicle Identification Number  259
Vehicle thefts
  investigative guidelines  261
Victim  4
Video Image Printer  394
Voice identification
  use of  20
Voice print analysis   136
*Voir dire*  382

## W

Warrants   145
Wheel Search Method  64
Witnesses
  expert  381
  identification of suspect by  8
  interview of  51
  motivation  46
  search for  53
  sex factors  43
  teenagers  44
Wounds
  contact   240
  exit   241
  incised   239
  identification of  239,  242
  gunshot   240
  stab   240

## Z

Zone Search Method  62